Y0-BYA-111

Centralized Book Processing

A Feasibility Study Based on Colorado Academic Libraries

by

Lawrence E. Leonard
Project Director

Joan M. Maier
Assistant Project Director

Richard M. Dougherty
Principal Investigator

The Scarecrow Press, Inc.

Metuchen, N.J. 1969

SBN 8108-0263-5

The research on which this publication is based was supported by National Science Foundation Grant GN 588.

Table of Contents

Preface

In October 1966, the National Science Foundation awarded a grant for library research in the area of centralized processing to the University of Colorado Libraries and the Colorado Council of Librarians, a committee of the Association of State Institutions of Higher Education, Colorado. Phase I of the study, begun in February 1967, examined the feasibility of establishing a book processing center to serve the nine state-supported college and university libraries in Colorado. Support for Phase II funded a simulation study of the proposed Center, carrying the work to 30 April 1968, the conclusion of the feasibility project. In August 1968, The National Science Foundation funded Phase III, an operational book processing center on a one year experimental basis.

This report summarizes the results of the fourteen-month feasibility study--the Colorado Academic Libraries Book Processing Center project (CALBPC). The report is organized under nine major sections: I. Background; II. Participating Libraries--Operational Characteristics; III. Cost Analysis; IV. Business Office Procedures; V. The Book Processing Center; VI. Approval Plan Utilization; VII. Mathematical Model/Simulation; VIII. Attitude Survey; IX. Conclusions and Recommendations.

Section I includes a brief history of centralized processing, interest shown by academic librarians in centralized book processing (study and development, past and present, in Colorado and elsewhere), and a brief profile of the study's participating libraries.

Section II presents the data which describe the existing operational characteristics of each of the participating libraries. The characteristics considered include: (1) ordering patterns--current or retrospective, domestic or foreign, vendor or publisher, rush or regular; (2) processing time-lag--delay from the time a requester places his order until he is notified that the processed book is available for use; (3) title duplication--overlap among the libraries; (4) cataloging modifications--classification number, Cutter number, descriptive cataloging, subject entries, and added entries.

Section III summarizes the cost analysis of each library's technical services activities. A processing cost was calculated for each library by determination and summation of unit labor cost, supply cost, equipment and institutional overhead, transportation (footage) cost, and paperback binding cost. Labor costs were calculated by developing standard times for processing tasks using time observation, diary and flow process charting techniques. The labor cost for operations performed in each institution's Business Office is covered in Section IV.

The proposed Book Processing Center was analyzed in Phase II of the study, and the findings are presented in Section V. Included were operating specifications, and standardization decisions for cataloging and physical processing. Section VI considers utilization of a book approval plan as an aid to coordinated ordering and/or expediting the ordering cycle. A unit processing cost was calculated for the Center using minimum processing times obtained from the libraries. Section VII deals with mathematical simulations of proposed operations. A variety of processing operations were computer simulated using processing times, material frequency flows through the model, and category of worker as variable inputs to obtain a realistic picture of cost and other operational characteristics. The developed model is generalized and could be used by other libraries.

Section VIII reports the results of a questionnaire survey that was conducted at eight of the nine campuses to measure faculty attitudes to existing library services and their attitude toward a group of additional services which each library might offer in conjunction with the Center.

Section IX contains conclusions resulting from Phases I and II of this study, and recommendations for further study on this and similar library research projects.

Tables of summary data are included in the text of the report to support the findings and analysis of each Section. More detailed data summaries and forms used in collecting and analyzing the data are located in the appendices. A scope list of standardized technical processing activities used in library costs analysis and in developing the model is also included in the appendices.

Acknowledgments

The authors are indebted to many individuals who contributed to the success of this project. We appreciate especially the fine co-operation, consideration and forbearance of the library director and staff at each of the participating institutions:

Miss Phyllis Dunham	Adams State College
Miss Virginia L. Wilcox	Colorado School of Mines
Mr. Daniel A. Seager	Colorado State College
Mr. LeMoyne W. Anderson and Mr. Robert H. DeWitt, Acting Director during Mr. Anderson's leave of absence	Colorado State University
Mr. Graham H. Sadler and Mr. Richard Gobble	Fort Lewis College
Mrs. Charlene Alexis	Metropolitan State College
Mr. Edward H. Broadhead	Southern Colorado State College
Mr. Ralph E. Ellsworth	University of Colorado
Mr. Richard D. Hershcopf	Western State College

Time observation is a data collection technique to which very few on the staffs of the participating libraries had been exposed prior to the study. Although something less than traumatic, a stopwatch tends to have an unnerving effect on many individuals. We are grateful to all timed for their cooperation in conducting their work while "under the stopwatch."

Thanks are due to those individuals who met with us during our April 1967 East Coast tour, and whose comments and advice were of considerable assistance in planning a centralized processing system: Mr. David Remington, Alanar Book Processing Center, Williamsport, Pennsylvania; Mrs. Barbara Markuson and Mrs. Henriette Avram, MARC Project, Library of Congress, Washington, D. C.; Mr. Allen Sprow, Veterans Administration, Washington, D. C.; Mr. Richard Pfefferle, Nassau Library System, Long Island, New York; Mr. Guenter Jansen, Suffolk Cooperative Library System, Long Island, New York; Mr. Lawrence Buckland, Mr. William Nugent and Miss Ann Curran, Inforonics, Inc., Cambridge, Massachusetts.

The principal investigators, Dr. Ralph E. Ellsworth, Dr. Richard M. Dougherty, and Mr. Don S. Culbertson, were instrumental in the formulation, development, and direction of the project. Their guidance, criticisms, and suggestions in their interaction with members of the project staff and with participating library personnel contributed incalculably to the research and to the report.

Westat Research, Inc., a management consulting firm, developed the mathematical model for the proposed Center, simulated the system with a series of computer runs, and wrote Section VII of this report. Dr. Donald Searls and Mr. Vern Achtermann of the Denver, Colorado, office, and Dr. Edward Bryant, President of Westat Research, Inc., Bethesda, Maryland, provided invaluable assistance and advice throught Phase II of this project.

Special thanks to Mrs. LaVica Andre and Mr. Walter Weiss of the project staff for all of their valuable assistance throughout each phase of the study. Their interest in the project, their recommendations and comments, and the long hours which they worked contributed immeasurably to the study and to the final report. Special acknowledgment is due Mr. Edward Dewing who assisted greatly with the initial organization of the study, and with formulation of the data collection procedures. Ed died 10 April 1967 as a result of a tragic automobile accident.

A special thanks to the typists, Mrs. LaVica Andre, Mrs. Glenda DeSantis, Mrs. Jean O'Neil and Mrs. Jerri Riegler for their forbearance in the face of an avalanche of manuscript and even worse, frequent revisions and changes. Without their excellent typing and proofreading, the authors would still have only an almost illegible, cut and pasted mountain of paper.

The principal investigators, project staff, and the Colorado Council of Librarians wish to thank the National Science Foundation for their support of the feasibility study under Grant GN-588, with Amendment No. 1. Without Foundation support and the support of the Council of Librarians, this study could not have been conducted.

Lawrence E. Leonard
Joan M. Maier
Richard M. Dougherty

Boulder, Colorado
15 June 1968

I. Background

Historical

Melvil Dewey, library pioneer, visionary and innovator was an advocate of cooperative efforts among libraries. He held opinions on nearly every phase of library science and he did not hesitate to voice them. His thoughts regarding cooperative cataloging were well expressed both in speeches and in his writings. Speaking before the Conference of Librarians at Philadelphia in 1876, he said:

> About once in so long articles appear in different countries rehearsing the follies of the present system of doing the same thing over a thousand times, as we librarians do in cataloging books that reach so many libraries. But right here they all stop. There somehow seems to be an idea among certain leaders of our craft, that such a thing (cooperative cataloging) is wholly visionary, at least their failure to take any practical steps in the matter would seem to indicate such a belief.[1]

In an article on cooperative cataloging which appeared in _Library Journal_ in 1877, he stated:

> At the present time, if a specially valuable book is published it finds its way to at least a thousand different libraries, in all of which it must be catalogued. One of the highest salaried officers of each of these thousand libraries must take this book and examine it for the scores of points that only a cataloguer can appreciate the necessity of looking up. Then the title must be copied and revised. Perhaps a half day is spent in preparing a satisfactory note to append for the benefit of the readers, etc., etc. And all this work is repeated to a certain extent in each of the thousand libraries! Can librarians complain if practical businessmen call this sheer extravagance?[2]

Dewey's words have since been repeated countless times, though evidently not often enough. The broad aims of cooperative and centralized cataloging which he constantly supported, have only recently started to be put into practice.

The concept of cooperative cataloging was proposed by Charles Coffin Jewett in 1850. He urged the Smithsonian Institution to begin accumulating stereotype blocks of its cataloging and that of other contributing libraries to be used in producing printed catalogs of different libraries, joint catalogs of two or more libraries, and possibly a union catalog of all libraries in the country.[3, 4] No positive action was taken by the Smithsonian, but Jewett's proposal influenced the thinking of Dewey and his contemporaries, and through their action, and that of Herbert Putnam, then Librarian of Congress, led to the card catalog service begun in 1901 by the Library of Congress.[5]

Centralized processing is, by scope, by definition, and by the calendar, a more recent phenomenon than is cooperative cataloging. A processing center can be defined as:

> A single agency which processes materials for a wider group of libraries. This may be, among other types, a library system with its branch or departmental libraries, a central agency such as a state or county library agency, some arrangement among a group of independent library systems whereby they agree to set up and operate such a center cooperatively, or where independent libraries contract to purchase this service from some other established library... an agency ordering, receiving, cataloging, and preparing materials for two or more libraries.[6, 7]

Centralized processing can be defined as:

> Those steps whereby library materials for several independent libraries, either by contract or informal agreement, are ordered, cataloged, and physically prepared for use by library patrons, these operations being performed in one location with billing, packing, and distribution to these same libraries.[8]

Although there were isolated examples of centralized processing in the early 1900's, processing centers as such came into existence in the 1940's, grew in number in the 1950's, and have proliferated during the 1960's. These centers serve public and school libraries almost without exception.

A July 1966 survey (revised to Spring 1967), by the Regional Processing Committee of the American Library Association, identified 63 processing centers or groups acting in a centralized processing capacity.[9] At that time there was at lease one operating center in each of 31 states in the U. S. Several additional states are now planning centralized processing centers. If these centers become part of regional cooperative programs, the profession will be well on its way to achieving the oft discussed, but little developed library communication networks, both at the regional and national level.

An exhaustive literature search indicated that there are no centers now performing book processing for a group of closely associated academic libraries.[10] As book prices and processing costs have continued to rise, academic librarians have begun to show greater interest in exploring the feasibility of such centers. There is every indication that this interest will accelerate, particularly if other studies demonstrate, as has the Colorado study, that centralized processing is a viable approach to the problems now faced by many academic librarians.

Other College/University Studies

Several studies on centralized processing other than the Colorado Academic Libraries Book Processing Center (herein referred to as CALBPC) feasibility study are now in progress or have recently been completed:

The Council on Library Resources has awarded grants to the New England Board of Higher Education to design and develop a mechanized Regional Library Cataloging and Processing Center for six academic institutions in the New England region[11] (Universities of Connecticut, Maine, Massachusetts, New Hampshire, Rhode Island and Vermont). Inforonics, Inc., of Cambridge, Massachusetts is conducting the study. The Center will probably begin in a batch process mode which may evolve into a time share system. Labels for pockets, cards, and spines, catalog card sets, and accounting procedures are the first products envisioned. Cost data were not included in the initial study.

California academic libraries have examined the question of centralized processing both at the junior college and college level. The junior college study recommended "that a processing center for junior college libraries in Southern California (or the entire state) be implemented...;" and that a study be made to determine whether there should be processing centers in both Northern and Southern California, or only one center to serve the entire state.[12] The state colleges did not recommend centralized processing, but felt instead that more economy could be achieved through a program of coordinated collection building, "automatic purchase programs," mechanization of bibliographic information for production of cataloging records and extension of Library of Congress services.[13] The Institute for Library Research, University of California, is now studying the possibility of an automated center for cooperative cataloging and serials control to be established at the California State Library.[14]

Florida State University's Library School conducted a study to determine the feasibility of "preparing all or some of the junior college (acquisitions and/or cataloging) records on a centralized basis with the aid of data processing equipment."[15] The study involved nineteen of the colleges in the state.

Other states considering centralized processing for academic libraries include Illinois, Indiana, Kansas, Nevada, and Ohio.[16] New York now has several public library processing centers which process books for one or more college libraries. Nelson Associates has recommended greater activities.[17] A recent Arthur D. Little, Inc. study explored the feasibility of one library processing center to serve all institutions of the State University of New York; the study recommended the establishment of a center.[18] A study conducted by Rice Estes also recommends centralized processing as one of nine cooperative efforts for seven academic libraries in Brooklyn.

Individual academic libraries in New York, Ohio and California are already participating in public library processing centers. A junior college library is participating in the processing activities at the Monterey County, California, Center, and three college libraries utilize the services of the Ohio State Library Statewide Center.[19] College libraries also participate in the Suffolk County[20] and Westchester Library Systems. One library system in the Finger Lakes region of New York is establishing a processing center to serve college libraries in the area.[21]

Planning in Colorado

At the 1941 Colorado College and Head Librarians Conference, Colorado's academic librarians expressed interest in the possible establishment of a center which would acquire and process materials for the participating libraries. In April, 1941, a special committee was appointed to outline alternative approaches to a study of centralized cataloging and other technical processes, including centralized book buying.[22]

Their Committee on Centralized Technical Processes and Book Buying formulated 208 questions regarding the feasibility and desirability of cooperation in technical services, and recommended 58 studies to obtain answers to these questions. The proposed studies were broad in scope, ranging from "the bibliographic needs of library clientele, the use of the catalog and the possibilities of various printed bibliographies as catalogs, through studies of the present library collections and practices, to the future of college libraries."[23] Although several reports and many sound recommendations resulted from the committee's efforts, the proposed studies were not carried out. A year or two after the Committee's first report was released, several key people left the state. Without these motivating forces, progress eventually ground to a halt.

A study financed by the Council on Library Resources at the request of the Colorado Council of Librarians, a committee of the Association of State Institutions of Higher Education in Colorado, was conducted by Donald Oehlerts in 1962. Oehlerts investigated the possibility of establishing a technical processing center to serve state-supported academic libraries. Direct transmission of interlibrary loans by special courier was also considered in this study.[24] The study recommended the establishment of a processing center, a teletype network for use in communicating interlibrary loan and other bibliographic information, and the organization of a courier circuit. The courier service was subsequently established and presently makes a round trip delivery from Fort Collins to Denver twice weekly, stopping at nine libraries along the way. It provides rapid interlibrary loan service among the participating libraries. A plan is now under study to make the courier service a daily run between Fort Collins and Pueblo, serving a considerably increased number of participants.

CALBPC

In late 1965, the National Science Foundation was approached to determine their interest in funding the Processing Center project. Based on NSF's favorable reaction, a formal proposal was prepared for submission to the Foundation. The project to be conducted was outlined in three phases: Phase I was data collection and evaluation; Phase II, systems design; and Phase III, an operational center on a one-year trial basis.

In October 1966, the National Science Foundation awarded the University of Colorado and the Colorado Council of Librarians a grant of $54,000 to conduct a one-year study (Phase I) concerning practicability of establishing a book processing center in Colorado.[25, 26] The member libraries of the Council contributed $11,200 to the study. A grant of $27,500 was awarded in June 1967 to conduct Phase II of the study.

Libraries of the nine state-supported Colorado academic institutions participated in the feasibility study. They were: Adams State College, Alamosa; Colorado School of Mines, Golden; Colorado State College, Greeley; Colorado State University, Fort Collins; Fort Lewis College, Durango; Metropolitan State College, Denver; Southern Colorado State College, Pueblo; University of Colorado, Boulder; Western State College, Gunnison.

The center as originally proposed would serve the nine state-supported college and university libraries and, if successful, would expand its operation to include interested private academic institutions in Colorado. The objective of such a center will be to order for delivery to the central point books requested by the participating libraries, to catalog, classify, process and prepare the books for use, maintain appropriate records, and to forward processed books and catalog cards to the participants. Disposition of the bibliographic data generated through technical processing of titles will be examined in the operational study (Phase III). The services proposed included forwarding a record of titles processed to the Bibliographical Center for Research in Denver and to the Library of Congress for inclusion in the regional and national union catalogs. Possibilities of using machine readable records was to be investigated during Phase III (e. g., production of a book catalog of member library holdings, issuance of periodic acquisitions lists, bibliographies, etc.). Another aspect would include testing of L. C. 's MARC II output as a data base.

Scope of the Study

Phase I. Following several preliminary meetings involving the investigators and staff of the nine member libraries, Phase I of the study was begun 1 February 1967. The tasks to be performed during the first phase concentrated on data collection and evaluation. The principle purpose was to ascertain whether a centralized operation could perform more effectively and economically than each library processing its own material could with these particular libraries in this geographic region.

During Phase I, the following information was compiled for each library: (1) ordering patterns; (2) title duplication; (3) cataloging modification; (4) processing time-lags; (5) processing times; (6) unit processing costs; (7) business office procedures and costs. A survey of faculty attitudes toward existing and proposed services was also conducted at each institution. A list of technical processing activities was compiled for identification of similar procedures at each institution, in order to insure uniform collection and analysis of data.

Phase II. Phase II was begun in September, overlapping with several Phase I tasks, i. e., tabulation and analysis of data, and the attitude survey. Phase II was intended to identify operating requirements for the proposed center and to design a prototype system. Data were analyzed and reduced to workable systems design specifications. These tasks were accomplished through development of decision flow charts, work flow diagrams, and flow process charts. Organizational patterns and space requirements for the center were also recommended. A subcontract was let to Westat Research, Inc., Denver, Colorado, a management consulting firm, to construct a mathematical model of the developed system, and to simulate the system on a computer using Phase I data and findings as variable input to the system.[27] A unit processing charge was calculated on a basis that would make the center self-supporting. Other products of the Phase II study were: generalized system design; personnel staffing requirements; method for measuring processing time lagр equipment and facility requirements needed for the Center's operation.

Phase III[a]. The Colorado Academic Libraries Book Processing Center will operate on an experimental basis for one year. During the trial period, the effectiveness of the Center will be measured to determine whether the requirements outlined have been met and anticipated benefits have been achieved. Modifications will be made as necessary, based on continuous examination of internal processes and developed products. The working relationship and exchange of data between the Processing Center, the Bibliographical Center for Research and other institutions in the emerging regional bibliographical network will be established during this trial operational period. An enlightening "before" and "after" picture of a processing center operation will be an objective of the Phase III trial period.

Institutional Profiles

The reader should understand from the outset that the purpose of this report has not been to develop a case study of the nine participating institutions. The object of the institutional analyses was to develop a composite of the requirements and operating characteristics of the nine institutions and the data are not identified with any particular institution. In order to give the reader some idea of the types of libraries involved in the study, a brief description of each institution is presented below.

The participants of the CALBPC study were two state universities and seven colleges. The seven colleges will be referred to as Group I institutions and the two universities as Group II institutions. This grouping is of particular value in Section VIII, the survey of faculty attitudes.

Statistics used to characterize the two categories of institutions are:

[a]Note: Phase III was funded by the National Science Foundation in August 1968. This report is, however, concerned only with Phase I and II of the study.

	Group I[a] (7 Institutions)	Group II[a] (2 Institutions)
Enrollment, Full-time	21, 488	38, 005
Faculty, Full-time	1, 173	3, 118
Library Budget	$ 988, 170	$ 1, 950, 510
Library Book Budget	$ 354, 425	$ 660, 988
Library Collection	689, 628 vols.	1, 214, 380 vols.

[a] See figures in the Statistical Profile.

The geography of the state has a significant bearing on the design and development of a processing center as the Rocky Mountains divide the state into two parts. Most of the population and institutions are located on the eastern slope of the mountains. However, Adams State College, Fort Lewis College, and Western State College are located west of the continental Divide. This has produced a certain amount of isolation from the other institutions. Figure 1. 1 presents a statistical profile of each institution.

Adams State College (ASC) was originally a normal school but its programs have undergone a great deal of expansion and it now offers a masters degree in education. To a large extenet, the college is intended to serve students from the southern part of the state, particularly in the area of the San Luis Valley. The present library facilities are overcrowded and a new library building is being planned.

Colorado State College (CSC) is one of the better known teacher training institutions in the country. Like most schools, it has undergone a great deal of growth and now occupies two campuses, one in town and a newly developing campus on the edge of the community. CSC now offers both masters and doctoral degrees in a wide variety of subjects and also offers extension courses in Denver. The present library is extremely overcrowded and a new library building is now in the planning stage.

Colorado School of Mines (Mines) has earned a reputation as one of the nation's outstanding institutions for the education of mining and petroleum engineers. The school offers a number of masters and doctoral degrees in the engineering disciplines. The present library building, occupied over ten years ago, has not outgrown its present space facilities. The library's collection includes a wealth of primary source materials: original mining reports, maps, metallurgical reports, geophysics, petroleum, and geology sources, and a great deal of significant material concerning the history of mining.

Colorado State University (CSU) is one of the fastest growing institutions in the state. Colorado State University was formerly Colorado A & M but the educational programs have been significantly broadened. CSU occupies three campuses with many modern buildings, and more under construction. Among the many doctoral programs offered are atmospheric science, radiation biology and watershed management. The library collection was centralized when the new building was opened in 1965. At present the library facilities are ample except for cramped quarters for the technical processing divisions.

The University of Colorado (CU) is the largest institution in the state and is, in many ways, the largest in the Rocky Mountain region. The University is situated at the foot of the mountains, 25 miles from the Denver metropolitan area. Consequently its resources are readily available to a large percentage of the state's population. A number of governmental research organizations have made their headquarters in the Boulder area. These include: The Environmental Science Services Administration; The National Bureau of Standards, Boulder Laboratories; The National Center for Atmospheric Research; Ball Brothers Research Corporation; Dow Chemical, Rocky Flats Division; and International Business Machines Corporation. The university presently offers advanced degrees in 65 disciplines and doctoral degrees in 45 fields of study. The library system consists of eight departmental libraries, two center libraries located in Denver and Colorado Springs, and the medical library located at the Medical Center in Denver.

Fort Lewis College (FLC) the institution farthest from Denver is located in Durango, Colorado, a national tourist mecca. The college is set on a mesa with a spectacular view of the San Juan Mountains. Fort Lewis became a liberal arts college after operating for many years as a technical junior college. The first baccalaureate degrees were awarded in 1964. In March, 1967, the library moved into a new library/audio-visual/classroom building. Since becoming a liberal arts school, the library has been deeply involved in a program

Figure 1.1 Statistical Profile of the CALBPC Participants

	Institution				Library					
Institution	yr. of founding[a]	student enrollment	size of fac. and research staff[e]	distance from the proposed center	vols. held 6/30/67[e]	vols. added 1/66 - 6/30/67[e]	library book budget[b]	prof. staff (FTE)[b]	clerical staff (FTE)[b]	student asst. (FTE)[b, g]
ASC	1925	2, 132	113	239	113, 599	10, 012	$ 38, 142	4. 9		8. 8
CSC	1890	6, 589	324	52	269, 906	12, 858	$100, 958	13. 0	8. 0	23. 0
CSM	1874	1, 538	174	20	95, 352	4, 733	$ 20, 091	6. 0	9. 0	2. 8
CSU	1879	11, 848	1, 377	48	408, 421	35, 583	$332, 869	22. 0	37. 0	6. 5
CU	1877	26, 157[c]	1, 741	--	805, 959	67, 492	$328, 119	51. 5	84. 1	49. 0
FLC	1927	1, 399	79	356	51, 426	9, 631	$ 68, 459	3. 0	2. 0	5. 0
MSC	1965	2, 443[d]	125	27	8, 310	4, 466	$ 45, 000	2. 0	1. 0	3. 3
SCSC	1933	5, 061	243[f]	141	50, 185	12, 204	$ 52, 105	6. 0	6. 0	4. 8
WSC	1911	2, 326	115	228	100, 850	4, 014	$ 29, 670	5. 0	4. 0	9. 5

a. American Colleges and Universities, 9th ed. Washington, D. C., American Council on Education, 1964.
b. American Library Association. Library statistics of colleges and universities 1965-66: Institutional data. Chicago, A. L. A., 1967.
c. Institutional Research Office, University of Colorado. Figures are for the fall term, 1967. Included are all four campuses, Boulder, Denver Center, Medical Center, and Colorado Springs.
d. College Blue Book, 12th ed. Los Angeles, California, College Planning Programs, Ltd., 1968.
e. Information supplied by each institution.
f. College's Bulletin, 1967-68.
g. U. S. Office of Education, "College and University Library Resources and Facilities," 1965-66.

of retrospective book buying.

Metropolitan State College (MSC) is considerably different from the other schools. MSC, popularly called Metro, is located in downtown Denver and is the newest addition to the four-year colleges. Metro will award its first baccalaureate degrees in the spring of 1969. In its short existence, the college has operated in rented quarters. The school offers both two-year vocational programs and a four-year liberal arts program. A contract with the Denver Public Library has given students access to library services in order to supplement the college library during its early period of growth. Because of the lack of space and staff, Metro has utilized the services of a commercial firm to process the majority of its books. Like Fort Lewis College, a large share of the book purchasing has been retrospective.

Southern Colorado State College (SCSC) was formerly a general and technical community junior college. SCSC awarded its first Bachelor degrees in 1965. There are two campuses, one in the heart of the city of Pueblo and a new campus on the edge of the town. The library/classroom building was the first structure completed on the new campus and was occupied in the fall of 1966. The college awards Associate of Arts and BA degrees.

Western State College (WSC) is located in Gunnison, a community of 4,100, an isolated part of the state, on the western slope. Although primarily a liberal arts college, masters programs are offered in social studies, English, education, speech, science, music, and business education. A new library building was opened in 1966.

Notes

1. Dewey, Melvil Statement made at the Conference of Librarians, Philadelphia, 1876, reported in Library Journal 1:118, Nov. 1876.

2. Dewey, Melvil "Co-operative cataloging." Library Journal 1(4-5):170, Jan. 1877.

3. Jewett, Charles C. "A plan for stereotyping catalogs by separate titles; and for forming a general stereotyped catalog of public libraries in the United States." (In: Proceedings of the American Association for the Advancement of Science, 1850, vol. 4. Washington, S. F. Baird, 1851, p. 165-176.)

4. Jewett, Charles C. Smithsonian Report on the Construction of Catalogues of Libraries... Washington: Smithsonian Institution, 1852, 78 p.

5. Dewey, Melvil "Printed catalog cards from a central bureau." Library, 2d Series, 2:130-134, (January 1901).

6. Mullen, Evelyn Day "Guidelines for establishing a centralized library processing center." Library Resources and Technical Services 2(3):171 (Summer 1958).

7. American Library Association, Resources and Technical Services Division, Regional Processing Committee "Guidelines for centralized technical services." Library Resources and Technical Services 10(2):233 (Spring 1966).

8. Hunt, James R. "The historical development of processing centers in the United States." Library Resources and Technical Services 8(1):54 (Winter 1964).

9. American Library Association, Regional Processing Committee "Regional processing centers; a preliminary list." 1 July 1966; revised to Spring 1967, 8 p.

10. Leonard, Lawrence E. Cooperative and centralized cataloging and processing: a bibliography, 1850-1967, University of Illinois Graduate School of Library Science, Occasional Papers, No. 93. Urbana, July 1968, 89 p.

11. Council on Library Resources "Grant to New England Board of Higher Education to help six-state, inter-university library cataloging project." Recent Developments, no. 216, for release 1 February 1967.

12. Moore, Everett L. "Processing center for California junior college libraries--a preliminary study." Library Resources and Technical Services 9(3):316, (Summer 1965).

13. California State Colleges, Committee of Library Development, Second report to the Chancellor "Recommendations for the support of California state college libraries." December 1965.

14. California, State Library, Memorandum from Mrs. Carma Leigh, dated 27 June 1967; subject: Automated center for cooperative cataloging and serials control to be established at California State Library, 2 p.

15. "Study on centralization." Library Resources and Technical Services 10(1):50 (Winter 1966).

16. Branscomb, Lewis C. "The Ohio College Library Center." The Rub-Off 18(2):6 (Mar.--Apr. 1967).

17. Nelson Associates, Inc. Feasibility of School and college library processing through public library systems in New York State. N.Y.: Nelson Associates, Inc., 1966.

18. Arthur D. Little, Inc. A plan for a library processing center

for the State University of New York, Report to the Office of Educational Communications, State University of New York (Rept. C-69541), Nov. 1967, 127p .

19. Bundy, Mary Lee "Behind central processing." Library Journal 88:3540 (1 Oct. 1963).

20. The Suffolk Cooperative Library System, Descriptive brochure, 1967, 8 p.

21. Catalogers (LC) "Eleven college libraries in beautiful Finger Lakes area beginning cooperative processing center" (classified advertisement). Library Journal 93(2):214 (15 Jan. 1968).

22. Colorado College and Head Librarians Conference, Special Committee on Centralized Technical Processes and Book Buying First Report, August 1942; Second Report, February 1943.

23. Wright, W. E. "Review (of Colorado College and Head Librarians Conference, Special Committee on Centralized Technical Processes and Book Buying)." Library Journal 68:244 (15 March 1943).

24. Oehlerts, Donald E. A study to determine the feasibility of establishing a cooperative technical processing program and direct transmission of Interlibrary loans. Denver, Colorado: Association of State Institutions of Higher Education in Colorado, 1962.

25. Dougherty, Richard M. "A central processing center for Colorado Academic Libraries." The Colorado Academic Library 3(3-4):4-6 (Summer and Fall 1966).

26. "Colorado academic librarians to get central processing." Library Journal 92:956, 964-965 (1 March 1967).

27. Ellsworth, Ralph E. and Richard M. Dougherty A proposal to National Science Foundation for support of development of an Academic Libraries Cooperative Processing Center for all Colorado colleges and universities. Stage I: Design of the system, Proposal 65. 5. 242 as revised March, July 1966.

II. The Participating Libraries - Operational Characteristics

Introduction

In order to identify the technical processing requirements of the nine participating libraries and to assess the manner in which a processing center, as well as other cooperative projects might affect each participant's operating procedures, extensive studies focusing on present procedures, time lags and costs were conducted at each library. These studies provide the "before" basis of a "before and after centralization" comparison.

The raison d'être of centralized processing is that books will be provided to member libraries faster, at a lower cost, and with a comparable or higher level of cataloging and processing; otherwise, why bother. It is this "now" picture of procedural analysis, cataloging products, speed of processing, and unit processing costs with which Section II and III of this report are concerned.

Data for Section II were collected at each participating library to identify ordering patterns, unique local cataloging practices, and processing time lags. Data were also gathered on the title duplication among the participants. Samples were drawn systematically from the files of each library in sufficient quantity to satisfy the statistical precision limits of the investigation. A sample size was generally selected to insure a confidence level of 99% with a variation of no more than ± 5% in the percentages estimated. That is, samples drawn from the files possess an average value which is within these specified limits (± 5%) of the true average value of the information contained in the file. Samples drawn from the American Book Publishing Record also approximate the distribution within these limits of the 30, 050 titles announced in the January-December 1966 issues of BPR. Because of the subject stratification within BPR, a systematic sample proved to be more efficient than a random sample.

Ordering Patterns

A close approximation of the type of materials which the Book Processing Center can expect to handle may be made from an appraisal of the current ordering patterns of each participant: i. e., what is the ratio of domestic orders to foreign orders, current to retrospective, rush to regular, vendor to publisher, etc. ? Also, are there discernable trends in ordering from certain publishers and vendors?

Methodology: The outstanding order file at each library was sampled. The sample drawn was examined and compared with data from the time lag study (750 titles from each library) discussed later in this section. As the processing time data were randomly selected--data slips gathered as books were processed--and as the time data carried all of the ordering pattern information, it was decided to code the time lag data for use not only in computing the processing lag, but also in tabulating information regarding ordering patterns. Consequently, the initial sample was used primarily as a correlation cross-check with the time lag data.

Sampling Procedure

The order file samples were drawn from a finite population (number of orders on file). The size of each file was estimated by compressing the order slips within each file drawer, measuring the compressed files and randomly selecting one inch of order slips from each file drawer to be counted. Random selection was made using a table of random digits.[1] For each group of titles counted, the number of foreign imprints was noted to provide a preliminary estimate of the proportion of foreign imprints on order. The proportion of foreign imprints ordered at each library was known to exceed the proportion of rush orders; hence the foreign order proportion was used in the sample size calculation, as it was utilized both in foreign and rush order estimates.

The information needed to estimate a proportion is the relative frequency with which an event has occurred. If an event occurs "x" times out of "n" trials, the relative frequency of its occurrence is $\frac{x}{n}$

and this sample proportion is used as an estimate of the total population proportion. Since the probability of a success (a foreign title) remains the same from trial to trial and the trials are independent for practical purposes, use of the binomial distribution is justified. Using a normal curve approximation of the binomial distribution, a sample size was computed that satisfied the predetermined level of precision.

According to Cochran,[2] approximate sample sizes for proportions may be computed using the formula

$$n_o = \frac{t^2 pq}{d^2} \qquad (1)$$

where n_o = sample size

t = abscissa of the normal curve that cuts off an area "a" at the tails

p = preliminary estimate of the proportion

q = $1 - p$

d = allowable error.

The above formula may be used provided N, the total number of titles on order, is large compared to the sample size. If the sample constitutes only an appreciable amount of the total population, say 5%, the sample size may be adjusted by using

$$n = \frac{n_o}{1 + \frac{n_o}{N}} \qquad (2)$$

As the project wished to establish results with a probability of 0. 99 and an error of less than 0. 05, the sample size required to give this degree of accuracy is (substituting into formula (1))

$$n_o = \frac{(2.58)^2 pq}{(0.05)^2} = 2663pq \qquad (3)$$

The library with the most significant holdings and acquisitions program in foreign titles exhibited a preliminary foreign to domestic title ratio of 40:60, based on the first sample drawn. Hence its p value in formula (3) is . 4 and its q value is . 6.

Substituting in formula (3), $n_o = 2663 (.4) (.6) = 639$.

A sample of 750 titles, more than large enough to meet the precision requirement for this portion of the study was collected at each library using the sampling procedure outlined above which follows the systematic sampling procedures suggested by Cochran[3] and Kish.[4] Records randomly selected were xeroxed and then refiled. This permitted the project staff to retain a permanent record of all titles selected.

Ideally the samples should have been drawn simultaneously at each library to measure ordering patterns at a single point in time for all libraries. In theory, the pattern should remain constant throughout the year, but as ordering is a cyclic process, and patterns vary with the type of request and the budget balance, some error may have been introduced by the delay in sampling--three months lapsed from the time the first library was sampled until the sampling process was completed.

Data summary and analysis: All of the sample data were coded and keypunched. Tabulations were initially printed on an IBM 407 accounting machine; computer programs were later written to cross-relate data elements, and to tabulate and print results using a CDC 6400 computer.

Figure 2. 1 summarizes the existing ordering patterns for the nine libraries. Rush orders account for only 1. 7% of the total orders placed by the libraries. It is unlikely that the libraries would place rush orders with the Center. They would generally prefer to order directly from publishers if the title is not locally available. But the very low frequency for rush orders suggests that standardized processing procedures can accommodate most orders.

Of all orders placed, 92. 8% were for domestic imprints, either current or retrospective. For our purposes, a current title was defined as a 1965 or later imprint; a retrospective title was defined as a 1964 or earlier imprint. Foreign titles account for 7. 2% of all orders and the majority of these were placed by the university libraries. The college libraries ordered very few foreign titles.

Most of the libraries placed a far greater percent of their orders with vendors than with publishers; 79. 5% to vendors as compared to 20. 5% to publishers. The usual reasons cited for the preference for vendors were procedural economies and reduction of paperwork.

Figure 2. 2 contains ordering patterns for the individual libraries, and volumes added to their collections during fiscal year 1967. The ratio of current domestic to other imprint categories varies inversely with the size of the collection. Hence the larger institutions will not benefit from centralized processing of current imprints as much as will the smaller institutions. The colleges will benefit by not having to process foreign language titles.

Figure 2. 1
Summary of Libraries' Ordering Patterns

Type of Order	Percent by Type	Percent by Category
Rush Orders: Current	0. 9%	
Rush Orders: Retrospective	0. 8%	1. 7%
Domestic: Current	49. 4%	
Domestic: Retrospective	43. 4%	92. 8%
Foreign Current	3. 4%	
Foreign: Retrospective	3. 8%	7. 2%
Order Placed Through Vendor (Current)	41. 6%	
Order Placed Through Vendor (Retrospective)	38. 0%	79. 5%
Order Sent to Publisher (Current)	11. 2%	
Order Sent to Publisher (Retrospective)	9. 2%	20. 5%

Processing Time-Lag Study

An important aspect of processing library materials, one which often receives too little attention, is the time lag from receipt of an order in a library to the date the requester is notified that his book has been processed and is ready for use.

Processing time-lag (also referred to as "throughput") will be

Figure 2. 2
Ordering Patterns of Each Participating Library (Percentage)

Type of Order	Library 1	2	3	4	5	6	7	8	9
Rush Orders: Current	0. 0	0. 2	0. 1	3. 2	1. 7	0. 0	0. 6	1. 8	0. 2
Rush Orders: Retrospective	0. 0	0. 1	0. 0	2. 4	1. 0	0. 0	1. 0	2. 3	0. 0
Domestic: Current	49. 7	71. 4	30. 0	55. 8	67. 5	37. 6	54. 7	31. 0	47. 2
Domestic: Retrospective	48. 2	26. 8	57. 3	40. 7	26. 0	59. 2	44. 3	35. 7	52. 5
Foreign: Current	1. 7	1. 8	4. 4	0. 8	4. 4	1. 6	0. 9	14. 4	0. 2
Foreign: Retrospective	0. 4	0. 0	8. 3	2. 7	2. 1	1. 6	0. 1	18. 9	0. 1
Order Placed Through Vendor (Current)	42. 8	71. 2	33. 9	34. 5	54. 7	26. 8	23. 5	39. 6	47. 0
Order Placed Through Vendor (Retrospective)	45. 3	24. 3	62. 3	25. 3	18. 1	45. 6	22. 8	46. 3	51. 9
Order Sent to Publisher (Current)	8. 2	2. 0	0. 5	22. 1	17. 5	12. 4	32. 1	6. 0	0. 4
Order Sent to Publisher (Retrospective	3. 7	2. 5	3. 3	18. 1	9. 7	15. 2	21. 6	8. 1	0. 7

	1	2	3	4	5	6	7	8	9
Number volumes added to collection FY 1967	4, 014	9, 631	35, 583	12, 858	4, 733	12, 204	10, 012	67, 492	4, 466

an important factor to the successful operation of a processing center. Books must flow through the central operation as rapidly as possible for several reasons: (1) the participating libraries will want to receive requested books with minimum delay; (2) snags and delays cost money and decrease overall operating efficiency; (3) space will be limited and there will be little room for storage; (4) one purpose for establishing a central processing operation is to reduce existing processing delays.

Four basic processing check points were considered in the study: (1) date a request was received in the library; (2) date the library placed an order with a vendor; (3) date the book arrived in the library; and (4) date the processed book was forwarded to the Circulation Department. The lag between the first and second dates is a factor over which a processing center would have no control; this time period was considered, however, as one of the facets of the attitude survey (see Section VIII of the report). However, this lag will have a counterpart in a central operation: the lag between receipt of an order and its placement with a vendor or publisher. This lag can not be compared on a 1:1 basis as there are many factors at each library which might delay the order: e. g. , budgetary limitation, staffing, complexity of order, priority assignment, etc. The remaining lags--between dates two and three, and three and four--can be compared directly between each library's performance and that of a centralized operation. These are the mean processing lags which a center must at least meet, and which must be beat if the flow of materials is to be improved.

Methodology of data collection: The purpose of the processing time-lag study was explained during the 13-17 February 1967 library visits. Files and forms to be used at each library were identified, the required processing dates were enumerated and the forms best suited for recording the four processing dates were selected. A member of each library's technical processing staff was assigned responsibility for recording the dates and saving the slips for the study staff. A follow-up letter was sent one week later to all library directors, notifying each library when to begin recording the required data.

The date that a request is received by the library is not normally recorded. Each library began stamping this date on all orders as they were received. Processing dates were noted as each request was ordered, received, and cataloged. The slips were accumulated over a three month period. At the end of this period the study staff collected the slips and examined them to determine whether there were 250 slips with a complete processing cycle. (See sample size determination below).

Several libraries which could not provide 250 usable slips were asked to continue the study. Completed orders were selected at random from those libraries which had accumulated more than 250 slips. In the final tabulation, 250 titles were used for the seven smaller institutions and 500 titles for the two larger institutions.

The methodology may have skewed the results somewhat as no specific batch of titles was monitored throughout the entire cycle. With minor exceptions, slips were collected as titles which had entered the system after the beginning of the time-lag study were processed. If anything, the processing time-lags presented in the following tables are lower than could be expected if a specific group of 250 titles had been tagged and monitored until the entire group had completed the order-catalog-processing cycle.

Processing time lags were determined in calendar days for the three processing intervals for each of the slips provided: (1) request to order placed; (2) order placed to book received; and (3) book received to book cataloged. The total processing cycle was also calculated for each slip.

Sample Size

If "x" is the mean of a random sample of size "n", the relationship of the theoretical sampling distribution of $\bar{x}$ (mean of the sample means), the mean μ (population mean) and the standard deviation $\sigma_{\bar{x}}$ (population standard deviation) is:

$$\sigma_{\bar{x}} = \frac{\sigma}{\sqrt{n}}$$

(sample standard deviation)
(n = number in the sample)

If n is large, the theoretical sampling distribution of $\bar{x}$ can be approximated with a normal curve.

Chosing a confidence coefficient of 0.99, it can be stated with a probability of .99 that the following inequality will hold

$$-2.58 < \frac{\bar{x} - \mu}{\sigma / \sqrt{n}} < 2.58$$

Rearranging terms and substituting the sample standard deviation s for σ:

$$-2.58 \frac{s}{\sqrt{n}} < \bar{x} - \mu < 2.58 \frac{s}{\sqrt{n}}$$

Since $\bar{x}$ is used as a point estimate of μ, the error is the difference between the two:

$$-2.58 \frac{s}{\sqrt{n}} < \text{error} < 2.58 \frac{s}{\sqrt{n}}$$

Hence, it can be stated with a probability of .99 that the error will be less than

$$\text{error} = 2.58 \frac{s}{n}$$

Solving for n:[5]

$$n = \left(\frac{2.58s}{E}\right)^2$$

Choosing to set the error at less than 5 days (average cycle time within 5 days of the correct value) and estimating the sample deviation to be 30 days based on a pilot sample:

$$n = \left(\frac{2.58 \times 30}{5}\right)^2 = 239$$ which was rounded to 250.

Data summary and analysis: A summary of the gross processing time lag for each library is represented in Figure 2.3. Each time lag is recorded in calendar days representing the three major lags. Total processing time is also shown for each library.

One relevant delay time not included in the table is the delay for orders sent through each institution's Business Office. This delay--receipt of orders from library, until forwarding of orders to a vendor--might add seven calendar days or more to the processing time lag. In some instances, librarians thought two or more weeks delay was not uncommon.

At the time of the data collection, one library contracted virtually all of its ordering, cataloging and book processing to a commercial firm. As the collection is being built on a priorities basis, the date from request to placement of an order had little meaning. When the books are received, they are completely cataloged; therefore, only the total processing lag at Library #2 is quite atypical.

The time lag from placement of an order until receipt (Figure

2. 3) is high for the university libraries, a reflection of the percentage of foreign orders processed. College libraries ordered primarily domestic imprints, which are more readily obtained and, consequently, their mean time for this processing lag is significantly less. There is considerable variation in processing times which appears to reflect differences in internal policy, staffing patterns and

Figure 2. 3

Processing Time Lag Summary
(In Mean Calendar Days)

Library	Order Requested to Order Placed	Order Placed to Book Received	Book Received to Book Cataloged	Total Processing Time
1	94	61	219	374
2	1	38	26	65
3	12	80	188	280
4	57	56	91	205
5	62	43	22	126
6	28	45	80	153
7	24	52	73	148
8	23	79	21	123
9	--	--	227	227
*Summary mean	38*	57*	90*	189**

Based on a sample of 250 titles at the seven smaller institutions and 500 titles at the two larger institutions.

*Summary mean is calculated using mean time lags for Libraries 1 through 8.

**Total processing mean is calculated using all nine libraries.

procedural efficiency at each institution. The processing lag which indicates the least variance is the lag over which each library has the least control--the lag between placement of an order and receipt of the book. Figure 2. 4 summarizes the mean processing lags by library, illustrating the time lags experienced by libraries when different categories of books are ordered, i. e., domestic and foreign imprints, both current and retrospective.

Figure 2.4
Mean Processing Time Lag for Each Category of Delay

	Library									
	1	2	3	4	5	6	7	8	9	Mean*
Current Domestic Title										
Order requested to order placed	92	0	4	66	63	29	25	20	0	35
Order placed to book received	55	36	83	48	40	52	49	68	0	53
Book received to book cataloged	183	26	184	81	21	76	86	19	230	77
Total time-requested through cataloged	330	62	271	195	124	157	160	107	230	161
Current Foreign Title										
Order requested to order placed	0	0	0	63	0	20	0	26	0	26
Order placed to book received	0	75	109	164	0	60	0	120	0	116
Book received to book cataloged	0	13	209	203	0	69	0	32	0	44
Total time-requested through cataloged	0	88	318	430	0	149	0	178	0	187
Earlier Domestic Title										
Order requested to order placed	98	3	7	43	57	27	23	26	0	29
Order placed to book received	66	45	79	66	48	41	54	77	0	64
Book received to book cataloged	253	25	190	102	24	83	56	20	226	107
Total time-requested through cataloged	417	73	276	211	129	151	133	123	226	193
Earlier Foreign Title										
Order requested to order placed	34	0	1	63	78	16	0	20	0	25
Order placed to book received	137	0	84	57	89	51	0	96	0	89
Book received to book cataloged	590	0	176	111	6	71	0	26	0	65
Total time-requested through cataloged	761	0	261	231	173	138	0	142	0	177

* Mean in last column calculated from raw data of all libraries. Mean for each library calculated using the number of titles processed for each category of order as the basis of the mean computation.

Title Duplication Among the Libraries

The proportion of current purchasing overlap among the participating libraries is an aspect of considerable importance to the determination of feasibility of centralized processing. A reasonable level of title duplication must exist to insure batch processing of multiple copies of titles.

Methodology of data collection: Using the January-December 1966 issues of American Book Publishing Record, a systematic sample was drawn by clipping every thirtieth entry from BPR and taping it to a printed data collection card (see Figure 2. 5). The sample was systematically selected to take advantage of the subject stratification within BPR. Entries were taken from all sections, including juvenile and fiction titles.[6]

One requirement set for the study was that the estimate of purchasing overlap (EP) must fall within 4% of the actual percentage (AP) with a confidence level of . 99.

$$P\,[\,|EP - AP| \leq 0.04] \geq 0.99 \qquad (1)$$

where P is the probability (to be greater than or equal to . 99) and EP - AP is the maximum error (to be less than or equal to 4%).

Using the normal approximation to the binomial distribution, (1) becomes

$$P\,\left[\,|Z| \leq \frac{0.04}{\sqrt{AP\,(1 - AP)/n}}\right] \geq 0.99 \qquad (2)$$

where Z is the root of the normal distribution.

For P = 0. 99 the value of Z is 2. 58 and (2) becomes

$$2.58 \leq \frac{0.04}{\sqrt{AP\,(1 - AP)/n}}\,;\quad n \geq AP\,(1 - AP)\left(\frac{2.58}{0.04}\right)^2$$

Assuming the worst case (requiring the largest n) AP = . 5, then

$$n \geq (.25)\,(4128) \geq 1032 \text{ titles}$$

This indicated a sampling fraction of 1/30 or a sample of 1, 208 titles of the 30, 050 announced in 1966. Each title was then checked at all of the participating libraries. In addition to the duplication check, the data collector noted whether the library had modified the LC classification and descriptive cataloging and, if so, how; series treatment was also recorded.

Figure 2. 5
Data Collection Card

Front

	OO	CO	PC	SL	
ASC			O		O
CSC	O		O		O
CSM	O		✓		
CSU			O	O	O
CU	O		✓		O
FLC			✓		
MSC			O		
SCSC			✓		
WSC			✓		

REDLICH, Fredrick Carl,
1910- 616. 89
The theory and practice of psychiatry [by] Fredrick C. Redlich, Daniel X. Freedman. New York, Basic [c. 1966] xii, 880p. 25cm. Bibl.
[RC454. R4] 66-13833 12. 50
I. Psychiatry. I. Freedman, Daniel X., joint author.
Comprehensive view of the field addressed to students and practitioners of psychiatry.

Back

	S	CALL # MOD #	CL #	CU #	DESC MA	DESC AD	DESC SU	DESC OT	MONO SO	MONO CT	MONO CS	DUP C #	SL C	
ASC														
CSC														
CSM		616. 89 R248th					✓				✓	1		
CSU														
CU									O		✓	1		
FLC											✓	1		
MSC														
SCSC		616. 89 R24t									✓	1		
WSC		616. 89 R248t									✓	1		

Data summary and analysis: Figure 2. 6 shows the percentage of titles in the 1966 BPR which were purchased by each library. Not surprisingly, the figures correlated closely with the size of the institution, library budget, emphasis in collection building, and scope of the curriculum.

Figure 2. 7 presents the actual number of BPR sample titles found at each of the libraries. Title overlap may be compared between any two institutions through use of this matrix; e. g., of the

Figure 2. 6

Percent of Titles Announced in 1966 Purchased by Each Library

Library	Percentage
# 1	9. 0
# 2	16. 1
# 3	41. 3
# 4	17. 6
# 5	2. 8
# 6	18. 0
# 7	9. 0
# 8	47. 8
# 9	5. 4

Figure 2. 7

Title Overlap Matrix

Library	# 1	# 2	# 3	# 4	# 5	# 6	# 7	# 8	# 9
# 1	108	34	69	51	13	50	28	78	18
# 2	34	194	140	82	12	84	33	147	29
# 3	69	140	498	152	21	161	59	408	50
# 4	51	82	152	212	15	98	48	154	31
# 5	13	12	21	15	34	12	5	24	5
# 6	50	84	161	98	12	217	38	176	32
# 7	28	33	59	48	5	38	108	61	12
# 8	78	147	408	154	24	176	61	576	52
# 9	18	29	50	31	5	32	12	52	65

1, 208 titles in the BPR sample, there were 408 common titles held by both Library # 3 and Library # 8. Library # 1 held 108 of the 1, 208 titles in the sample; # 2 had 194; # 3 had 498; # 4 had 212; # 5 had 34; # 6 had 217; # 7 had 108; # 8 had 576; # 9 had 65.

When a title is ordered by one of the participating libraries, the probability that it will be ordered by any other library in the system can be determined by examining Figure 2. 8 and comparing the second library against the first. The matrix was calculated using the existing BPR data. Probability is represented on a scale from 0 (there is no chance that an event will occur) to 1. 0 (there is 100% chance that an event will occur). As an example, assume that Library

Figure 2. 8

Probability of Title Duplication Between Two Libraries

	#1	#2	#3	#4	#5	#6	#7	#8	#9
#1	1. 0	. 32	. 64	. 47	. 12	. 46	. 26	. 72	. 17
#2	. 17	1. 0	. 72	. 42	. 06	. 43	. 27	. 76	. 16
#3	. 13	. 28	1. 0	. 31	. 04	. 32	. 12	. 81	. 11
#4	. 24	. 39	. 72	1. 0	. 07	. 46	. 23	. 72	. 16
#5	. 38	. 35	. 61	. 44	1. 0	. 35	. 15	. 70	. 14
#6	. 23	. 39	. 74	. 45	. 06	1. 0	. 18	. 81	. 15
#7	. 25	. 30	. 54	. 44	. 04	. 35	1. 0	. 55	. 12
#8	. 13	. 25	. 74	. 27	. 04	. 30	. 11	1. 0	. 09
#9	. 27	. 45	. 77	. 48	. 08	. 52	. 19	. 80	1. 0

#5 orders a title; the probability that Library #8 will order that same title is . 70 or 70%. Or assume that Library #8 orders a title; the probability that Library #5 will order the same title is . 04 or 4%.

The expected number of duplicate copies of a title that will be ordered within the system is an important consideration. Assume that an order is initiated by one library, how many additional orders for that title could a center expect to receive from the other libraries? This is a critical question for any group of libraries contemplating centralized processing, as the relative success or failure of a center will depend to a large extent on the number of duplicate copies ordered and processed.

Figure 2. 9 lists the expected rate of order duplications and total of expected orders for copies of a title by other libraries, if placed by each of the indicated libraries. For example, if a title is ordered by Library #9, the Center can expect 3. 523 other orders for that title, making a total of 4. 523 copies ordered. If Library #8 orders a title, the Center could expect 1. 910 other orders for the same title, making a total of 2. 910 copies ordered. The average expected number of order duplications is 2. 818 indicating that the Center can expect 3. 818 requests for any title ordered.

Figure 2. 9
Expected Title Duplication Level

Expected Number of Order Duplications (Excluding Multiple Copies)		
Library	#1	3. 157
	#2	2. 892
	#3	2. 129
	#4	2. 976
	#5	3. 147
	#6	3. 000
	#7	2. 630
	#8	1. 910
	#9	3. 523
Center		
Average expected number of order duplications 2. 818		

Total Expected Orders for a Title (Excluding Multiple Copies)		
Library	#1	4. 157
	#2	3. 892
	#3	3. 129
	#4	3. 976
	#5	4. 147
	#6	4. 000
	#7	3. 630
	#8	2. 910
	#9	4. 523
Center		
Average expected orders for copies of a title 3. 818		

These figures are based on the assumption that only one copy is ordered by each library. Should one or more libraries order multiple copies, the duplication factor would naturally increase. Generally the college libraries ordered one copy only of a given title; but as the university libraries frequently ordered additional copies, the duplication figures have been understated.

Cataloging Modification

The Processing Center will use Library of Congress catalog copy to the maximum extent possible in cataloging and processing books. The policy regarding cataloging with L. C. copy will be to accept the classification, descriptive cataloging and subject analysis without modification. Titles with L. C. copy will be processed by clerks trained to process books using the unmodified L. C. copy.

The extent of modification of L. C. copy in each of the participating libraries was measured in order to determine how often a conflict would arise when a library accepts unmodified L. C. cataloging. Two of the nine libraries are classified by the Dewey Decimal System and one classified by Dewey with only a few types of materials classed according to L. C. These three libraries are not included in the call number modification summary figures or in the shelf list conflicts. One of these three libraries has since begun classifying by L. C.; the directors of the libraries still using Dewey have agreed to adopt L. C. once the Processing Center becomes operational.

The six libraries using L. C. classification had changed from Dewey to L. C. classification, and began reclassification projects on October 1958; July 1962; November 1963; July 1965; September 1965. One library was established in October 1965, and began with the L.C. system. All of the six had used L. C. for some time and had reclassified at least a part of their collections.

Methodology of data collection: The types and frequency of cataloging modifications were analyzed, using the *Book Publishing Record* sample titles as the data base. As the *BPR* titles were checked against the public catalog, note was made by the data collector of modifications in the classification number, Cutter number, descriptive cataloging, subject cataloging, treatment of monographic series (classed together or classed separately; standing order or not a standing order), and the number of copies processed. The call number, if different from the *BPR* entry, was also noted on the back of the collection card. The shelf list was then checked to locate information not found on the main entry card in the public catalog and to determine the reason for call number modification (e. g., was there a conflict between the suggested L. C. number and a class number the library had assigned earlier; was the number simply changed to fit a particular subject emphasis in the collection; or was the number modified to conform to a local library policy).

The data cards for which there were no corresponding titles in the collection were arranged by the L. C. classification number printed in the BPR entry. After the public catalog and in-process file had been checked against all BPR titles in the sample, the shelf list was checked for possible conflicts, i. e., if the titles had been processed into the library, would there have been a call number conflict between the L. C. number indicated in the BPR entry and a number already assigned to a title.

Data summary and analysis: Figure 2. 10 summarizes the processing modifications identified in the nine libraries. Of the 2, 016 titles identified in the libraries, 9. 5% were on order, 3. 9% were in process and 86. 5% were in the collection. All cataloging modification figures are based on the 86. 5% of the titles identified, as this is the percent of titles actually cataloged at the time of the survey.

The study showed that 88% of the L. C. assigned numbers were accepted with no modification. Of the 12% modified, Cutter number modification accounted for the majority of the changes and most of the changes were performed at Library #6 (see Figure 2. 11).

Monographic series accounted for 21% of those titles processed (for purpose of the study, monographic series were identified as those titles published at regular or irregular intervals which have some connection, such as subject, form, authorship, or publication, and are identified as monographic serials rather than periodicals). As the Center will process monographic series, the method of ordering (standing order or titles ordered individually) and the treatment (classed together or classed separately) were examined. Of the 21% monographic series received, 18. 75% were classed separately and 2. 2% were classed together. As the Center will follow L. C. Catalog copy in classifying titles processed, those libraries which have not followed L. C. 's treatment of a particular series must continue to order the title through a vendor or publisher rather than through the Center. Were the Center to receive the order, the L. C. suggested class number would be assigned, and a conflict in classification would result. Standing orders accounted for only 4. 53% of the total orders received. Unless the Center were to accept standing orders, this 4. 53% would continue to be ordered independently by each library.

The total BPR sample (1, 208 titles) was checked against the shelf list at the six libraries using the L. C. classification system

Figure 2. 10

Summary of Modification in L. C. Classification and Cataloging Among the Nine Participating Libraries

Percent of:	
1. BPR sample titles that were:	
a. On order	9. 57%
b. In process	3. 92%
c. Cataloged	86. 51%
2. Call number modification - total	12. 18%
a. Classification number only	0. 28%
b. Cutter number only	10. 58%
c. Classification and Cutter number	1. 32%
d. No modification	87. 82%
3. Cataloging modification - total	4. 70%
a. Added entry only	0. 98%
b. Subject entry only	0. 40%
c. Added and subject entry	3. 32%
d. No modification	95. 30%
4. Monographic series - total	20. 99%
a. Classed together	0. 29%
b. Classed separately	16. 17%
c. Standing orders	4. 53%
(1) classed together	1. 95%
(2) classed separately	2. 58%
d. Not a serial	79. 01%
5. Shelf list conflicts	0 conflicts in 1587 volumes

and no conflicts were found. Conflicts which had been expected were: (1) for a book already in the collection, a change in classification number because the number had been assigned to a title previously processed into the collection; and (2) for a book not in the collection, a conflict between the L. C. number provided in the BPR entry, and a number already used by the library.

As no conflict was identified, a tentative plan to maintain a shelf list of each library's holdings was abandoned. The survey demonstrated that call numbers assigned by L. C. will fit into each library's collection with little or no conflict.

Summary of Results

The survey of the operational characteristics of the participat-

Figure 2.11
Percent Modification of L. C. Classification and Cataloging at Each Participating Library

Percent of:	1	2	3	4
1. BPR sample titles that were:				
a. On order	18.52	0.52	0.00	0.00
b. In process	1.85	12.88	1.00	1.88
c. Cataloged	79.63	86.60	99.00	98.12
2. Call number modification total -2a -2c	Dewey	9.52	2.84	Dewey
a. Classification number only	---	1.19	0.20	---
b. Cutter number only	---	4.76	2.03	---
c. Classification and Cutter number	---	3.57	0.61	---
d. No modification	---	90.48	97.16	---
3. Cataloging modification	8.14	1.79	0.16	2.39
a. Added entry only	0.00	0.00	0.20	0.96
b. Subject entry only	1.16	0.60	0.00	0.96
c. Added entry and subject entry	6.98	1.19	0.41	0.47
d. No modification	91.86	98.21	99.39	97.61
4. Monographic series total 4a -4c	20.93	22.02	21.30	18.66
a. Classed together	2.33	0.00	0.00	0.48
b. Classed separately	17.44	22.02	15.42	14.83
c. Standing orders 4c total (1) - (2)	1.16	0.00	5.88	3.35
(1) Classed together	0.00	0.00	3.04	2.39
(2) Classed separately	1.16	0.00	2.84	0.96
d. Not a serial	79.07	77.98	78.70	81.34
5. Shelf list conflicts	---	0	0	---

ing libraries reveals that a centralized agency could be established without seriously disrupting the present procedures of the libraries. While adjustments would be necessary, it is clear that for the type of materials which the libraries are acquiring, the vast majority can be processed and added to a collection without conflict in the records. The libraries would not have to establish preliminary checks, and the books could be handled without assuming that each was in conflict.

The relatively high proportion of current domestic titles ordered by the college libraries suggest the desirability of joint purchasing and cataloging if a method for coordinating orders can be estab-

5	6	7	8	9
5. 88	46. 36	0. 93	9. 03	23. 08
0. 00	0. 00	20. 37	3. 64	0. 00
94. 12	53. 64	78. 70	87. 33	76. 92
0. 00	67. 80	Dewey	1. 79	2. 00
0. 00	0. 00	---	0. 20	0. 00
0. 00	64. 41	---	0. 99	2. 00
0. 00	3. 39	---	0. 60	0. 00
100.00	32. 20	---	98. 21	98. 00
21. 88	3. 39	45. 88	2. 39	4. 00
3. 13	1. 69	1. 18	1. 79	2. 00
6. 24	0. 00	0. 00	0. 00	2. 00
12. 51	1. 70	44. 70	0. 60	0. 00
78. 12	96. 61	54. 12	97. 61	96. 00
21. 88	22. 88	16. 47	23. 46	2. 00
0. 00	0. 00	0. 00	0. 20	2. 00
18. 75	22. 88	16. 47	15. 11	0. 00
3. 13	0. 00	0. 00	8. 15	0. 00
3. 13	0. 00	0. 00	2. 58	0. 00
0. 00	0. 00	0. 00	5. 57	0. 00
78. 12	77. 12	83. 53	76. 54	98. 00
0	0	---	0	0

lished that will not impinge on freedom of selection by faculty and librarians. It would no doubt be possible to reduce the lag time from the time an order is submitted to a vendor until a book is received, since a local vendor would be in a better position to create an inventory that approximated the types of materials the colleges were likely to order.

The low frequency of rush orders also suggests the desirability of a centralized operation since the vast bulk of materials added to collections can be handled in a routine fashion. Rush materials could be handled on a special basis at a central operation or could continue to be ordered and processed by each library.

The low rate of foreign material acquisitions at the college libraries suggest the desirability of pooling cataloging resources at the central agency in order to make the most effective use of language capabilities. Moreover, as programs requiring special language skills are initiated within the state's schools the benefits of pooling language capabilities will increase significantly.

Although there is no assurance that a centralized agency would process materials more rapidly than they are processed under the present systems, the present average lag of six months does permit considerable leeway for improvement.

Notes

1. Pearson, E. S. "Random Sampling Numbers." Tracts for computors, no. XXIV. Department of Statistics, University College, University of London.

2. Cochran, W. G. Sampling techniques. N. Y.: Wiley, 1963.

3. Cochran, ibid.

4. Kish, L. Survey sampling. N. Y.: Wiley, 1965.

5. Freund, John E. Modern elementary statistics, 2d ed. Englewood Cliffs, N. J.: Prentice-Hall, 1960, p. 220.

6. BPR exludes: (a) Federal and State Government publications; (b) subscription books; (c) dissertations; (d) second, third, fourth, etc. printings or impressions; (e) serials, quarterlies, and other periodicals; (f) pamphlets under forth-nine pages. Only paperback fiction titles under $1. 00 were excluded from the sample drawn.

III. Analysis of Current Library Operations - Times and Costs

Introduction

> Libraries do not have devices at present by which they can accurately measure their administrative effectiveness or social significance. The next ten years will witness the development of a body of costs and measurements for various types of library service which will meet adverse criticisms and enable the library to justify its support upon a basis of substantial facts, rather than of unproven assumptions. To a philosophy of action and specific objectives will be added accurate measures of performance--all of which are essential to sustained progressive achievement.[1]

This prediction was ventured by Louis Round Wilson in an article, "The next fifty years," written in 1936. Three decades later, the millennium still is out of sight, though articles on cost analysis abound in the literature.

Before data collection could begin at each library, it was necessary to prepare a thesaurus of all technical processing tasks performed at the nine libraries. Several published sources were utilized initially to compile the thesaurus or "Key to Functions Performed."[2 - 9]

At the beginning of the study, the project team visited each library to explain to the technical services staff what the study entailed. As work progressed, data on specific processing activities were obtained from interviews with the head librarian and the supervisory personnel in each of the libraries. A tape recorder was used to document interviews whenever this was possible.

The "Key to Functions Performed" was revised twice on the basis of information gathered during the time studies and from the data obtained during the initial diary studies. The diary studies were particularly helpful in improving the precision of the terminology used in the Key. Conversations with individual staff members attempting to fill out the diary forms revealed several defects in the first and second versions. The third version was actually used in the data gathering process.

Other forms needed to conduct the study were prepared in advance of the time observation phase of the study. These forms were the diary study explanation, the diary form, the "Flow Process Chart," the "Technical Processing Operations Timed" form, and the "Time Study Observation Sheet." The diary form "Daily Time-Function Record," was based on one used by Hendricks' _Comparative Costs of Book Processing,_ pp. 85-86. The other forms were based on examples found in the literature.[10-13.]

Flow Process Charting

In order to acquire a clear understanding of the tasks performed and the sequence of work flows in each technical services department, a member of the project first interviewed the head of the department and then the individual to be timed. On the basis of these interviews, the list of technical processing operations to be timed was drafted. After observing the procedures followed at each work station, the first draft of the flow process charts for each procedure was prepared and a scale floor plan of the technical processes work area was drawn. A sample of each form used locally in technical processing was also collected.

The time observation studies were then conducted, after which the flow process chart was reexamined and each step identified by type of operation, using the symbols provided on the chart. The distance traveled in feet during the performance of the operation was calculated from the work layout drawings.

The completed flow process charts were inspected carefully for errors by the supervisor. The charts were also compared with the diary study results, time observation sheets, and the local forms in order to detect omissions or inconsistencies in the data. In the narrative, the level of personnel performing the functions was also specified as well as the type of equipment used. (A sample flow process chart is shown in Figure 3.1.)

Diary Studies

The purpose of the diary study was to obtain mean times for

Figure 3. 1
Flow Process Chart

Library:			Summary	Pres Meth	Prop Meth	Diff
Subject Charted: Acquisitions			Operation	112		
Present Method Proposed	Man Chart Material	Sheet 1 of 16	Transportation	46		
			Inspection	2		
			Delay	0		
Chart Begins: Periodical Clerk opens mail bag.			Storage	1		
Chart Ends: Files them in "direct order" file.			Distance in feet	3, 394		
Charted by J. M. M.		Date 6/1/67				
			Total steps	161		

Dist in Feet	Time in Min	Step #	Process Description
			Sorting Mail
		1	Periodical Clerk opens mail bag and removes contents.
		2	Separates into three categories: 1) books, 2) magazines, and 3) enveloped mail.
32		3	Delivers book packages to Student Assistant's work table. Note: Boxes are left in the receiving room directly.
115		4	Delivers enveloped mail to Secretary in Library Office.
		5	Secretary sorts mail into seven categories: 1) first class, 2) bills or renewal notices, 3) personal mail for staff members, 4) publishers' brochures and catalogs, 5) periodicals that the Student Assistant did not recognize, 6) college catalogs, and 7) items to confer with the Librarian about.
		6	Opens first envelope of category number 1 mail.
		7	Reads contents and sets aside. Note: Repeats steps 6 and 7 until all of category number 1 is handled. Repeats steps 6 and 7 for category number 2.
		8	Opens first envelope of category number 4.
		9	Secretary examines and sets aside. Note: If a brochure, usually throws it in wastebasket. Note: Repeats steps 8 and 9 for categories 6 and 7.
132		10	Delivers category number 3 mail to staff member(s).
115		11	Delivers category number 5 to Periodical Clerk.

Figure 3. 1 (Continued)

Library________ Sheet 2

Subject Charted: Acquisitions of 16

Date 6/1/67

Dist in Feet	Time in Min	Step #	Process Description
		12	Confers with Librarian about cateogries numer 1, 2 and 7.
124		13	Takes publishers catalogs to filing cabinet in Cataloging Room.
		14	Arranges them alphabetically.
		15	Files them removing superseded catalogs when found.
15		16	Takes superseded catalogs to waste basket.
139		17	Returns to office.
			Checking Bibliographies
6		18	Student Assistant takes bibliography (Choice, Publishers Catalog, etc., that a faculty member has marked for desiderata) and marking pen to public catalog from reference service desk.

Flow Process Chart

Library:

Subject Charted: Cataloging (Exact LC cards)

Present / Proposed Method	Man / Material Chart	Sheet 1 of 9

Chart Begins: Student Assistant matches newly received books with LC cards and multiple-order slips.

Chart Ends: Secretary (or Student Assistant) types Monthly Acquisitions List.

Charted by L. Leonard Date 6/1/67

Summary

	Pres Meth	Prop Meth	Diff
Operation	91		
Transportation	26		
Inspection	4		
Delay			
Storage			
Distance in feet			

Total steps 121

Dist in Feet	Time in Min	Step #	Process Description
		1	Student Assistant matches newly received books with LC cards and multiple-order slips in outstanding orders file.

Figure 3. 1 (Continued)

Library ________________ Sheet 2 of 9

Subject Charted: Cataloging (Exact LC cards) Date 6/1/67

Dist in Feet	Time in Min	Step #	Process Description
			Note: Books which have cards in file are delivered to hold shelf for checking. Those for which LC cards are on order, but not yet received, are placed on hold shelves arranged alphabetically by author. Books for which no LC copy was located in verification procedure are delivered to Cataloger's Office. Pink, blue and yellow multiple-order slips are placed in book.
		2	Places books with LC cards on hold shelf for checking. Note: Student Assistant checks incoming LC cards against books on LC hold shelves, and places books on hold shelf as LC cards are matched with the books.
16		3	Clerk-typist walks to LC copy hold shelf.
		4	Checks to see that exact LC copy has been sent for each book. Note: If there is any discrepancy, gives books to Cataloger.
16		5	Carries books with exact LC copy to her desk.
30		6	Carries books with near LC copy to Cataloger's Office.
		7	Places books on Cataloger's desk.
30		8	Clerk-typist returns to her desk.
		9	Picks up book.
		10	Removes multiple-order slips and LC cards from book.
		11	Turns to verso of title page in book.
		11A	Types call number on pink notification slip.
		12	Types LC call number and accessions number on main entry and shelf list cards. Note: Gets accessions number from verso of title page. Stamped on bottom of page as part of the Acquisitions check-in procedure.
		13	Types LC call number, subject headings, and added entries on appropriate cards in set.
		14	Types circulation card. Note: Types accessions number on upper right corner

Figure 3. 1 (Continued)

Library ______ Sheet 2 of 9

Subject Charted: Cataloging (Exact LC cards) Date 6/1/67

Dist in Feet	Time in Min	Step #	Process Description
			of circulation card.
		15	Types card pocket. Note: Types accessions number on upper right corner of card pocket.
		16	Places cards and multiple-order slips in card pocket.
		17	Places pocket in book.

tasks that involve large frequency variability that tend to make direct time observations difficult (e. g., original cataloging, bibliographic searching, bindery procedures, etc.). Diary times used in the labor cost analysis are identified as such in the labor computation tables. (See Appendix 3. 5) Information from the diary study was also checked against the flow process charts to verify the level of personnel who performed each function. This information was later used in computing labor costs.

During each time-study visit, the project member met with all supervisors and personnel who would be involved in the diary study. The "Key to Functions Performed" and the procedure for completing the "Daily Time-Function Record" were carefully explained.

A representative cross section of personnel were assigned to the diary study; however, it was not required that two people performing the same functions be part of the study, as in the case of two typists preparing sets of L. C. cards. The technical processing departments in most of the colleges were too small to exclude any staff member from the diary study with the exception of student assistants who were assigned repetitive jobs such as arranging catalog cards or pasting pockets. In the latter case only one student was chosen for the study, preferably the student who worked the most hours in the library. Any line librarian, including the head librarian, who performed supervisory functions concerning technical processes, was included in the diary study. If a supervisor was involved with technical processing tasks only a portion of his total work day, he entered this information on the appropriate area of the diary record and used function #47 (other general activities) with a description of the other duties he performed. Other persons assigned part-time to technical services functions filled out the diary record in the same manner. (See revised "Key to Functions Performed" Figure 3. 2, and sample diary form, Figure 3. 3 following the discussion of diary studies; the rest of the Diary Study Packet can be found in Appendix 3. 1.)

Figure 3. 2

Revised Key
Colorado Academic Libraries Book Processing Center
Technical Processing - Monographs and Monographic Series
Key to Functions Performed

Function Number	Acquisitions
1	Sorting of Acquisitions mail
1. 1	Typing purchase request cards
2	Bibliographic checking - verification
3	Assign dealer and fund
4	Prepare multiple-order record
4. 1	Burst multiple-order forms
5	Type purchase requisition, purchase order or letter order.
6	Typing (general) - correspondence, claims, etc.
7	Revise, sign and mail request to dealer
8	Filing
9	Revision (general)
10	Check reports from dealer
11	Inquiries
12	Receiving routine
13	Bookkeeping
14	Clear order files
15	Notify requestor
16	Other Acquisitions work (specify)
	Cataloging
17	Order LC cards or other unit cards
18	Receive and arrange LC cards

Figure 3. 2 (Continued)
Revised Key to Functions Performed

Function Number	
18. 1	Receive and arrange LC proof slips or proof sheets
19	File LC proof copy
20	Match LC cards or proof copy and books
21	Collate books
21. 1	Write sourcing information in book
22	Accession (number and/or record)
23	Catalog and classify with LC cards/copy
24	Type call number, added entries
25	Revise LC card sets or locally reproduced sets
25. 1	Add copies or volumes
26	Original cataloging and classifying
27	Type master card
27. 1	Type card sets
27. 2	Type modification on a card or proof slip
27. 3	Type authority cards
28	Revise master card (or typed card sets)
29	Reproduce card sets
30	Type circulation card
31	Type pocket
32	Mark call number on spine of volume
33	Paste pocket and date due slip. Paste gift plate
33. 1	Paste biographical and review material in book
34	Property stamp
34. 1	Place plastic jacket on book
34. 2	Prepare paperbound books for bindery
35	Sort shelf list and catalog cards (also: authority cards, cross-references, etc.)
36	File shelf list and catalog cards (also: authority cards, cross-references, etc.)
37	Revise filing of shelf and catalog cards (also: authority cards, cross-references, etc.)
37. 1	Revise completed books before forwarding to Circulation
38	Catalog maintenance (other than filing)
38. 1	Revision (general)
39	Other cataloging work (specify)
	General Activities
40	Book selection
40. 1	Prepare periodic acquisitions lists
41	Professional reading
42	Reporting
43	Staff meetings
44	Supervision of personnel
45	Personal business
46	Sick leave, vacation

Figure 3. 2 (Continued)
Revised Key to Functions Performed

Function Number	
47	Other general activities (specify)
48	Time spent keeping this record

The diary study was conducted during two five-consecutive work day periods. During the first diary study a member of the project was available to answer questions posed by participants and to observe that forms were properly completed. A great deal of ambiguity was eliminated from the "Key to Functions Performed" as a result of these communications. The second study was run two months later, but no member of the investigation team was present. The forms were mailed to the head librarian with instructions for their completion and return to the Project Office.

The diary forms for the unsupervised study were compared with results of the supervised study; no significant differences could be detected in the manner in which the charts were filled out or the time totals for the functions performed. This was true even though a few changes in personnel and changes in duties assigned had transpired between the two studies.

Time Observations

Time observation is a method well suited to determining the unit time required to perform repetitive tasks when small time intervals are involved. This was the method used to arrive at the unit times for the majority of tasks measured during this phase of the study.

Before beginning the timing, the investigator first questioned the subject to insure that he (the investigator) understood what was going to be done and the reason for it. Next, he timed several sample work cycles to insure that all steps identified were in proper sequence and that each operation was in fact being performed. Observations were then recorded to the nearest second on a "Time Study Observation Sheet," using a stop watch.

Figure 3. 3
Colorado Academic Libraries Book Processing Center
Daily Time - Function Record

Date 17 July 1967

Library State College Name J. Jones
Department Cataloging Position Asst. Cataloger

Minutes	Function Key	Number Items Handled	Function Key	Number Items Handled	Function Key	Number Items Handled	Function Key	Number Items Handled
Hour	8:00		9:00		10:00		11:00	
05	#26	3 Books	#45					
10								
15			#21.1	25 Books				
20								
25					#37	300 Cards		
30								
35			#37					
40								
45					# 26			
50								
55							#26	5 Books
60	#45							

Record in the appropriate time space the number of items handled or processed while performing one function. If work schedule is other than 8:00 a. m. - 5:00 p. m., consider the columns as 1st through 8th hour of work.

Function Key	Number Items Handled	Function Key	Number Items Handled	Function Key	Number Items Handled	Function Key	Number Items Handled
1:00		2:00		3:00		4:00	
#23				#23	10 Books	#26	4 Books
		#23	21 Books				
		#43					
				#37.1	22 Books		
		#45					
						#48	

The distance traveled in performing a task was noted but not used in the computation of the mean times. Movement was omitted since it is a factor independent of the time required to complete a task. The number of items handled in a given operation or series of steps were also recorded. Occasionally the person timed did not follow the same sequence for each cycle. The importance of these variations was discussed with the employee and, if necessary, recorded as irregularly performed operations.

A personal rating factor in the form of a time allowance was recorded on each observation form to account for worker variations from the "normal time" taken to perform the task. Normal time is the time required by an individual familiar with a work routine to complete one repetition or cycle of this routine working at a normal pace. It is equivalent to the observed time (watch reading) multiplied by the rating factor (a subjective percentage factor assigned by the observer to compensate for deviation from the subject's normal working pace). Most individuals timed were judged to be performing over their normal working speed; therefore, such ratings as 110% (1. 10), 125% (1. 25), etc., were assigned. A person who was nervous and consequently made an excessive number of errors received ratings in the range of 85% (0. 85) or 90% (0. 90).

Each time observation was recorded on the "Time Study Observation Sheet" (see Figure 3. 4). Readings were recorded in the horizontal R (watch reading) line as the subject completed each cycle or timed element of a cycle. The recordings were later converted to decimal fractions of minutes and entered in the T (time) line above each corresponding R reading. If it were not possible to obtain forty cycles during a single timing session, the observations were continued the following day. In some cases, there were not enough books or orders placed to provide forty observations even though the task was important. When this occurred, as many cycles as possible were timed and the data were later supplemented by the diary studies or by standard times located in published sources. Occasionally it was necessary to return to the library to complete the time observations. When all readings had been taken, the T values were summed and $\overline{T}$ (the mean observed time) was calculated for

Figure 3. 4

Time Study Observation Sheet

Library: No. 6

Operation Filing shelf lists

Time Started 8:35 Time Finished 8:50

Observer JM Date 5-10-67

Student Assistant

Allowances RF 1. 15%

Standard Time . 2895 min.

Units/hour

Function (67)

No.	Elements		1	2	3	4	5	6	7	8	9	10	ΣT	$\bar{T}$	RF	NT	
1	Takes drawer and file box to	T	. 68														
	work table	R	. 41														
2	Files each shelf list card (re-	T	. 07	. 23	. 13	. 20	. 23	. 13	. 08	. 10	. 23	. 27					
	moving temp. card slips)	R	. 4	. 14	. 8	. 12	. 14	. 8	. 5	. 6	. 14	. 16					
		T	. 15	. 20	. 22	. 18	. 08	. 28	. 17	. 18	. 25	. 12					
		R	. 9	. 12	. 13	. 11	. 5	. 17	. 10	. 11	. 15	. 7					
		T	. 20	. 28	. 15	. 22	. 13	. 12	. 15	. 25	. 17	. 08					
		R	. 12	. 17	. 9	. 13	. 8	. 7	. 9	. 15	. 10	. 5					
		T	. 18	. 10	. 07	. 13	. 13	. 08	. 10	. 12	. 08	. 22					
		R	. 11	. 6	. 4	. 8	. 8	. 5	. 6	. 7	. 5	. 13					
		T	. 23	. 08	. 23	. 08	. 08	. 12	. 08	. 13	. 13	. 12					
		R	. 14	. 5	. 14	. 5	. 5	. 7	. 5	. 8	. 8	. 7					
		T	. 22	. 20	. 08	. 13	. 07	. 15	. 10	. 07	. 07	. 20					
		R	. 13	. 12	. 5	. 8	. 4	. 9	. 6	. 4	. 4	. 12					
		T	. 17	. 15	. 30	. 10	. 23	. 15	. 15	. 17	. 23	. 18					
		R	. 10	. 9	. 18	. 6	. 14	. 9	. 9	. 10	. 14	. 11					
		T	. 13	. 10	. 25	. 33	. 32	. 40	. 25	. 20	. 33	. 12	13. 29				
		R	. 8	. 6	. 15	. 20	. 19	. 24	. 15	. 12	. 20	. 7	80	. 17	1. 15	. 196	
3	Replaces two drawers	T	. 17														
		R	. 10														
4	Obtains two more drawers	T	. 17														
		R	. 10														

ΣT = 13. 29

Readings = 80

Standard Time = (NT) (1. 4771)

= (. 196) (1. 4771) = . 2895

each task. This mean time multiplied by RF (the personal rating factor) yielded NT (the normal time). Functions which are not appliable to all books processed are multiplied by a frequency factor other than 1.00 to produce an adjusted mean time (see Discussion of Frequencies). The timing and flow process charting phase of the data collection were conducted during March, April, May, June and July.

Each institution's business office personnel were also interviewed during the field trips with the exception of the University of Colorado Libraries which maintains its own internal accounting system. Each interview was taped and a collection of business office forms used in book procurement were obtained. A discussion of the business office studies is included in Section IV.

Sample Size for Time Observations

The number of time observations required to achieve the desired reliability is independent upon the variance of the times recorded of the subject performing the task under study. A large variation in a group of readings for a small number of timed work cycles would indicate that more readings are required, assuming homogenity in the task elements.

The sample size, "n," must be large enough to predict at a selected confidence level that the sample approximates the population "μ" within defined limits. Population here is defined as the total number of repetitions in performance of a task over a finite period of time.

Based on estimation procedures outlined in Modern Elementary Statistics,[14] initial timings of the more commonly performed functions were taken at two libraries, one large and one small, using forty observations as the sample size (N=40).

The variance of these observations was computed by substituting into the following formula:

$$s^2 = \frac{n \sum_{i=1}^{n} X_i^2 - \left(\sum_{i=1}^{n} X_i \right)^2}{n\,(n-1)}$$

The standard error was computed:

$$s_{\overline{X}} = \frac{s}{\sqrt{n}}$$

The mean for each function: $\overline{X} = \frac{\Sigma X}{n}$. At a 95% confidence level, the real mean would fall within the range expressed as $\overline{X} \pm 1.96\ s_{\overline{X}}$.

The results of the calculations for several of the selected functions are summarized below:

Function #11 - Filing in order file (Library #8)

$s = .0575$

$s_{\overline{x}} = .00909$

$\overline{X} = .466 \quad 1.96\ (s_{\overline{X}}) = .0178$

μ is between $.47 \pm .02$ at 95% C. L.

Function #23 - Pulling encumbrance cards (Library #8)

$s = .615$

$s_{\overline{x}} = .009723$

$\overline{X} = .31125 \quad 1.96\ (s_{\overline{X}}) = .01906$

μ is between $.31 \pm .02$ at 95% C. L.

Function #60 - Pasting pockets (Library #6)

$s = .0594$

$s_{\overline{x}} = .009391$

$\overline{X} = .35425 \quad 1.96\ (s_{\overline{X}}) = .01841$

μ is between $.35 \pm .02$ at 95% C. L.

The degree of variability occurring with forty observations was considered to be acceptable. Therefore, this sample size was adhered to whenever it was practical to apply it. Up to one hundred observations were taken on very brief cycle functions such as property stamping, preliminary sorting of cards for the public catalog, assigning vendors to order cards, etc. As mentioned earlier, in a few cases it was not possible to time forty cycles. When this occurred the observations were supplemented with data from the diary studies. However, forty observations was the standard sample size used, and every effort was made to time at least forty cycles of repetitive functions.

Standardized Technical Processing Activities

Once the "Key to Functions Performed" (the activity list used in the diary study) was refined, and the scope of each activity was adequately defined in depth, the "Key" was redesignated "Standardized Technical Processing Activities" (STPA) (see Figure 3. 5 for list, and Appendix 3. 2 for scope of activities). The study staff used the standard activities identified as the basis for the detailed time study and cost analysis work conducted at each library. The study of technical services activities included analysis of a diversity of tasks ranging from single elements to an entire routine. Consequently, to collect useful, comparable data, the units (elements, operations, processes, etc.) to be measured were divided into three categories: (1) activities that are performed in the same manner by all libraries, i. e., filing cards, opening mail, etc.; (2) activities that may be performed by alternative methods, but which all produce essentially the same result, product, or action, i. e., preparing multiforms by typing, photography, or xerography, etc.; (3) activities that can be more meaningfully measured as composite routines, i. e., claiming procedures, accessioning routines, etc.

Analysis in the "Activities" compilation is limited to the acquiring and processing of monographs and monographic series, thus omitting activities associated with technical processing of periodicals. Functions which have no processing center counterpart or a substitution activity--e. g.: library--sort and file catalog cards, center--update book catalog--are also eliminated from the list.

Figure 3. 5
Standardized Technical Processing Activities

I. Acquisitions
  A. Preliminary Activities
    1. Open, sort and distribute incoming mail
    2a. Review book order requests
    2b. Review selection media
    3. Select titles to be ordered
    4. Type library order request card
  B. Bibliographic Searching - Checking
    5. Search and verify bibliographic information
  C. Orders Placement
    6. Assign vendor and fund

7. Prepare multiple order record
8. Type purchase requisition, etc.
9a. Revise typing
9b. Sign and mail requests
10. Burst forms
11. File forms in appropriate files
12. Encumbrance or prepayment routine

D. Receiving, Billing
13a. Unpack books; check against packing list or invoice
13b. Check outstanding order file
14. Check in serials on Kardex
15. Collate books
16. Book return procedure (incorrect shipment, defective copy, approval books)
17. Book accessioning routine
18. Write sourcing information
19. Prepare gift record form
20. Book distribution routine
21. Prepare receiving report
22. Prepare invoices for payment
23. Expenditure routine

E. Post-Cataloging
24. Clear in-process file
25. File forms, etc., in completed records or discard
26. Requestor notification routine
27. Periodic accessions list routine

F. Miscellaneous Activities
28. Vendor status routine
29. Claims routine
30. Cancellations routine
31. Out-of-print order routine. This routine was not subdivided in the CALBPC study as it served its purpose in labor cost analysis, and for comparison of similar activities among the participating libraries. It will, however, be too broad an activity in analyzing the technical processes functions of a single library in a minutely detailed study.
32. Process inquiries
33. General typing - correspondence, etc. (specify)
34. General revision (specify)
35. General filing (specify)

G. Other Acquisitions Activities
36. Other acquisitions activities not listed above (specify)

II. Cataloging

A. Pre-Cataloging
37. Sort books, assign and distribute
38. Search for LC copy; verify bibliographic information
39. Order LC cards or other unit cards
40. Receive and arrange LC cards
41. Receive and arrange LC proof slips or proof sheets
42. File LC copy (cards or proof)
43. Match LC cards or proof copy and books
44. Added copies/added volumes routine

Figure 3. 5
Standardized Technical Processing Activities (Cont.)

B. LC Cataloging
   45. Catalog and Classify with LC cards/copy
C. Original Cataloging
   46. Original cataloging and classifying
   47. Shelf listing (for 44, 45 and 46)
D. Card Reproduction and Processing
   48. Type complete card sets
   49. Type master card
   50. Revise master card
   51. Type modification on a card or proof slip
   52a. Reproduce card sets (other than typing)
   52b. Sort cards into sets
   53. Type call number, added entries
   54. Revise typing on card sets
   55. Prepare authority cards
   56. Prepare cross-reference cards
E. Mechanical Book Processing
   57. Prepare circulation card
   58. Prepare book pocket
   59. Mark call number or place label on spine of volume
   60. Affix pocket and date due slip. Affix gift plate
   61. Affix biographical and review material in book
   62. Stamp property marks
   63. Affix plastic jacket to book
   64. Paperback books--library binding routine
   65. Revise completed books before forwarding to circulation
F. Card Filing
   66. Sort and alphabetize shelf list and all catalog cards
   67. File shelf list and all catalog cards
   68. Revise filing of shelf list and all catalog cards
G. Miscellaneous Activities
   69. Route card sets to departmental libraries
   70. Paperback books--bindery routine (preparation)
   71. Paperback books--bindery routine (receiving)
   72. Catalog maintenance (other than filing)
   73. General typing (specify)
   74. General revision (specify)
   75. General filing (specify)
   76. Other cataloging activities not listed above (specify)

Even with these limitations, the standardized activities represent a comprehensive description of functions performed by the majority of libraries in the country. Activities that are not included can be added locally and others modified to meet local needs. A library can also subdivide any of the activities in order to collect data that more nearly satisfies its particular needs.

Data Analysis of the Member Libraries

Time observation data, data derived from the other methodological approaches and information pertaining to each library's procedures were analyzed to yield comparative unit cost figures. Five major factors were studied to calculate the unit cost for book processing at each library: labor, supplies, overhead, transportation (the total distance moved in the work flow), and binding.

Symbols and Formulas

1. Unit Labor Cost

a. Mean Times (a) - In order to obtain mean fimes from the raw data recorded on the time observation sheets, it was necessary to convert the readings to decimal times, and key the steps or blocks of steps to coordinate with the tasks identified in the STPA list.

If a function was found to be split into several distinct steps sometimes performed by different people or in combination with portions of other tasks, it was labeled with the appropriate function number with a subscript denoting the sequence of the step. Next, a mean time was calculated for each sub-function by summing the observed times and dividing by the number of items handled or cycles performed, whichever was appropriate for that particular function.

This information was transferred to another sheet so that all sub-functions could be cumulated to yield a total mean time for each function. (See Figure 3. 6) These mean times were then recorded on the labor computation chart of the library being analyzed.

b. Simulated Times - By comparing the labor chart with the flow process chart and the diary studies it was possible to identify which remaining functions could be labeled NA (not applicable), which could bc labeled AF (accomplished by another function), and which functions needed additional timing. Data from the diary studies were used if an adequate number of entries had been recorded to approximate a time observation session, (noted by a d following the diary time in the labor chart). Times still lacking were obtained by averaging the observed times gathered at other libraries in the study. Times calculated by this last method are distinguished by parenthesis (see Figure 3. 7).

Figure 3. 6
Mean Times (in minutes)

Calculation of Mean Times by Sub-Function for One Library
Numerator = total time in minutes and hundredths of minutes
Denominator= number of observations or number of items handled

Function Step	Mean	Description
1	$\frac{18.16}{65} = .279$	Sorts mail
4	$\frac{25.66}{40} = .641$	Types purchase request card
5_1	$\frac{9.63}{120} = .080$	Stamps search key on card
5_2	$\frac{10.22}{120} = .085$	Alphabetizes cards
5_3	$\frac{7.55}{76} = .099$	Writes in date on cards
5_4	$\frac{28.78}{50} = .575$	Searches public catalog
5_6	$\frac{28.43}{50} = .568$	Searches B. I. P.
5_7	$\frac{3.42}{50} = .068$	Circles B. I. P. at bottom of each card
5_8	$\frac{44.22}{50} = .884$	Searches C.B.I. for remaining titles
5 Total	2. 359	Search and verify bibliographic info.
7	$\frac{27.48}{40} = .678$	Types order form
8	$\frac{18.38}{5} = 3.676$	Examines invoice, types requisition, stamps signature, staples
9	$\frac{33.12}{40} = .828$	Posts orders
10	$\frac{7.75}{40} = .193$	Bursts forms
11	$\frac{.95}{2} = .475$	Files requisition file copy

Figure 3.7
Labor (L)
Unit Cost Calculation for Technical Processing Activities

Acquisitions

Library No. 3

Key: AF = Another function incorporated this activity at this library.

NA = Not applicable (not performed at this library).

( ) = Simulated data

+ = Standardizing factor (1.4771)

g_1 = Student Assistant

g_2 = Clerk (full-time)

g_3 = Professional

d = Data taken from the diary

	a	b	c	d	f	g	h	i
	Observed Mean Time	Frequency	Adjusted Time	Personal Rating Factor	Standard Time+	Category of Worker	Wage/ Minute	Cost of Activity
1. Open, sort and distribute incoming mail.	(.410)	1.000	.410	1.10	.6662	2	.0362	.024
2. Review book order requests; review selection media.	.429 d	1.000	.429	1.10	.6970	3	.0813	.057
3. Select titles to be ordered.	AF	---	---	---	---	-	---	---
4. Type library order request card.	NA	---	---	---	---	-	---	---
5. Search and verify bibliographic information.	2.990	1.000	2.990	1.20	5.2998	2	.0362	.192
6. Assign vendor and fund.	.395	1.000	.395	1.15	.6709	3	.0813	.054
7. Prepare multiple order record.	3.735	1.000	3.735	1.17	6.4549	2	.0362	.234
8. Type purchase requisition, etc.	2.268	.054	.122	1.10	.1982	2	.0362	.007

c. Frequencies (b) - All labor functions for each library were evaluated to determine to what extent a given function was performed for each book moving through the system. (See Figure 3. 8 and Frequency Computation Chart in Appendix 3. 3) Not all books are subjected to the same functions 100% of the time, so that a frequency of less than 1. 00 had to be established. Proportions such as gift books compared to purchases, hardbacks to paperbacks, added volumes compared to new titles, all affect the frequency with which a function is performed. Percentages based on the statistics collected were calculated and entered on the labor chart. For example, if every book received a pocket, the frequency was 1. 00, whereas a paperback book may have represented only 15% of the total number of books processed or . 15 in the frequency column. The mean time multiplied by the frequency produced the adjusted time (c) for each function. c = a x b

d. Personal Rating Factor (d) - The rating factor for each function was recorded on the time sheet when the observations were completed. At the same time each function was keyed according to one of three categories of personnel performing the function: #1 - Student Assistant; #2 - Clerk and #3 - Professional.

e. Standardizing factor (e) - Voos has listed the following elements which affect labor productivity and which are difficult to obtain through direct time observations and diary study data.[15]

These elements are:

unproductive time	16. 3 %
supervision	6. 5 %
administration	3. 8 %
instruction	5. 7 %
p =	32. 3 %

The standardizing factor was computed from the formula:[16]

$$e = \frac{100}{100 - p} \quad \text{where } p = 32.3$$

$$e = 1.4771$$

f. Standard Times (f) f = c x d x e - Standard times for each activity were calculated by multiplying the adjusted time (c) by the personal rating factor (d) and standardizing factor (e). A table of the standard times for each library was compiled. A mean standard time for each function was computed using the standard library times. The high and low standard times for each function and the mean of all

Figure 3. 8
Frequency Computation
Acquisition

* The use of these functions varied widely.
** Proportions were estimated when no statistics were available.

Assumption: Volumes processed entered the system during a given fiscal year.

Activity Description	Frequency Percentage Formula
1. Open, sort and distribute incoming mail.	1
2. Review book order requests; review selection media.	$\frac{\text{titles purchased}}{\text{volumes processed}}$
3. Select titles to be ordered.	Same as # 2
*4. Type library order request card.	Same as # 2
5. Search and verify bibliographic information.	Same as # 2
6. Assign vendor and fund.	Same as # 2
7. Prepare multiple order record.	Same as # 2
*8. Type purchase requisition, etc.	$\frac{\text{purchase req. prepared}}{\text{volumes processed}}$
9. Revise typing. Sign and mail requests.	Same as # 8
10. Burst forms.	Same as # 2
11. File forms in appropriate files.	Same as # 2
12. Encumbrance or prepayment routine.	Same as # 2
13. Unpack books; check against packing list or invoice. Check outstanding order file.	Same as # 2 ⟶ 1 (if gifts are handled this way)
14. Check in serials on Kardex.	$\frac{\text{added volumes}}{\text{volumes processed}}$
*15. Collate books.	0 ⟶ 1
16. Book return procedure (incorrect shipment, defective copy, approval books).	$\frac{\text{volumes returned}}{\text{volumes processed}}$
17. Book accessioning routine.	0 or 1
*18. Write sourcing information.	0 or 1
19. Prepare gift record form.	$\frac{\text{gift volumes received}}{\text{volumes processed}}$
20. Book distribution routine.	1
*21. Prepare receiving report.	Same as # 2

standard times calculated for each function are summarized in the table of generalized standard times. (See Figure 3. 9 and Generalized Standard Times Summary in Appendix 3. 4) Having worked with, calculated and recalculated the data, it is suggested that the best pro-

Figure 3.9
Generalized Standard Times Summary

Acquisitions

Activity Description	Normalized			Standardized		
	Low	High	Mean	Low	High	Mean
1. Open, sort and distribute incoming mail.	.321	1.348	.646	.474	1.990	.954
2. Review book order requests; review selection media.	.472	.942	.823	.697	1.391	1.215
3. Select titles to be ordered.	---	---	---			---
4. Type library order request card.	.675	2.563	1.470	.997	3.786	2.171
5. Search and verify bibliographic information.	1.599	13.624	4.274	2.362	20.123	6.313
6. Assign vendor and fund.	.069	1.732	.481	.102	2.559	.711
7. Prepare multiple order record.	.613	15.293	2.800	.906	22.590	4.136
8. Type purchase requisition, etc.	.352	14.176	6.213	.519	20.939	9.177
9. Revise typing. Sign and mail requests.	.118	1.679	.757	.174	2.480	1.118
10. Burst forms.	.148	3.746	.861	.218	5.533	1.272
11. File forms in appropriate files.	.373	2.521	1.523	.550	3.724	2.250
12. Encumbrance or prepayment routine.	.485	1.090	.740	.716	1.610	1.094
13. Unpack books; check against packing list or invoice. Check outstanding order file.	.654	6.064	2.878	.966	8.957	4.252

cedure in computation would be to multiply the observed mean time (a) by the personal rating factor (d) to produce a normal time. Multiply the normal time by the standardizing factor (e) to obtain a standard time for each function. Then multiply the standard time by the function frequency to produce an adjusted time which can be further used in unit labor cost computation.

g. Wages-per-minute (h) (See Figure 3. 10) (Raw statistics reported in days were converted to hours by multiplying them by eight.) For each of the three categories of personnel ($g_{1, 2, 3}$) the total actual productive hours of work performed during the fiscal year 1966-67 were calculated by summing the total hours of vacation (W_v) time and paid holidays authorized (W_h), and sick leave (W_s) taken. $W_v + W_h + W_s = W_u$ This sum (W_u) was subtracted from the total amount of official hours worked (W_t) to obtain the actual amount of productive time (W_p). $W_t - W_u = W_p$ The total wages paid to each category ($H_{1, 2, 3}$) were divided by the total productive hours worked ($W_{p1, p2, p3}$) to obtain the productive wage cost per hour (H_h). $\frac{H_{1, 2, 3}}{W_{p1, p2, p3}} = H_h$ The wage cost per hour was then divided by 60 to obtain the wage cost per minute (h). $\frac{H_h}{60} = h$ The wage cost per minute per category was entered on the labor chart for each library according to the category of personnel performing a given function.

h. Unit labor Cost per Function (i) - The unit cost obtained for each function was calculated by multiplying the value for standard time (f) by the wages per minute (h). $i = f \times h$.

i. Total Unit Labor Cost (L) $\Sigma i = L$ - The total unit labor cost was calculated by summing the unit costs for each function. (See Figure 3. 7; labor cost charts for each library are in Appendix 3. 5)

3. Unit Supply Cost (See Figure 3. 11) (S) - The annual supply budget (B_s) divided by the total volumes processed (P) in FY 1967 gave the unit supply cost. $\frac{B_s}{P} = S$

4. Unit Overhead Cost (O) - Two categories of overhead were considered: equipment and institutional.

a. Equipment Overhead (See Figure 3. 12, 3. 13) - Equipment overhead was calculated as the sum of the funds spent on new equipment

Figure 3. 10
Wages-Per-Minute Cost (h)

Library	G_1 Number of Personnel	G_2	G_3	W_v Hours Vacation			W_s Hours Sick			$W_t - W_h$ Total Work Hours Reported (Less Paid Holidays)			W_p Productive Hours		
	Stdt.	Clerk	Prof.	Stdt.	Clerk	Prof.	Stdt.	Clerk	Prof.	Stdt.	Clerk	Prof.	Stdt.	Clerk	Prof.
# 1	--	2 x 120	2 x 160	--	240	320	--	80	48	1, 903	3, 810	4, 000	1, 903	3, 490	3, 632
# 2	7	3. 7 x 120	2. 66 x 160 FTE	--	444	426	--	44	72	2, 500	6, 755	5, 120	2, 500	6, 267	4, 622
# 3	--	15 x 120	16 x 160	--	1, 800	1, 600	--	1, 390	716	12, 307	30, 000	18, 840	12, 307	26, 810	16, 524
# 4	24	7 x 120	4 x 160	--	840	640	--	164	80	13, 000	9, 800	9, 400	13, 000	8, 796	8, 680
# 5	--	2 x 120	2 x 160	--	240	320	--	120	95	579	3, 165	3,894. 6	579	2, 805	3, 479. 6
# 6	2 3/4 FTE	6 1/2 x 120	2 x 160	--	780	320	--	472	40	4, 748	14, 348	3, 984	4, 748	13, 096	3, 624
# 7	10	1 x 120	1. 433 x 160	--	120	229. 3	--	40	40	5, 463	1, 440	2, 704	5, 463	1, 280	2, 434. 7
# 8	--	46 36 x 80 8 x 120 2 x 160	16 x 160	--	4, 160 2, 880 960 320	2, 560	--	4, 266. 4	812	13, 807	87, 648	31, 880	13, 807	79, 221. 6	28, 508
# 9	. 25	. 55 x 120	1. 25 x 160	--	66	200	--	68. 2	51. 7	520	1, 144	2, 600	520	1, 009. 8	2, 348. 3

Figure 3.10
Wages-Per-Minute Cost (h)
(Cont.)

Library	H Total Wages Paid			H_h Productive Wage Cost per Hour			h Productive Wage Cost per Minute		
	Student	Clerk	Professional	Student	Clerk	Prof.	Student	Clerk	Prof.
#1	$ 1,600.00	$ 5,605.20	$ 17,820.00	$0.8408	$1.6061	$4.8899	$0.0140	$0.0268	$0.0815
#2	3,500.00	10,500.00	24,248.00	1.4000	1.6754	5.2462	0.0233	0.0272	0.0874
#3	17,539.00	58,272.00	80,630.00	1.4251	2.1735	4.8797	0.0238	0.0362	0.0813
#4	13,455.20	22,456.00	37,300.00	1.0350	2.5529	4.2972	0.0172	0.0425	0.0716
#5	725.00	6,650.00	13,417.00	1.2522	2.3708	3.8559	0.0209	0.0395	0.0643
#6	3,613.00	20,598.00	16,500.00	0.7610	1.5721	4.5528	0.0127	0.0262	0.0759
#7	5,742.00	2,205.00	11,570.00	1.0511	1.7227	4.7521	0.0175	0.0287	0.0792
#8	18,364.00	171,303.00	129,785.00	1.3300	2.1623	4.5525	0.0222	0.0360	0.0759
#9	519.20	3,828.46	10,576.18	0.9985	3.7913	4.5038	0.0166	0.0632	0.0751

(O_p) during the year prorated over a use period of one year according to the expected life span, the rental charges for equipment (O_r), and the amount of depreciation allowance (O_d) on equipment for the year considered. This sum was divided by the total volumes processed (P) during FY 1968 to obtain the equipment overhead per book.

$$O_e = \frac{O_p + O_r + O_d}{P}$$

b. Institutional Overhead (Oi-u) (See Figure 3. 14) - Institutional overhead was defined to include: Building depreciation or rent plus maintenance, insurance (fire, theft), light, heat, water and power, telephone, and janitorial service.

The total square footage (X) assigned to technical services was calculated from the floor plan; this sum was multiplied by the institutional overhead in square feet to obtain the total institutional overhead cost (O_{i-t}) for technical processing. This product was divided by the total number of volumes processed to obtain the institutional overhead per book. $(O_{i-u})\ (X) = O_{i-t}$ $\quad \frac{O_{i-t}}{P} = O_i$

Equipment overhead per book and the institutional overhead were summed to yield the total unit overhead cost. (See Figure 3. 15) $O = O_e + O_i$

5. Transportation

a. Definition: Transportation is defined as the cost associated with the distance a book moves through the system.

b. Rate of walking speed for the average worker. The sum of the feet recorded in the distance column on each flow chart was calculated (j) : On the basis of timed observations the rate of speed of the average worker in feet per minute was calculated to be 241. 2 feet (s = 241. 2 feet per minute).

c. Total transportation cost in dollars. - The total distance (j) divided by 241. 2 (s) gave the number of minutes required for transportation (t). $t = \frac{j}{s}$

Summing the wages per minute ($h_{1, 2, 3}$) for each category of worker for each library gave the total wages per minute paid (h_t).

The total transportation cost in dollars (T_c) was calculated by multiplying the total wages per minute by the number of minutes used in transportation. $T_c = (t)\ (h_t)$

Figure 3.11
Supplies Cost (S)

Library	B_s Annual Supply Budget	P Volumes Processed	S Unit Supply Cost
#1	$ 632.85	4,014	$ .1577
#2		9,631	(.2918)*
#3	6,000.00	35,583	.1686
#4	5,136.33	12,858	.3995
#5	705.00	4,733	.1489
#6	4,949.25	12,204	.4080
#7	3,000.00	10,012	.2996
#8	12,137.10	67,492	.1798
#9	2,555.58	4,466	.5722

* ( ) indicates a simulated cost due to the fact that no exact figure could be obtained

Figure 3.12
Overhead on Equipment

$$O_e = \frac{E + D + A}{P}$$

O = Overhead on equipment
E = Equipment cost per annum
P = Total books processed in FY 1967
c = Capital outlay for equipment for technical processes in FY 1967

ℓ = Estimated life span of the equipment purchased
A = Contract services (such as xerox*) per annum
D = Depreciation in dollars per annum on equipment held prior to FY 1967

$E = \frac{c}{\ell}$

$O = \frac{E+D+A}{P}$

* prorate if such equipment is shared with another department

Figure 3. 13
Equipment Overhead (O_e)

Library	Capital Outlay	Life-Span In Years	O_p Equipment Cost per Year	O_r Contract Services	O_d Depreciation	P Total # of Books Processed FY 1967	$O_p + O_r + O_d$	O_e Equipment Overhead
#1	171. 50	(20)*	8. 58	---	(840. 93)*	4, 014	849. 51	. 2106
#2	261. 00	10	26. 10	96. 24	(1803. 38)*	9, 631	1, 925. 72	. 2000
#3	740. 00	(20)*	37. 00	3337. 00	(840. 93)*	35, 583	4, 214. 93	. 1185
#4	2431. 00	10	243. 10	---	(840. 93)*	12, 858	1, 084. 03	. 0843
#5	590. 10	19	31. 06	(24. 43)*	(840. 93)*	4, 733	896. 42	. 1894
#6	(493. 05)*	(20)*	24. 65	---	(840. 93)*	12, 204	865. 58	. 0709
#7	235. 00	15	15. 67	---	(840. 93)*	10, 012	856. 60	. 0856
#8	4243. 73	(20)*	212. 19	8565. 45	465. 19	67, 492	9, 242. 83	. 1369
#9	1207. 65	(20)*	60. 38	98. 00	254. 23	4, 466	412. 61	. 0924

* ( ) indicates a simulated figure as no exact data was available

Figure 3. 14
Institutional Overhead (O_i)

Library	O_{i-u} Institutional Overhead in Dollars per Square Foot	X Total Square Footage	O_{i-t} Total Institutional Overhead Cost	P Volumes Processed	O_i Institutional Overhead per Book
#1	$(2. 47)*	992. 00	$ 2, 450. 24	4, 014	. 6104
#2	(2. 47)	1, 920. 00	4, 742. 4000	9, 631	. 4924
#3	(2. 47)	4, 776. 00	11, 796. 72	35, 583	. 3315
#4	(2. 47)	1, 728. 02	4, 268. 2094	12, 858	. 3319
#5	(2. 47)	1, 258. 00	3, 107. 2600	4, 733	. 6565
#6	(2. 47)	1, 792. 00	4, 426. 2400	12, 204	. 3627
#7	(2. 47)	1,228. 75	3, 035. 0125	10, 012	. 3031
#8	. 9071	12, 182. 85	11, 051. 0632	67, 492	. 1637
#9	4. 0400	525. 00	2, 121. 0000	4, 466	. 4749

* ( ) indicates a simulated cost due to the fact that no exact figure could be obtained. $\frac{.9071 + 4.0400}{2} = 2.47$

Figure 3. 15
Unit Overhead Cost (O)

Library	O_i Institutional	O_e Equipment	O Total
#1	$. 6104	. 2106	$. 8210
#2	. 4924	. 2000	. 6924
#3	. 3315	. 1185	. 4500
#4	. 3319	. 0843	. 4162
#5	. 6565	. 1894	. 8459
#6	. 3627	. 0709	. 4336
#7	. 3031	. 0856	. 3887
#8	. 1637	. 1139	. 2776
#9	. 4749	. 0924	. 5673

d. Unit Transportation Cost. (See Figure 3. 16) - A sample study of the number of books transported on a book truck at various times of the day and on different days yielded a "batching" factor of 85, i. e. an average of 85 books are transported at one time. Therefore, the unit transportation cost (T) was obtained by dividing the total transportation cost (T_c) by 85.

6. Unit Binding Cost (prorated) for Paperbacks (M) (See Figure 3. 17)

a. A paperback is defined as a commercially published monograph or a title in a monographic series that arrives from the vendor bound in a paper cover.

b. Unadjusted Unit Bindery Cost - The total amount spent on binding during FY 1967 (B_m) divided by the number of paperback volumes bound (V) yielded the binding cost per book (B_c). $\frac{B_m}{V} = B_c$

c. Frequency - The total number of paperbacks bound (V) divided by the total books processed (P) in FY 1967 yielded the percentage (b) of paperbacks processed that were also bound. $\frac{V}{P} = b$

d. Adjusted Unit Binding Cost - The average binding cost (B_c) per volume multiplied by the percentage of paperbacks bound (b) yielded the unit binding cost for paperbacks (M). $(B_c)\ (b) = M$

7. Total Unit Processing Cost (C) (See Figure 3. 18) - The summation of the costs for labor (L), supplies (S), overhead (O), transportation (T), and binding (M) produced the Unit Processing Cost (C) for each library. $C = L + S + O + T + M$

Comparative Analysis of the Data

The data presented in this chapter have been used for several purposes. In Section V, data are used to compare the costs of CALBPC with those of the individual libraries, and in Section VII the data are used in the model simulation studies. In this Section the investigators concentrated on four questions: 1) the factors that produced the disparity in processing costs between the participating libraries; 2) the advantages of task specialization that a central operation could provide; 3) present staff utilization patterns; and 4) the utility and limitations of the standard technical processing activities developed as a part of the project.

Figure 3. 16
Transportation (T)

Library	j	t	h_a	t_c	T
# 1	5966	24. 7350	. 1223	3. 0251	. 0356
# 2	4389	18. 1968	. 1379	2. 5093	. 0313
# 3	7724	32. 0237	. 1413	4. 5249	. 0532
# 4	4426	18. 3502	. 1313	2. 4094	. 0283
# 5	3978	16. 4928	. 1247	2. 0567	. 0242
# 6	3593	14. 8966	. 1148	1. 7101	. 0201
# 7	4326	17. 9356	. 1254	2. 2491	. 0265
# 8	8730	36. 1946	. 1341	4. 8537	. 0571
# 9	1392	5. 7712	. 1549	. 8940	. 0105

Key:
j = total feet recorded on flow chart
$t = \frac{j}{241.2}$ = time in minutes required for transportation (241. 2 feet per minute is the speed of the average worker)
h_a = average wage per minute
t_c = total transportation cost in dollars per minute
$T = \frac{t_c}{85}$ (85 is used as the batching factor)

Figure 3. 17
Binding Cost (M)

Library	B_m Amount spent on binding during FY 67	V Number of Volumes Bound	B_c Unadjusted Unit binding cost per Volume	P Total Books Processed	b Percentage of Paperbacks Also Bound	M Adjusted Unit Binding Cost
# 1		367	*(1. 19)	4, 014	. 091	. 1083
# 2		0	---	---	---	---
# 3	$1, 683. 86	1, 427	1. 18	35, 583	. 040	. 0472
# 4	813. 15	695	1. 17	12, 858	. 054	. 0632
# 5		0	---	---	---	---
# 6		0	---	---	---	---
# 7		500	(1. 19)	10, 012	. 049	. 0583
# 8	5, 022. 68	2, 972	1. 69	67, 492	. 044	. 0744
# 9		0	---	---	---	---

* ( ) simulated as no exact figure was available

Figure 3. 18
Summary Cost Sheet
Cost of Processing per Volume (in dollars) by Member Library

Library	L	S	O	T	M	C
# 1	$3. 412	$. 158	$. 821	$. 036	$. 108	$4. 54
# 2	3. 010	. 292	. 692	. 031	---	4. 02
# 3	2. 807	. 169	. 450	. 053	. 047	3. 53
# 4	4. 965	. 400	. 416	. 028	. 063	5. 87
# 5	6. 691	. 149	. 846	. 024	---	7. 71
# 6	1. 809	. 408	. 434	. 020	---	2. 67
# 7	2. 775	. 300	. 389	. 026	. 058	3. 55
# 8	3. 568	. 180	. 278	. 057	. 074	4. 16
# 9	1. 490	. 572	. 567	. 010	1. 850(U)	4. 49
Average	3. 392	. 292	. 544	. 032	. 367	4. 50
CALBPC	$2. 346	$. 292	$. 310	$. 057	$. 092	$3. 10

Volume predicted for C. A. L. B. P. C. is 119, 505, based upon the sum of the volumes added to each member library in FY 1967 (i. e., 160, 993) prorated by the average percentage of new titles added (i. e., 74. 23%).

Key:
L = Labor Cost
S = Supply Cost per Book
O = Overhead (Equipment and Institutional)
T = Transportation Factor
M = Commercial Binding Cost for Paperback Books Prorated
U = Cost per Volume of Utilizing a Commercial Firm for Processing
C = Cost of Processing per Volume per Member Library

Factors that affected local book processing costs

As can be seen from Figure 3. 17 a considerable disparity exists between the low cost of $2. 67/volume at institution # 6 and the $7. 71/volume calculated for institution # 5. Many factors contributed to produce this range, the most significant of which are discussed in the following paragraphs.

Personnel

The staffing pattern observed at some of the libraries inhibits effective utilization of personnel. In some cases the libraries are not provided sufficient non-professional support. Consequently, professional staff members must make up the difference. On the other hand, one or two libraries have made extensive use of students, thus lowering the unit cost, but increasing staff training problems. The frequent turn over in student workers has also reduced staff effectiveness.

One explanation for the high percentage of student assistants at several institutions is a State Civil Service restriction on number of clerks within an institution, forcing libraries to rely upon student help or to assign professionals to perform clerical jobs. The objective should be to achieve a balance between professional and non-professional staff.

Processing procedures

Efficiency of technical processing departments has a significant effect on the unit cost per volume processed. Some of the libraries maintain procedures that others once followed and have discarded, e. g. , sourcing of books, maintenance of accession records, excessive handling of materials, etc.

Records proliferation and maintenance

Several of the libraries maintain more records and files than they actually need. Many of these files were established to provide useful information or to provide information for a specific project. However, the files have continued to exist, and as the libraries have grown, file maintenance costs have increased proportionately.

Work layout and work flow

The effectiveness of the technical services work areas and the design of individual work stations varies from library to library. The technical services layouts in some of the libraries are extremely effective. In others they are equally poor. A catalog area that forces a cataloger to walk 150 feet each time she wishes to consult a record results in miles of walking over a period of one year; or an outstanding order file that forces a clerk to balance a tray on her knee while she processes a book is not conducive to high production. In one or two cases a library has run out of space and of necessity has been forced to decentralize its operations; the results have not usually been desirable.

Staff specialization

The advantages of staff specialization were vividly underscored by an analysis of the diary study data for original cataloging and classification. As mentioned earlier, the diary study method was employed in collection of the original cataloging/classification data. The diary times, as reported by the catalogers, for the two samples are summarized in Figure 3. 19. Possibly the greatest weakness to the diary study technique is that the precision of the measurements is unknown. The investigators estimate that the error could be as great as plus or minus five minutes; nevertheless, the study appears to provide a useful statistic.

The variation in the reported times can be attributed to a number of factors: (1) The difficulty of the material to be cataloged; (2) the language of the material; (3) depth of subject analysis, i. e., a scientific treatise as compared to an English literature title; or (4) a cataloger's conception of original cataloging. The task of original cataloging/classification was defined in the STPA list; however, investigators occasionally observed that some catalogers reported books as originally cataloged even when LC copy was discovered during the cataloging process.

In order to insure that the data were reasonably reliable, the results were compared against the production statistics of the catalogers at institution # 8. The cross check supported the reliability of the diary study data. Extrapolating the times reported by cataloger number one, for example, 7, 000 books could have been cataloged in one work year. During the preceeding 12 months, roughly 5, 095 books were cataloged and classified. But this level of production accounted for only 75% of this individual's time. The remainder was spent training and orienting new catalogers.

The observed times of catalogers two and three at institution # 8 are considerably higher than the times reported by most of the other catalogers. These differences can be explained in part by the fact that these catalogers process foreign language materials almost

Figure 3. 19
Cataloging Times*

		Sample I		Sample II		Overall Average Time
Insti- tution	Cata- loger	[b]N	$X = \frac{\Sigma X_1}{N}$ (time/book)	[b]N	$X_2 = \frac{\Sigma X_2}{N}$ (time/book)	$X_T = \frac{\Sigma X_1 + \Sigma X_2}{N_1 + N_2}$
1	#1		None	32	15. 8	15.8
2	#1	55	17. 4		None	17. 4
3	#1	58	18. 4	76	12. 1	14. 8
	#2	2	15. 5	49	11. 9	12. 1
4	#1	2	30. 0		None	30. 0[a]
	#2	49	13. 2	67	18. 8	16. 4
	#3		None	4	20. 0	20. 0[a]
5	#1	48	30. 7	14	22. 1	28. 7
8	#1	70	9. 1	96	14. 1	12. 0
	#2	33	34. 5	78	22. 3	26. 0
	#3	93	23. 5	75	30. 2	26. 5

[a] Sample too small to be meaningful
[b] N = Number of books cataloged

* Original cataloging diary times as reported by catalogers. Observations have not been standardized.

exclusively whereas cataloger one processes principally English literature materials.

On the basis of the diary data, the investigators believe that when the processing center is put into operation a two price system should be considered--one for foreign language titles cataloged, and one for English language materials.

The data were also analyzed according to the tasks performed by each of the catalogers who participated in the study and the amount of time devoted to each task. (See Figure 3. 20) The figures as presented overstate the precision of the methodology. When figures such as . 6 of one percent are cited, all this implies is that a cataloger in a particular institution devoted time to that task; whether the actual figure is . 6 or 6 percent is not important.

The catalogers in the largest institution spend approximately 63% of their time performing original cataloging and classification whereas catalogers in the smaller schools are able to devote only about 25% to 30% of their time to cataloging. (See Figure 3. 20) This

Figure 3. 20
Tasks Performed by Catalogers Who Participated in the Diary Studies

Task	Time Spent on Tasks (%)					
	Institution					
	# 1	# 2	# 3	# 4	# 5	# 8
Receive and arrange LC proof slip or sheets	15. 6					
Bibliographical checking - verification					2. 6	
Match LC cards or proof and books					. 7	
Collate books	. 8	1. 5			. 7	3. 0
Catalog and classify with LC cards/copy		9. 1	11. 2	18. 8	3. 1	
Revise LC card sets or locally reproduce sets	1. 1	2. 3		3. 7	12. 6	
Original cataloging and classifying	22. 5	32. 3	29. 4	26. 5	28. 6	63. 0
Type master card			. 6			
Type modification on a card or proof slip	2. 0					
Type authority cards	2. 0		3. 6			
Revise master card	. 6	7. 8				
Type circulation card				. 2		
Property stamp, sort shelf list, cards, etc.	2. 6			. 3		
File shelf list and catalog cards				1. 0		
Revise filing of catalog cards and shelf list			8. 6	4. 6	1. 6	
Revise completed books before forwarding to circulation	7. 8			4. 4	. 9	
Catalog Maintenance		2. 3	1. 4	1. 3	6. 8	. 2
Revision (general)			3. 7	8. 5	1. 1	. 4
Other catalog work (includes: rush books, check-in serials, catalog serials, reclassification, microfilm production)			13. 1	13. 3	14. 6	4. 4

Figure 3. 20
Tasks Performed (continued)

Task	Time Spent on Tasks (%)					
	Institution					
	#1	#2	#3	#4	#5	#8
Book selection		. 6				
Professional reading		2. 2	. 8		. 4	. 5
Staff meetings			2. 0	. 9		1. 7
Supervision of personnel	14. 8	. 6	1. 2	4. 7	3. 4	. 3
Personal business	6. 8	7. 9	8. 3	8. 3	5. 5	7. 4
Other activities (includes: meetings, classes, tours, consultations with staff, taking courses, teaching)	22. 1	22. 0	14. 0	5. 6	13. 1	16. 0
Keeping time record	. 6	2. 3	3. 2	. 6	5. 3	2. 3

does not mean that these catalogers are deliberately inefficient or that the library is poorly organized. The major problem is that in the smaller libraries catalogers must, of necessity, become jacks of all trades. Consequently a significant part of their time is occupied performing either professional tasks not directly related to cataloging or tasks that could be performed better by clerical workers. If a processing center were put into operation, an immediate benefit would be more effective utilization of professional catalogers. These advantages would be particularly apparent in the cataloging and classification of foreign language materials.

Overall staff utilization: A comparison of the level of technical services personnel (i. e., student assistant, clerk, or librarian) performing tasks at each library was made, the number of tasks each performs, and the frequency of each task performed. (See Figure 3. 21) All data for this comparison were obtained from each library's labor computation charts.

Data listed in the "Tasks Performed" column represent a physical count of technical processing tasks performed by each category of worker; the tasks were identified and categorized at each

Figure 3. 21
Comparison of Technical Services Personnel, Number of Activities Performed, and Frequency of Performance

Library	Category of Personnel	Tasks Performed	% Task Performed	Frequency of Performance	% Frequency of Performance
# 1	1	8	14. 6	26. 857	45. 0
	2	38	69. 1	26. 842	44. 9
	3	9	16. 3	6. 046	10. 1
	Total	55		59. 745	
# 2	1	11	26. 2	15. 066	32. 9
	2	23	54. 8	24. 881	54. 2
	3	8	19. 0	5. 917	12. 9
	Total	42		45. 864	
# 3	1	4	7. 8	9. 000	21. 5
	2	39	76. 5	22. 226	53. 1
	3	8	15. 7	10. 603	25. 4
	Total	51		41. 829	
# 4	1	12	20. 0	12. 033	26. 6
	2	38	63. 3	22. 325	49. 4
	3	10	16. 7	10. 862	24. 0
	Total	60		45. 220	
# 5	1	9	16. 7	21. 196	44. 8
	2	28	51. 8	15. 861	33. 4
	3	17	31. 5	10. 316	21. 8
	Total	54		47. 373	
# 6	1	9	19. 6	13. 756	31. 6
	2	31	67. 4	21. 359	49. 1
	3	6	13. 0	8. 408	19. 3
	Total	46		43. 523	
# 7	1	31	60. 8	26. 628	59. 4
	2	8	15. 7	5. 317	11. 9
	3	12	23. 5	12. 863	28. 7
	Total	51		44. 808	
# 8	1	11	18. 6	15. 504	26. 9
	2	44	74. 6	40. 636	70. 5
	3	4	6. 8	1. 488	2. 6
	Total	59		57. 628	
# 9	1	17	45. 9	22. 494	60. 7
	2	5	13. 5	1. 082	2. 9
	3	15	40. 6	13. 482	36. 4
	Total	37		37. 058	

Figure 3. 21
Comparison of Technical Services Personnel (continued)

Library	Category of Personnel	Tasks Performed	% Task Performed	Frequency of Performance	% Frequency of Performance
CALBPC	1	4	8. 2	4. 000	11. 6
	2	42	85. 7	28. 153	82. 2
	3	3	6. 1	2. 100	6. 2
	Total	49		34. 253	

Category of Personnel:
1. Student Assistant
2. Clerk (full-time)
3. Professional Librarian

library, using the STPA list. Frequency of performance was calculated using the frequency of occurrence of each processing task, based on the frequency computation, Figure 3. 8; i. e., all books receive mechanical processing but only a certain percent (or frequency) require original cataloging.

Not surprisingly, the labor cost of technical processing agrees in most instances with the category of personnel assigned to the task; libraries using a high percentage of student assistance realize a lower unit labor cost; moreover those libraries which require the fewest tasks in their technical processing also reflect lower unit labor costs.

Staff utilization is indicated by the percent of activities performed by each category, and the variance between this figure and the percent of frequency of performance. The "% Task Performed" column is a straight computation based on the percent of activities performed by each category. The "% Frequency of Performance" column reflects the processing involvement percentage of each category of worker. In Library #7 for example, student assistants are assigned to 60. 8% of the processing tasks, with a working time involvement of 59. 4%; clerks assignment/involvement ratio is 15. 7% to 11. 9% and the librarian computation at #7 is 23. 5% to 28. 7%. This analysis again bore out the advantages of increased size, where task specialization is possible. At institution #8 professional librarians account for approximately three percent of the tasks performed.

Standard Technical Processing Activities and Standard Times

Data comparability was achieved through the development and use of the STPA list. The activities list was initially used in the structured diary study and was modified further for use in the time observation study, the time and cost computations, and in computer simulation of the proposed processing center.

The standardized times recorded in Figure 3. 9 and Appendix 3. 4 represent the time required to perform each task described in the STPA. Variations in methods used by the participating libraries in accomplishing tasks account in part for the variation in times recorded for a given activity. For example, consider activity #59, "Mark call number or place label on spine of volume." The standard time per volume for this activity ranges from a low of 1. 19 minutes at one library to a 3. 28 minutes at another library with a mean of 2. 12 minutes overall. If all libraries used exactly the same method for labeling the spine of a book, the variation in time could be explained as a reflection of the competence level and efficiency of the individuals labeling books at each library. However, five distinct methods of spine labeling were identified at the nine libraries, each of which is categorized within the #59 activity--labeling using: (1) Se-Lin labeler; (2) typed self-adhesive label coated with plastic glue; (3) hand lettering with an electric stylus; (4) hand lettering with india ink; (5) cloth tape covering the bottom portion of the book's spine with hand lettering on cloth tape. Variations in procedure also exist within any given method. For example, using a Se-Lin labeler: (a) some libraries type a continuous strip of numbers for all books on a truck or shelf, before labeling the books; (b) others type a strip for only a small group of books; (c) some place a cut label on the spine without truncating the corners of the label; (d) others truncate the four corners; (e) some iron the labels on one at a time; (f) others iron the labels on groups of books as one step; etc., etc.

Variation in unit times can also be attributed to policy decisions regarding technical processing activities at individual libraries. For example, function #5, Figure 3. 9 "Search and verify bibliographic information," produced a time range per title from 2. 36 minutes to 20. 12 minutes with a mean standard time of 6. 31 minutes. The policies within acquisitions departments account for much of this variance. A library may search a few bibliographic sources and either process the order with an estimate of price, or return the order to the requester for additional information. Another library may search every bibliographic source it owns to verify the entry, searching to the bitter end and exhausting its sources; consequently increasing its unit searching time.[17] Variance in all of the above times may also be affected by the quantity and quality of the bibliographic sources available to a library for bibliographic searching.

The standardized activities list can be used by other libraries to measure their own processing costs. Because of local procedural and policy variations, the investigators developed cost ranges rather than one "precise" figure for each variation. Although some precision is sacrificed, this was not viewed as critical. The idle time associated with most library operations more than negates the effect of precise measurements; i. e., breaks occur between task cycles increasing the unit time. For example, a library clerk can charge out 180 books per hour (a standard time of 20 seconds/charge), but if only 120 books are borrowed by patrons during a 60 minute period the time per actual loan is 30 seconds; therefore, a unit time is realistic only as long as a worker is not idle. In all but a few library situations idle time can be expected. A time range for tasks performed should provide an effective measuring tool for library system studies.

Notes

1. Wilson, Louis Round "The next fifty years." *Library Journal* 61:256-257, 1936.

2. Hendricks, Donald D. *Comparative costs of book processing in a processing center and in five individual libraries.* Springfield, Ill., Illinois State Library, May 1966, 89 p.

3. Miller, Robert A. "Cost accounting for libraries: acquisition and cataloging." *Library Quarterly* 7:511-536, (Oct. 1937).

4. Oller, Kathryn "A time study of the Urbana (Illinois) Free Library." University of Illinois Library School, *Occasional Papers*, no. 16, Nov. 1950, 11 p.

5. Reichmann, Felix "Costs of cataloging." *Library Trends* 2:290-317 (Oct. 1953).

6. Rider, Fremont "Library cost accounting." Library Quarterly 6:331-381 (Oct. 1936).

7. Tauber, Maurice F. and associates Technical services in libraries. N.Y., Columbia University Press, 1953.

8. Wulfekoetter, Gertrude Acquisitions work: processes involved in building library collections. Seattle, Wash., University of Washington Press, 1961.

9. Wynar, Bohdan S. and Harold R. Malinowsky, eds. Cost analysis study, Technical Services Division, University of Denver Library. University of Denver Graduate School of Librarianship, Studies in Librarianship, no. 4, 1965.

10. Barnes, Ralph M. Motion and time study: design and measurement of work, ed. 5. N.Y., Wiley, 1963.

11. Dougherty, Richard M. and Fred J. Heinritz Scientific management of library operations. N.Y., Scarecrow Press, 1966.

12. Mundel, Marvin E. Motion and time study: principles and practice, ed. 3. Englewood Cliffs, N.J., Prentice-Hall, 1960.

13. Schultheiss, Louis A., Don S. Culbertson and Edward M. Heiliger Advanced data processing in the university library. N.Y., Scarecrow Press, 1962.

14. Freund, John E. Modern elementary statistics, ed. 2. Englewood Cliffs, N.J., Prentice-Hall, 1960, p. 212.

15. Voos, Henry "Standard times for certain clerical activities in technical processing." Ph.D. Thesis, Rutgers, The State University, New Brunswick, N.J., 1964, p. 94.

16. Dougherty, Richard M. and Fred J. Heinritz Scientific management of library operations. N.Y., Scarecrow Press, 1966, p. 113.

17. Fristoe, Ashby "Bitter end; the searching process." Library Resources and Technical Services 10:91-95 (Winter 1966).

IV. Institutional Bookkeeping Systems and Their Effect on Book Procurement

The first three sections of this report have explicated technical processes within each of the cooperating libraries, demonstrating how these processes might be accomplished more efficiently through a centralized service. Section IV explores the effect on book procurement of institutional bookkeeping procedures external to the authority and operation of the libraries. These business office procedures both limit and define the character of the acquisition routines employed within the library of that institution. It will be shown in Section IV that there is considerable variation and much duplication of work relating to accounting, both in the library and in the business office on each campus.

This phase of the study is not intended to provide hard figures relating to waste or cost savings, but rather to demonstrate a method by which bookkeeping procedures can be analyzed vertically in an academic institution. One point to bear in mind is that the library is not completely free to determine its own most efficient mode of operation.

If the institution imposed inefficient procedures upon an internal agency in order to achieve institution-wide uniformity, one solution compatible to both the purposes of the institution and the internal agency (in this case, the library) may be to turn over these library functions to an outside agency such as a processing center.

The advantages of the proposed CALBPC bookkeeping system over the present methods of operation are revealed by the labor cost analysis simulation reported later in this section. In summary these are:

1. Economy of operation due to the elimination or combination of functions performed by the library and the business office through the use of computerized records.

2. Comprehensive record keeping on book procurement available from a central point, and therefore useful as

a data base. Up-to-date record keeping at any step in the book procurement process.

Current Procedures Affecting Book Procurement

The study of the business office procedures presented a different set of problems to the project team. In this phase of the study the investigators worked with individuals who were not directly concerned with library operations. Yet the project could not remove these operations from the scope of the study, since CALBPC may possibly perform some of the operations now performed by business office personnel as well as by library staff.

In order to investigate business procedure costs as they relate to book procurement, it was necessary to devise a different methodology than that used to study library procedures. A combination of interviews and a cost analysis based upon simulated data was employed. The interviews were conducted in the respective business offices with either the business manager, the purchasing agent or both as the principal resource person. Occasionally other staff members took part in the interview. Each tape was subsequently analyzed and a business procedures résumé was written based upon the tape and upon forms collected during the interview. Each of these résumés was analyzed to produce the following description of accounting activities.

Description of Accounting Activities: The purpose of this phase of the investigation was to determine if the establishment of a centralized book purchasing operation for the nine state-supported senior colleges would reduce the costs of maintaining accounting records and reduce the amount of duplicated effort. Each of the functions presently performed at nine schools could be performed once at the Center. Financial reports generated at the Center would be designed to satisfy the needs of each institution. The actual business procedures required for library book procurement would be performed at the Center.

Eight of the nine libraries purchase books through their institutional business office, which in turn is responsible to State Accounts and Control. The other library maintains its own bookkeeping department; all operations except issuing checks and auditing are perform in the library. Central accounting is responsible for issuing vouchers and auditing. Most of the explanation which follows pertains to the eight libraries under the state accounting system. The topics covered are divided into two main categories: encumbering and expending. Expending was further subdivided into: verifying, vouchering, data processing, warranting, clearing statements, closing the Fiscal Year and retiring records.

Encumbering: Basically two different procedures for encumber-charges were identified, although a number of local variations were observed such as the use of multiple 3 x 5 forms and purchase order forms to perform the same task.

Procedure I--A library initiates an order by preparing a purchase order form. This form may vary from one to eight parts. The titles to be ordered are either itemized directly on the purchase order form or else the 3 x 5 multiform slips are attached to the purchase order. The Purchasing Office approves the purchase order and forwards one copy to the Data Processing Department for encumbering. At least one copy is filed by vendor and one by purchase order number. One copy is returned to the library as an information copy. Four libraries do not use this procedure.

The four exceptions prepare a requisition form upon which the Purchasing Office issues a purchase order. Two of the libraries itemize each title on the requisition form and the Purchasing Office in turn itemizes the titles on the purchase order. The other two libraries attach copies of the multiform slips to their requisitions to provide the Purchasing Office with the information required.

One library must request permission from the Governor's Office to place institutional memberships and subscription orders. This library also secures bids on periodical subscriptions. None of the other institutions are required to perform these routines.

All of the libraries except one maintain ledgers of encumbrances and expenditures. One system is mechanized; that is, the data are coded onto punch cards. The amount and date encumbered, number of copies, amount and date expended, account code, and vendor code are recorded on a card. Once every two weeks encumbrance and expenditure cards are sent to Central Accounting where a budget audit is run. Central Accounting returns the cards with a budget report listing each separate transaction.

Those libraries that maintain manual ledgers also list bibliographic and requester information. Each locally administered fund is ledgered separately.

Procedure II--For a standing order, rush, prepaid or confirming purchase the library first acquires the material and the invoice before preparing the purchase order. The invoice and purchase orders are then sent to the Business Office which makes the encumbrance and expenditure in a single operation. Three libraries use Procedure II for most of their book purchases.

Expending. Verifying: Most of the libraries inspect the books received against either the invoice or a packing slip. When all the items on an invoice have been accounted for, the library stamps "received," the date, authorizes payment and forwards it to the Business Office for payment. If the Business Office receives an invoice directly, it is forwarded to the library. Five libraries follow this procedure.

The libraries that maintain full ledgers log in the invoice. At one institution the Business Office retains all invoices until the library notifies it that all items have been received. The Business Office then routes the invoice to the library for verification. In such cases the receiving clerk routes the completed invoice to the bookkeeper in the order department, who summarizes the invoice for payment and sends it on to Central Accounting.

In a few cases, the Business Office requests that the library issue a receiving report as verification of goods or services received. At one institution the Business Office provides the mailroom clerk with a receiving report (a carbon copy of the purchase order) to use when the books arrive. The mailroom clerk sends this report to the library with the books. The library does not normally receive the invoice. The mailroom clerk upon receipt of the receiving report checks the items received against this report, and returns it to the Business Office to initiate payment. If books arriv[e] without a receiving report, the library prepares one.

At another library the Business Office sends the invoice and receiving report forms to the library which lists the items received on the receiving report. The library then routes the invoice and the receiving report back to the Business Office for payment. Two other libraries prepare receiving reports but they perform the verification on the invoice itself.

The Business Office compares the invoice (and receiving report, if used) with the purchase order, and if the two documents agree both are forwarded to Accounting to be vouchered. If the amount of the invoice exceeds the amount on the purchase order, a new purchase order may be issued to cover the difference; or a supplemental purchase order is prepared if the amount exceeds the encumbrance by as much as 5%. One institution issues a supplemental order only if the amount is exceeded by $10.00. Three libraries handle their own change orders.

Vouchering: After a purchase order is verified, it is matched with others addressed to the same vendor for the current accounting period, and the voucher prepared lists all outstanding charges to the vendor. The invoice is always attached to the first copy of the voucher. Another copy of the invoice is attached to the third copy of the voucher. Practice varies in the use of supporting documents such as copies of the purchase order and receiving report. The first and second copy (Remittance Advice) of the voucher is sent to Data Processing before forwarding to State Accounts and Controls. The third copy is retained for the institution's permanent file. Some institutions file by voucher number, others by vendor's name.

At one library the voucher is charged against a special service fund, and a specially designed three part form is utilized as follows: Copy 1--sent to vendor with a check drawn on the service fund, Copy 2--attached to purchase order along with individual 3 x 5 slips representing the books supplied by the vendor, and Copy 3--sent to the state with the regular voucher for reimbursement. The State voucher form is processed as follows: Copy 1--sent to State Accounts and Control, Copy 2--sent to State along with the voucher form attached, Copy 3--filed numerically by voucher number as the permanent record, and Copy 2 of the State voucher is returned with a warrant for the amount of reimbursement.

One library forwards a requisition and invoice to the Business Office after it has received the merchandise or service. At this time the Business Office prepares a purchase order in six parts, two of which are sent to the State Purchasing Agent for approval. A voucher is then prepared by the regular procedure.

Data Processing: After a purchase order is approved, it is sent to Data Processing where an encumbrance card is punched. When the merchandise is received, the Accounting Office prepares a voucher and sends a copy to Data Processing to punch an expenditure card. The encumbrance and expenditure cards are used to prepare a budget summary report for each department. The voucher is returned to the Accounting Office to be filed either by vendor or by voucher number.

At three libraries, Data Processing encumbers and expends at the same time since the library does not send encumbrance information to the Business Office until the order is completed.

Warranting: After Data Processing processes a voucher, the Business Office forwards the first and second copy, attaching a copy of each of the purchase order(s) listed on the voucher and the pertinent invoice(s) to State Accounts and Controls. This office issues a warrant for the total amount on the voucher, attaches the second (Remittance Advice) copy of the voucher to it, and sends it to the vendor. The original copy of the voucher, the second copy of the warrant and the invoice(s) are then filed permanently.

Two libraries forward their receiving reports as well as the above mentioned documents. These are also filed permanently. Warranting does not apply to one library since purchase orders for library books and periodicals are paid from a special fund.

Clearing Statements: Upon receipt of a statement, the library tries to determine if the merchandise has been received. If so, the statement is forwarded to the Business Office with an "information found" noted on it. If the items have not been received, the library originates a tracer letter to the vendor. The Business Office prepares a voucher, if lacking, for any statements covering books that have been received.

At one library the library assistant checks the Business Office records as well as the library's records to determine disposition of the statement.

Closing the Fiscal Year: All but one institution cancels its outstanding purchase orders at the end of the fiscal year. The exact closing date varies from June 15 to September 1. The Business Office issues new purchase orders against the new fiscal year's budget if the library still wishes to acquire the items or services. One library is permitted to carry some encumbrances over to the new fiscal year.

Retiring Records: There is no standard state-wide procedure. For the most part, the purchase orders and vouchers are stored. One library indicated that all punched card records would be stored eventually on magnetic tape. Another library's purchasing office reretains a numerical and an alphabetical file (by vendor) of all purchase orders and vouchers for seven years.

Institutional Bookkeeping Systems: Labor Cost Analysis Simulation

This portion of the study was conducted to determine if the establishment of centralized book purchasing for the nine state-supported senior colleges is likely to save labor costs and other duplicative costs for the state in terms of accounting and associated record keeping. The hypothesis is that each of the nine colleges are performing functions which could be performed once by computer at the Center. The reports generated by the Center would fit into the reporting system at each institution, but all business procedures required for all library book procurement would be performed at the Center.

The standard times, functions performed, volume, and salary data used in this investigation were obtained during Phase I of the feasibility study.

The investigators hypothesized that the functions cited in Figure 4.1 can be performed at the Center more efficiently than they are presently performed through use of the following methods:

1. The Center will issue a two part 3 x 5 card order form for use by all libraries.
2. The six part multiple order form will be created by

photocopy from the order card submitted by the member library.

3. Accounting functions $^{t}2$, 3, 5, 6, 7, 8, 9, 10 will be done on data processing equipment. (See Figure 4. 1)

The Center could serve as jobber and processor for the bulk of domestic and foreign in-print titles procured by the member libraries during its first year of operation (FY 1968-69). Depending upon the success of its first year of operation, the Center may expand the scope of materials it handles to include out-of-print, and other specialized titles.

Methodology: The project attempted to develop a methodology for evaluating business office operations. Although the cost figures and times are intended to be conservative, it is the belief of the investigators that the figures are reasonably accurate. The simulated times used are based on comparable operations, i. e., time used to prepare a purchase order in the library was substituted for preparing the purchase order in the business office. The times required to prepare warrants were also simulated, and filing times are also independent of location. Some of the business managers would not have been enthusiastic about a team of librarians performing time studies in their offices; but all interviewed were cooperative in furnishing the project with forms and information.

Figure 4. 1 is keyed in two ways, according to the numbered steps below and according to the formula or symbols introducing each step.

Key to Symbols used in Explanation and in Figure 4. 1:

t = Unit time in minutes for a single function
t_U = Total unit time
T = Total time in minutes, man hours, and work days (one work day = 8 hours)
Fractions of minutes are expressed in decimals.
L = Library
B = Business Office
M = Maintenance (receiving room)
S = State Accounting Office
V = Total volumes of books ordered during FY 1966-67
V_I = Total volumes ordered by one institution
O = Orders for books placed during FY 1966-67
w = Wage per minute
W = Total wages
C_I = Total labor cost to institution

C_U	=	Total unit (per book) cost
C_U - L	=	Unit labor cost to institution
C_U	=	Average unit labor cost over all the institutions
CALBPC	=	Colorado Academic Libraries Book Processing Center
NA	=	Not applicable
AFL	=	A function of the library (i. e., a task performed by the Library Staff)
SYSTEM	=	CALBPC and cooperating libraries
L-SYSTEM	=	Function retained by a library member of the CALBPC SYSTEM
CALBPC-L	=	Library functions to be performed by CALBPC
CALBPC-BS	=	Business Office and State Accounting functions to be performed by CALBPC

Explanation of Figure 4. 1:

Institutional

$t_1 - t_{14}$	1. Obtained standard unit times for each function performed by each library. Those functions which affected the procurement of a book were selected.
	2. Substituted in reasonable minimum times for Business Office and State Accounts and Controls times which were not obtained by direct observation. Note: In some instances a function was performed both by the library and the business office.
t_L	3. Obtained sum of the times for the functions performed by each library.
t_{BS}	4. Obtained sum of the times for the functions performed by the Business Office and by the State Accounting Office.
$t_L + t_{BS} = t_U$	5. Summed t_L and t_{BS} to obtain the total unit time to procure each book at each library.
	6. Obtained statistics on the total volumes purchased and the number of purchase orders placed at each institution. Note: Where statistics on orders placed were not available, this quantity was estimated by sampling the number of titles listed on invoices for that institution and dividing the total volumes purchased by the average titles listed on an invoice.
$t_L \cdot V = T_L$	7. Obtained total library time spent on book procurement by multiplying unit library time by the

total number of volumes purchased.

$t_{BS} \cdot O = T_{BS}$	8. Obtained total Business Office and State Accounting time spent on book procurement by multiplying unit business office and state time by the number of orders placed.
$T_L + T_{BS} = T$	9. Added total library time and total business office and state time together to obtain total institutional time spent on book procurement.
w_L	10. Obtained average wage per minute paid to a full time clerk at each library.
$w_L \cdot T_L = W_L$	11. Calculated total wages paid by each library by multiplying the total time spent by the average wage per minute.
w_{BS}	12. Obtained average wage per minute paid by State Civil Service to bookkeepers and accountants (See Figure 4. 2).
$w_{BS} \cdot t_{BS} = W_{BS}$	13. Calculated total wages paid by Business Office and State Accounting Office by multiplying the total time spent by the average wage per minute.
$W_L + W_{BS} = C_I$	14. Calculated total labor cost to each institution by adding total wages spent by library and by Business Office and State Accounting Office.
ΣC_I	15. Obtained the total labor cost incurred by all nine libraries by adding their individual total labor costs.
$\frac{C_I}{V_I} = C_U$	16. Calculated the unit labor cost per institution by dividing the total labor cost by the number of volumes purchased.
$\frac{\Sigma C_I}{\Sigma V}$	17. Obtained the average unit cost over all institutions by summing the total cost to each institution and dividing the total by the sum of all volumes purchased in FY 1967.
CALBPC	
$t_1 - t_{14}$	18. Hypothesized standard times based on time observations obtained during the study of the nine libraries, on times in published studies, and on times obtained by conferring with operating centers processing books for public and school libraries.
	19. Since the purchase request cards, etc., would

continue to be handled by the member libraries although in a modified way, institutional average time is used as total unit library time within the CALBPC system hereafter referred to as L-SYSTEM time.

20. Determined the volume of books to be handled by the Center for two periods, one for FY 1968-69 and the other for FY 1969-70.

    a. Took 119, 505 volumes based upon the sum of the volumes added to each member library during FY 1966-67 (160, 993 volumes) prorated by the averaged percentage of new titles.

    b. Took 148, 801 because this was the total number of volumes purchased by the nine institutions during FY 1966-67.

21. Computed the number of orders placed by CALBPC by dividing the total volume by the expected number of titles to be handled per order (an average of 200 titles per order based on an examination of the approval system of billing with the regular system of billing).

$w_{L\text{-SYSTEM}}$ 22. Used the average unit wages (see Step 10) as an appropriate wage for the function performed by the libraries in the system: w_L.

23. Chose .0360 as the average salary per minute for library clerks at the Center as this is the average paid by C. U. (Rounded to .04 after computations performed).

w_{BS} - CALBPC 24. Computed the average salary per minute for accountants and bookkeepers at the University of Colorado to use as the average wage for such personnel at the Center (see Figure 4. 2).

25. Transferred L-SYSTEM time in t_1 column to L-SYSTEM time.

CALBPC-L 26. Added together those functions which are performed by library clerks at CALBPC: t_2 and t_3.

CALBPC-BS 27. Added those functions which are performed by bookkeepers at CALBPC: t_6, t_7, t_9, t_{12}, t_{13}, and t_{14}.

28. Computed total unit SYSTEM time by summing

total L-time, CALBPC-L time, and CALBPC-BS time.

29. Computed total L-SYSTEM time by multiplying t_1 by the total number of volumes handled.

30. Computed total CALBPC-L time by multiplying total unit CALBPC-L time by the total volumes handled.

31. Computed total CALBPC-BS time by multiplying unit CALBPC-BS time by the total orders placed.

32. Computed the total wages paid for t_1 by multiplying the total L-SYSTEM time by the average institutional wage, w_L.

33. Computed the total wages paid for CALBPC library clerks by multiplying the total CALBPC-L time by the average CALBPC library clerk wage.

34. Computed the total wages paid for CALBPC bookkeepers by multiplying the total CALBPC-BS time by the average CALBPC bookkeeper's wage.

C_{CALBPC} 35. Obtained the total wages paid by the CALBPC SYSTEM by summing the total L-SYSTEM wages, the total CALBPC-L wages, and the total CALBPC-BS wages paid.

$C_{U\text{-}CALBPC}$ 36. Obtained the unit cost for book procurement under the CALBPC SYSTEM by dividing the total wages paid by the total books handled by the system.

37. Prorated the total labor cost of processing all volumes by the traditional method by 80. 3 percent which is the percentage of the total volume load that CALBPC might assume during its first year of operation.

$C_I - C_{CALBPC} = C_s$ 38. Obtained the total amount saved by adoption of the CALBPC system by subtracting the total labor cost (prorated) for all nine institutions from the cost incurred by CALBPC.

$C_U - C_{U\text{-}CALBPC}$ 39. Obtained the amount saved per book ordered by subtracting the CALBPC unit labor cost from average unit labor cost over all institutions.

40. Calculated the Center's labor cost by summing L-SYSTEM, CALBPC-L and CALBPC-BS wages. Used the same volume level as the traditional system.

41. Calculated the Center's labor cost using a volume of 50% of the FY 1968-69 (119, 505 volumes) (or 40. 2% of the FY 1969-70, 148, 801 volumes) expected work load, i. e., 59, 752 volumes.

Conclusions: It should be noted that certain business and accounting functions are also being performed at the libraries. The labor costs for these functions are presented in the labor cost analysis of the member libraries in Section III of this report. These functions, as per the STPA List, are: #8 (typing the purchase requisition and/or purchase order), #11 (filing forms), #12 (encumbering), #22 (verification), #23 (expending), #35 (correspondence pertaining to procurement) and #36 (checking statements). The CALBPC system would perform all bookkeeping functions, thus eliminating duplication of effort.

Other library functions would be abbreviated or eliminated by the adoption of the CALBPC System. These are #4 (typing library order request card), #6 (assigning vendor and fund), and #7 (preparing multiple order record), #21 (preparing receiving report), #28 (noting reports from dealers), #29 (claiming outstanding orders), and #30 (cancelling orders).

The total average unit cost for library book procurement is calculated to be $. 32, and the total institutional cost is $47, 184. 55 per annum. In order for the existing system to be compared with CALBPC'S first year of operation, the total institutional cost, $47, 184. 55, must be prorated to 80. 3%, since CALBPC's first year volume level is expected to be 119, 505 whereas the existing system's volume level is 148, 801 (119, 505 is 80. 3% of 148, 801). The CALBPC System unit cost for functions relating to business procedures is $. 08 per book (or an average of $. 80 per invoice if an invoice listed ten books) or a total of $9, 603. 32, for the first year of operation. Therefore, $47, 184. 55 prorated by 80. 3% is $37, 889. 19. The latter figure minus $9, 603. 32 equals $28, 285. 87, the amount estimated to be saved by the system during its first year. An estimated saving of

$. 24 per book (or $28, 285. 87 total) would accrue to the State by the adoption of the CALBPC System, from the change in business procedures alone.

In order to analyze the savings expected from the establishment of the CALBPC Bookkeeping System as compared to the present system, it is necessary to bear in mind that one function, No. 4, Type Purchase Request Card, will be performed at each of the libraries. A portion of another function, No. 5, Searching, may also be performed in the library to verify the "in-print" status of a title unless the title was published in the current year or is cited from an up-to-date buying list. Since the degree of verification will vary from library to library according to local policies, this function was not included in the analysis in Figure 4. 1. To simulate this cost for each library a frequency of one check for each title was assumed and a standard time of . 31 minutes was multiplied by the local wage rate of the category of personnel who typically performs the Books in Print check. This information was entered in Figure 4. 3. This cost was added to the proposed CALBPC Bookkeeping Cost. The typing of the purchase request had already been calculated as part of the cost of $. 08. The revised total CALBPC cost was subtracted from that of the present bookkeeping system to provide the unit savings in dollars per library expected by the adoption of the CALBPC Bookkeeping System.

As the Center changes from an experimental design to a functional organization, its efficiency is likely to improve, resulting in still greater savings to the State. Moreover, local bookkeeping for books and periodicals procured outside of the Center, as well as for books ordered through the Center, may be feasible and certainly desirable if duplication in these procedures can be eliminated. CALBPC could produce budget report information on a demand basis for any "local" or "Center" fund whenever the need arose. This is not always possible under the systems now operating.

Figure 4. 1
Labor Cost Analysis of Business Procedures Relating to Book Procurement

(1) FY 1966-67	(2) Column	t_1 Purchase Request Card	t_2 Assign Vendor and Fund	t_3 Multiple Order Form (3'' x 5'')
# 1	1	L 2. 63	L . 10	L 1. 30
# 2	2	L . 83	L . 48	L . 86
# 3	3	NA	L . 52	L 4. 96
# 4	4	L . 14	L . 56	L 1. 13
# 5	5	L 1. 15	L . 08	L 13. 43
# 6	6	L . 77	L . 40	L . 99
# 7	7	L 1. 40	L . 15	L . 70
# 8	8	NA	L 1. 97	L . 70
# 9	9	L 3. 62	NA	L 1. 18
Institutional Total	10	10. 53	4. 26	25. 24
Institutional Average	11	1. 27	. 47	2. 81
CALBPC SYSTEM (18)	12	L-SYSTEM TIME (19)	CALBPC-L TIME	CALBPC-L TIME
FY 1968-69 (only 80. 3% of processing handled by Center)	13	1. 27	. 08	. 86
FY 1969-70 All processing handled by Center	14	1. 27	. 08	. 86
Experimental 50% of expected volume or 59,752	15	1. 27	. 08	. 86

Figure 4. 1 (continued)

Column	t_4 Requisition	t_5 Purchase Order	t_6 Encumbrance	t_7 Filing
1	L 1. 11	B (1. 30)*	B = (. 55) L = . 75	B = (. 84) L = 1. 82
2	L . 07	B (1. 30)	AFL	B = (. 84) L = 2. 06
3	L . 66	B (1. 30)	NA	B = (. 84) L = 2. 94
4	L . 41	B (1. 30)	AFL	B = (. 84) L = 1. 98
5	L 2. 38	B (1. 30)	B (. 86)	B = (. 84) L = 7. 12
6	NA	L . 40	B = (. 55) L = . 07	B = (. 84) L = . 92
7	L 1. 30	B (1. 30)	B = (. 86) L = . 44	B = (. 84) L = 3. 45
8	L . 03	NA	L . 55	B = (. 84) L = 2. 08
9	L . 83	B (1. 30)	B = (. 55) L = . 01	B = (. 84) L = . 76
10	10. 46	9. 49	5. 19	30. 68
11	1. 16	1. 05	. 58	3. 41
12			CALBPC-BS TIME *	CALBPC-BS TIME *
13	NA	NA	. 55	. 42
14	NA	NA	. 55	. 42
15	NA	NA	. 55	. 42

* Parentheses ( ) designate simulated times.

Figure 4. 1 (continued)

Col-umn	t_8 Receiving Report	t_9 Verification	t_{10} Vouchering	t_{11} Expending
1	L 1. 84	B = (. 48) L = . 22	B (1. 50)	B = (. 55) L = . 27
2	L 2. 21	B = (. 48) L = . 01	B (1. 50)	B (. 55)
3	L 1. 08	L . 01	B (1. 50)	B = (. 55) L = . 37
4	NA	L . 18	B (1. 50)	B = (. 55) L = 3. 26
5	NA	B = (. 48) L = 2. 60	B (1. 50)	B (. 86)
6	AFL	L (. 48)	B (1. 50)	B = (. 55) L = . 23
7	M = (. 48) L = . 48	B = (. 48) L = (. 48)	B (1. 50)	B = (. 86) L = . 36
8	NA	L . 33	NA	L . 11
9	NA	B = (. 48) L = .03	B (1. 50)	B (. 55)
10	6. 09	6. 77	11. 99	9. 63
11	. 68	. 75	1. 33	1. 07
12		CALBPC-BS TIME *		CALBPC-BS TIME * (part of verification)
13	NA	. 44	NA	---
14	NA	. 44	NA	---
15	NA	. 44	NA	---

* These functions would be incurred at the Business Office or State Accounting Office only twelve times per year when CALBPC issued its monthly statement.

Figure 4. 1 (continued)

Column	t_{12} Warranting	t_{13} Monthly Budget Report	t_{14} Clearing Statements	t_L (3) L-TIME
1	S (. 50)	B (. 04)	B (. 17)	10. 03
2	S (. 50)	B (. 04)	B = (. 17) L = (. 17)	6. 69
3	S (. 50)	B (. 04)	. 12	10. 66
4	S (. 50)	B (. 04)	L . 34	11. 66
5	S (. 50)	B (. 04)	B = (. 17) L = (. 17)	26. 93
6	S (. 50)	B (. 04)	B = (. 17) L = (. 17)	4. 43
7	S (. 50)	B (. 04)	B = (. 17) L = . 06	8. 82
8	B (. 50)	B (. 04)	L (. 17)	5. 93
9	S (. 50)	B (. 04)	B = (. 17) L = (. 17)	6. 59
10	4. 50	. 32	2. 38	91. 73
11	. 50	. 04	. 26	10. 19
12	CALBPC-BS TIME (also S)	CALBPC-BS TIME *	CALBPC-BS TIME	(25) L-SYSTEM TIME
13	. 50	. 04	. 17	1. 27
14	. 50	. 04	. 17	1. 27
15	. 50	. 04	. 17	1. 27

Figure 4. 1 (continued)

Column	t_{BS} B-TIME	(4) S-TIME	(5) $t_L + t_{BS} = t_U$ Total Time per Book	V Total Volumes FY 1966-67 — Volumes	(6) O Purchased — Orders Placed
1	5. 43	. 50	15. 96	3, 664	800
2	4. 88	. 50	12. 06	9, 606	125
3	4. 22	. 50	15. 39	34, 202	(1,487)
4	5. 22	. 50	17. 39	11, 833	3,306
5	6. 06	. 50	33. 48	3, 660	532
6	3. 65	. 50	8. 57	10, 204	671
7	6. 54	. 50	15. 85	6, 621	1,050
8	1. 38	---	7. 31	64, 745	(2,815)
9	5. 43	. 50	12. 52	4, 266	122
10	42. 79	4. 00	138. 52	148, 801	(10, 908)
11	4. 75	. 44	15. 39	16, 533	1,212
12	Σ(26) CALBPC-L	Σ(27) CALBPC-BS	Σ(28) SYSTEM TIME	SYSTEM VOLUME	
13	. 94	2. 12	4. 33	119, 505 ÷ (20A) 200	(21) 598
14	. 94	2. 12	4. 33	148, 801 ÷ (20B) 299	(21) 744
15	. 94	2. 12	4. 33	59, 752 75	797

Figure 4. 1 (continued)

Column	(7) $t_L \times V = t_L$ Total Library Time FY 1966-67		(8) $t_{BS} \times O = t_{BS}$ Total Business Office and State A. & C. Time	(9) $T_L + T_{BS} = T$ Total Book Procurement Time
	Hrs. Work Days Minutes	Hrs. Work Days Minutes	Hrs. Work Days Minutes	Hrs. Work Days Minutes
1	613 77 36753. 22		79 10 4742. 48	692 86 41495. 70
2	1070 134 64225. 72		11 1. 4 672. 14	1082 135 64897. 85
3	6078 760 364661. 72		117 14. 6 7024. 14	6182 773 370942. 37
4	2300 287 138005. 91		315 39 18922. 55	2615 326 156928. 46
5	1643 205 98554. 28		58 7 3487. 63	1701 212 102041. 92
6	753 95 45166. 99		46 5. 8 2781. 63	799 100 47948. 62
7	973 121 58381. 33		123 15 7387. 49	1096 137 65768. 81
8	6400 800 384028. 49		64 8 3869. 22	6465 808 387897. 71
9	468 59 28100. 14		12 1. 5 723. 23	480 60 28823. 37
10	20298 2537 1217877. 80		814 102 48867. 01	21112 2639 1266744. 81
11	2255 282 135319. 76		90 11 5429. 67	2346 293 140749. 42
12	(29) L-SYSTEM TIME	(30) CALBPC-L TIME	(31) CALBPC-BS TIME	SYSTEM TIME
13	2529 316 151759. 40	1867 233 112023. 99	21 3 1266. 74	4417 552 265050. 13
14	3149 394 188962. 39	2325 290 139486. 06	26 3 1576. 02	5500 687 330024. 46
15	1265 158 75879. 06	934 117 56011. 52	281 35 1688. 29	2226 278 133578. 87

Figure 4. 1 (continued)

Col-umn	(10) w_L Wages per Min. Full-Time Clerk	(11) $w_L \times T_L = W_L$ Total Wages Paid by Library FY 1966-67		
1	$ .03	$ 984.99 (unit cost .27)		
2	.03	1,746.94 (unit cost .18)		
3	.04	13,200.75 (unit cost .39)		
4	.04	5,865.25 (unit cost .50)		
5	.04	3,892.89 (unit cost 1.06)		
6	.03	1,183.38 (unit cost .12)		
7	.03	1,675.54 (unit cost .25)		
8	.04	13,825.03 (unit cost .21)		
9	.06	1,775.93 (unit cost .42)		
10	.33	44,150.70 (unit cost .38)		
11	.04	4,905.63		
12	(22) L-WAGE	(32) L-SYSTEM WAGES	(23) CALBPC-L WAGE	(33) CALBPC-L TOTAL WAGES
13	.04	5,493.69	.04	$ 4,032.86
14	.04	6,840.04	.04	5,021.50
15	.04	2,746.82	.04	2,016.41

Figure 4. 1 (continued)

Column	(12) w_{BS} Wages per Min. Paid by Business Office FY 1966-67	(13) $w_{BS} \times t_{BS} = W_{BS}$ Total Wages Paid by Business Office & State FY 1966-67	(14) $W_L + W_{BS} = C_I$ Total Labor Cost to Institution FY 1966-67	(16) $\frac{C_I}{V} = C_U$ Cost per Book
1	$. 06	$ 290. 24 (unit cost . 08)	$ 1275. 23	$. 35
2	. 06	41. 14 (unit cost . 01)	1788. 07	. 19
3	. 06	429. 89 (unit cost . 01)	13630. 64	. 40
4	. 06	1158. 06 (unit cost . 10)	7023. 31	. 59
5	. 06	213. 44 (unit cost . 06)	4106. 34	1. 12
6	. 06	170. 24 (unit cost . 02)	1353. 61	. 13
7	. 06	452. 11 (unit cost . 07)	2127. 66	. 32
8	. 06	234. 48 (unit cost . 01)	14059. 50	. 22
9	. 06	44. 26 (unit cost . 01)	1820. 19	. 43
10	. 55	3033. 85 (unit cost . 04)	47184. 55 (15)	3. 74
11	. 06	337. 10	5242. 73	. 32 (17)
12	(24) CALBPC-BS WAGE	(34) CALBPC-BS TOTAL WAGES	(35) SYSTEM LABOR COST	(36) SYSTEM COST PER BOOK
13	. 06	76. 76	9603. 32	. 08
14	. 06	95. 51	11957. 05 (40)	. 08
15	. 06	102. 31	4865. 55 (41)	. 08

Figure 4. 1 (continued)

Column	Total Labor Cost to Institutions Pro-rated for Comparison to CALBPC FY 1968-69	Total Labor Cost to Institutions Pro-rated for Comparison to CALBPC @ Half Expected Volume
10	$ 37, 889. 19 (37) ($ 47, 184. 55 pro-rated by 80. 3%)	$ 18, 949. 32 (41) ($ 47, 184. 55 pro-rated by 40. 2%)
12	Amount saved by (38) adoption of CALBPC System in one year	Amount saved per book in one year (39)
13	28, 285. 87	. 24
14	35, 181. 99	. 24
15	14, 083. 77	. 24

Figure 4. 2
Business Office Wage Rate

State of Colorado Civil Service:

* Accountants (Grade 24)

$660-$884 per month
Median Salary $ 773
Annual Salary $9, 276

* Bookkeepers (Accountant Clerk) (Grade 9)

$317-$425 per month
Median Salary $ 372
Annual Salary $4, 464

Legal holidays	11
Vacation	15
Total	26

Work days (52 5)	260
Less days off	-26
Actual work days	234

University of Colorado:

* Accountant

$444-$905 per month
Median Salary $ 726
Annual Salary $8, 712

* Bookkeeper (Clerk 4)

$375-$505 per month
Median Salary $ 441
Annual Salary $5, 212

Legal holidays	8. 0
Average vacation time $\frac{10 + 15}{2}$	12. 5
Total	20. 5

Work days (52 5)	260. 0
Less days off	-20. 5
Actual work days	239. 5

Figure 4. 2 (continued)

State of Colorado Civil Service:	University of Colorado:
Actual work minutes (8) (60) (234) = 112, 320	Actual work minutes (8) (60) (239. 5) = 114, 960
* Average annual salary $6, 870	* Average annual salary $6, 962
Salary per minute $. 0612	Salary per min. $. 0606

Figure 4. 3
Unit Saving Estimated by the Adoption of the CALBPC Bookkeeping System

Library	Cost of B. I. P. Check a	Present Bookkeeping System's Cost b	Total CALBPC Bookkeeping System's Cost c (a + . 08)	Unit Savings d (b - c)
1	. 01	. 35	. 09	. 26
2	. 01	. 19	. 09	. 10
3	. 01	. 40	. 09	. 31
4	. 01	. 60	. 09	. 51
5	. 02	1. 12	. 10	1. 02
6	N. A.	. 13	. 08	. 05
7	. 01	. 32	. 09	. 23
8	. 01	. 22	. 09	. 13
9	. 01	. 13	. 09	. 04

Adding each library's present bookkeeping cost to its unit labor cost (from Figure 3. 18) results in an estimated overall labor cost for procurement and processing (see Figure 4. 4).

Figure 4. 4
Overall Unit Labor Cost

Library	Library Labor Cost	Present Bookkeeping System's Cost	Unit Labor Cost Including Business Office Procedures
#1	3. 41	. 35	3. 76
#2	3. 01	. 19	3. 20
#3	2. 81	. 40	3. 21
#4	4. 96	. 60	5. 56
#5	6. 69	1. 12	7. 81
#6	1. 81	. 13	1. 94
#7	2. 78	. 32	3. 10
#8	3. 57	. 22	3. 79
#9	1. 49	. 13	1. 62

V. The Book Processing Center

Introduction

Based on data compiled in the investigation of the participants' operational characteristics, present processing costs, and existing framework of ordering (Sections II, III and IV), centralized processing appeared to offer considerable promise of savings in cost, time and staff. Design of the Book Processing Center was the next phase of the project. A center systems design was prepared utilizing two methods: traditional planning; and mathematical modeling simulation. Much of the data compiled earlier in the investigation was used in planning the operational configuration of the Center, and in providing variable input for computer simulation of the system.

In the following, the Center is described much as if it were a technical processing department of a very large library. It projects operating costs and savings to member libraries.

Once tentative specifications and costs were drawn up, the next step was to gain agreement by member libraries regarding the processing product the Center would provide and at what price. The utility of an approval plan concept to improve upon the services of the center and to promote the adoption of cooperative book selection with all its attendant advantages was also investigated.

The mathematical modeling of the Center provides two benefits: (1) a reliable method for initially predicting unit processing costs, staffing patterns, and processing time lags at various levels of processing; and (2) a management tool for decision making during Phase III of the study: establishment of the Center. The model also provides a means by which a library can simulate its technical services operations to derive data for improving its system.

Proposed Operating Specifications

The initial design phase of the Center had two major objectives:

to serve as a proposed guideline to the member libraries and to provide enough data so that a mathematical model could be constructed. After flow charting, the project team directed its attention to the problem of the availability of Library of Congress cataloging copy upon which the rapid flow of books through the system would depend. A cost analysis of the Center similar to that undertaken for each member library was completed as was a projection of the savings that might accrue.

Decision flow chart: The process of planning the Center on the basis of all data collected began with exhaustive flow charting of the proposed Center. Figure 5. 1 is a simplified version of the original flow chart, which is too lengthy to include in the final report.

L. C. cataloging copy: The availability of Library of Congress cataloging copy is of primary importance. In order to learn more about this, statistics on four categories of imprints were collected: (1) 1965+; (2) 1964 and earlier; (3) approval procurement (1967); and (4) countries cooperating in the shared cataloging program for the years 1966 and 1967.

The results of the investigation are summarized in Figure 5. 2. The methodology for collecting this data is explained below.

By Imprint Date 1965+: At Library #8 the technical services staff drew a sample of 442 titles to search for proof cards at the time of title receipt. For this sample, proof cards were located for 39. 6% of the titles. Another 6. 5% were represented in the National Union Catalog or the LC Printed Catalog from which card sets could be produced by a xerox camera enlargement process. Therefore, a total of 46. 1% of the titles received in the sample could be mass cataloged. This means that there is a . 461 chance of availability of L. C. copy for imprints up to two years old.

By Imprint Date 1964 or Earlier: Processing a sample of 604 titles received, proof cards were located for 5. 6% of the titles, 10. 6% could be provided from N. U. C. by xerographic enlargement, and an additional 74. 7% were located in the L. C. Printed Catalog. In other words there was a . 909 chance of availability of L. C. copy at the time of receipt of the books bearing imprints three years old or older.

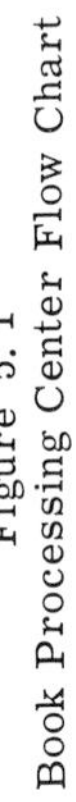

Figure 5.1
Book Processing Center Flow Chart

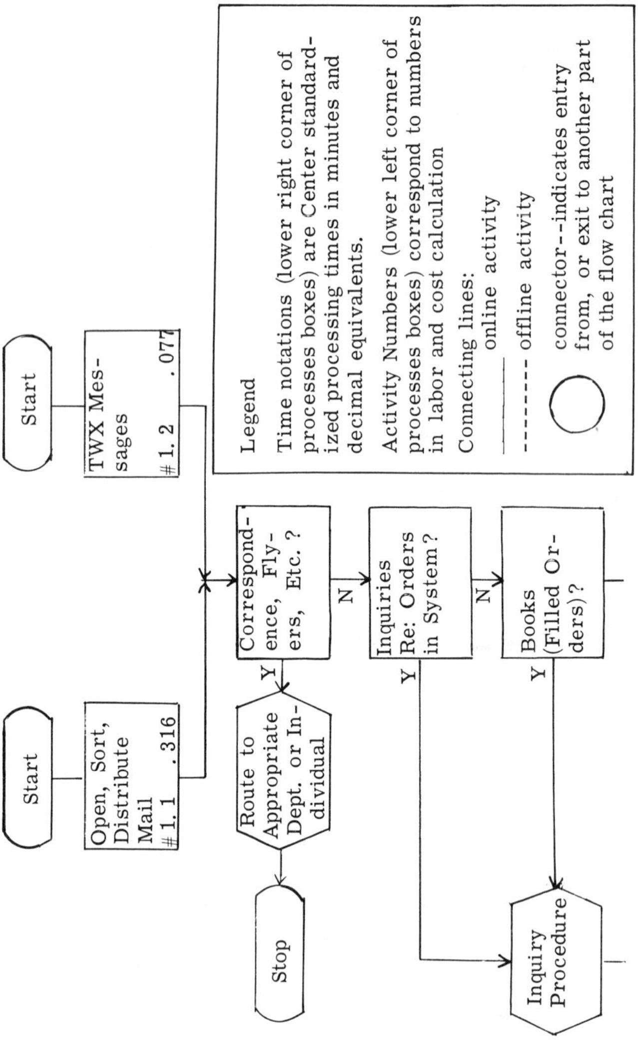

Start
Start
Open, Sort, Distribute Mail
1. 1 .316
TWX Messages
1. 2 .077
Correspondence, Flyers, Etc. ?
Y
N
Route to Appropriate Dept. or Individual
Stop
Inquiries Re: Orders in System?
Y
N
Books (Filled Orders)?
Y
Inquiry Procedure
Legend
Time notations (lower right corner of processes boxes) are Center standardized processing times in minutes and decimal equivalents.
Activity Numbers (lower left corner of processes boxes) correspond to numbers in labor and cost calculation
Connecting lines:
online activity
offline activity
connector--indicates entry from, or exit to another part of the flow chart

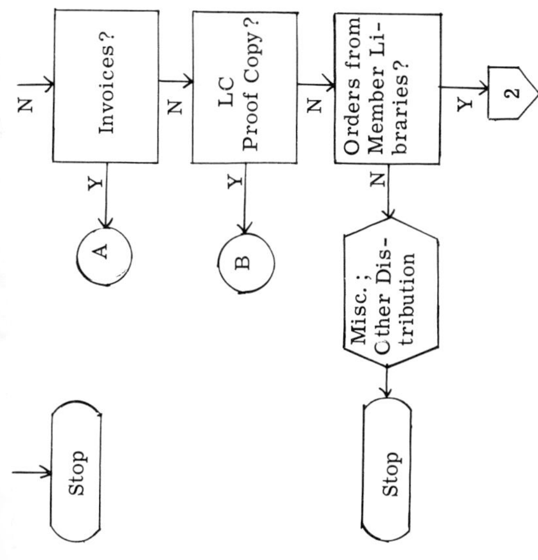
N
Invoices?
Y
A
N
LC
Proof Copy?
Y
B
N
Orders from
Member Li-
braries?
Y
2
N
Misc.;
Other Dis-
tribution
Stop
Stop

Figure 5.1 (continued)

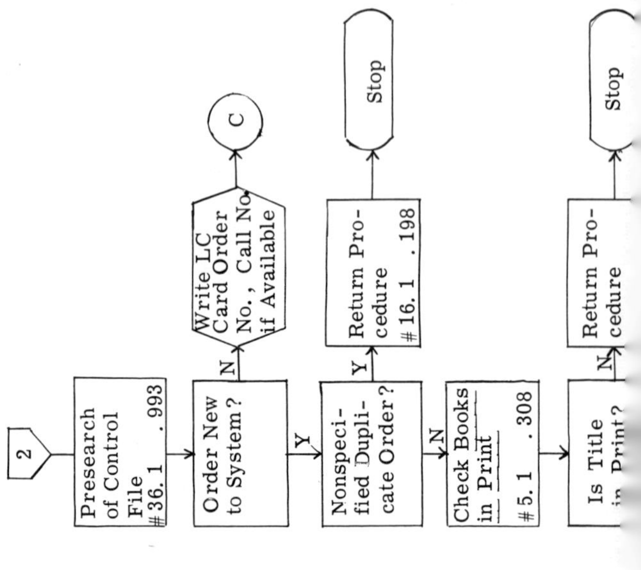

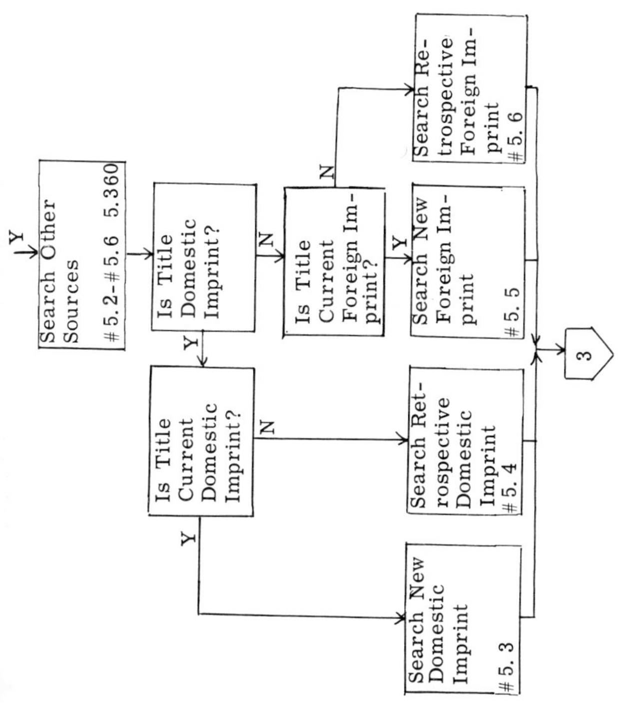
Y
Search Other Sources
5.2-# 5.6 5.360
Is Title Domestic Imprint?
Y
N
Is Title Current Domestic Imprint?
Is Title Current Foreign Imprint?
Y
N
Y
N
Search New Domestic Imprint
5. 3
Search Retrospective Domestic Imprint
5. 4
Search New Foreign Imprint
5. 5
Search Retrospective Foreign Imprint
5. 6
3

Figure 5.1 (continued)

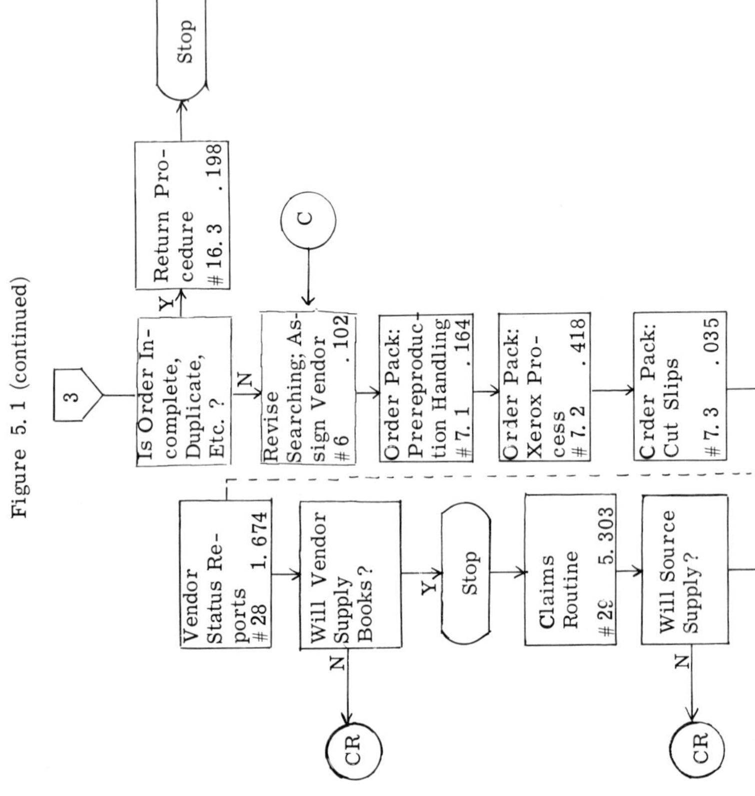

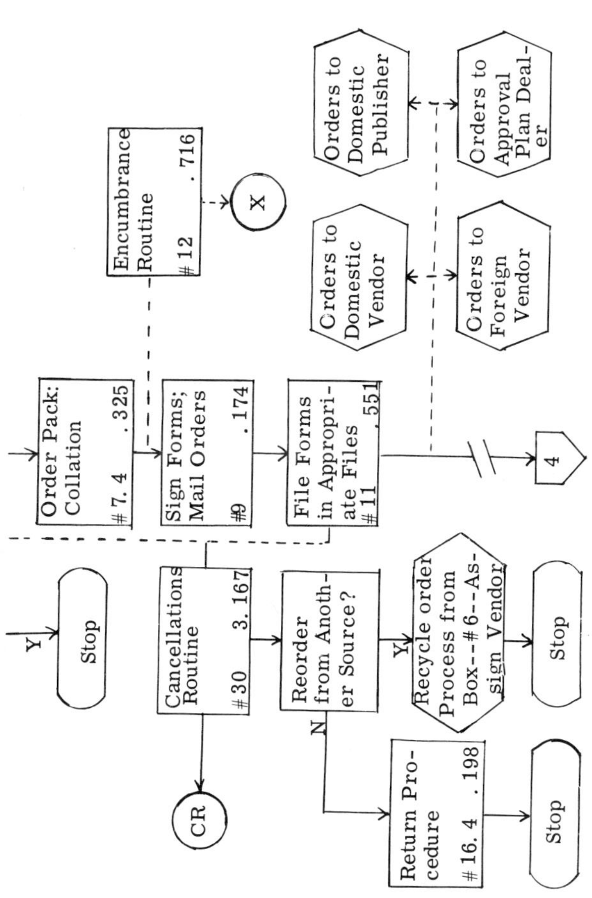
Y
Stop
Order Pack: Collation
7. 4 .325
Sign Forms; Mail Orders
#9 .174
File Forms in Appropri- ate Files
11 .551
4
Encumbrance Routine
12 .716
X
Orders to Domestic Vendor
Orders to Domestic Publisher
Orders to Foreign Vendor
Orders to Approval Plan Deal- er
Cancellations Routine
30 3. 167
CR
Reorder from Anoth- er Source?
N
Y
Recycle order Process from Box--# 6--As- sign Vendor
Stop
Return Pro- cedure
16. 4 . 198
Stop

Figure 5.1 (continued)

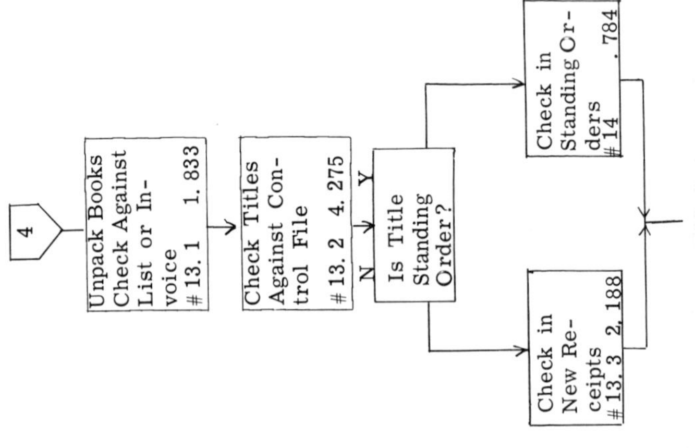

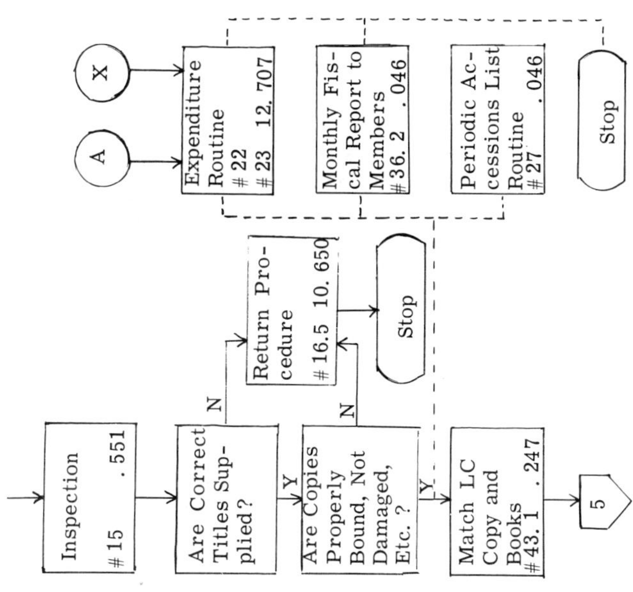
Inspection
#15 .551
Are Correct Titles Supplied?
N
Y
Are Copies Properly Bound, Not Damaged, Etc. ?
N
Y
Return Procedure
#16.5 10.650
Stop
Match LC Copy and Books
#43.1 .247
5
A
X
Expenditure Routine
#22
#23 12.707
Monthly Fiscal Report to Members
#36.2 .046
Periodic Accessions List Routine
#27 .046
Stop

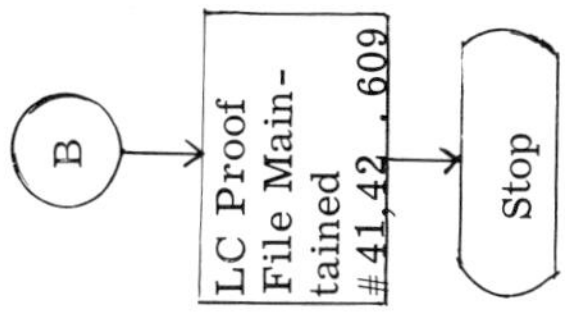
B
LC Proof File Maintained
#41,42 .609
Stop

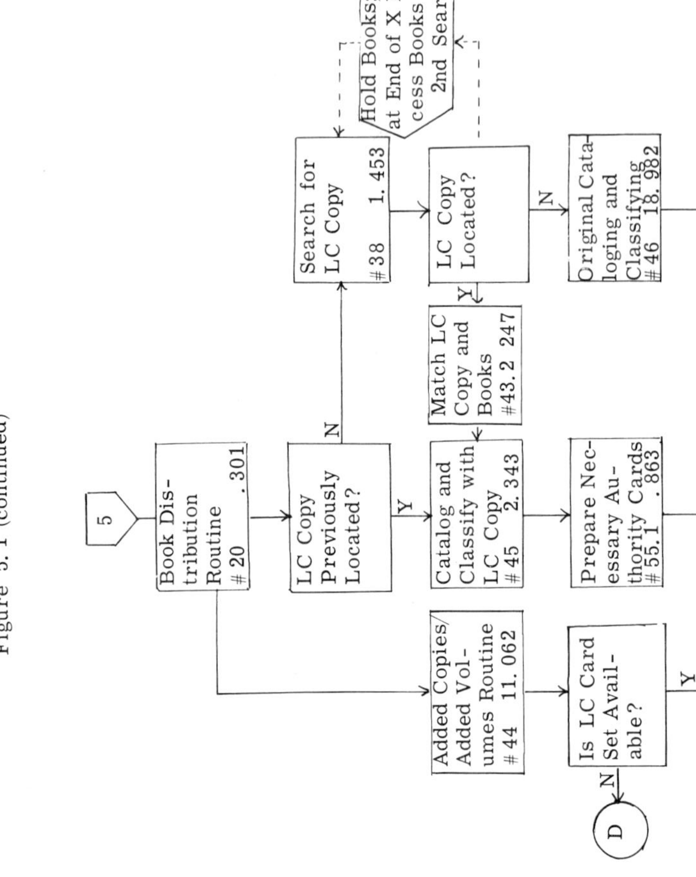

Figure 5.1 (continued)

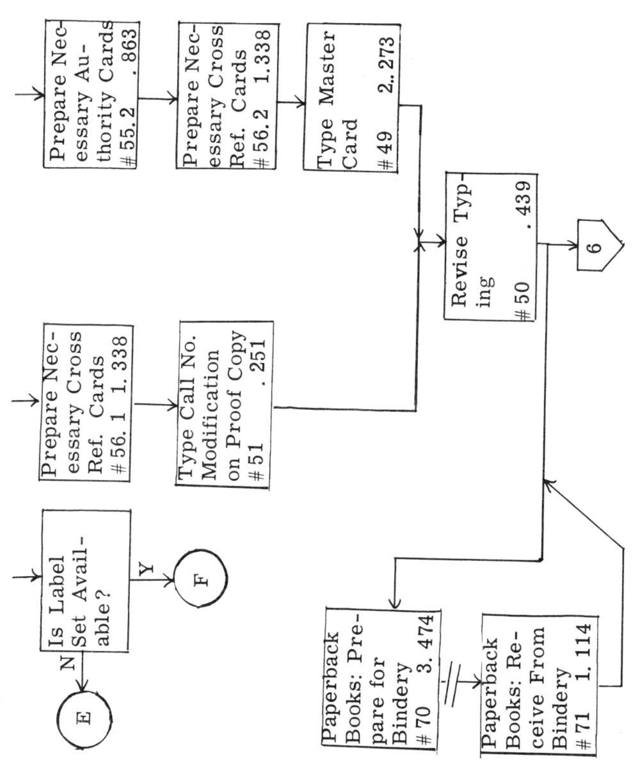
Is Label Set Available?
N
Y
E
F
Prepare Necessary Cross Ref. Cards #56.1 1.338
Type Call No. Modification on Proof Copy #51 .251
Prepare Necessary Authority Cards #55.2 .863
Prepare Necessary Cross Ref. Cards #56.2 1.338
Type Master Card #49 2..273
Revise Typing #50 .439
6
Paperback Books: Prepare for Bindery #70 3.474
Paperback Books: Receive From Bindery #71 1.114

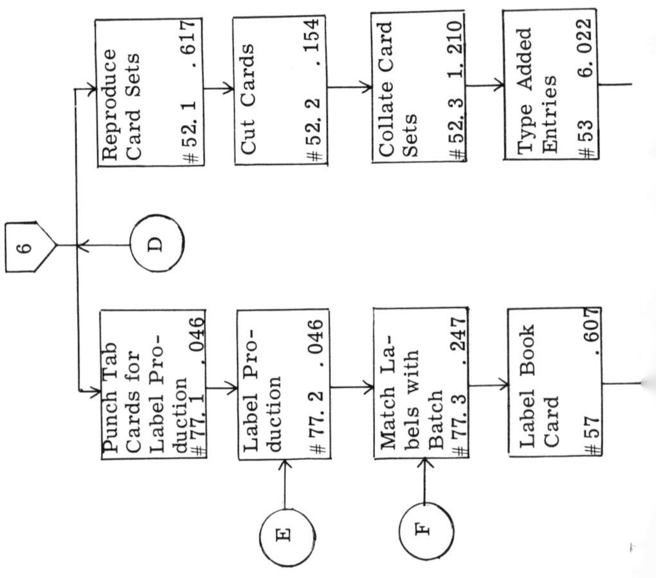

Figure 5. 1 (continued)

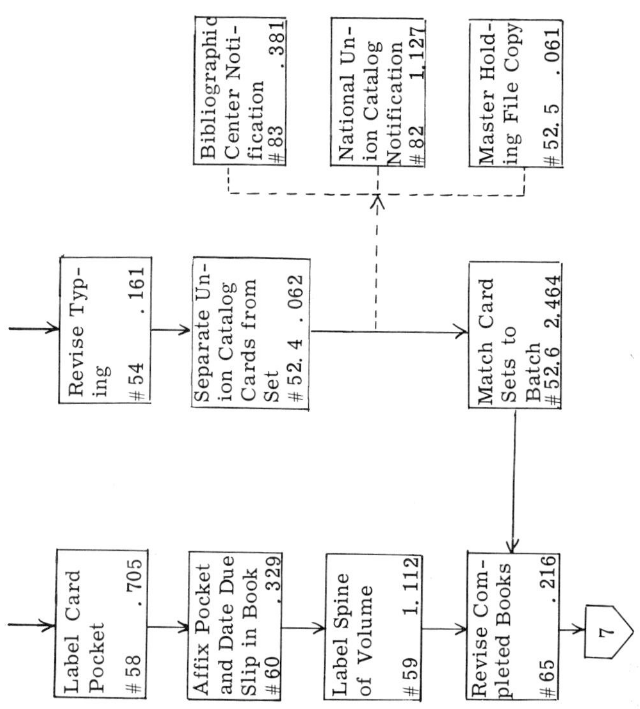
Label Card Pocket #58 .705
Affix Pocket and Date Due Slip in Book #60 .329
Label Spine of Volume #59 1.112
Revise Com- pleted Books #65 .216
7
Revise Typ- ing #54 .161
Separate Un- ion Catalog Cards from Set #52.4 .062
Match Card Sets to Batch #52.6 2.464
Bibliographic Center Noti- fication #83 .381
National Un- ion Catalog Notification #82 1.127
Master Hold- ing File Copy #52.5 .061

Figure 5. 1 (continued)

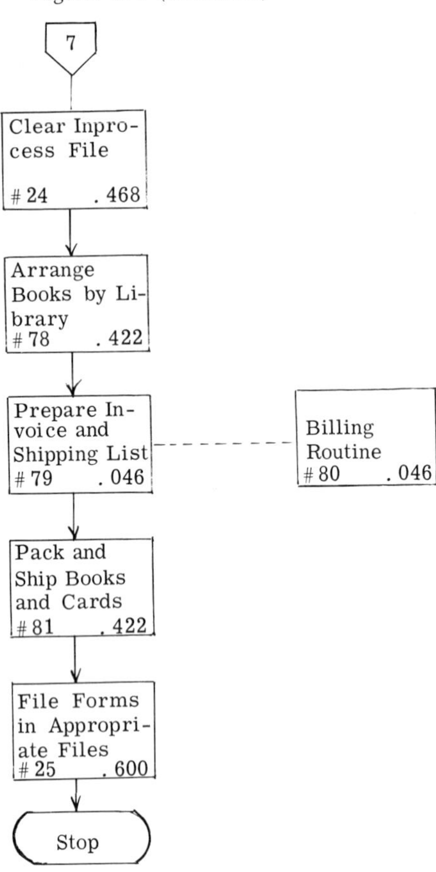

At the Time of Approval Procurement (1967): A sample of 657 titles received on approval were checked for proof cards with the result that 53. 4% of the titles had copy available.

Foreign Imprints (1966-1967): 168 imprints in English, French, German, Scandanavian, Dutch and Slavic, published in 1966/67, were searched for LC copy. LC copy was located for 26. 2% of these titles on the initial search.

The percentage of other 1966 and 1967 imprints in the sample for which LC copy was available totaled 33. 8% and the overall percentage for all 1966/67 imprints searched was 32. 7%.

The results of this test were sobering. In spite of all national efforts to accelerate the flow of cataloging copy to research libraries, copy is still available for only about one-half of the titles at the time they arrive. This type of delay has already reduced the effectiveness of the approval plans now in operation. It must be recognized that until the Library of Congress is able to shorten the lag time, the processing of a substantial number of books will be delayed. Moreover, as is shown in the next section, the processing cost is markedly affected by the availability of cataloging copy.

Figure 5. 2
Available Copy at Time of Receipt of Books

	Sample Size	Proof Copy	Xerox Copy or LC Cards	LC Copy	Total % Available
Imprints 1965+	442	175	29		
% Available		39. 6	6. 5		46. 1
Imprints 1964 and earlier	604	34	64	451	
% Available		5. 6	10. 6	74. 7	90. 9
Approval books (1967)	657	351			
% Available		53. 4			53. 4
Shared Cataloging countries (1966-67)	168	44			
% Available		26. 2			26. 2
Total of all other imprints 1966-67	940	328			
% Available		33. 8			33. 8
Grand total for all 1966 and 1967 imprints, foreign and domestic	1138	372			
% Available		32. 7			32. 7

Note: Data was supplied by Technical Services Personnel at Library #8.

Catalog card overrun: Catalog card reproduction and catalog card production overruns is a facet of centralized processing which will be studied in detail in an operational environment after the Center is established. Three alternatives are immediately apparent: (1) reproduce duplicate sets of cards when a copy of a title is ordered, basing the number of sets on the title/copy duplication factor identified in Figure 2. 9; (2) reproduce one set of cards for each copy of a title as the copies are ordered; and (3) order LC card sets as copies of titles are ordered. Alternative three may be discarded as an approach which, at present, is not practical because of cost and time lag.

In examining alternatives (1) and (2), the probability of duplication of copies of a single title ordered by member libraries must be considered. Based on the BPR title/copy duplication study, Section II, sample data were tabulated on the number of titles purchased by the member libraries as a cumulative percentage (see Figure 5. 3). Using a base figure of 774 titles, which was the number of titles found in at least one library of those studied, from the total BPR sample of 1, 206 titles, this analysis focuses on the advantages and disadvantages of alternative methods for handling card catalog inventories.

Figure 5. 3
Number of Titles Affected by Duplication of Orders
(Sample Size: 774)

Number of Institutions	Number of Titles Purchased	% Cumulated
1	220	28
2	209	56
3	138	77
4	112	88
5	58	95
6	28	99
7	5	99. 6
8	2	99. 8
9	2	100

Alternative (1): With regard to the additional sets of cards identified in Figure 5. 4 as "sets discarded," these card sets would be stored and used when additional orders were received. However, the problem with overruns is to identify the cutoff point after which more card sets would be stored than used. If too high a cutoff is selected, the waste in card reproduction and file maintenance of card sets can prove to be expensive. Examination of Figure 5. 4 indicates a cutoff at four card sets for each title.

Alternative (2): Reproduction of card sets as orders are received would be the better of the two approaches if an effective system can be instituted to effect coordinated ordering, i. e., if all or the majority of orders for copies of a title were received at one time. If however, there is no attempted coordination, the work involved in pulling a master card, running one set of cards, and returning the master card to the file may prove more expensive and time consuming than maintaining an overrun.

Figure 5. 4
Catalog Card Overruns

Catalog Card Sets: Overrun per Title	Sets Utilized (1)	Sets Discarded (2)	% Waste (3)	Additional Sets Needed (4)	% of Rework	Minimum Sets Reproduced (1) + (4)
9	6, 966	5, 339	76	----	---	6, 966
8	6, 192	4, 067	66	2	. 1	6, 194
7	5, 418	3, 397	63	6	. 3	5, 424
6	4, 644	2, 632	57	15	. 7	4, 649
5	3, 720	1, 895	51	52	2	3, 772
4	3, 096	1, 216	39	147	7	3, 243
3	2, 322	649	28	354	17	2, 676
2	1, 548	220	14	699	34	2, 247
1	774	0	0	1253	61	2, 027
	(batch)			(sequential)		

Support for a policy of card reproduction on demand is drawn from the percentage of titles member libraries buy that are not purchased by the University of Colorado, where the Center will be housed. (See Figure 5. 5) For approximately one-fourth of the orders received, a master card must be prepared, because it will not have been cataloged as part of the University Library system.

Card production methods: The Catalog Maintenance Unit of the C. U. Library compared card production by xerox and by flexowriter as both were being used simultaneously. The data in Figure 5. 6 shows rather conclusively that the xerox method is the faster of the two.

Prior to the processing center time study, both systems had been subjected to cost analysis. L. H. Gregory did the study on

Figure 5. 5
Percentage of Titles Purchased by Libraries Other Than C. U.

Library #	%
1	29
2	25
3	19
4	28
5	30
6	19
7	45
8	--
9	21

Figure 5. 6
Card Reproduction Time: Xerox and Flexowriter Methods Compared[1]

From	To	No. of Cards in Sample	Average Time in Days
	XEROX		
Copy placed in box by cataloger	Set produced by xerox	273	4. 99
Set produced by xerox	Card placed in prefile	273	10. 66
Cards placed in prefile	Cards filed	195	9. 87
	Total Time		25. 52
	FLEXOWRITER		
Copy placed in box by cataloger	Flexowriter input completed	188	29. 04
Flexowriter input completed	Cards placed in prefile	184	18. 42
Cards placed in prefile	Cards filed	115	10. 69
	Total Time		58. 15

xeroxing,[2] and Mr. James Stephens, Systems Analyst at the C. U. Library, completed the flexowriter cost study. The results are not available in final form; nevertheless, they do indicate that the flexowriter system is more expensive than the xerox method. The flexowriter system was abandoned at C. U. in March 1968.

At present C. U. continues to reproduce card sets by xerography. Since the time studies noted in the previous paragraph were completed, the library has begun to use a Xerox 2400. The effective output of this machine is considerably greater than the Xerox 720 that was formerly used. Card reproduction will be studied further. It is possible that a xerox/multilith process may be more economical.

CALBPC unit costs: The unit processing cost for the Center was calculated by the methodology used in calculating unit costs of the participating libraries (Section III). The minimum mean time observed for each activity applicable to Center activities was used as one factor in this calculation. Several standardized processing times obtained from the Nassau Library System Processing Center, Long Island, New York,[3] were substituted for those Center processing activities which had no comparable function in any of the nine participating libraries. (See Figure 5. 7)

Unit Labor Cost: The tasks analyzed were selected on the basis of the functions as indicated on the CALBPC decision flow chart. (See Figure 5. 1) The minimum mean time observed for each function was selected out of all data compiled at member libraries and recorded with its corresponding personal rating factor. The level of person performing the function at the Center was a matter of judgment on the projected Center's operation; however, full-time clerks were favored to perform most of the tasks.

Additional procedures which had not been previously identified on the STPA list were obtained by locating appropriate sub-functions from the mean time tables. For example, mean times for key punching obtained as part of the bookkeeping tasks at Library # 8 were used to simulate times for functions 36. 2 (monthly report to members) and 79 (invoice/shipping list production) for the Center. If such functions included sorting or filing tasks, times for these were extracted from time observation sheets or from the mean time tables also. In this manner, a simulated time was calculated from a summation of selected sub-functions that most nearly approximated the necessary Center function when taken as a unit. Voos' observed time and standardizing factor were used for function 60 (affix pocket and date due slip).

Frequencies: A frequency chart was prepared based on the participating library labor charts for those functions which were rele-

Figure 5. 7
Labor (L)
Unit Cost Calculation for Technical Processing Activities
Acquisitions

Library C. A. L. B. P. C.

Key: AF = Another function incorporated this activity at this library.
NA = Not applicable (not performed at this library).
( ) = Simulated data
+ = Standardizing factor (1. 4771)
g_1 = Student Assistant
g_2 = Clerk (full-time)
g_3 = Professional
d = Data taken from the diary.

	a	b	c	d	f+	g	h	i
Activity Description	Observed Mean Time	Fre-quency	Adjusted Time	Personal Rating Factor	Standard Time	Cate-gory of Worker	Wage/ Minute	Cost of Activity
1. Open, sort and distribute incoming mail.	. 249	1. 000	. 249	1. 07	. 3935	2	. 0360	. 014
2. Review book order requests; review selection media.								
3. Select titles to be ordered.								
4. Type library order request card.								
5. Search and verify bibliographic information.	3. 489	. 100	. 3489	1. 10	. 5669	2	. 0360	. 020
6. Assign vendor and fund.	. 063	1. 000	. 063	1. 10	. 1024	3	. 0759	. 008
7. Prepare multiple order record.	. 580	1. 000	. 580	1. 10	. 9424	2	. 0360	. 034
8. Type purchase requisition, etc.								
9. Revise typing. Sign and mail re-quests.	. 112	1. 000	. 112	1. 05	. 1737	2	. 0360	. 006
10. Burst forms.								
11. File forms in appropriate files.	. 324	1. 000	. 324	1. 15	. 5507	2	. 0360	. 020
12. Encumbrance or prepayment routine.	. 453	1. 000	. 453	1. 07	. 7160	2	. 0360	. 026

13. Unpack books; check against packing list or invoice. Check outstanding order file.	5. 200	1. 000	5. 200	1. 08	8. 2954	2	. 0360	. 299
14. Check in serials on Kardex.	. 483	. 0375	. 0181	1. 10	. 0294	2	. 0360	. 001
15. Collate books.	. 311	1. 000	. 311	1. 20	. 5512	2	. 0360	. 020
16. Book return procedure (incorrect shipment, defective copy, approval books).	6. 924	. 0061	. 042	1. 08	. 0671	2	. 0360	. 002
17. Book accessioning routine.								
18. Write sourcing information.								
19. Prepare gift record form.								
20. Book distribution routine.	. 191	1. 000	. 191	1. 07	. 3019	2	. 0360	. 011
21. Prepare receiving report.								
{22. Prepare invoices for payment. {23. Expenditure routine.	7. 966	1. 000	7. 966	1. 08	12. 7079	2	. 0360	. 458
24. Clear in-process file.	. 302	1. 000	. 302	1. 05	4. 6839	2	. 0360	. 169
25. File forms, etc., in completed records or discard.	. 369	1. 000	. 369	1. 10	5. 9955	2	. 0360	. 216
26. Requestor notification routine.								
27. Periodic accessions list routine.	. 028	1. 000	. 028	1. 10	. 0460	2	. 0360	. 002
28. Vendor status routine.	. 985	. 1576	. 1552	1. 15	. 2637	2	. 0360	. 010
29. Claims routine.	3. 264	. 0347	. 1133	1. 10	. 1840	2	. 0360	. 007
30. Cancellations routine.	1. 864	. 0369	. 0688	1. 15	. 1168	2	. 0360	. 004
31. Out-of-print order routine.								
32. Process inquiries.								
33. General typing - correspondence, etc. (specify).								
34. General revision (specify).								
35. General filing (specify).								
36. Other acquisitions activities not listed above (specify).								
36. 1. Pre-search of control file	. 611	1. 000	. 611	1. 10	. 9928	2	. 0360	. 036
36. 2. Monthly report to members.	. 028	1. 000	. 028	1. 10	. 0455	2	. 0360	. 002
						Sub-total		1. 365

Figure 5. 7 (continued)

Cataloging

Activity Description	a Observed Mean Time	b Fre- quency	c Adjusted Time	d Personal Rating Factor	f Standard Time	g Cate- gory of Worker	h Wage/ Minute	i Cost of Activity
37. Sort books, assign and distribute.								
38. Search for LC copy; verify biblio- graphic information.	. 895	. 7423	. 6644	1. 10	1. 0795	2	. 0360	. 039
39. Order LC cards or other unit cards.								
40. Receive and arrange LC cards.								
41. Receive and arrange LC proof slips or proof sheets.								
42. File LC copy. (cards or proof)	. 458	. 468	. 2143	. 90	. 2849	2	. 0360	. 010
43. Match LC cards or proof copy and books.	. 290	. 229	. 0664	1. 15	. 1128	2	. 0360	. 004
44. Added copies/added volumes routine.	. 373	. 2501	. 9329	1. 09	1. 0169	2	. 0360	. 037
45. Catalog and classify with LC cards/ copy.	1. 510	. 6497	. 9810	1. 05	1. 5214	2	. 0360	. 055
46. Original cataloging and classifying.	14. 081 d	. 1002	1. 411	1. 10	2. 2926	3	. 0759	. 174
47. Shelf listing (for 44, 45, and 46).								
48. Type complete card sets.								
49. Type master card.	1. 304	. 1002	. 1307	1. 18	. 2278	2	. 0360	. 008
50. Revise master card.	. 270	. 1002	. 0205	1. 10	. 0334	2	. 0360	. 001
51. Type modification on a card or proof slip.	. 155	. 1002	. 0155	1. 10	. 0253	2	. 0360	. 001
52. Reproduce card sets (other than typing). Sort cards into sets.	1. 489	1. 000	1. 489	1. 10	2. 4193	2	. 0360	. 081

53. Type call number, added entries.	3.810	1.000	3.810	1.07	6.0217	2	.0360	.217
54. Revise typing on card sets.	.095	1.000	.095	1.15	.1613	2	.0360	.006
55. Prepare authority cards.	1.168	1.000	1.168	1.00	1.7252	2	.0360	.062
56. Prepare cross-reference cards.	1.648	1.000	1.648	1.10	2.6777	2	.0360	.096
57. Prepare circulation card.	.357	1.000	.357	1.15	.6058	1	.0222	.013
58. Prepare book pocket.	.415	1.000	.415	1.15	.7049	1	.0222	.016
59. Mark call number or place label on spine of volume.	.655	1.000	.655	1.15	1.1126	1	.0222	.025
60. Affix pocket and date due slip.	Standard Time (Voos)							
Affix gift plate.	.2030	1.000	.2030	1.10	.3298	1	.0222	.007
61. Affix biographical and review material in book.								
62. Stamp property marks.								
63. Affix plastic jacket to book.								
64. Paperback books--library binding routine.								
65. Revise completed books before forwarding to circulation.	.127	1.000	.127	1.15	.2158	3	.0759	.016
66. Sort and alphabetize shelf list and all catalog cards.								
67. File shelf list and all catalog cards.								
68. Revise filing of shelf list and all catalog cards.								
69. Route card sets to departmental libraries.								
70. Paperback books--bindery routine (preparation).	2.138	.0704	.1505	1.10	.2446	2	.0360	.009
71. Paperback books--bindery routine (receiving).	.685	.0704	.0482	1.10	.0786	2	.0360	.003
72. Catalog maintenance (other than filing).								

Figure 5. 7 (continued)

Cataloging

Activity Description	a Observed Mean Time	b Fre-quency	c Adjusted Time	d Personal Rating Factor	f Standard Time	g Cate-gory of Worker	h Wage/ Minute	i Cost of Activity
73. General typing (specify).								
74. General revision (specify).								
75. General filing (specify).								
76. Other cataloging activities not listed above (specify).								
77. Label production.	. 201	1. 000	. 201	1. 10	. 3266	2	. 0360	. 012
78. Arrange books by library.	. 2605	1. 000	. 2605	1. 10	. 4233	2	. 0360	. 015
79. Invoice/shipping list production.	. 028	1. 000	. 028	1. 10	. 0455	2	. 0360	. 002
80. Billing.	. 028	1. 000	. 028	1. 10	. 0455	2	. 0360	. 002
81. Packing and mailing.	. 2605	1. 000	. 2605	1. 10	. 4233	2	. 0360	. 015
82. Union catalog (arrange and file).	. 6938	1. 000	. 6938	1. 10	1. 1273	2	. 0360	. 041
83. Bibliographic Center notification.	. 235	1. 000	. 235	1. 10	. 3818	2	. 0360	. 014
						Sub-total		. 981
					Acquisitions			1. 365
					Cataloging			. 981
					ΣL			2. 346

vant to CALBPC. The frequencies for each function were averaged for the nine libraries to obtain a composite frequency per function. Tasks peculiar to the Center's operation, identified as 36. 2 and 77-83, were each assigned frequencies of 1. 0 because they pertained to every book coming through the system.

Standard Times: The CALBPC standard times were then calculated using the same methodology already described in Section III.

Wage Rate: The wage scale in use at the University of Colorado was used as the CALBPC rate.

Unit Cost: The standard time multiplied by the appropriate wage rate yielded the unit cost per function, which, when summed, produced the total unit labor cost for CALBPC. This figure was entered on the Summary Cost Sheet (Figure 3. 18). For convenience the CALBPC portion of this table is reproduced here.

Figure 5. 8
CALBPC: Summary of Cost Factors

Labor	Supplies	Overhead	Transportation	Binding	Cost
$2. 35	. 29	. 31	. 06	. 09	$3. 10

The unit supply cost and unit overhead cost for the nine libraries were averaged to obtain estimates for the Center. The figure for transportation was based upon the physical layout at the University of Colorado. The unit bindery fee was based on a study of bindery charges at the University of Colorado. The five factors were then summed to obtain the unit book ordering and processing cost of $3. 10 for CALBPC, as noted in Figure 5. 8.

Cost Savings: Certain functions such as those pertaining to the initiation of book orders and checking in shipments of books must be performed by the cooperating libraries. This means that a share of their present unit processing cost is retained. The costs of such functions, summarized from the unit labor charts, are shown in Figure 5. 9.

The costs of functions retained were entered in Figure 5. 10, then added to the CALBPC processing fee of $3. 10 to obtain the esti-

Figure 5. 9
Cost of Functions Retained by Libraries Which Participate in Centralized Processing

Library	Cost of Functions Retained	Functions												
		1	2	4	(5)*	61	62	63	65	66	67	68	69	72
1	$. 672	x		x	x	x	x		x	x	x	x		
2	. 689	x	x	x	x		x		x	x	x	x		x
3	. 922	x	x		x		x		x	x	x	x		x
4	. 677	x	x	x	x		x		x	x	x	x		x
5	. 658	x		x	x		x	x	x	x	x	x		x
6	. 449	x	x	x			x	x		x	x	x		x
7	. 513	x		x	x	x	x		x	x	x	x		x
8	. 230	x			x		x		x	x	x	x	x	x
9	. 484	x	x	x	x		x	x	x	x	x	x		x

Average Cost = $. 588

* Function 5 may be partially retained or not at all depending upon local policy. Only the cost for checking Books in Print was included in the Cost of Functions Retained.

mated full processing cost to member libraries. From this amount was subtracted the unit processing cost for each library to obtain the unit dollar savings on processing.

A discount advantage expected through the use of combined ordering and a larger volume of ordering is conservatively estimated at 5% of the average current book price of $7. 69, or $. 384. This amount, when added to the unit savings on processing, provides an estimate of the amount saved on total unit processing for each library. A similar calculation was made with a discount advantage of 10%. It will be noted that two libraries would not except a savings under the 5% discount advantage, but all except one library would save under the 10% discount advantage. Savings for seven libraries ranged from $. 45-$4. 34 by the first method, and $. 83-$4. 72 by the second method.

Insofar as anticipated volume at the Center is concerned, the unit saving shown in Figure 5. 11 is substantial. This level of savings

Figure 5. 10
Unit Savings to Member Libraries Through the Use of Centralized Processing

Library	Unit Cost of Functions Retained by Library	Plus CALBPC's Unit Cost of $3. 10	Unit Cost of Present System	Unit Savings on Processing	Unit Savings with 5% Discount Advantage ($. 384)*	Unit Savings with 10% Discount Advantage ($. 769)*
1	$. 672	$3. 772	$4. 540	$. 768	$1. 152	$1. 537
2	. 689	3. 789	4. 020	. 231	. 615	1. 000
3	. 922	4. 022	3. 530	-. 492	-. 108	. 277
4	. 677	3. 777	5. 870	2. 093	2. 477	2. 862
5	. 658	3. 758	7. 710	3. 952	4. 336	4. 721
6	. 449	3. 549	2. 670	-. 879	-. 495	-. 110
7	. 513	3. 613	3. 550	. 063	. 447	. 832
8	. 230	3. 330	4. 160	. 830	1. 214	1. 599
9	. 484	3. 584	4. 490	. 906	1. 290	1. 675

*The average book price of $7. 69 was the basis for calculating the average discount allowances beyond those already enjoyed by member libraries. This average is quoted from "An Analysis of Abel Approval Plan at the University of Nebraska Libraries, 1966-67" (unpublished typewritten manuscript prepared July 13, 1967). This analysis was based upon 8865 titles.

would not be realized until after the one year trial operating period. For the total system, an estimated $117, 785 would be saved per year. That is an amount greater than the majority of the book budgets of the cooperating libraries. If the 10% discount advantage is used in the calculation, $159, 488 would be the projected saving--a difference of $41, 703. It is clear that every effort should be made to obtain the best possible discounts consonant with good service and to eliminate or combine labor functions where feasible. As orders become better coordinated and as the copy per volume ratio increases, unit costs will drop substantially. The copy per title variable was tested by a mathematical model. The results underscore the potential savings that can be realized by ordering multiple copies. The cost of processing one volume per title is $2. 96 whereas the cost of processing six volumes per title is $2. 33 (See Figure 7. 9).

Figure 5. 11
Estimated Savings in Processing Costs at Member Libraries Through the Establishment of CALBPC

Library	Total Volumes Processed by Libraries	% of Books That Might be Processed	Total Volumes Processed	Less 15% for Local Ordering (Rush Orders, Standing Orders, etc.)	Projected CALBPC Unit Savings (Incl. 5% Discount Advantage)*	Projected CALBPC Unit Savings (Incl. 10% Discount Advantage)*	Total Annual Savings (or Loss) by Establishment of CALBPC	Total Annual Savings (or Loss) by Establishment of CALBPC
	a	b	c (a x b)	d	e	f	g (d x e)	g (d x f)
1	4, 014	52	2, 070	1, 760	$1. 15	$1. 54	$ 2, 028	$ 2, 705
2	9, 631	75	7, 250	6, 162	. 62	1. 00	3, 790	6, 162
3	35, 583	32	11, 080	9, 410	-. 11	. 28	-1, 016	2, 607
4	12, 858	57	7, 319	6, 221	2. 48	2. 86	15, 409	17, 804
5	4, 733	76	3, 598	3, 075	4. 33	4. 72	13, 333	14, 517
6	12, 204	54	6, 500	5, 520	-. 50	-. 11	-2, 732	- 607
7	10, 012	54	5, 406	4, 596	. 45	. 83	2, 054	3, 824
8	67, 492	100**	67, 492	----	1. 21	1. 60	81, 935	107, 920
9	4, 466	61	2, 720	2, 313	1. 29	1. 68	2, 984	4, 556
Total	160, 993		113, 435	106, 549			$117, 785	$159, 488

*Entered from Figure 5. 10 in Section V.
**Library #8 is 100% because the Center will be located there.

Standardized processing times: Supplementary to the cost information provided to the member libraries on their own operation are two figures pertaining to standardized processing times. There are also two ways of computing standard times, one with the frequency of use of each function multiplied with the other factors, and the other, omitting frequency considerations altogether. The latter method is a practical form of presenting data because it enables another library to use the times cited and to introduce its own frequencies. Appendix 5. 1 lists the Overall Standard Times with the frequencies omitted from the computation.

As a means of comparing one library to another among those who participated in the study, the sums of the acquisition and cataloging standard times from the labor charts are shown in Figure 5. 12. The number of steps recorded on the flow process chart are also shown. These times include frequencies as well as the personal rating factor and the standardizing factor (1. 4771). The Center's projected time proved to be twenty-one minutes below the average total time; one library's time was four minutes less than the Center's and another library's was eighty-seven minutes greater.

Standardization Decisions

Standardization of many of the participants' processing routines is a significant element in the design and successful implementation of centralized book processing. Exception procedures resulting from lists of local modifications may well render a center ineffective and uneconomical. Establishment of a set of well defined, workable specifications is the only realistic approach to the organization and operation of a processing center.

In order to determine what processing "product" would be acceptable to the member libraries, the following steps were taken:

1. Nine copies each of two current American imprints were selected.
2. A copy of the two titles was sent to each library in September, 1967, along with instructions requesting them to catalog the books and return them to the Project Office with all documents generated during this process. LC copy was provided with one book, and the other was to receive

Figure 5. 12
Comparison of the Number of Steps Used in Technical Processes Per Library and the Standard Unit Book Processing Time

Note: The unit time is the product of the observed mean time, frequency, personal rating factor and standardizing factor (1. 4771).

Library	Steps: Acquisitions	Steps: Cataloging	Total Steps	Unit Time: Acquisitions	Unit Time: Cataloging	Total Time
# 1	132	290	422	27. 494	70. 282	97. 776
# 2	161	121	282	28. 469	43. 328	71. 797
# 3	255	239	494	28. 462	35. 444	63. 906
# 4	303	295	598	46. 308	62. 434	108. 742
# 5	177	248	425	94. 016	56. 354	150. 370
# 6	151	169	320	18. 403	41. 266	59. 669
# 7	141	184	325	30. 662	43. 281	73. 943
# 8	628	342	970	33. 463	69. 161	102. 624
# 9*	133	87	220	28. 680	14. 167	42. 847
Σ	2, 081	1, 975	4, 056	335. 957	435. 717	771. 674
Mean	231	219	450	37. 328	48. 413	85. 742
		Center's Time		37. 727	25. 846	63. 573

Average number of steps:

Acquisitions	231
Cataloging	219
Total	450

Average unit processing time:

Acquistions	37. 328 minutes
Cataloging	48. 413 minutes
Total	85. 742

* Uses commercial book processing

original cataloging.

3. After receiving all nine sets, the investigators compared the books, their card sets, and documents with the information on the flow charts, the business office procedure summary, and with the forms collected during the field trips.
4. A comparison chart of all functions pertinent to forms used and to the physical appearance of each library's processed books was drafted. (See Appendix 5. 2)
5. On the basis of this information and the cost projections previously calculated for CALBPC, a proposal of functions that the Center could perform was entered at the bottom of the chart.
6. A meeting of representatives from each member library and project staff was held in November, 1967. Each library was sent a copy of the "Functions Comparison" chart a week prior to this meeting. (See Appendix 5. 2) Technical services personnel from each library were invited to accompany the head librarians so that they might evaluate the processing "product" that the Center was proposing and express their views to the group.
7. On the basis of group consensus at this meeting, CALBPC was able to draw up a list of specifications for centralized processing acceptable to all member libraries. These specifications are shown in Figure 5. 13.

Figure 5. 13
Specification Sheet Colorado Academic Libraries Book Processing Center

Order Request Card: Two part order request, similar to CU's to facilitate searching. Second copy remains at requesting library.

Multiple-Order Record: Participating libraries will be notified whenever a basic title is ordered centrally.

Orders Placement Procedure: One copy of multiform will be sent to vendor. Encumbrance card punched for each title.

Library Accounting Procedure: Each participating library will receive a monthly statement of its account. The statement will include: (1) encumbrances, (2) expenditures, and (3) free balance.

Receiving-Payment Procedure: Checks from member libraries will be recorded on punched cards and forwarded to the business office for payment. Expenditure data will be punched; and collated against encumbrance cards. Invoices and accounting slip will be forwarded for payment.

Classification: Library of Congress.

Cuttering: Library of Congress.

Author and Subject Heading Authority: Library of Congress for both author and subject.

Authority and Cross-Reference Cards: Believe this can be better accomplished at the local library.

Catalog Card Reproduction and Processing: Xerox reproduction using die cut stock; cards photo reproduced six-up; power cut to size. May use perforated stock four-up. Subject headings will be in red. Pattern of capitalization follows tracing on Library of Congress card. Call number will be formulated same on everything.

Example: DS
35
W4
1966

Sourcing Information: Local operation.

Accessioning Procedure: No accessioning. (Copy numbers will be used to distinguish multiple copies ordered by one library.)

Book Pocket: Pocket with self-adhesive, machine-printed label (call number, title), pasted inside front board. Hinged if flyleaf contains a map.

Spine Label: A self-adhesive, machine-printed label applied with plastic glue coating.

Date Due Slip: Yes, located inside front flyleaf opposite pocket.

Circulation Card: One circulation card. Call number and title.

Property Stamp: None.

Plastic Jacketing: None.

Biographical-Review Information: None. Book jackets will be forwarded with book.

Paperback Books: Cataloged and forwarded to a commercial bindery when a paperback is received instead of hardback, or when requested by a library. Prebounds will be ordered from a dealer when so requested. A binding equivalent to "permabound" in quality is available.

Periodic Accessions List: Special lists produced by computer as by-products will be one goal, but development of such a system will take some time.

Notes

1. Hewitt, Joe, Head, Catalog Maintenance Unit, University of Colorado. Typewritten manuscript of results of time in process study completed November 28, 1966, 2 p.

2. Gregory, L. H. "Xerox card production, cost breakdown per card," Typewritten manuscript, 1967, 5 p.

3. Times obtained by phone conversation with Mr. Richard Pfefferle, Chief of Technical Processing, Massau Library System.

VI. Approval Plans and Centralized Processing

Definition

Rather than investigate all types of approval plans as they might affect centralized processing, a comprehensive plan used by large university libraries was chosen for analysis. A "comprehensive approval plan" is defined as book selection from copies supplied by publishers or dealers to libraries according to selection criteria (specifications) agreed upon between a library and a supplier.

Many libraries of all types engage in small or limited approval plans. These are usually restricted to certain publishers or narrow subject specializations. Some publishers whose offerings cover a wide range of subjects offer their own approval plans with sizeable discounts as one inducement.

The purpose of this section is twofold:

1. To determine if the approval plan technique is an efficient means of acquiring new books for CALBPC.
2. To determine if a plan could be used to serve the bibliographic needs of all member libraries in terms of cooperative book selection of basic titles for greater economy and speed of procurement.

The following topics will be discussed: a general description of an existing approval program; an investigation of the approval programs at the Colorado State University and University of Colorado Libraries; a determination of the quality and suitability of the plan for the libraries served; and conclusions and recommendations as to CALBPC's use of approval plans.

Limitations of the Study

This study is based upon archival data. It was undertaken after the scheduled investigations were completed in order to supplement the operational data needed to establish the proposed Processing Center. While it would have been helpful if the records had been fuller, the combined records at C. U. and C.S.U. provided sufficient data to in vestigate the topics selected for study.

Description of a Comprehensive Approval Program

One of the better known approval plan dealers is based in the Pacific Northwest. He initiated his approval program in 1960. Now he serves more than ninety academic libraries.[1] This dealer offers, in effect, three different plans for English language publications, and has recently added foreign language titles to the program. The four plans are:

1. E. L. A. P. --English Language Approval Plan: this includes books from the United States, the United Kingdom, and the Continent. The domestic plans are all modifications of E. L. A. P.
2. F. L. A. P. --Foreign Language Approval Plan: this includes titles from Continental publishers only.
3. A. L. A. P. --Academic Library Approval Plan: provided for smaller libraries.
4. V. O. L. A. P. --(under development) provided for vocational and community colleges.

Within each plan a library may profile its own requirements in terms of subject inclusions and exclusions, academic level, publisher, reprint vs. original, nationality of the imprint, paperback vs. cloth, date of imprint, standing orders already in force, and price range of items. In short, the dealer does a considerable amount of screening before the library receives its shipment of approval books. Assuming the profile is sufficiently precise and the dealer adheres to it, the advantages claimed for this plan are:

1. The labor and supply cost of creating the multiform for each title are eliminated.
2. No funds are encumbered until the book has been examined and added to the collection. Of course, some libraries use a block encumbrance on their approval plan for budget control.
3. Shipping charges to the library are paid by the dealer.
4. The lag between publication and receipt of the book tends to be less than it is when the book is ordered by traditional procedures.
5. The L. C. order number is included on the multiform for the convenience of those libraries which order L. C. cards. The letter classification can be used to sort the books for the examination shelves.

6. Librarians can spend more time on examining books for their intellectual content and less time on the mechanics of book procurement.

7. The plan provides flexibility and permits the library to take advantage of sudden availability of large amounts of money, such as occasionally occur with federal grants or end-of-the-fiscal year budget surpluses.

8. Finally, the efficiency and speed of this method permits a larger portion of the total budget to be allocated to books or to service to patrons.

Claims 1, 2, 3, and 5 appear clearly acceptable. They relate to the purely mechanical features of approval plans. Advantages 6 and 7 will depend upon policy decisions within an individual library. This study focuses on claims 4 and 8.

These operational features had not been verified locally through intensive study, even though both C. S. U. and C. U. have operated comprehensive approval plans since the fall of 1965. Moreover, there is very little on approval plans in the literature. The Spring 1968 issue of Library Resources and Technical Services has "A Symposium on Approval Order Plans and the Book Selection Responsibilities of Librarians" based on material presented to a workshop sponsored by the College Division of the Pacific Northwest Library Association on August 23, 1967. The articles emphasize suspicion among academic librarians that approval plans are not developed with sufficient quality-controls and that, under the influence of these plans, librarians may abdicate their duty to select books for their libraries. However none of these articles includes or cites any statistical studies which substantiate these fears.

Operation of the Plan in Two Settings

For purposes of comparison, the following aspects of the operation of an existing approval plan were studied at C. S. U. and C. U.:

1. Specifications of the individual library's plan.
2. Examination procedures.
3. Budgetary importance.
4. Handling procedures with regard to time lags in processing, shelf list comparisons, variations in cataloging.

5. The quality of the plan.

Specifications: Because the profile of C. U. was more restrictive than that of C. S. U., it was convenient to compare C. S. U.'s specifications against C. U.'s policy, point by point. The selection policy of *Choice: Books for College Libraries* is given in Figure 6.1 to provide information for the section on quality of the approval plan.

Standing order policies: C. U. has retained most of the separate standing orders that were in force prior to the acceptance of the plan. The order clerk relies on the serials check-in records to indicate which titles would constitute a duplication and should, therefore, be returned. C. S. U., since the inception of its approval plan, has endeavored to eliminate as many standing orders as possible except for certain society publications. It will be shown in the comparison of handling procedures that standing orders for serials reduce the efficiency of the approval plan.

The comparison in Figure 6.2 indicates a solid area of agreement in the selection policies of all three; but, there is greater agreement between the two libraries as to their approval profiles than there is between either of the approval profiles and *Choice*. A more precise investigation of the correlation between the plan and *Choice* appears later in this section.

As to areas of disagreement it is possible that the need of both libraries could be satisfied by a composite plan housed at CALBPC, excluding those subject fields of interest to C. S. U. only. For example, C. U. does not wish to receive medical books because the Medical Library handles its technical services completely independently of the central library. C. S. U., on the other hand, needs a large number of medical books for its veterinary program and could therefore retain the medical portion of its plan.

Examination procedures. General handling at both libraries

1. Transportation to the library is paid by the approval dealer.
2. Books are shipped weekly and returned weekly so that each shipment is on display in the Acquisitions area approximately five working days.
3. Books arrive in boxes containing approximately thirty volumes per box.
4. A separate "invoice" is included in each volume. This is a

Figure 6.1
Specifications for Titles Supplied Under the Approval Plan:[2] General

C. U.	C. S. U.	*Choice: Books for College Libraries* (Selection Policy)[3]
1. Titles supplied should reflect scholarly American imprints to meet the research needs of an academic institution. "A scholarly American Book" designates that general body of publications which is bought by most university and college libraries, and which is published by responsible American presses.	1. Same as C. U.	1. Same as C. U.
2. Only current American imprints are acceptable.	2. Same as C. U.	2. Same as C. U. plus the University of Toronto and McGill University Presses.
3. Titles published simultaneously in Britain and the United States are acceptable; however, a volume bearing the American imprint should be supplied.	3. Same as C. U.	3. Not significant.
4. British, and other foreign imprints, will be accepted only if it can be determined from the book itself that the title is indeed to be published in the United States.	4. Same as C. U.	4. Not significant.

5. Publications of foreign universities are not acceptable. (Note: the restrictions against foreign publications are necessary because many of the titles are received on a "Standing Order" basis from foreign dealers. Receipt of the titles on the approval plan results in duplicate titles and extra work for everyone.)	5. See # 2.	5. Same as C. U. except as indicated in # 2 above.
6. Titles which are merely distributed by an American publisher are not acceptable. Exception: Israeli publications distributed by Davey. Science librarians wanted to see these titles on approval.	6. Titles distributed by an American publisher are acceptable.	6. Same as C. U.
7. Titles in reprint are not acceptable. Slips may be sent to the library for a check. Slip should include as much of the original imprint information as is available from the book itself. (Note: C. U. Library has, on the average, 40-50% of titles supplied in reprint. Exclusion of the physical volumes means less bulk to return to the dealer.	7. See # 2. Slips on expensive and foreign titles may be sent to the library. Also slips on business law.	7. Reprints are reviewed according to how long the book is out-of-print and whether the editors think it needs a re-evaluation.

Figure 6. 1
Specification: Exclusions (continued)

C. U.	C. S. U.	Choice: Books for College Libraries (Selection Policy)
1. Excludes medicine except nursing; includes "Introduction to. . ." titles and basic texts only. Pharmacy: includes graduate level only.	1. Excludes these L. C. classifications: RK--Dentistry; RT--Nursing; RV--Botany, Thomsonian, and Eclectic Medicine; RX--Homeopathy; RZ--Miscellaneous Schools and Arts.	1. Excludes certain advanced texts particularly in the science and technology fields.
2. Excludes agriculture except as it relates to botany.	2. Includes agriculture.	2. Excludes gardening, home economics, and vocational literature. Includes business and elementary engineering because these subjects are taught in many junior colleges and in some liberal arts colleges.
3. Excludes cookbooks, general household manuals, anything on food products such as would relate to home economics courses. These fields are covered by programs at C. S. U.	3. Includes cookbooks.	3. See # 2.
4. Excludes fiction.	4. Excludes fiction except westerns.	4. Includes fiction.
[illegible]	5. Same as C. U.	5. Same as C. U.

6. Excludes law books issued by publishers who limit themselves to this field.	6. In the humanities and social sciences the tendency is to publish reviews of more books that are suitable only at the senior year or first year graduate level.

Figure 6. 1 (continued)
Specifications: Standards of Acceptance by Level

Each title received on the approval plan is given an educational rating by the approval dealer. The various levels are outlined below.

Levels	Institutional Acceptance		Choice
	C. U.	C. S. U.	
1. High school	no	no	no
2. Freshman/Sophomore level in college. Titles in this classification are recognized by "Introduction to. . . " "Basic, " "Contemporary, " "Readings in . . " and preface statements specifying freshman level materials.	no	no	yes
3. Junior/Senior level in college. Titles in this classification are recognized by such terms as "Advanced, " "Casebook on, " "Readings in advanced. . . " and preface statements specifying junior level materials.	yes	yes	yes
4. Graduate level. This includes material published by university presses, the Consultants Bureau, and other responsible presses.	yes	yes	yes

Figure 6. 1
Specifications: Standards of Acceptance by Level (continued)

Levels	Institutional Acceptance C. U.	Institutional Acceptance C. S. U.	Choice
5. Graduate level. This includes general but scholarly material. Text is well documented, intended for specialized and limited interests.	yes	yes	limited
6. Titles about which there might be a reasonable doubt should be supplied. Approval dealer should lean towards inclusion of questionable titles rather than exclusion.	yes	yes	Yes, to the extent that some negative reviews are published.

Figure 6. 2
Points of Similarity and Dissimilarity in Selection Policies

Specifications	C. U. vs C. S. U.		C. U. vs Choice		C. S. U. vs Choice	
	Similar	Dissimilar	Similar	Dissimilar	Similar	Dissimilar
General	5	2	5	0	5	2
Exclusions	3	3	3	3	2	4
Level	6	0	4	2	4	2
Total	14	5	12	5	13	6
Percent	74	26	70	30	58	42

five-part 3"x 5" multiform which indicates the list price, the library's net price, the L. C. classification, the L. C. main entry when available, and the L. C. order number. If a book must be returned, this slip accompanies it--thus it never enters the library's accounting system; the slip also serves as a credit memo.

C. U. The week's shipment arrives on Thursday. A clerk places it on display shelves according to broad L. C. classification and checks the invoice slips against the outstanding order file, the card catalog, and the Kardex. Duplicates are set aside temporarily so that faculty and library staff may select them for purchase.

During the period September 1965 to March 1968, 2, 368 titles, of an estimated 22, 199 titles received on approval, were rejected. This amounted to a rejection rate of 11%. Although rejection statistics were not kept on a monthly basis, the order librarian observed that the rejection rate has dropped from about 17% to about 7% between the inception of the plan and March 1968. The rejection rate is an important index to the effectiveness of the library's selection profile and the approval dealer's ability to predict what the library needs.

Study of a 10% sample of the 2, 368 rejected titles, showed that 46% were standing orders, 19% were duplicates (on order), and 35% had no reason given on the slip. Most of those in the last group were popular non-fiction, new editions of standard works, foreign, very expensive, or highly esoteric.

An invoice is created by xeroxing the upper right hand corner of each slip and attaching an adding machine tape listing the prices. In this manner an average of 214 books can be processed on one invoice. This batching procedure eliminates much of the summarizing of invoices required by the regular invoicing procedures, in which an invoice listing a single title may require almost as much bookkeeping time as one listing several hundred books. Keypunching for individual titles is likewise eliminated.

C. S. U. The handling is similar to that at C. U. except that the books are shelved by broad subject areas according to the five subject divisions of the library: Life Sciences, Social Sciences, Physical Sciences, Humanities, and Reference. Each of these divisions is staffed by a subject specialist whose duty it is to select the books in his division each week, and to acquaint the faculty with the plan. Because subject specialists screen incoming books, the plan at C.S.U. receives more consistent scrutiny than does the C. U. plan.

Approval expenditures: The proportion of the book budget allocated to the plan is three to four times greater at C. S. U. than at C. U. and has increased during each of the three years the plan has been operating. (See Figure 6. 3.) By contrast, C. U. 's participation has remained at the six to eight percent level. C. U. does not allocate specific budgets; however, it does set up target amounts for over two hundred individual academic departments and research groups.

Figure 6. 3
Approval Plan vs. Total Book Budget Allocations

	1965-66*	1966-67	1967-68
Amount spent on Approval Plan at:			
C. U.	$ 45, 700	$54, 207	($ 52, 594)**
C. S. U.	51, 000	67, 736	90, 000
Amount Allocated to Total Book Budget at:			
C. U. (Boulder Campus)	$666, 505	$715, 805	$635, 149
C. S. U.	333, 000	350, 000	362, 000
% of Total Book Budget Spent on Approval Plan at:			
C. U.	6. 9	7. 6	8. 3
C. S. U.	15. 3	19. 4	24. 9

*C. U. began receiving books in September 1965; C. S. U. in November 1965.
**July-March only.

Comparison of handling procedures: C. S. U. has saved all the approval plan invoice slips for books purchased since the inception of the plan whereas C. U. has not retained a similar file nor has either library retained any record of rejected titles. However, the C. S. U. file was considered to be comprehensive enough (15, 925 slips) to yield statistically valid samples for studying three basic types of data:

1. Lag times in procurement and processing.
2. The correlations between the approval plan's subject emphasis and the shelf list of each institution.
3. The degree of agreement between C. S. U. and C. U. as to call number and serials handling of approval titles.

Sample sizes were computed for both extreme specificity and normal specificity in order that the sample would satisfy the purpose intended.

Extreme specificity: The number of approval slips in the total universe was 15, 925. The extreme number of cateogries to be used in gathering the statistics was 21 (the number of L. C. major classifications most used at either library).

$N_p = 15,925 \qquad \frac{N_p}{21} = 759 \qquad \theta = .50$ (worst possible case)

A sample size on 759 at the .05 confidence level was calculated as follows:

$$\sigma_p = \sqrt{\frac{\theta(1-\theta}{N} \times \frac{N_p - N}{N_p - 1}}$$

$$.05 = \sqrt{\frac{(.50)(.50)}{N} \times \frac{759 - N}{758}}$$

$$.0025 = \frac{.25}{N} \times \frac{759 - N}{758}$$

$$.0025 = \frac{189.75 - .25N}{758N}$$

$$\begin{aligned} 1.895N + .25N &= 189.75 \\ 2.145N &= 189.75 \\ N &= 88.4132 \\ 21N &= 1,857 \end{aligned}$$

Therefore, a sample size of at least 1, 857 is necessary to insure a confidence level of .05 for that degree of specificity.

For a confidence level of .01 employing the entire universe the equation is:

$$\sigma_p = \sqrt{\frac{\theta(1-\theta)}{N} \times \frac{N_p - N}{N_p - 1}}$$

$$.01 = \sqrt{\frac{.25}{N} \times \frac{15,925 - N}{15,924}}$$

$$.0001 = \frac{3981.25 - .25N}{15,924N}$$

$$1.5924N + .2500N = 3,981.25$$
$$1.7424N = 3,981.25$$
$$N = 2,214.8$$

The sample size suitable for comparing the 21 subject (L. C.) percentages represented in the approval plan would be 2, 215.

Normal specificity: It was projected that no more than four strata or categories would be used in the time lag or Choice portions of the study. Therefore, the average number of slips in each category, assuming uniform distribution, would be $\frac{N_p}{4}$ or 3, 981. The sample size required for 3, 981 slips at the . 05 confidence level was computed as:

$$\sigma_p = \sqrt{\frac{.25}{N} \times \frac{3,981 - N}{3,980}}$$

$$.05 = \sqrt{\frac{.25}{N} \times \frac{3,981 - N}{3,980}}$$

$$.0025 = \frac{995.25 - .25N}{3,980N}$$

$$9.95N + 25N = 995.25$$
$$10.20N = 995.25$$
$$N = 97.585$$
$$4N = 390.3$$

Therefore, a sample valid, at the . 05 confidence level, for normal specificity would need to be at least 390. This is also the sample size at the . 025 confidence level for the total universe:

$$.025 = \sqrt{\frac{.25}{N} \times \frac{15,925 - N}{15,924}}$$

$$.000625 = \frac{3,981.25 - .25N}{15,924N}$$

$$9.9525N + .2500N = 3,981.25$$
$$10.2025N = 3,981.25$$
$$N = 390.2$$

An N of 390 permits a . 025 confidence level for statistical results for which there is no stratification and an . 05 confidence level for results employing up through four strata. An N of 2, 215 permit between an . 05 and an . 01 confidence level for results requiring up to twenty-one strata.

After the sample sizes were computed, the next step in data collection was to prepare the samples. Readying the large sample involved alphabetizing the entire approval slip file of 15,924 items for later comparison to the annual indices of _Choice._ The sample of 390 slips was selected by pulling every fifteenth slip, mounting them on the coding forms (see Figure 6.12), xeroxing them and returning them to the file so that they could be checked in _Choice_ along with the other slips. A second sample of 2,008 items was taken by recording the L.C. class on every seventh slip in the large sample.

To investigate 1) the elapsed time between the publication of the book and the library's receipt of it; 2) the elapsed time between receipt of the book and the completion of its preparation for public use; and 3) the elapsed time between the date processed and the date reviewed in _Choice,_ it was necessary to obtain four dates for each item in the sample. These were: (1) date of publication, (2) date of receipt, (3) date of filing in shelf list, and (4) date reviewed in _Choice._ The source for the first date was _Forthcoming Books,_ searched for the years 1964-67. After the search for date #1 was completed, the C.S.U. card catalog was checked for the call number and main entry, after which the shelf list was checked for date #3. Finally issues of _Choice_ for the period 1965 to February 1968 were searched for date #4. Of course, it was not possible to obtain all four dates for all 390 titles; however, the data were sufficiently complete to yield the three lag time averages for C.S.U.

At C.U. the card catalog and shelf list were checked to obtain date #3 so that the lag times could be averaged for that library as well. Since it was not possible to find out the date of receipt of approval books at C.U., it was assumed that the date indicated on the dealer's slip would serve both libraries. Both libraries were served by the same dealer, so it is probable that there is no significant difference in the receipt date. (See Figure 6.4.)

In Figure 6.5, Approval Plan Lag Times vs. General Lag Times, it will be observed that there is a radical difference between the C.U. lag times taken from Figure 2.3, Processing Time-Lag Summary, and the C.U. approval plan lag times. The explanation is that the former lag times were computed from slips recording the date each book was sent to circulation rather than the date the shelf list was filed. "General Lag Times" figures incorporate

Figure 6. 4
Approval Plan Lag Times (in Calendar Days)

	Publication Date To Receipt Date	Receipt Date to Processing Date	Processing Date to Date Reviewed in Choice	Total Waiting Time
C. S. U.	69. 5	103. 1	121. 6	172. 1
C. U.	69. 5	100. 2	125. 4	169. 7

Figure 6. 5
Approval Plan Lag Times Vs. General Lag Times (in Days)

	Publishing Date to Date Received*	Book Received to Book Cataloged	Total Processing Time
C. S. U. --Approval	69. 5*	103. 1	172. 6
C. S. U. --General	92. 0**	188. 0	280. 0
Difference	22. 5	84. 9	107. 4
% of Difference	24. 5%	45. 2%	38. 3%
C. U. --Approval	69. 5*	100. 2	125. 4
C. U. --General	102. 0**	21. 0	123. 0
Difference	32. 5	79. 2 (overage)	2. 4 (overage)
% of Difference	31. 9%	---	---
Approval Plan Lag Times Vs. Current Domestic Lag Times			
C. S. U. --Approval	69. 5*	103. 1	172. 6
C. S. U. --Cur. Dom.	87. 0**	184. 0	271. 0
Difference	17. 5	80. 9	98. 4
% of Difference	20. 1	43. 9	32. 5
C. U. --Approval	69. 5*	100. 2	125. 4
C. U. --Cur. Dom.	88. 0**	19. 0	107. 0
Difference	18. 5	81. 2 (overage)	18. 4 (overage)
% of Difference	21. 0%	---	---

The Current Domestic Lag Times were taken from Figure 2. 4.

* "Publishing Date to Date Received" is comparable to "Order Requested to Order Placed" and "Order Placed to Book Received" if approval plan receipts are considered to be a general order-request.

** 92. 0 is the sum of 12. 0 and 80. 0 from Figure 2. 3. These are the lag times in days reported for "Order Requested to Order Placed" and "Order Placed to Book Received."

102. 0 is the sum of 23. 0 and 79. 0
87. 0 is the sum of 4. 0 and 83. 0
88. 0 is the sum of 20. 0 and 68. 0

all routines undertaken at the library for technical processing including any approval routines in force. The approval plan lag times consider just those books procured on the approval plan.

Concerning the extra time taken on approval titles, if an approval title arrives at C. U. before the proof card is received from the Library of Congress, it is held until the card is matched to the book, unless there is a rush request. The processing time on approval books is much longer than average at C. U. because their system is geared to the availability of L. C. copy at the time the book is received.

The approval plan provides new books to the two libraries 20% faster than they typically obtain them by traditional methods. It also speeds up cataloging at C. S. U. by 43. 9%. The apparent failure to speed C. U. 's cataloging is due to differing methods of collecting the data, i. e., taking the date of completion from the shelf list instead of having it recorded on the order slip as the book passes through the system. In the final definition, processing is incomplete for a given title until the cards are filed in the public catalog(s). At C. U. the shelf list cards are filed on an average of three weeks after the book is routed to the circulation department.

To compare the C. S. U. shelf list with that at C. U., it was decided to use the L. C. Classification and to convert any Dewey portions of either into L. C., and a cross-reference chart from Dewey to L. C. was prepared. (See Figure 6. 6.) C. U. had begun to use L. C. Classification in 1958 and C. S. U. in 1962. Fifty-eight percent of the C. U. shelf list and 70. 7% of the C. S. U. shelf list are now in L. C.

If one inch of cards is taken to equal 100 titles, it is possible to estimate the size (in titles) of each collection per classification and to calculate the percentage of titles in each classification for each library. Since the L. C. -classed titles represent, in large measure, the newer acquisitions in each library, it was useful to retain separate figures for each classification system as possibly more valid to the current acquisition program than the overall percentages of the collections.

A sample of 2, 215 titles systematically pulled from the approval slips was tallied for L. C. classification and the percentages were

Figure 6. 6
Cross-Reference and Conversion Chart from Dewey to L. C. Classifications

Dewey	L. C. Equivalent	Dewey	L. C. Equivalent
000 - 009	A	572 - 573	G
010 - 029	Z	574 - 599	Q
030 - 069	A	600 - 609	T
070 - 079	P	610 - 619	R
080 - 089	A	620 - 629	T
090 - 099	Z	630 - 639	S
100 - 299	B	640 - 649	T
300 - 319	H	650 - 659	HF
320 - 329	J	660 - 699	T
330 - 339	H	700 - 736	N
340 - 349	K	737	C
350 - 354	H	738 - 779	N
355 - 358	U	780 - 789	M
359	V	790 - 791	G
360 - 369	H	792	P
370 - 379	L	793 - 799	G
380 - 389	H	800 - 899	P
390 - 399	G	900 - 909	D
400 - 416	P	910 - 912	G
417	C	913	C
418 - 499	P	914 - 919	G
500 - 569	Q	920 - 929	C
570	G	930 - 969	D
571	C	970 - 989	E-F
		990 - 999	D

calculated. The shelf list size, percentage, and the approval dealer receipt percentage data according to the L. C. Classification are represented in Figures 6. 7 and 6. 8.

The shelf list measurements served to indicate the relative size of the two collections by title: 124, 600 estimated titles for C. S. U. as compared to 282, 300 for C. U. The same comparison can be made for each L. C. class by adding two zeroes to each measurement figure in each "Grand Total" column.

It was now possible to calculate correlations on the percentages represented below using the equation:

$$r = \frac{N\Sigma XY - \Sigma X\Sigma Y}{\sqrt{[N\Sigma X^2 - (\Sigma X)^2][N\Sigma Y^2 - (\Sigma Y)^2]}}$$

where N = 21 (the number of L. C. classes used)
X = one shelf list
Y = the other shelf list or approval dealer receipts

The results of these calculations were as follows:

X	Y	r
C. S. U. Total Shelf List	C. U. Total Shelf List	. 904
C. S. U. L. C. Shelf List	C. U. L. C. Shelf List	. 967
C. S. U. Total Shelf List	Dealer Sample	. 899
C. S. U. L. C. Shelf List	Dealer Sample	. 921
C. U. Total Shelf List	Dealer Sample	. 914
C. U. L. C. Shelf List	Dealer Sample	. 929

It should be emphasized that this is a broad subject analysis and that two factors would tend to polarize the approval plan receipts around the subject emphases of the institution it serves--the fact that the dealer specializes in scholarly books; and the fact that the institutional profile would tend to screen out undesirable subject acquisitions if the librarians had not done so. Therefore, at least in terms of subject emphasis, the approval plan seems reasonably well suited to each institution under study. The highest correlation, . 97, occurred between the C. S. U. and C. U. shelf lists. It points to the desirability of cooperative selection of basic materials in those subject classifications where the percentages are most nearly alike. (See Figure 6. 7)

Figure 6.7
Shelf List Comparison*

LC Class	C.S.U. Shelf List						C.U. Shelf List					
	Total LC (in inches)	Additional Dewey	Grand Total	% of Total	% of Total That is LC	% of Total That is Dewey	Total LC (in inches)	Additional Dewey	Grand Total	% of Total	% of Total That is LC	% of Total That is Dewey
A	9.9	0.8	9.8	.006	.005	.001	24	10.2	34.2	.007	.005	.002
B	70.0	36.5	106.5	.060	.040	.020	191	141.0	332.0	.068	.039	.029
C	8.5	1.6	10.1	.006	.005	.001	23	89.2	112.2	.023	.005	.018
D	77.0	23.5	100.5	.057	.044	.013	262	101.5	363.5	.074	.053	.021
E-F	61.5	17.0	78.5	.045	.035	.010	169	47.5	216.5	.044	.034	.010
G	23.1	27.7	50.8	.029	.013	.016	56	115.5	171.5	.035	.011	.024
H	105.5	62.7	168.2	.095	.060	.035	254	183.0	437.0	.090	.052	.038
HF	17.5	11.0	28.5	.016	.010	.006	59	35.0	94.0	.019	.012	.007
J	26.5	11.5	38.0	.022	.015	.007	73	49.5	122.5	.025	.015	.010
K	1.5	13.0	14.5	.008	.001	.007	7	25.0	32.0	.007	.002	.005
L	34.4	73.0	107.4	.061	.019	.042	117	210.0	327.0	.067	.024	.043
M	37.5	---	37.5	.021	.021	---	70	18.0	88.0	.018	.014	.004
N	41.0	---	41.0	.023	.023	---	110	71.0	181.0	.037	.022	.015
P	340.0	8.7	348.7	.198	.193	.005	841	548.0	1389.0	.285	.173	.112
Q	160.5	70.2	230.7	.131	.091	.040	306	205.0	511.0	.105	.063	.042
R	50.5	32.5	83.0	.047	.029	.018	43	51.0	94.0	.019	.009	.010
S	65.5	52.0	117.5	.067	.037	.030	19	15.0	34.0	.007	.004	.003
T	73.5	62.2	135.7	.077	.042	.035	95	88.0	183.0	.038	.020	.018
U	4.0	2.0	6.0	.003	.002	.001	8	6.0	14.0	.003	.002	.001
V	1.0	0.2	1.2	.001	.001	---	8	1.5	9.5	.002	.002	---
Z	38.0	10.2	48.2	.027	.022	.005	88	45.2	133.2	.027	.018	.009
Total	1246.0	516.3	1762.3	1.000	.707	.293	2823	2056.1	4879.1	1.000	.579	.421

* Measurements were taken April 1968.

Figure 6. 7
Shelf List Comparison (continued)

The L. C. Shelf Lists Analyzed Separately as to Class

L. C. Class	C. S. U. Percentages X	C. U. Percentages Y	X-Y
A	. 007	. 008	-. 001
B	. 056	. 068	-. 012
C	. 007	. 008	-. 001
D	. 062	. 093	-. 031
E-F	. 049	. 060	-. 011
G	. 019	. 020	-. 001
H	. 085	. 090	-. 005
HF	. 014	. 021	-. 007
J	. 021	. 026	-. 005
K	. 001	. 002	-. 001
L	. 028	. 041	-. 013
M	. 030	. 025	+ . 005
N	. 033	. 039	-. 006
P	. 273	. 298	-. 025
Q	. 129	. 108	+ . 021
R	. 041	. 015	+ . 026
S	. 052	. 007	+ . 045
T	. 059	. 034	+ . 025
U	. 003	. 003	----
V	. 001	. 003	-. 002
Z	. 030	. 031	-. 001
	1. 000	1. 000	

Figure 6. 8
L. C. Distribution in the Approval Sample

L. C. Class	Titles in Sample	Percentage in Sample
A	5	. 002
B	179	. 089
C	15	. 007
D	171	. 085
E-F	121	. 060
G	38	. 019
H	163	. 081
HF	66	. 033
J	112	. 056
K	11	. 005
L	66	. 033
M	30	. 015
N	101	. 050
P	412	. 205
Q	292	. 145
R	96	. 048

Figure 6. 8
L. C. Distribution in the Approval Sample (continued)

L. C. Class	Titles in Sample	Percentage in Sample
S	19	. 009
T	79	. 039
U	5	. 002
V	---	---
Z	27	. 013
Total	2, 008	1. 000

As the approval dealer Sample Code Key illustrates (See Figure 6. 12), a record was made of the call number and the method of handling all the 390 titles in the sample at each institution. Since 58 of the titles were owned by C. S. U. alone, only 332 titles could be compared: 293 monographs and 39 serials. Three tables, below, contrast the result of this study with that of the BPR Sample discussed in Section II. LC call numbers are taken as the standard in both studies; however, this part of the study was intended to focus on the extent of conflict between the two libraries in their use of LC call numbers.

Call number modifications pertain either to the class or cutter numbers rather than the addition or elimination of the year of the edition. The majority of modifications were in the P-class (literature). Serial modifications related to differences in processing monographic serials, i. e., classed together or classed separately, with or without analytics, etc.

Figure 6. 9
Percentage of Variation in the Total Sample

	Call No.	Serial Handling
Number of items out of 332	53	20
% of modification	16	6

Figure 6. 10
Percentage of Variations: Monograph Vs. Serial

	Call No.	Serial Handling
Number of monographic items in 293	33	11
Number of serial items in 39	30	77
Total modification	53	16

Figure 6. 11
Percentage of Variation from LC in BPR Sample

	Call No. Modification	Serial Modification
C. S. U.	2. 84	21. 30
C. U.	1. 79	23. 46

Figure 6. 12
Sample Code Key

Class No.

319

Author
Shryock, John K
Title
The origin and development of the state cult of Confucius.

L. C. No.
66-21765

Invoice No.
CST 22167

BL A5R (1932)

595	Publisher Paragon			Pub. Date 1966	
Mar 7'67	Edition	Vols.	Copies 1		Approved
Date Received 10-18-66	Invoice Date	The Libraries Colorado State University Fort Collins, Colo. 80521			Fund H
List Price 10. 00-1	Net Price 9. 00				

Duplicate Invoice

Item--(Circle correct code)
*Type of Pub'n. 1 mono 2 serial
*Library 1 2 3 4 5 6 7 8 9
*Ordered 1 vendor 2 direct
3 approval dealer 4 gift

Figure 6. 12
Sample Code Key (continued)

*Standing order 0 no 1 yes
*Handling 1 classed separate
2 classed together
Cycle time (month-day-year)
Date pub. ______ ______
*date rec'd. ______ ______
*date filed-SL ______ ______
date reviewed
in *Choice* ______ ______
LC class __________
List price __________
*Price paid __________
Publisher code __________
(* data collected in the field)

Of 39 serials in the sample, serial handling variations were found in twenty files, or 51% of the serials processed. As to call number modification differences in 30 out of the 39 serials were detected between the two libraries. This constituted 77% of the serial titles. It is apparent that although the serial titles constitute only 12% of the titles owned by both libraries, there is greater variation in handling of serials than in monographs. The *BPR* study also indicates that serials present difficulties in terms of arriving at a standard acceptable to both libraries.

Of the titles not procured by C. U., three were reprints of titles already in C. U. 's collection. There were ten reprints in the total sample of 390 titles. The retrospective buying program of C. S. U. in the humanities and social sciences accounts for their purchase of reprints. The other 55 titles not in the C. U. collection would have been rejected because they did not conform to the C. U. 's profile. The fifty-eight titles not purchased by C. U. suggests that there is an 85% area of agreement between the use of the approval plan at C. U. and C. S. U. This percentage is higher than that resulting from the analysis of the specifications. In Figure 6. 2, where the profile of one library was compared to that of the other library and each compared to *Choice's* profile, the percentages there were 74% similarity between C. U. and C. S. U., 70% between C. U. and *Choice*, and 58% between C. S. U. and *Choice*.

Quality of the plan: Because of the interest of the smaller state colleges in the careful selection of basic titles and because of the financial impracticality of a comprehensive approval plan at these colleges, we decided to study the extent to which the approval plan at C. S.U. would serve as a basic selection tool for CALBPC. Since practically all member libraries, particularly the smaller ones, use *Choice* as a selection tool, it was chosen as one criterion of quality for the approval plans now in use at C. S. U. and C. U. Figure 6. 4 indicates that the lag from the time a book that has been received on approval is processed to the time it is reviewed in *Choice* is 121. 6 to 125. 4 days. This means that if the approval plan were as reliable for bringing quality books into the collection as *Choice* is in reviewing them, the Center would save time by using an approval plan, rather than *Choice*, without sacrificing quality.

The author entries in two full years of *Choice*, March 1966 to February 1968, were compared with the entire universe of approval plan titles. In the first year the percentage of the approval dealer's titles appearing in *Choice* was 40. 4%. For the second year the percentage increased to 45. 1%.

The delay between publication dates and the review dates was studied. Three 5% samples of the titles reviewed in each of three issues in *Choice* (March, July/August, and November, 1967) were systematically selected from the indices. For each title in each sample, the publication dates were searched in *Forthcoming Books*. If no date were listed, the date was estimated as December of the year of publication in order to give *Choice* the benefit of the doubt. The lag times for each sample were averaged:

Sample	Average Lag Time in Months
A	9. 5
B	8. 9
C	9. 2

One of the investigators queried the editor of *Choice* to determine if any advance information on the titles selected could be procured. The answer indicated that the reviewing was farmed out to a great many faculty and library personnel around the country, and it was not possible for even the editor to know what the final selection for each issue would be until press time. The lag figures above indicate that Choice was not appropriate as a current awareness tool for screening the approval titles.

The 40.4 and 45.1 percentages of Choice titles represented in the approval plan suggests that either the plan's profile would need adjusting to catch more of these titles, or the approval dealer should tighten his own bibliographic screening, or both. It is possible that some of the Choice titles might have been rejected by C.S.U. since it is a university rather than a college and since it is technically oriented. On the other hand, there has been a concerted effort over the past five years at C.S.U. to strengthen the humanities and the social science areas of the collection. Subject specialists on the library staff have also monitored the plan during this period.

Budget Planning Information

The sample of 390 was analyzed to determine the discount rates afforded on the approval plan at C.S.U. from November 1965 to June 1967:

Discount Rates on the Approval Plan

	No discount	10%	20-25%	30%
Percentage of titles in sample	14.9	62.6	0.7	21.8

The approval dealer representative reported that an average of 10 to 20% discount is normal for the plan since scholarly presses are not noted for sizeable discounts and the dealer pays the shipping charges on approval books one way.

In 1967 at the University of Nebraska a study of their approval plan was undertaken to determine the average price of books in the humanities, science and technology, and social studies.[4] The study, based on 8,865 titles purchased during one fiscal year, provides information useful to individual libraries in apportioning the book budget among the various academic divisions of their institution and also in controlling and balancing expenditures of general funds such as an approval plan budget. Figure 6.13 abstracts information from the Nebraska study.

Figure 6. 13
Average Book Prices by Typical Academic Discipline* as Analyzed from the Approval Plan, 1966-67

Discipline	LC Classifications	Average Price	Composite Average
General Library			
General Bibliography	A998-8999	$ 9. 91	
General Periodicals	AP	40. 50	
General Works	A-AM, AS-AZ	10. 34	
			$10. 27
Agriculture:			
Agriculture	S-SD, SH	8. 70	
Home Economics	TX	7. 53	
Veterinary Science	SF	10. 78	
			8. 78
Humanities:			
General Humanities	GT500-2370, P only, PN1-1999	6. 08	
Architecture	NA	11. 07	
Art	N only, NB-NK	9. 57	
Classics	PA	6. 56	
English	PE, PN6011-6525, PR, PS, PZ	5. 05	
German	PB, PD, PF-PM, PT	5. 90	
Journalism	PN4700-5639	6. 10	
Music	All M's	6. 80	
Philosophy	B-BD, BH-BX	6. 25	
Romance Languages	PC, PQ	5. 42	
Speech	PN2000-4321	6. 09	
			6. 57
Science and Technology:			
General Science	Q only, R-RA, RD-RF, RJ, RM, T, TR	11. 57	
Botany	QK	12. 50	
Chemistry	QD, TN, TP	14. 45	
Engineering	TA-TL, TS, TT	11. 30	
Geology	QE	10. 88	
Mathematics	QA, QB	8. 31	
Microbiology	RB, RC, RG	7. 86	
Pharmacy	RS	10. 07	
Physics	QC	10. 47	
Zoology	QH, QL, QM, QP, QR	10. 24	
			10. 81

* Abstracted from "Analysis of the Approval Plan at the University of Nebraska Libraries, 1966-67."

Figure 6. 13
Average Book Prices (continued)

Discipline	LC Classifi-cations	Average Price	Composite Average
Social Studies:			
General Social Studies	CT, H only, U-V	6. 24	
Anthropology	GN, GR, GT1-485, 2400-7070	5. 29	
Economics	HA-HE, HG-HJ	7. 21	
Business Organization	HF	7. 45	
Geography	G-GF	9. 18	
History	C-CS, all D's, E-F	6. 63	
Political Science	all J's	5. 78	
Psychology	BF	6. 42	
Social Work	HV	5. 36	
Sociology	HM-HT, HX	5. 83	
Teachers College	GV, all L's, Z4-997	5. 93	
Law	all K's	7. 21	
			$ 6. 52
	Overall Average		$ 7. 69**

** Based on 8, 865 titles.

Conclusions

In the light of the budgetary importance of the comprehensive approval plan at each institution, it must be very carefully monitored to insure that quality as well as efficiency result from its use. Profiling alone cannot screen the books sufficiently. The foregoing study indicates that the comprehensive approval plan is efficient, economical, leads to better service, and has some relevance to the acquisition of quality books. The study also indicates that a more controlled study of quality needs to be conducted. On the basis of the Choice comparison, the comprehensive plan would not be suitable for selection of basic books for undergraduate collections unless the specifications could be restructured to improve its agreement with Choice.

Uniform classifying and handling of serials is a major problem in centralized processing of approval titles. The Center might render more satisfactory service by treating monographic series on an individual title basis, with an added entry for series. It would be up to the individual library to handle any Kardex or authority record it might wish to maintain for such a series. In those few cases where the item is actually classed together by the member library, in opposition to LC, it would be better to let the member library order the title directly; or the member library could change the call number upon receipt of the book from the Center. From a practical standpoint the Center could not maintain a series authority file for all member libraries to cover those rare incidences of call number conflict in series handling (6% according to the sample).

Elimination of the preparation of the multiform (order pack) and of the search for the LC number speeds the library's handling of approval books. Although both C. U. and C. S. U. have different formats for their multiforms, which differ from the dealer's as well, there seems to be no important problem created by the use of the two kinds of forms in each order file. This experience on the part of these two large libraries would suggest that the format of order slips is not very important.

Another point of efficiency is the speed with which approval plan titles are dispatched from the publisher to the library so that they can be made available to the public when the demand for them is greatest.

A chief advantage of the approval plan in terms of operation is its simplified bookkeeping. Only titles actually purchased have to be entered into the accounting system. Moreover, every book so ordered is provided its own invoice. There is none of the tedious waiting for and matching of invoices. Also the fact that each invoice lists only one title makes the system more amenable to automated accounting procedures.

Notes

1. Morrison, Perry D. "A Symposium on Approval Order Plans and the Book Selection Responsibilities of Libraries." Library Resources and Technical Services 12:133 (Spring, 1968).

2. Based on a typewritten manuscript prepared by Abigail Dahl-Hansen, Order Librarian, C. U. Library, correspondence between the Approval dealer and the Acquisitions Department, C. S. U. Library,

and interviews with pertinent personnel at both libraries.

3. Gardener, Richard K. "Choice: Books for College Libraries, Its Origin, Development, and Future Plans." *Southeastern Librarian* 15(1):71-2 (Spring, 1965).

4. *Ibid.*

VII. A Generalized Stochastic Model for Simulating the Operation of a Book Processing Center

Introduction

A generalized stochastic model for a book processing center was developed and programmed (for the CDC 3600 computer using FORTRAN IV) in order to study the behavior of a proposed system under a variety of alternative conditions. The model was generalized in order to have the capability of:

1. adding or deleting tasks performed;
2. accommodating different employee levels by task;
3. accommodating different costs;
4. accommodating different proportions for flows of orders through the system;
5. accommodating different ratios of number of copies per title ordered at one time;
6. accommodating different times required for a task;
7. accommodating different levels of inputs in terms of orders per unit of time; and
8. accommodating different batch sizes which affect the delay of an order through the system.

The model is stochastic in the sense that it cannot predict the course or time required for any particular order but, since the operations of the system can be described by probability distributions, it can predict the behavior of the system as a whole under numerous situations with a large input of orders.

Under varying alternative inputs the model will:

1. provide staffing requirements for each task;
2. determine materials costs for each task;
3. determine order-delay times through the system;
4. determine average unit costs;
5. show the effects of operating policy changes; and
6. provide a management tool for monitoring the system once it is in operation.

Variable inputs to the model included:

1. The mean observed times pertaining to the functions the Center will perform were multiplied by the personal rating factor and by the standardizing factor to obtain generalized standardized times. Times were calculated without regard to frequency because the frequency factors will be handled as transition probabilities (see below). The standard times were reported as high, low, and mean (see Figure 3. 9) so that the effect of changing the times could be evaluated.
2. Most of the functions are performed on batches of books, cards, etc. An individual book or order is delayed because it must wait for work to be performed on other items in its batch. Therefore, the amount of delay time due to batching was simulated for different batch sizes. Those functions affected by batching were so designated on the flow chart.
3. In addition to considering the delay time from the point of an individual book or order, it was also important to determine where the entire flow or any portion of it would be delayed until a certain preceding function was performed. Therefore, the concepts "off-line" and "on-line" were used as criteria. For example, the bookkeeping procedures (Functions 12, 22-23) are off-line because the performance of these tasks does not delay the ordering or processing of the book or any function. Bookkeeping can be conducted at the same time that the main flow of tasks is being carried out. A "no" is entered on the chart for delay time encountered for such functions; or "yes" if delay time is a concomitant to an on-line procedure (see Figure 7. 5).
4. Some functions pertain to handling titles, the rest to the physical volume (copies of books). For example, searching a purchase request card is a title function but marking spines is a volume function. Any bibliographic procedure applies to multiple copies of the same title, whereas the physical handling must be done on a per volume basis. This duplication factor was varied in order to study the Center's capability to accomplish a greater volume output with less work on indi-

vidual titles. The duplication factor was ranged from 1.0 to to 3.0 in .5 title increments.

5. To determine the effect of different levels of operation upon the system, a range of from 40,000 to 200,000 volumes, with increments of 20,000 volumes, was inputed to the computer.
6. Within the flow chart there are branches in the flow of work. Some books or orders are served by a sub flow of activities whereas the remainder continues to follow the main flow. For example, many foreign titles may have to be diverted to a holding area to be re-searached for LC copy, while the bulk of books received move unimpeded through the system. Consequently, the proportion of books or orders going to each branch had to be identified wherever these splits occurred in the flow chart. Otherwise, the design would be predicated on the false assumption that every book or order is handled in exactly the same way throughout the system. The transition probabilities are expressed as percentages and are based upon frequency data and statistics compiled during the field investigations. The advice of the supervisory personnel in technical processes at the University of Colorado Library was solicited because the volume level and processing procedures of that library approximate that of the proposed Center more nearly than does that of any of the other member libraries.
7. The four categories of personnel--student assistants, full-time clerks, library assistants, and full-time professionals--were selected and the wage rates prevailing at the University of Colorado were adopted to correspond to each category.
8. Supplies supportive of each of the Center's functions were identified and costs per thousand projected. Supplies such as pencils and typewriter ribbons, that could not be allocated to any specific task were classed as miscellaneous supplies and prorated over all tasks. Supply costs for ordering threshholds from 40,000 to 200,000 volumes were tabulated.
9. Overhead, binding, and transportation--The cost figures pre-

viously calculated for CALBPC were used.

The output of the model was as follows:

1. The proportion of ordered volumes processed through each task: mathematically this figure is the expected number of times an order receives the task processing. When orders always move ahead and do not recycle through a task, this expected number is equal to the proportion of orders processed at each task.
2. The number of units processed through each task: "units" in this case generally refers to volumes; however, for certain indicated tasks, such as cataloging, the unit processed is a title. The ratio of copies per title will be dependent upon the number of orders for new titles that are initiated at the same time. Tasks for which the number of units processed refers to titles rather than to volumes are indicated by an asterisk on the computer print-out.
3. The employee level, man-hours required and man-years of effort for each task: employee levels are inputs to the model, but are printed with the manpower requirements for convenience. Man-hours are derived from items processed by a task and processing time requirements. Man-years are developed from the number of available man-hours in a year. For this section of the study, 1820 hours constitute a man-year.
4. Labor costs for each task: this shows man-hours converted into salary costs and is dependent upon the previously chosen employee level. Salary costs include accruals for leave, etc., unless the level represents hourly wages.
5. Supply costs for each task: miscellaneous supplies such as pencils, erasers, etc., are included in overhead. Supply costs cover punch cards, catalog card sets, forms etc. Most tasks have no supply costs associated with them.
6. Total labor and supply costs for each task.
7. The average times and costs for the above per volume ordered: because of cancellations and various return procedures not all volumes ordered will be received and processed.

8. The average times and costs per volume processed: volume processed refers to those actually received and sent to the requesting library.
9. Average total cost, including overhead.
10. Cumulative average delay or elapsed time in minutes by task: this time is a function of the batching policy and assumes that when a batch arrives at a task, staffing is such that work can be started immediately. Lag times for orders in the hands of vendors are not included, but are shown in Figures 2. 3 and 2. 4.
11. Labor times and costs summarized by employee level: these figures cumulate tasks utilizing the same employee level.

In addition, an option will provide the above output for any subset of tasks that might be considered a group or a separate department, such as acquistions functions only, mechanical processing only, etc.

Construction of the Model

The book processing center system is composed of a number of tasks which may or may not be performed at the same physical location. Orders pass from task to task and take different paths through the system, depending upon the results of the preceding task. For example, the separate paths taken after the search for LC copy has been completed is dependent upon whether or not copy is found.

Some of the tasks are off-line in the sense that the order does not pass directly through them; they take place at the same time as other tasks and for mathematical purposes can be viewed as though they are parallel with other tasks. Examples of these are the encumbrance and other bookkeeping routines.

A flow diagram of the system indicating the separate tasks and their paths through the system is presented in Figure 7. 1. Off-line tasks are indicated by using broken lines instead of solid lines. Figure 7. 2 relates the computer task numbers, which must run sequentially, to the activity numbers used in the STPA. Both numbers are shown on the flow diagram.

A few of the tasks indicated serve a mathematical purpose only. These are called "dummy" tasks. The Start, end of processing, and end tasks fall into this category.

Figure 7. 1
Book Processing Center Flow Chart

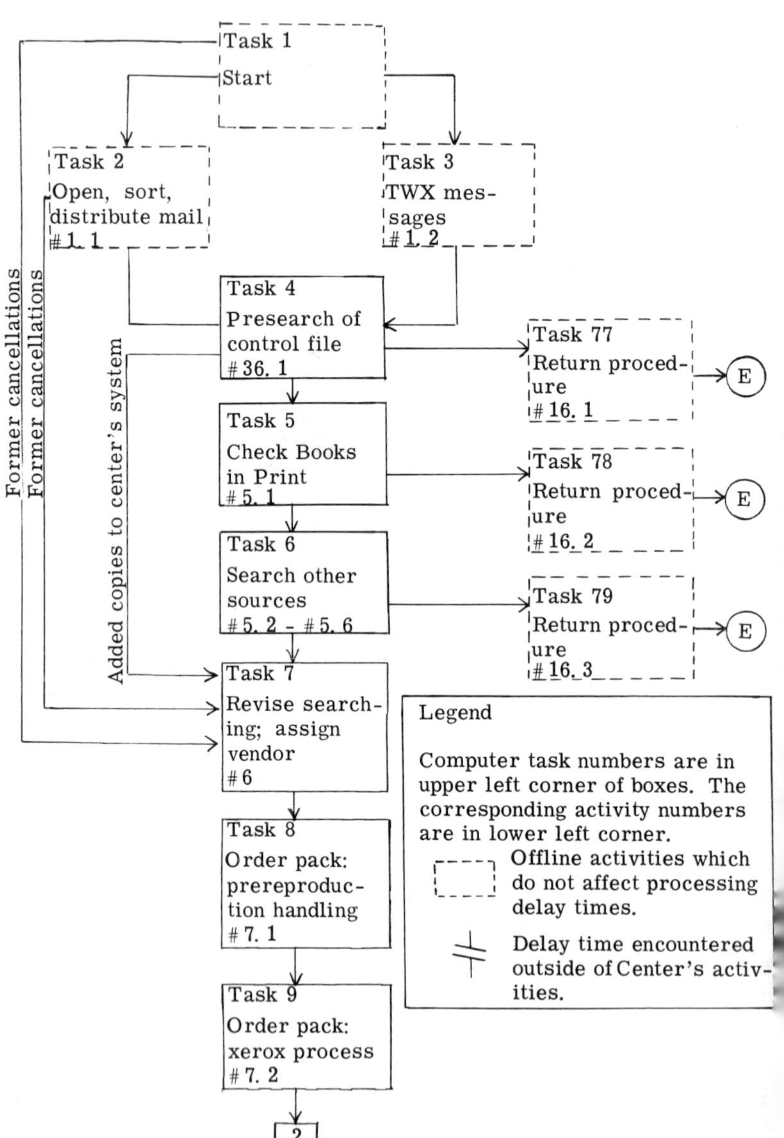

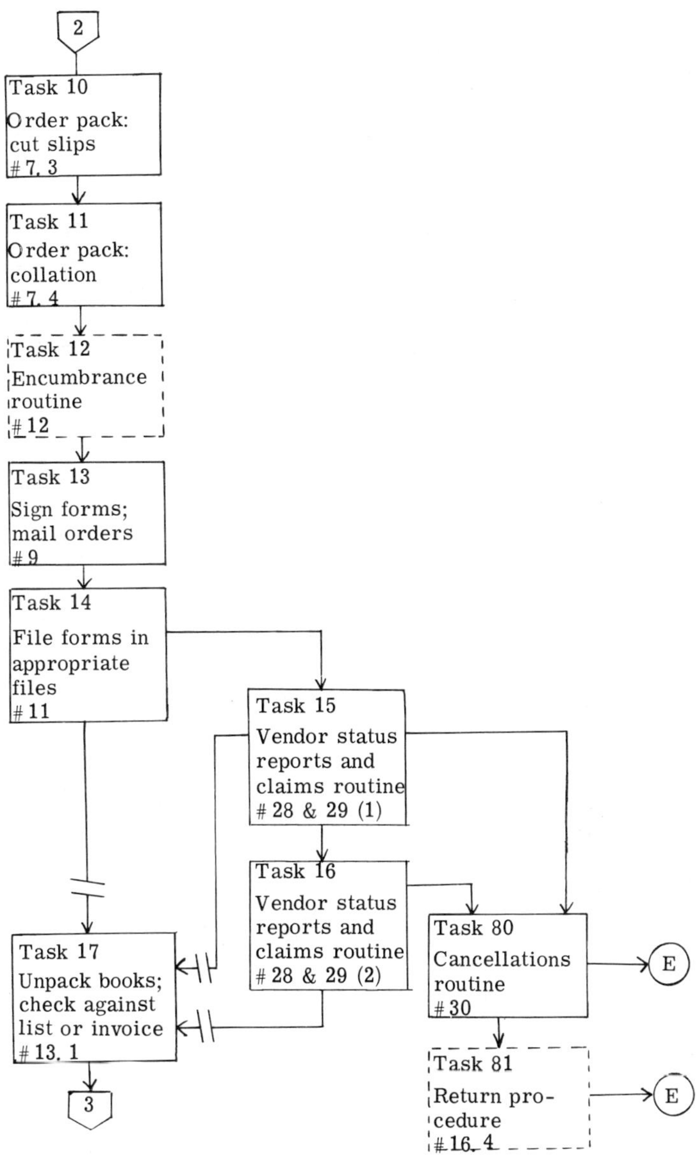
2
Task 10
Order pack:
cut slips
7. 3
Task 11
Order pack:
collation
7. 4
Task 12
Encumbrance
routine
12
Task 13
Sign forms;
mail orders
9
Task 14
File forms in
appropriate
files
11
Task 15
Vendor status
reports and
claims routine
28 & 29 (1)
Task 16
Vendor status
reports and
claims routine
28 & 29 (2)
Task 80
Cancellations
routine
30
E
Task 17
Unpack books;
check against
list or invoice
13. 1
3
Task 81
Return pro-
cedure
16. 4
E

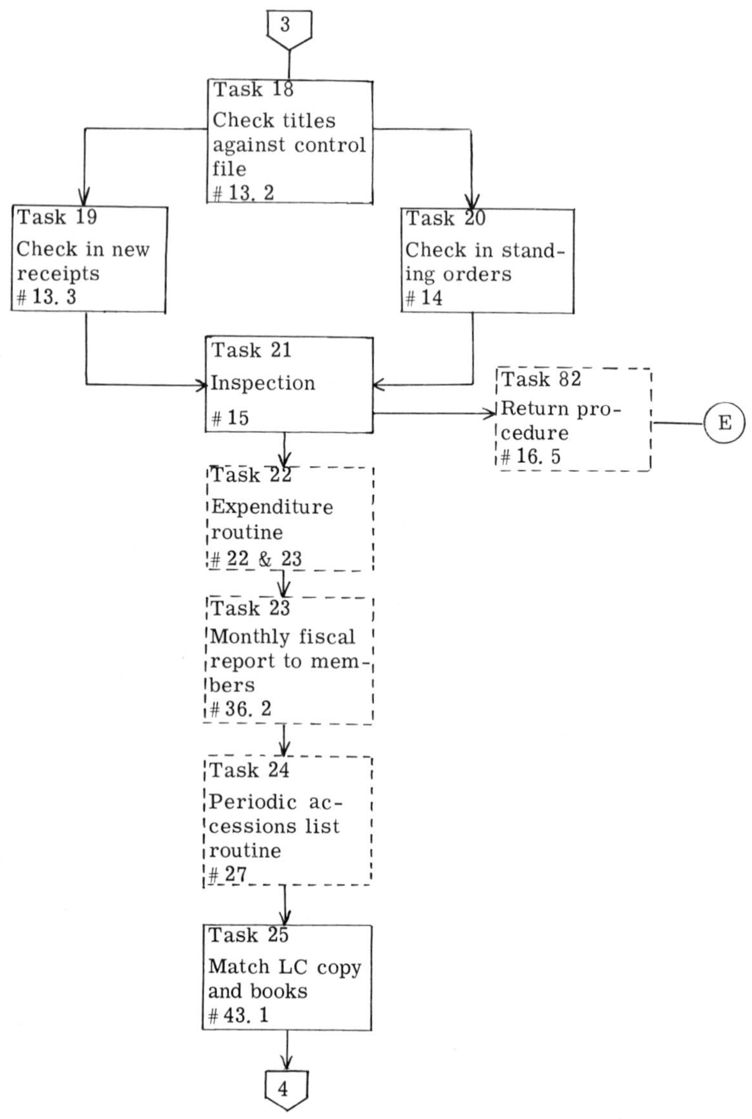
3
Task 18
Check titles against control file
13. 2
Task 19
Check in new receipts
13. 3
Task 20
Check in standing orders
14
Task 21
Inspection
15
Task 82
Return procedure
16. 5
E
Task 22
Expenditure routine
22 & 23
Task 23
Monthly fiscal report to members
36. 2
Task 24
Periodic accessions list routine
27
Task 25
Match LC copy and books
43. 1
4

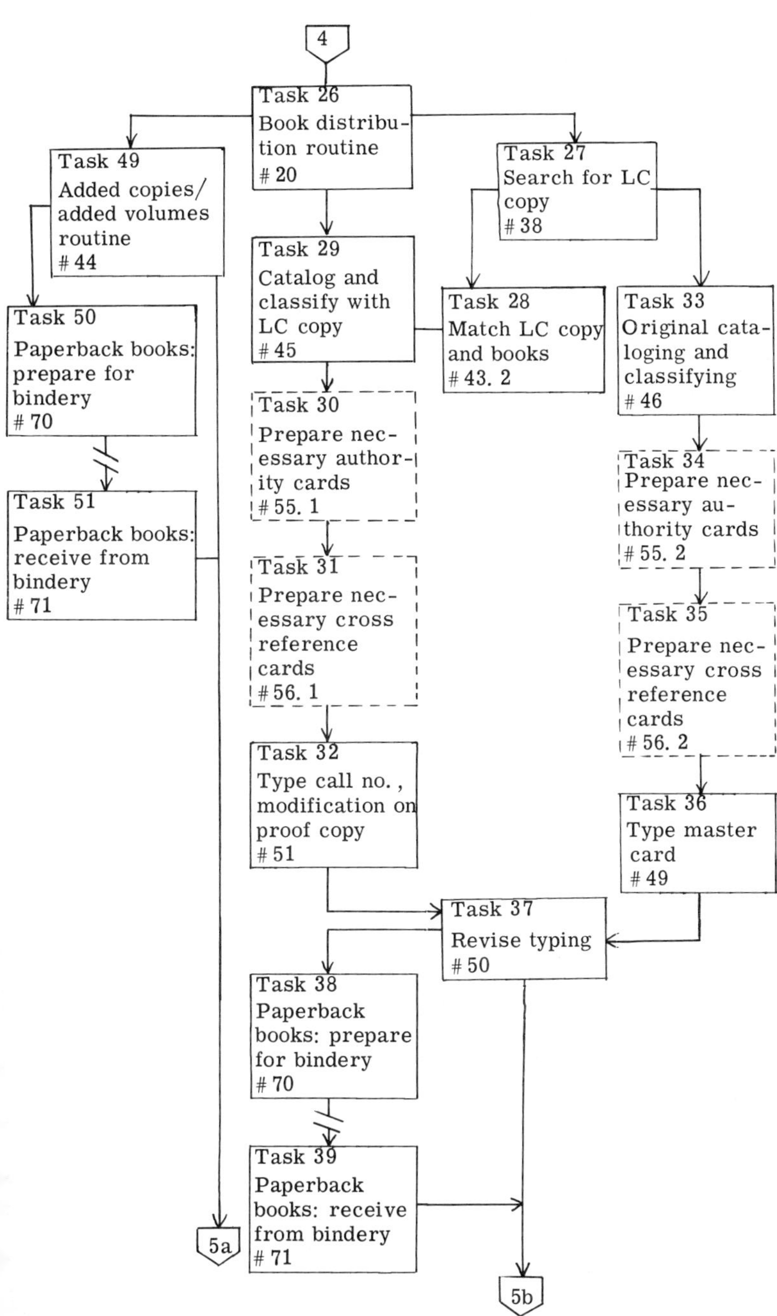
4
Task 26
Book distribution routine
20
Task 49
Added copies/ added volumes routine
44
Task 27
Search for LC copy
38
Task 29
Catalog and classify with LC copy
45
Task 28
Match LC copy and books
43. 2
Task 33
Original cataloging and classifying
46
Task 50
Paperback books: prepare for bindery
70
Task 30
Prepare necessary authority cards
55. 1
Task 34
Prepare necessary authority cards
55. 2
Task 51
Paperback books: receive from bindery
71
Task 31
Prepare necessary cross reference cards
56. 1
Task 35
Prepare necessary cross reference cards
56. 2
Task 32
Type call no., modification on proof copy
51
Task 36
Type master card
49
Task 37
Revise typing
50
Task 38
Paperback books: prepare for bindery
70
Task 39
Paperback books: receive from bindery
71
5a
5b

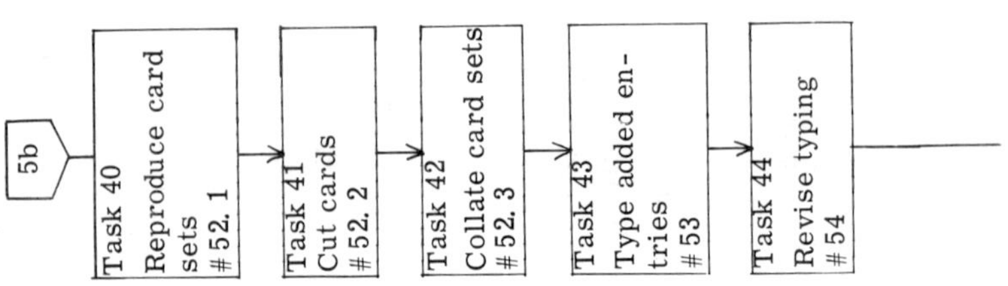
5b
Task 40 Reproduce card sets #52.1
Task 41 Cut cards #52.2
Task 42 Collate card sets #52.3
Task 43 Type added en- tries #53
Task 44 Revise typing #54

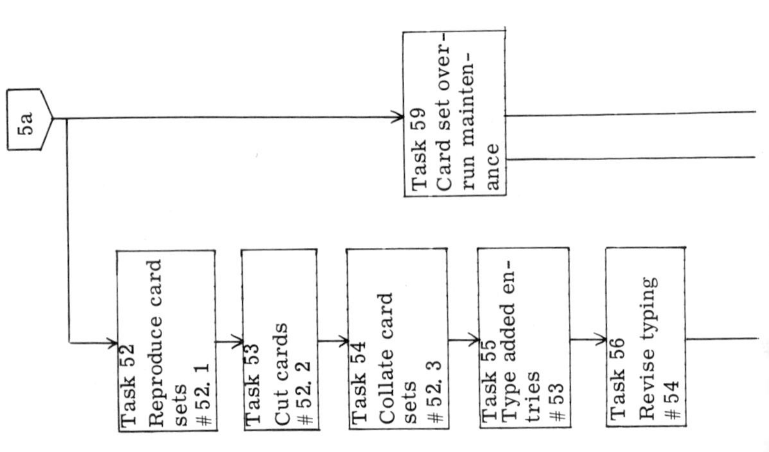
5a
Task 59 Card set over- run mainten- ance
Task 52 Reproduce card sets #52.1
Task 53 Cut cards #52.2
Task 54 Collate card sets #52.3
Task 55 Type added en- tries #53
Task 56 Revise typing #54

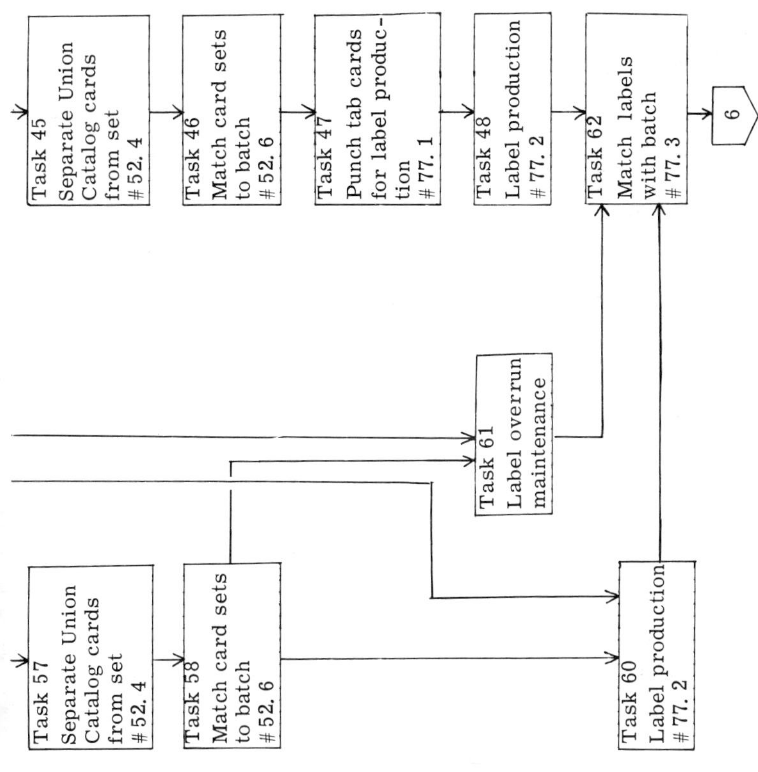
Task 45
Separate Union
Catalog cards
from set
52. 4
Task 46
Match card sets
to batch
52. 6
Task 47
Punch tab cards
for label produc-
tion
77. 1
Task 48
Label production
77. 2
Task 62
Match labels
with batch
77. 3
6
Task 61
Label overrun
maintenance
Task 57
Separate Union
Catalog cards
from set
52. 4
Task 58
Match card sets
to batch
52. 6
Task 60
Label production
77. 2

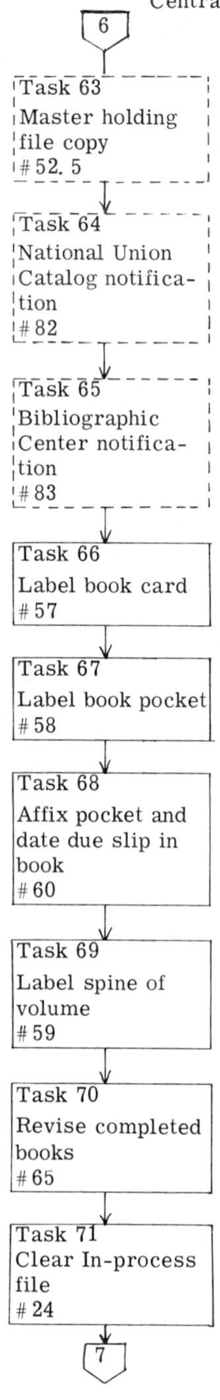
6
Task 63
Master holding file copy
52. 5
Task 64
National Union Catalog notification
82
Task 65
Bibliographic Center notification
83
Task 66
Label book card
57
Task 67
Label book pocket
58
Task 68
Affix pocket and date due slip in book
60
Task 69
Label spine of volume
59
Task 70
Revise completed books
65
Task 71
Clear In-process file
24
7

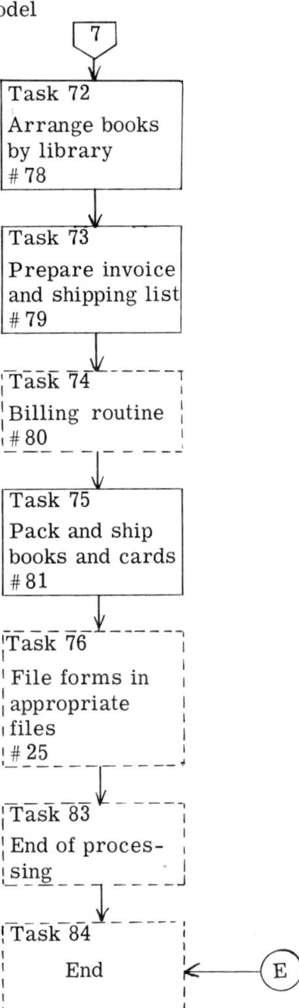
7
Task 72
Arrange books by library
78
Task 73
Prepare invoice and shipping list
79
Task 74
Billing routine
80
Task 75
Pack and ship books and cards
81
Task 76
File forms in appropriate files
25
Task 83
End of proces-sing
Task 84
End
E

Figure 7. 2
Relationship of Computer Task Number to Activity Number

Computer Task Number	Activity Number	Task Description
1	---	Start
2	1. 1	Open, Sort, Distribute Mail
3	1. 2	TWX Messages
4	36. 1	Presearch of Control File
5	5. 1	Check Books In Print
6	5. 2-5. 6	Search other Sources
7	6	Revise Searching; Assign Vendor
8	7. 1	Order Pack: Prereproduction Handling
9	7. 2	Order Pack: Xerox Process
10	7. 3	Order Pack: Cut Slips
11	7. 4	Order Pack: Collation
12	12	Encumbrance Routine
13	9	Sign Forms; Mail Orders
14	11	File Forms in Appropriate Files
15	28&29(1)	Vendor Status Reports & Claims Routine
16	28&29(2)	Vendor Status Reports & Claims Routine
17	13. 1	Unpack Books: Check Against List or Invoice
18	13. 2	Check Titles Against Control File
19	13. 3	Check in New Receipts
20	14	Check in Standing Orders
21	15	Inspection
22	22&23	Expenditure Routine
23	36. 2	Monthly Fiscal Report to Members
24	27	Periodic Accessions List Routine
25	43. 1	Match LC Copy & Books
26	20	Book Distribution Routine
27	38	Search for LC Copy
28	43. 2	Match LC Copy and Books
29	45	Catalog and Classify with LC Copy
30	55. 1	Prepare Necessary Authority Cards
31	56. 1	Prepare Necessary Cross Reference Cards
32	51	Type Call No., Modification on Proof Copy
33	46	Original Cataloging and Classifying
34	55. 2	Prepare Necessary Authority Cards
35	56. 2	Prepare Necessary Cross Reference Cards
36	49	Type Master Card
37	50	Revise Typing
38	70	Paperback Books: Prepare for Bindery
39	71	Paperback Books: Receive from Bindery
40	52. 1	Reproduce Card Sets
41	52. 2	Cut Cards
42	52. 3	Collate Card Sets
43	53	Type Added Entries
44	54	Revise Typing
45	52. 4	Separate Union Catalog Cards from Set
46	52. 6	Match Card Sets to Batch
47	77. 1	Punch Tab Cards for Label Production
48	77. 2	Label Production

Figure 7. 2 (continued)

Computer Task Number	Activity Number	Task Description
49	44	Added Copies/Added Volumes Routine
50	70	Paperback Books: Prepare for Bindery (Added Copies)
51	71	Paperback Books: Receive from Bindery (Added Copies)
52	52. 1	Reproduce Card Sets (Added Copies)
53	52. 2	Cut Cards (Added Copies)
54	52. 3	Collate Card Sets (Added Copies)
55	53	Type Added Entries (Added Copies)
56	54	Revise Typing (Added Copies)
57	52. 4	Separate Union Catalog Cards from Set (Added Copies)
58	52. 6	Match Card Sets to Batch (Added Copies)
59	---	Card Set Overrun Maintenance (Added Copies)
60	77. 2	Label Production (Added Copies)
61	---	Label Overrun Maintenance (Added Copies)
62	77. 3	Match Labels with Batch
63	52. 5	Master Holding File Copy
64	82	National Union Catalog Notification
65	83	Bibliographic Center Notification
66	57	Label Book Card
67	58	Label Card Pocket
68	60	Affix Pocket and Date Due Slip in Book
69	59	Label Spine of Volume
70	65	Revise Completed Books
71	24	Clear In-Process File
72	78	Arrange Books by Library
73	79	Prepare Invoice & Shipping List
74	80	Billing Routine
75	81	Pack & Ship Books and Cards
76	25	File Forms in Appropriate Files
77	16. 1	Return Procedure
78	16. 2	Return Procedure
79	16. 3	Return Procedure
80	30	Cancellations Routine
81	16. 4	Return Procedure
82	16. 5	Return Procedure
83	---	End of Processing
84	---	End

As indicated above, the program of the model is generalized so that completely new and different tasks can be accommodated simply by adding and renumbering tasks. The program, without modification, can handle up to 99 different tasks. A larger number could be accommodated with simple modification.

Figure 7. 3
Transition Probabilities Governing Passage of Requests Through the System

Present Task	Next Task 1	2	3	4	...	j	...	n-1	END
1	0	p_{12}	p_{13}	p_{14}	...	p_{1j}	...	p_{1n-1}	p_{1n}
2	0	0	p_{23}	p_{24}	...	p_{2j}	...	p_{2n-1}	p_{2n}
3	0	0	0	p_{34}	.	p_{3j}	.	p_{3n-1}	p_{3n}
4	0	0	0	0	.	p_{4j}	.	p_{4n-1}	p_{4n}
.	.	.	.	.	.	.	.	.	.
.	.	.	.	.	.	.	.	.	.
.	.	.	.	.	.	.	.	.	.
i	0	0	0	0	...	p_{ij}	...	p_{in-1}	p_{in}
.	.	.	.	.	.	.	.	.	.
.	.	.	.	.	.	.	.	.	.
.	.	.	.	.	.	.	.	.	.
n-1	0	0	0	0	...	0	...	0	1. 00
End	0	0	0	0	...	0	...	0	1. 00

The mathematical development of the model is based upon a transition matrix which attaches probabilities to the passage of orders from one task to another. The tasks can be so defined that the order always progresses to a higher numbered task. While this is not essential, it leads to efficiencies in computer time since a simpler and more exact matrix inversion routine can then be utilized.

For a general form of the model assume a set of tasks $\{i\}$, $i = 1, 2, \ldots, n$ with probabilities governing the passage of an order from task i to task j. A matrix of such probabilities is called a "transition matrix." If all transitions except for the ending task, are to a higher numbered task, the matrix has zeros on the diagonal and below the diagonal except for the ending task which has a 1. 00 on the diagonal. The entries in the upper diagonal may or may not be zero depending upon the transitions that are possible. Figure 7. 3 illustrates a transition matrix in which transitions are to higher numbered tasks. The first integer of the subscripts refers to the row task and the second integer refers to the column task.

Since the entries in the matrix are probabilities, each p_{ij} is such that $0 \leq p_{ij} \leq 1$ for all i and j. Also, the sum of the p_{ij} for a given i must equal one, $\sum_j p_{ij} = 1$. A matrix exhibiting these properties is called a stochastic matrix. When an entry on the diagonal is equal to one ($p_{ii} = 1$), the task is called an absorbing task. That is, once the order has reached this task, it will remain there. For the simulations in this study only the ending task is considered to be an absorbing task. All other absorbing tasks, such as the return procedure tasks, have transition probabilities of 1.0 to the ending task, thus making them non-absorbing tasks. This procedure does not affect the results but it does simplify the computer presentation of the results.

In order to utilize Markov chain theory in the simulation of the system, the probability that an order will pass from task i to task j must not be dependent on the path of the order prior to its arrival at task i. If the system itself does not possess this property, it is still possible to construct a matrix of transition probabilities with the Markov property by adding tasks. An example of where this was required occurs in the added-copy flow.

Where possible, inputs for the simulations were derived from actual measurements at the nine libraries in the study. Other data were entered on the basis of subjective judgment when data were not available. For instance, how many volumes would require original cataloging? This figure had to be based on a set of assumptions-- what titles are ordered, how soon after publication are the titles ordered, how current is the L. C. card copy distribution system. Transitions for tasks such as cataloging can only be estimated until actual operations are begun.

Three basic sets of transition probabilities were used in the computer simulations. These are presented in Figure 7.4. Eighty-four tasks were defined. Adding or deleting tasks (up to 99) or changing the order of the flow (transition probabilities) is readily accomplished by changing the input to the program and does not involve a program change. In Figure 7.4 the column of expected transitions represents the best judgment as to transitions to be encountered in

Figure 7. 4
Matrix of Transition Probabilities

Computer Tasks From	To	Activity Numbers From	To	Low	Expected	High
1	2	--	1. 1	0. 950	0. 960	0. 970
1	3	--	1. 2	0. 015	0. 010	0. 005
1	7	--	6	0. 035	0. 030	0. 025
2	4	1. 1	36. 1	0. 990	0. 995	1. 000
2	7	1. 1	6	0. 010	0. 005	0. 000
3	4	1. 2	36. 1	1. 000	1. 000	1. 000
4	5	36. 1	5. 1	0. 635	0. 690	0. 745
4	7	36. 1	6	0. 350	0. 300	0. 250
4	77	36. 1	16. 1	0. 015	0. 010	0. 005
5	6	5. 1	5. 2-5. 6	0. 985	0. 990	0. 995
5	78	5. 1	16. 2	0. 015	0. 010	0. 005
6	7	5. 2-5. 6	6	0. 985	0. 990	0. 995
6	79	5. 2-5. 6	16. 3	0. 015	0. 010	0. 005
7	8	6	7. 1	1. 000	1. 000	1. 000
8	9	7. 1	7. 2	1. 000	1. 000	1. 000
9	10	7. 2	7. 3	1. 000	1. 000	1. 000
10	11	7. 3	7. 4	1. 000	1. 000	1. 000
11	12	7. 4	12	1. 000	1. 000	1. 000
12	13	12	9	1. 000	1. 000	1. 000
13	14	9	11	1. 000	1. 000	1. 000
14	15	11	28&29(1)	0. 200	0. 200	0. 200
14	17	11	13. 1	0. 800	0. 800	0. 800
15	16	28&29(1)	28&29(2)	0. 200	0. 200	0. 200
15	17	28&29(1)	13. 1	0. 650	0. 650	0. 650
15	80	28&29(1)	30	0. 150	0. 150	0. 150
16	17	28&29(2)	13. 1	0. 750	0. 750	0. 750
16	80	28&29(2)	30	0. 250	0. 250	0. 250
17	18	13. 1	13. 2	1. 000	1. 000	1. 000
18	19	13. 2	13. 3	0. 940	0. 960	0. 980
18	20	13. 2	14	0. 060	0. 040	0. 020
19	21	13. 3	15	1. 000	1. 000	1. 000
20	21	14	15	1. 000	1. 000	1. 000
21	22	15	22&23	0. 970	0. 980	0. 990
21	82	15	16. 5	0. 030	0. 020	0. 010
22	23	22&23	36. 2	1. 000	1. 000	1. 000
23	24	36. 2	27	1. 000	1. 000	1. 000
24	25	27	43. 1	1. 000	1. 000	1. 000
25	26	43. 1	20	1. 000	1. 000	1. 000
26	27	20	38	0. 300	0. 330	0. 350
26	29	20	45	0. 350	0. 370	0. 400
26	49	20	44	0. 350	0. 300	0. 250
27	28	38	43. 2	0. 700	0. 750	0. 800
27	33	38	46	0. 300	0. 250	0. 200
28	29	43. 2	45	1. 000	1. 000	1. 000
29	30	45	55. 1	1. 000	1. 000	1. 000
30	31	55. 1	56. 1	1. 000	1. 000	1. 000

Figure 7. 4 (continued)

Computer From	Tasks To	Activity Numbers From	To	Low	Expected	High
31	32	56. 1	51	1. 000	1. 000	1. 000
32	37	51	50	1. 000	1. 000	1. 000
33	34	46	55. 2	1. 000	1. 000	1. 000
34	35	55. 2	56. 2	1. 000	1. 000	1. 000
35	36	56. 2	49	1. 000	1. 000	1. 000
36	37	49	50	1. 000	1. 000	1. 000
37	38	50	70	0. 100	0. 070	0. 040
37	40	50	52. 1	0. 900	0. 930	0. 960
38	39	70	71	1. 000	1. 000	1. 000
39	40	71	52. 1	1. 000	1. 000	1. 000
40	41	52. 1	52. 2	1. 000	1. 000	1. 000
41	42	52. 2	52. 3	1. 000	1. 000	1. 000
42	43	52. 3	53	1. 000	1. 000	1. 000
43	44	53	54	1. 000	1. 000	1. 000
44	45	54	52. 4	1. 000	1. 000	1. 000
45	46	52. 4	52. 6	1. 000	1. 000	1. 000
46	47	52. 6	77. 1	1. 000	1. 000	1. 000
47	48	77. 1	77. 2	1. 000	1. 000	1. 000
48	62	77. 2	77. 3	1. 000	1. 000	1. 000
49	50	44	70	0. 060	0. 060	0. 060
49	52	44	52. 1	0. 940	0. 940	0. 940
49	59	44	---	0. 000	0. 000	0. 000
50	51	70	71	1. 000	1. 000	1. 000
51	52	71	52. 1	1. 000	1. 000	1. 000
51	59	71	---	0. 000	0. 000	0. 000
52	53	52. 1	52. 2	1. 000	1. 000	1. 000
53	54	52. 2	52. 3	1. 000	1. 000	1. 000
54	55	52. 3	53	1. 000	1. 000	1. 000
55	56	53	54	1. 000	1. 000	1. 000
56	57	54	52. 4	1. 000	1. 000	1. 000
57	58	52. 4	52. 6	1. 000	1. 000	1. 000
58	60	52. 6	77. 2	1. 000	1. 000	1. 000
58	61	52. 6	---	0. 000	0. 000	0. 000
59	60	---	77. 2	0. 000	0. 000	0. 000
59	61	---	---	1. 000	1. 000	1. 000
60	62	77. 2	77. 3	1. 000	1. 000	1. 000
61	62	---	77. 3	1. 000	1. 000	1. 000
62	63	77. 3	52. 5	1. 000	1. 000	1. 000
63	64	52. 5	82	1. 000	1. 000	1. 000
64	65	82	83	1. 000	1. 000	1. 000
65	66	83	57	1. 000	1. 000	1. 000
66	67	57	58	1. 000	1. 000	1. 000
67	68	58	60	1. 000	1. 000	1. 000
68	69	60	59	1. 000	1. 000	1. 000
69	70	59	65	1. 000	1. 000	1. 000
70	71	65	24	1. 000	1. 000	1. 000
71	72	24	78	1. 000	1. 000	1. 000
72	73	78	79	1. 000	1. 000	1. 000

Figure 7. 4 (continued)

Computer Tasks From	To	Activity Numbers From	To	Low	Expected	High
73	74	79	80	1. 000	1. 000	1. 000
74	75	80	81	1. 000	1. 000	1. 000
75	76	81	25	1. 000	1. 000	1. 000
76	83	25	---	1. 000	1. 000	1. 000
77	84	16. 1	---	1. 000	1. 000	1. 000
78	84	16. 2	---	1. 000	1. 000	1. 000
79	84	16. 3	---	1. 000	1. 000	1. 000
80	81	30	16. 4	0. 250	0. 250	0. 250
80	84	30	---	0. 750	0. 750	0. 750
81	84	16. 4	---	1. 000	1. 000	1. 000
82	84	16. 5	---	1. 000	1. 000	1. 000
83	84	---	---	1. 000	1. 000	1. 000
84	84	---	---	1. 000	1. 000	1. 000

the operating system. The high and low columns refer to higher and lower values for probabilities of paths that orders may take. These are expected to provide a range within which actual transitions would occur.

Four levels of employee--student, clerk, library assistant, and professional librarian--were considered as possible alternatives for each task. These are shown in Figure 7. 5. The program will handle up to 10 levels, reflecting different salary scales.

Generalized standard times were developed for each task and are also presented in Figure 7. 5. The development of the standard times was discussed in Section III of this report.

For the simulations, the times were considered the same for a task regardless of level of employee used. However, the program will accommodate different times for each level of employee. It may be, for example, that a professional will perform the same task faster (or slower) than a clerk.

Also included in Figure 7. 5 is a column indicating whether or not each task would contribute to the delay time encountered by an order in the system. Delay time is considered as starting after the order has been opened and is waiting for processing at task 4, which is a pre-searching task. Tasks which are not considered as delaying the order are basically the "off-line" tasks which go on concurrently

Figure 7. 5
Task Inputs for Wage Scale-Standard Time-Delay Time-Processing Unit

Computer Task Number	Activity Number	Wage Scale	Generalized Standard Times (in Minutes)	Delay Time Encountered	Processing Unit
1	---	2	. 000	No	Volume
2	1. 1	2	. 316	No	Volume
3	1. 2	2	. 077	No	Volume
4	36. 1	2	. 993	Yes	Volume
5	5. 1	2	. 308	Yes	Title
6	5. 2-5. 6	3	5. 360	Yes	Title
7	6	4	. 102	Yes	Title
8	7. 1	2	. 164	Yes	Volume
9	7. 2	2	. 418	Yes	Volume
10	7. 3	2	. 035	Yes	Volume
11	7. 4	2	. 325	Yes	Volume
12	12	3	. 716	No	Volume
13	9	2	. 174	Yes	Volume
14	11	2	. 551	Yes	Volume
15	28 & 29(1)	2	6. 977	Yes	Volume
16	28 & 29(2)	2	3. 489	Yes	Volume
17	13. 1	2	1. 833	Yes	Volume
18	13. 2	2	4. 275	Yes	Title
19	13. 3	2	2. 188	Yes	Title
20	14	2	. 784	Yes	Title
21	15	3	. 551	Yes	Volume
22	22 & 23	3	12. 707	No	Volume
23	36. 2	2	. 046	No	Volume
24	27	2	. 046	No	Volume

Task Inputs for Wage Scale-Standard Time-Delay Time Processing Unit (continued)

Computer Task Number	Activity Number	Wage Scale	Generalized Standard Times (in Minutes)	Delay Time Encountered	Processing Unit
25	43. 1	2	. 247	Yes	Title
26	20	2	. 301	Yes	Volume
27	38	3	1. 453	Yes	Title
28	43. 2	2	. 247	Yes	Title
29	45	3	2. 343	Yes	Title
30	55. 1	3	. 863	No	Title
31	56. 1	2	1. 338	No	Title
32	51	2	. 251	Yes	Title
33	46	4	22. 879	Yes	Title
34	55. 2	4	. 863	No	Title
35	56. 2	2	1. 338	No	Title
36	49	2	2. 273	Yes	Title
37	50	3	. 439	Yes	Title
38	70	2	3. 474	Yes	Volume
39	71	2	1. 114	Yes	Volume
40	52. 1	2	. 617	Yes	Volume
41	52. 2	2	. 154	Yes	Volume
42	52. 3	2	1. 120	Yes	Volume
43	53	2	6. 022	Yes	Volume
44	54	3	. 161	Yes	Volume
45	52. 4	2	. 062	Yes	Volume
46	52. 6	2	2. 464	Yes	Volume
47	77. 1	2	. 046	Yes	Volume
48	77. 2	2	. 046	Yes	Volume
49	44	2	. 600	Yes	Volume
50	70	2	3. 474	Yes	Volume

51	71	2	1.114	Yes	Volume
52	52.1	2	.617	Yes	Volume
53	52.2	2	.154	Yes	Volume
54	52.3	2	1.210	Yes	Volume
55	53	2	6.022	Yes	Volume
56	54	3	.161	Yes	Volume
57	52.4	2	.062	Yes	Volume
58	52.6	2	2.464	Yes	Volume
59	---	1	.000	Yes	Volume
60	77.2	2	.046	Yes	Volume
61	---	1	.000	Yes	Volume
62	77.3	2	.247	Yes	Volume
63	52.5	2	.061	No	Volume
64	82	2	1.127	No	Volume
65	83	2	.381	No	Volume
66	57	2	.607	Yes	Volume
67	58	2	.705	Yes	Volume
68	60	2	.329	Yes	Volume
69	59	2	1.112	Yes	Volume
70	65	3	.216	Yes	Volume
71	24	2	.468	No	Volume
72	78	2	.422	Yes	Volume
73	79	2	.046	Yes	Volume
74	80	3	.046	No	Volume
75	81	2	.422	Yes	Volume
76	25	2	.600	No	Volume
77	16.1	1	.198	No	Volume
78	16.2	1	.198	No	Volume

Task Inputs for Wage Scale-Standard Time-Delay Time Processing Unit (continued)

Computer Task Number	Activity Number	Wage Scale	Generalized Standard Times (in Minutes)	Delay Time Encountered	Processing Unit
79	16.3	1	.198	No	Volume
80	30	1	3.167	Yes	Volume
81	16.4	1	.198	No	Volume
82	16.5	3	10.650	No	Volume
83	---	2	.000	No	Volume
84	---	2	.000	No	Volume

Wage Scale

1 Student Assistant	$1.33 Hour
2 Clerk	2.13 Hour
3 Library Assistant	2.72 Hour
4 Professional	4.55 Hour

with other processing. Delay time is considered to be a function of the number of items that are batched together before transfer to the next task.

The delay time while the order is in the hands of the vendor is considered out of the system and is not accounted for in the program. Figure 2. 3 and Figure 2. 4 present average times for this delay.

Figure 7. 5 contains, in addition, a column indicating the processing unit for each task. In general, the unit is the individual volume ordered; however, a few tasks are performed only on a title basis for duplicate volumes being ordered at the same time. A factor is used to convert volumes to titles for these tasks, the volume/ title reduction factor. This factor can be varied for different runs of the program. Its actual value in practice will depend upon the degree to which ordering is coordinated among the libraries.

Figure 7. 6 shows anticipated supply costs per thousand for different materials and ordering thresholds. For example, orders of circulation cards under 60, 000 would cost $3. 00 per thousand whereas orders of over 200, 000 would cost $1. 60 per thousand. On the same table, overhead in actual dollar amounts is shown for different threshold levels of ordered volumes.

In Figure 7. 7 average numbers of supply units per task per unit processed are presented. The unit processed may be either a volume or a title depending upon the task.

Mathematical Notes

The mathematical methodology used in this investigation was developed by Dr. Donald T. Searls of Westat Research Inc., Denver, Colorado.

The mathematical model employed for the system simulation can be described as a special type of Markov chain model with modifications. The system we are considering is viewed as having n tasks of which r are non-absorbing tasks. Since we are considering only one absorbing task, an artifical ending task, $r + 1 = n$. The stochastic matrix of transition probabilities P is represented diagrammatically in Figure 7. 3. A Q matrix is formed by deleting the row and

Figure 7. 6
Cost of Supplies Per Thousand Based on Varying Ordering Thresholds

Supply Item	Ordering Thresholds (Thousands)								
	40	60	80	100	120	140	160	180	200
Purchase Request Card	$ 4. 50	$ 4. 20	$ 4. 15	$ 4. 10	$ 4. 05	$ 4. 00	$ 3. 95	$ 3. 90	$ 3. 85
Order Pack	3. 60	3. 40	3. 40	3. 35	3. 35	3. 30	3. 30	3. 25	3. 25
Catalog Card Sets (6 Cards Per Set)	105. 00	99. 63	99. 13	98. 63	98. 13	97. 63	97. 13	96. 63	96. 13
Catalog Cards	5. 00	4. 64	4. 60	4. 55	4. 50	4. 45	4. 40	4. 35	4. 30
Ektafax Carbons	6. 00	5. 54	5. 50	5. 45	5. 40	5. 35	5. 30	5. 25	5. 20
Label Sets (3 Per Set) (Incl. Die Cost of $60. 00)	9. 00	8. 50	8. 25	8. 10	8. 00	7. 93	7. 88	7. 83	7. 80
Book Pockets	6. 25	5. 00	4. 60	4. 55	4. 55	4. 50	4. 50	4. 45	4. 45
Circulation Cards	3. 00	2. 50	1. 95	1. 90	1. 85	1. 80	1. 75	1. 65	1. 60
Date Due Slips	2. 60	2. 50	2. 45	2. 40	2. 35	2. 30	2. 25	2. 20	2. 15
Punch Cards	1. 00	0. 95	0. 94	0. 92	0. 91	0. 90	0. 89	0. 88	0. 86
Overhead	$32, 900	$43, 300	$51, 600	$58, 400	$63, 400	$68, 900	$74, 600	$81, 000	$87, 800

Note: Miscellaneous Supplies, Bindery Costs, Transportation, and LC File Maintenance are included in Overhead Figures.

Figure 7. 7
Average Supply Units Required Per Task Per Unit Processed

Computer Task No.	Activity No.	Purchase Request Cards	Order Pack	Catalog Card Sets	Catalog Cards	Ektafax Carbons	Label Sets	Book Pockets	Circulation Cards	Date Due Slips	IBM Card Sets
2	1. 1	1									
3	1. 2	1									
8	7. 1		1								
12	12										2
22	22 & 23										1
23	36. 2										1
30	55. 1				1/2	1/4					
31	56. 1				1/2	1/4					
34	55. 2				1/3	1/4					
35	56. 2				1/3	1/4					
36	49				1/3						
40 & 52	52. 1			1							
48 & 60	77. 2						1				
66	57								1		
67	58							1			
68	60									1	

column from P which include the absorbing task. Q then refers only to non-absorbing transitions and since we have defined the tasks so that processing always moves forward, Q can be characterized as

$$Q = \{q_{ij}\}$$

where $$q_{ij} = 0, \text{ for } j \le i.$$

We assume that the q_{ij} are dependent only on the task i, so that the stochastic matrix is a representation of a Markov chain.

Let $p_{ij}^{(m)}$ be an entry of the matrix found by multiplying the matrix P by itself m times. That is $P^m = \{p_{ij}^{(m)}\}$. The entries $p_{ij}^{(m)}$ represent the probabilities of transition from task i to task j in exactly m steps.

If for each transition task i there exists an integer h such that $p_{ij}^{(h)} > 0$ where j is the absorbing task, Q^m will converge to the null matrix and $(I + Q + Q^2 + \ldots + Q^{m-1})$ will converge to the inverse $(I-Q)^{-1}$. The matrix $(I-Q)^{-1}$ is called the "fundamental matrix" of the

Markov chain. These results may be found in Kemeny and Sneil, Finite Markov Chains, D. Van Nostrand Co., Inc., Princeton, 1960, Chapter III.

The above results are general results for a Markov chain. For this particular application since there are zeros on the diagonal and below the diagonal of Q,

$$Q^m = 0$$

and

$$(I-Q)^{-1} = \sum_{h=0}^{m-1} Q^h$$

where

$$Q^o = I.$$

This latter feature permits the use of a simple and more exact inverse routine in the program.

We are primarily interested in the first row of $(I-Q)^{-1}$ which shows the expected number of times that an order is processed at each task. In this case this is also equal to the proportion of all orders processed at each task.

This first row of $(I-Q)^{-1}$ will be designated as a vector, V, with dimensions equal to the number of non-absorbing tasks.

Let u be a scalor equal to the number of volumes initially ordered; then, let

$$V_1 = uV$$

which is a vector representing the number of volumes processed by each task.

Let R be a vector with zeros for tasks for which the volume is the unit of processing and 1/reduction factor for tasks for which the title is the unit of processing.

Let V_2 be the vector resulting from multiplying corresponding elements of R and V_1. V_2 becomes a vector representing numbers of volumes or titles processed at the appropriate tasks.

Man-hour requirements are developed by multiplying elements of V_2 by unit processing times for the appropriate employee level. Costs are derived by a multiplication of man-hours by salary costs.

Materials costs are developed by checking elements of V_2 for appropriate tasks against the cost thresholds and making the corresponding unit cost multiplication.

The elapsed time computations involve a multiplication for appropriate tasks of the batch size multiplied by the unit processing time multiplied by corresponding elements of V.

Analysis of the Simulation Studies

For each of the simulation runs all input parameters except one were held constant. In this manner it was possible to measure the impact of one parameter at a time. For example, the input parameter varied in Figure 7. 8 is the number of volumes requested, ranging from 50, 000 to 500, 000 volumes. This simulation shows that the cost per volume processed when 50, 000 volumes are requested, will be $2. 78 per volume; but when the number is increased to 500, 000, the unit cost drops to $2. 24 per volume. It should be noted that this simulation assumes that an average of two copies of each title are ordered and processed together.

The cost per volume processed when titles are ordered and processed one at a time is shown in Figure 7. 9. The spread between the cost of single copy processing ($2. 96/volume) and the cost when six copies are processed together ($2. 33/volume) emphasizes the advantage of coordinated ordering. Until experience is gained, the actual volume/title factor will not be known.

The difference between the $3. 10/volume charge calculated in Section III and the charge of $2. 96 produced by the model simulation was caused by two factors. First, the supplies charge per volume for CALBPC calculated for Section III was $. 29, based upon an average of supply costs of the nine cooperating libraries, whereas the Center supply cost per volume may more nearly approximate the supply cost at Library No. 8--$. 19 per volume. The mathematical model considers the actual supply thresholds, function by function, which provides a more precise estimate. Second, the cost analysis in Section III could not take into account the attrition of requests as they pass through the system via cancellations and returns. Any order that entered the system could exit only at Function No. 16 (Return Procedure, Figure 7. 10).

The man power requirements for the Center are estimated to be sixty-one man years with a volume/title factor of one. But the staffing requirement is reduced to forty-six man years when the volume/title factor increases to six.

Figure 7. 8
Book Processing Center Simulation
Variable: Volumes Requested

Variable	Return Procedures							
	Pre-Search		Bip Check		Full Search		Cancell-ations	
Vol. Requested	Volume	%	Volume	%	Volume	%	Volume	%
50K	483	1. 0	333	0. 7	330	0. 6	1, 954	3. 9
75K	724	1. 0	500	0. 7	494	0. 6	2, 931	3. 9
100K	965	1. 0	666	0. 7	659	0. 6	3, 908	3. 9
130K	1255	1. 0	866	0. 7	857	0. 6	5, 081	3. 9
160K	1544	1. 0	1066	0. 7	1055	0. 6	6, 253	3. 9
200K	1930	1. 0	1332	0. 7	1319	0. 6	7, 817	3. 9
250K	2413	1. 0	1665	0. 7	1648	0. 6	9, 771	3. 9
500K	4826	1. 0	3330	0. 7	3297	0. 6	19, 542	3. 9

Figure 7. 9
Book Processing Center Simulation
Variable: Volume/Title Factor

Variable	Return Procedures							
	Pre-Search		Bip Check		Full Search		Cancella-tions	
V/T Factor	Volume	%	Volume	%	Volume	%	Volume	%
1. 0	1285	1. 0	866	0. 7	857	0. 6	5081	3. 9
2. 0	1255	1. 0	866	0. 7	857	0. 6	5081	3. 9
3. 0	1255	1. 0	866	0. 7	857	0. 6	5081	3. 9
4. 0	1255	1. 0	866	0. 7	857	0. 6	5081	3. 9
5. 0	1255	1. 0	866	0. 7	857	0. 6	5081	3. 9
6. 0	1255	1. 0	866	0. 7	857	0. 6	5081	3. 9

Figure 7. 10
Book Processing Center Simulation
Variable: Low, Expected, & High Transitions
to Request Return Procedures

Variable	Return Procedures							
	Pre-Search		Bip Check		Full Search		Cancella-tions	
Return Proc.	Volume	%	Volume	%	Volume	%	Volume	%
Low	376	0. 3	261	0. 2	261	0. 2	5164	4. 0
Expected	1255	1. 0	866	0. 7	857	0. 6	5081	3. 9
High	4141	3. 2	2791	2. 1	2699	2. 1	4815	3. 7

Note: The Expected Transitions to the Preliminary Search--BIP Check--Full Search Return Routine show a total of 2. 3%.
For the Low Return run, the return procedures total 0. 7%.
For the High Return run, the return procedures total 7. 4%.

Figure 7. 8 (continued)

Constants: Expected Transitions
Title/Volume Factor (2. 0)

Book Returns		Volumes Completely Processed		Cost Per Copy Ordered	Cost Per Copy Processed	Man/Yrs. Required	Total Cost
Volume	%	Volume	%	$	$	Man/Yr.	$(000)
938	1. 9	45, 962	91. 9	2. 55	2. 78	20	128
1407	1. 9	68, 944	91. 9	2. 47	2. 69	30	185
1876	1. 9	91, 926	91. 9	2. 47	2. 69	40	247
2439	1. 9	119, 502	91. 9	2. 37	2. 58	52	309
3002	1. 9	147, 080	91. 9	2. 35	2. 56	64	376
3752	1. 9	183, 850	91. 9	2. 32	2. 53	80	465
4690	1. 9	229, 813	91. 9	2. 23	2. 43	100	558
9380	1. 9	459, 625	91. 9	2. 06	2. 24	201	1028

Figure 7. 9 (continued)

Constants: Volumes Requested (130K)
Expected Transitions

Book Returns		Volumes Completely Processed		Cost Per Copy Ordered	Cost Per Copy Processed	Man/Yrs. Required	Total Cost
Volume	%	Volume	%	$	$	Man/Yr.	$(000)
2439	1. 9	119, 502	91. 9	2. 72	2. 96	61	354
2439	1. 9	119, 502	91. 9	2. 37	2. 58	52	309
2439	1. 9	119, 502	91. 9	2. 26	2. 46	49	294
2439	1. 9	119, 502	91. 9	2. 20	2. 39	47	286
2439	1. 9	119, 502	91. 9	2. 17	2. 36	46	282
2439	1. 9	119, 502	91. 9	2. 14	2. 33	46	278

Figure 7. 10 (continued)

Constants: Volumes Requested (130K)
*Expected Transitions
Volume/Title Factor (2. 0)

Book Returns		Volumes Completely Processed		Cost Per Copy Ordered	Cost Per Copy Processed	Man/Yrs. Required	Total Cost
Volume	%	Volume	%	$	$	Man/Yr.	$(000)
2479	1. 9	121, 459	93. 4	2. 40	2. 57	53	313
2439	1. 9	119, 502	91. 9	2. 37	2. 58	52	309
2311	1. 8	113, 243	87. 1	2. 28	2. 62	49	296

The availability of Library of Congress cataloging copy will affect the performance of the Center. When copy is not available, the cost of cataloging is increased and the speed in which books are readied for use is reduced. As is shown in Figure 7. 11, if copy is located before a book is ordered, the labor cost per volume processed is $2. 17; if copy is not located until after the book is received, the cost of processing is increased to $2. 23 per volume. If copy is not found even after additional searching is performed and the title must be cataloged originally, the cost per volume goes to $3. 95 per volume.

Another alternative investigated was the cost of volumes processed without additional searching. As can be seen from Figure 7. 11, the cost of labor/volume is reduced from $3. 95 to $3. 89. This difference indicates that if a reliable set of predictors could be formulated, it might be cheaper to catalog some books originally bypassing the additional searching routine.

The effect of batching and the delays that batching cause were also analyzed. Figure 7. 12 shows that almost no delay time is incurred when a title is hand-carried through the system (a batching factor of one). Of course, this alternative would be economical for RUSH requests only. On the other hand, as the batch size increases beyond 100 volumes, the elapsed times also increases more rapidly. This analysis suggests that batches that can be accommodated by a book truck will be most economical without producing intolerable delay times.

Finally, it should be reiterated that the intention has been to develop a generalized model that can be used by other organizations to analyze their operations. Libraries differ in organizational structures and in the types of materials they process. The model developed as part of this investigation can accommodate many different situations. Task boxes in the model can be changed, added, or subtracted. For example, in this study foreign language imprints have been combined with English language materials in both bibliographic searching and cataloging, but the model can separate these two categories of materials.

The text of the mathematical model is available from the University of Colorado Libraries for cost of reproduction and mailing. Requests should be addressed to CALBPC Coordinator, University of Colorado, Norlin Library, Boulder, Colorado 80302.

Figure 7. 11
Path Analysis

Description of Path	Time (Min.)	Labor Cost
1. Request Returned After Full Search	7. 2	$0. 30
2. Request Cancelled	22. 4	0. 81
3. Book Returned	29. 0	1. 20
4. Added Volume/Copy Routine	44. 1	1. 71
5. LC Cataloging (Copy Located at Time of Ordering)	54. 5	2. 17
6. LC Cataloging (No Copy Located at Time of Ordering)	55. 9	2. 23
7. Original Cataloging (Copy Known Not to be Available)	76. 8	3. 89
8. Original Cataloging (Search for Copy but None Found)	78. 2	3. 95

Task Paths

1. 1-2-4-5-6-79
2. 1-2-4-5-6-7-8-9-10-11-13-14-15-16-80
3. 1-2-4-5-6-7-8-9-10-11-12-13-14-17-18-19-21-82
4. 1-2-4-7-8-9-10-11-12-13-14-17-18-19-21-22-23-24-25-26-49-52-53-54-55-56-57-58-60-62-63-64-65-66-67-68-69-70-71-72-73-74-75-76-83-84
5. 1-2-4-5-6-7-8-9-10-11-12-13-14-17-18-19-21-22-23-24-25-26-29-30-31-32-37-40-41-42-43-44-45-46-47-48-62-63-64-65-66-67-68-69-70-71-72-73-74-75-76-83-84
6. Same as 5 except, delete Task 25 and add Tasks 27 & 28
7. 1-2-4-5-6-7-8-9-10-11-12-13-14-17-18-19-21-22-23-24-26-33-34-35-36-37-40-41-42-43-44-45-46-47-48-62-63-64-65-66-67-68-69-70-71-72-73-74-75-76-83-84
8. Same as 7 except, add Task 27

Note: Refer to Figure 7. 1 for Description of Path Tasks
Refer to Figure 7. 5 for Task Times and Wage Scale

Figure 7. 12
Elapsed Time With Varying Batch Size

Transition Probability	Batch Size	Requests Rec'd Thru Mail Orders		Unpack Books Thru End of Proc.	
		Hours	Days	Hours	Days
Expected	1	. 098	. 012	. 453	. 057
Expected	25	2. 453	. 307	11. 315	1. 414
Expected	50	4. 907	. 613	22. 628	2. 829
Expected	100	9. 813	1. 227	45. 257	5. 657
Expected	150	14. 720	1. 840	67. 885	8. 486
Expected	200	19. 625	2. 453	90. 513	11. 314
Expected	250	24. 532	3. 066	113. 142	14. 143
Expected	500	49. 063	6. 133	226. 283	28. 285

VIII. Library User Attitude Survey

Introduction

The sheer volume of literature reporting library and information use studies would indicate that the user of libraries and information centers is an intensively studied individual. But so far the user of information has not been adequately described in quantitative terms. The information professions have learned a great deal about users but not enough to remove the uncertainties from information systems design and development.

Countless studies have been conducted using one or a combination of the following methodological techniques: (1) study of library circulation records by tracing specific withdrawals, (2) study of reference questions, (3) direct observations, (4) diary studies, (5) questionnaires, (6) interviews, and (7) reference counts.[1]

Among the types of data which have been obtained using these techniques are: (1) frequency and degree of exposure to information and its sources; (2) reason for the exposure; (3) performance of the information system; (4) user's value judgments regarding the system's performance; and (5) respondent's general communication skills, information use patterns and overall use of library services.[2]

The methodology employed in this investigation represents a slightly different approach to the problem. Those who participated in the survey were asked to indicate not only their reaction to existing library resources and services but also their attitudes toward a variety of suggested services that a library might offer.

The purpose of the survey was to measure the attitudes of faculty toward library resources and services, and to develop a data instrument that could be used to assess the impact of services introduced as part of a proposed bibliographic network.[3] Another objective was to gain insight as to the level of faculty awareness of library services. In other words, do faculty know what services their library offers, and if so, do they use them?

The project team did not attempt to measure current library use patterns in each of the institutions. This approach was considered but not pursued because too many critical variables could not be adequately controlled. For example, it is far simpler to measure out-of-library use (books and periodicals checked out, articles xeroxed, items borrowed through inter-library loan, etc.) than to measure in-library use, i. e., material read but not formally borrowed. Moreover, the heterogenity and the dispersed geographic distribution of the users compounded the problems. Precise measurement of use patterns and attitudes is not often achieved even when the group studied is relatively homogeneous in interests and educational background. For state-of-the-art reviews of use studies, the reader should consult Herner and Herner and A. S. Barber.[4, 5]

In the CALBPC investigation, great emphasis was placed on the attitudes of faculty toward the library. It is the investigators' contention that faculty user attitudes play a major role in the ultimate success or failure of a library service. If a library is not responsive to user needs, the long range results will be inevitable. Moreover, if library services are under-utilized because users are either unaware of available services, this condition may also evoke dissatisfaction. It was hoped that the results of the survey would provide guidance in setting network program priorities.

The attitude survey was structured to provide information on several aspects of library operations: (1) Existing library resources--what are faculty attitudes toward the adequacy of library collections in satisfying teaching and research needs? Are the opinions of college faculty the same as those working at the universities? (2) Existing library services--how do faculty feel about them? Do these services adequately meet faculty bibliographical needs in research and instructional programs? Are faculty aware of services now offered? (3) Possible library services--what priorities would faculty attach to a variety of services that might be offered if a bibliographical network were put into operation? Which do the faculty feel are the most significant and least significant services in furthering their research and instructional programs? What services other than those suggested would users prefer to see initiated as a part of the network?

Study Methodology

The universe to be investigated was defined as full-time faculty and faculty status personnel at the participating institutions. These included all administrative, research, and professional personnel, both teaching and non-teaching. Librarians were excluded from the study, although they fell within the universe to be sampled.

One of the institutions did not wish to participate in the survey and withdrew from the feasibility study in November, 1967. This reduced the Group I institutions (colleges) to six with eight institutions in all participating in the survey. The survey was conducted over an eight month period running concurrently with other Phase I and Phase II tasks.

Initially, a questionnaire was developed for distribution to the participating institutions. Two types of questions were employed in the data instrument. The first part of the questionnaire concentrated on attitudes toward present services, adequacy of collections, and questions that would produce information on user awareness. Throughout this section, the questions were structured so that respondents answered according to a significance scale, such as, never important, rarely important, sometimes important, usually important, or always important; yes, no, or in part; or never, rarely, sometimes, usually, or always. The sequence of the multiple answers was staggered to lessen the bias of "order effect."

The second section dealt with proposed services and was structured differently. It had been the investigators' intention to use a force-choice structure which would cause a respondent to assign priorities to the twelve services listed, ranking them from 1 to 12, the most through least significant services. This approach was abandoned when the project's consultant, Dr. Donald Chase, Chase and Associates, Bethesda, Maryland, advised that other surveys have consistently shown that respondents encounter difficulty in ranking the significance of more than four or five items. As a substitute, he recommended that a scale ranging from very significant to very insignificant be employed for each service proposed and that a point scale from one to five be used. This approach permits the ranking of any of the services from "1 - very significant" to "5 - very significant" with a neutral position "3," and shadings "2 - somewhat significant" and "4 - somewhat insignificant." (See Appendix 8. 1 for questionnaire.)

Once the initial questionnaire had been designed, a pilot survey was conducted at one Group I and one Group II institution. The random sample size was established arbitrarily at 10 for the Group I institution and 21 for the Group II institution. A transmittal packet containing the questionnaires, a letter of instruction, and a suggested cover letter were sent to the head librarian at the two institutions. The librarian at the Group I institution employed telephone follow-ups and was able to distribute 9 out of the 10 questionnaires. The project staff conducted a telephone follow-up for the 21 questionnaires distributed at the other institution and also sent additional copies with hand-written notes to non-returnees. In all, 16 returns of the 21 questionnaires were received.

The results of the pilot study were forwarded to the project's consulting psychologist. After a critique of the pilot data instrument, the questionnaire was revised on the basis of the consultant's suggestions. The questionnaire was revised seven times before the actual survey. Even so, eight questions had to be modified during the data tabulation to facilitate coding.

On the basis of the pilot survey, it was decided that telephone interviews should be conducted in order to validate the final questionnaires. The telephone interview was structured in order to provide a codeable record of the interview. This was accomplished by means of an interview check list. (See Appendix 8. 2)

The project's consultant was asked to evaluate the proposed interview validation procedure. Since time would not permit an interview with each respondent, the consultant recommended that the investigators interview five percent of the sample. It was his view that this number would be sufficient for purposes of questionnaire validation. This is the approach the project team adopted. Of those in the original sample, 11.9% were interviewed. (See Figure 8. 1.) The interviews in both the pilot and the actual surveys varied from 15 minutes to 45 minutes, depending upon the willingness of the subject to discuss library services.

Figure 8. 1
Telephone Interview Questionnaire for Validation

Library	No. in Sample	Number Inter-viewed	% of Faculty Interviewed
1	35	5	14. 3%
2	24	5	20. 8%
3	157	18	11. 5%
4	97	10	10. 3%
5	52	6	11. 5%
7	34	5	14. 7%
8	195	22	11. 3%
9	38	4	10. 5%
Totals	632	75	11. 9%

Samping procedure: Once the instrument had been revised, the survey subjects were selected. The following method was used:

1. The total number of personnel according to the definition of the universe was obtained from the Office of the Academic Dean at each institution.
2. The eight institutions participating in the attitude survey were divided into two groups, Group I for the state colleges, and Group II for the state universities.
3. The formula:

$$\sigma_p = \sqrt{\frac{\theta\ (1 - \theta)}{N_s} \times \frac{N_{ps} - N_s}{N_{ps} - 1}}$$

where: N = sample size
θ = .50
σ_p = .05
N_{ps} = 930 (Group I) or 3118 (Group II)

was used to compute the total sample size for Group I and for Group II. The formula assumed the worse possible outcome in terms of answers, i. e., $\theta = .50$ so that the maximum sample size for a confidence level of 95% would result; that is, the variance of the population mean would be within 5%. Use of the above formula yields an overestimate when sample calculation is for a stratified population, as was the case in this instance.

4. After computing the group sample size, the sampling ratio

was calculated for each institution within the Group by means of the formula:

$$\frac{N_s \text{ total}}{N_{ps} \text{ total}}$$

5. The sampling ratio multiplied by the population size yielded a sample size for each institution. (See Figure 8. 2.)

An address list was prepared by drawing a random sample from the faculty roster of each institution. The address list and a packet of instructions were then sent to the head librarian at each institution. In addition, a letter of instruction for initiating the follow-up procedure was furnished. After the librarian had returned the completed questionnaires to the project office, a series of follow-up letters were sent as required, spaced about ten days apart. As it became apparent that the original subject selected was not appropriate, i. e. , a visiting professor or a person on leave, another subject was randomly selected and sent a questionnaire using the same procedure as had been employed for the total sample. In all, the substitution procedure represented 3. 9% of the total sample.

Questionnaire response: The project team attempted to obtain as high a return rate as was possible. In all, three follow-up letters were distributed, and where necessary, a letter was sent to a respondent's home address if it were determined that the subject was on leave or worked primarily at home. As the reader can see from Figure 8. 3, the response rate from the initial questionnaire was 76. 6%, which was remarkable in itself; after the third follow-up, the return rate totaled 96. 5% of the 632 questionnaires distributed; 555 or 88% returned usable questionnaires.

Every attempt was made to obtain a response, if not a completed questionnaire, from all subjects in order to minimize the biases introduced by non-response. (See Figure 8. 4.) The investigators' hypothesized that most of those who did not respond considered themselves non-library users. To a certain extent, this hypothesis was borne out, though not completely. Of the 77 who did not return questionnaires, 36 or 48% stated that they did not use the library. An examination of library No. 8's circulation file did not produce any con

Figure 8. 2
Sample Size for Each Institution

Institution	Population Size N_{ps}	Sampling Ratio $\frac{N_s}{N_{ps}}$	Sample Size N_s
# 1	115	. 301	35
# 2	79	. 301	24
# 4	324	. 301	97
# 5	174	. 301	52
# 7	113	. 301	34
# 9	125	. 301	38
Total	930		280

Group I - State-Supported Institutions of Higher Learning Having a Faculty of Less Than 500 Members

Institution	Population Size N_{ps}	Sampling Ratio $\frac{N_s}{N_{ps}}$	Sample Size N_s
# 3	1377	. 114	157
# 8	1741	. 114	195[a]
Total	3118		355

Group II - State-Supported Universities Having a Faculty of Over 1000 Members

[a] Sample reduced from 198 to 195 at # 8 as three questionnaires from this institution could not be located for coding. Total sample for Group II institutions was reduced to 352.

Figure 8. 3
Cumulative Response Rate: 632 Questionnaires

Response After:	Number Returned	Percent Returned	Number Usable	Percent Usable
Initial Mailing	484	76. 6%	449	71. 0%
1st Follow-up	574	90. 8%	530	83. 9%
2nd Follow-up	599	94. 8%	549	86. 9%
3rd Follow-up	610	96. 5%	555	87. 8%

Figure 8. 4
Reasons Cited by Subjects for Not Returning the Questionnaires

Reason Cited for Non-response	Institution 1	2	3	4	5	7	8	9	Totals no.	%
Does not use library	2		7	6	2	1	14	5	37	48. 1%
Invalid substitution				1					1	1. 3%
New on Campus	1	1	6	4			2		14	18. 2%
Does not have time to complete the form		1	2				2		5	6. 5%
Hostile to survey				1					1	1. 3%
Unable to make contact with individual		1	2	3	1		10	2	19	24. 7%
Totals	3	3	17	15	3	1	28	7	77	100. 0%

tradictory evidence. Several respondents apologetically indicated that the questionnaire had become buried on their desk, or like most questionnaires had simply been dumped into the wastebasket. Then too, one respondent became aggravated by the project team's persistence. In all, only 3% of the total sample did not respond to the questionnaire.

Once all of the questionnaires had been received the responses to each question were tabulated according to their date of return, (see Figure 8. 3) that is, the initial questionnaire, the first follow-up, and so on. The responses were then cross-checked to insure that the follow-up procedure itself had not biased the responses. Th check indicated no significant differences and so few questionnaires were returned as a result of the third follow-up that this small nur ber did not significantly affect the response percentages. (See Appendix 8. 8 for tabulation of questions according to time of return.)

Questionnaire validation: The project staff examined all questionnaires and selected those which were most in need of validatio that is, questionnaires containing question marks, write in remarks or incomplete answers. Additional questionnaires were randomly selected to increase the validation sample size for each participat institution to ten percent. Invalid answers were noted and correct answers substituted. Those questions identified in the validation process as being ambiguous or misleading to some respondents were later checked against the remainder of the questionnaires to insure that there were no significant variations in the response pattern. The cross-check suggests that the responses to questions 4, 12, 13, 18, 19, 25, and 29 should be interpreted cautiously as there is some doubt of their reliability. For tabulation purposes, "Possible Services" on pages 3 and 4 of the questionnaire were numbered, continuing the numerical sequence of pages 1 and 2. Thus C. (Union Library Acquistions List) was redesignated as question 25; and G. (Periodical Contents Service) became question 29. Questions A - L became questions 23 - 34.

Question 4 asked users to indicate the relationship between bibliographic and reference sources and their own research activities. During the telephone interviews, respondents were more likely to state that they always needed bibliographic resources in their research activities whereas the profile of the overall sample showed that the majority of respondents noted that they either sometimes or usually needed bibliographical resources. As for the survey analysis, this did not make a great difference since the two most positive answers, usually and always, were analyzed as a unit.

The interviews also brought to light that some who had reported a satisfaction level with regard to interlibrary loan services had actually not used the service within the last year or two, and some respondents who had used the service once or twice could not actually remember whether the service was satisfactory. It is likely that there are fewer serious users of interlibrary loan services than suggested by the survey.

The responses to questions 14, 18, 19, 25, and 29 all can be accounted for by the fact that respondents either did not know that a particular service was offered, or did not understand what the service involved. For example, question 25 is concerned with the importance of union library acquistion lists. Once this concept was made clear, some users downgraded the importance of this service to their immediate needs. In this same vein, question 19 asked respondents to indicate whether or not their library provided specialized reference and research services in a subject area. Several of those interviewed stated that the service was not only available but that they had used the service. The bias imbedded is that more users have taken advantage of the reference services than the responses suggest.

Weaknesses in the methodology: The high response rate suggested that library users were sufficiently motivated to participate in the survey. The telephone follow-up interviews reinforced this impression. However, the interviews also revealed certain general difficulties with the questionnaire. In question 10, "Library resources and services in my subject area are adequate to the support of my teaching needs;" the choice of answers were yes, no, and in part. The respondents who do not teach were not provided with a choice.

The failure to provide enough response choices was evident in several questions as the respondent added the answer most applicable to him. Because write-ins occurred for several questions, additional answers were inserted in order to code the data. These included the following questions: 1. don't know - (f); 2. don't know - (e); 3. don't know - (e); 7. don't know - (d); 9. do not use - (f); 10. don't teach - (d); 11. don't know - (f); and 14. don't know if there is one - (e).

Problems with terminology and a lack of knowledge about the library were also detected. The telephone interviews revealed that several terms had been misinterpreted or were not understood at all. "Rush" as used in question 19 and 20 was confused with interlibrary loan service. "Union catalog" or "union acquistions list" on page 3 of the questionnaire was unfamiliar to several respondent Finally, the terms "current contents service" and "translation ser vice" (see questions 14, 15, and 18) were not understood by many respondents. In the latter case numerous respondents noted satisfac tion or dissatisfaction with a service that is not actually provided.

A sentiment frequently voiced during the interviews was for li braries to publicize services available to faculty and students and to explain what these services entail. Further, those interviewed wanted to know what could be expected from the library, particularly if a bibliographic network were implemented. The imponderable is--what weight can be attached to the attitudes of those who have not taken the trouble to learn how to use their libraries, or do not believe they need to use the library?

Some of the follow-up interviews revealed a reluctance on the part of respondents to criticize their library to an outsider. The respondent might give assurance that books were ordered and processed quickly enough, or that library services in general were perfectly satisfactory. In some cases this reaction may have represented the opinions of an individual who is not a frequent library user. Other respondents probably do not possess sufficient background to discriminate between good and poor library service.

The heterogenity of the universe sampled, representing a conglomeration of skills, specializations, and individual desires reduced the sensitivity of the study technique. One difficulty in attempting to measure attitudes of a heterogeneous academic community has been illustrated by a study performed at Southampdon University in England.[6] In this study, the library attempted to measure the impact of services that had been in operation for three years. Among the services organized was a Library Services Consultation Committee formed to act as a link between students and the library. Those students wishing to complain or offer suggestions could do so by addressing the Committee, and conversely, the library could use the Committee as a sounding board for changes in services, etc. The results of the study were essentially negative, i. e., no marked change in attitude could be observed. The investigators reported that it was not possible to detect whether there actually had been change in student attitudes toward the library or whether the research instrument developed was not sufficiently sensitive to detect the changes that had occurred.[7]

The attitude survey conducted in the present investigation runs the same set of risks in that many variables affect the attitudes and actions of teaching faculty and researchers, and the tool developed for the study may not measure those changes in attitude that occur after a bibliographic network is established.

Analysis of the Questionnaire

The data were analyzed in a variety of ways: (1) by size of institution; the six colleges were categorized into one group and the two universities into a second group; (2) by individual institution; and (3) by academic discipline. The institutions were grouped by size to permit identification of differences in attitudes among individuals employed in institutions which place different emphasis on teaching and research. The response tabulations are included as Appendices 8. 3, 8. 4, 8. 5, and 8. 6. Columns a - f correspond to responses a - f; and a - e to responses 1 - 5 for questions 23 - 34.

The analysis according to discipline was accomplished by dividing academic areas of interest into seven categories. These included administrative services, applied science, humanities, the sciences, social sciences, interdisciplinary areas, and vocational and technical fields of study. The areas were categorized according to information obtained from the _Guide to Graduate Study_,[8] _The College Blue Book_,[9] and the U. S. Office of Education, _Earned Degrees Conferred, 1964-65_.[10] The subject areas assigned to each of the groupings may be found in Appendix 8. 7.

Most of the analyses which follow concentrate on the extremes of answers, i. e., individuals who answered "never" or "rarely" to a question or those who answered "always" or "usually." It was assumed that individuals who checked the extremes held stronger negative or positive attitudes, and that analysis of the extremes would prove more meaningful.

A regression analysis correlation coefficient matrix was developed in order to study and identify relationships among respondent's attitudes. For the most part this analysis proved inconclusive as most of the "r" values range from minus .10 to plus .25. The primary reason for the low correlations was that multiple choice questions were employed to identify variations in relationships that the library profession presumes do exist. As more possible combinations are introduced through multiple choice structuring, the correlation coefficient is reduced in magnitude. The highest r^2 (r^2 % .52) value observed involved the use of the Rush request procedure and an individual's satisfaction with that service (questions 19 and 20). Those individuals who requested the fewest rushes were also those who were most satisfied with the service. The weakness of the group regression analysis is that it did not relate the attitudes of individuals but rather of individuals in agregate.

Results of the Survey

As already noted the survey was not designed to study the user _per se_. The investigation was directed more at learning how a library is used and in identifying the attitudes that faculty users hold regarding the library, and its services. However, the data have been coded so that future analysis could be keyed to the user. Data have been coded according to the following categories: highest degree held and/or second degrees at the same level; years of teaching experience; academic departmental affiliation and subject specialty; and location of the respondent, either at a branch or on the main campus. Moreover, the responses of individuals can be compared with the responses of others from his institution, academic discipline, or with those from other academic fields. But for the purposes of the present study, group reactions and attitudes toward the status of library collections and services has taken priority.

The collections: User attitudes toward the adequacy of library book collections were divided into two categories: (1) research collections, and (2) teaching collections. Respondents from Group I (colleges) and Group II (universities) institutions expressed practically identical attitudes toward teaching resources. Forty-five percent reported that the collections were adequate to support their teaching needs, and 40% felt the collections met their needs at least in part. Only 10% indicated that the current collections would not support their instructional programs.

With regard to research, respondents from the Group I institutions were less satisfied with the collections than those from the Group II institutions. Of the respondents, 58% of the Group II users indicated that their needs were either always or usually satisfied by existing collections whereas only 37% from the Group I institutions expressed this same degree of satisfaction. At the other extreme 10%

from the Group I institutions lamented that their research needs were never or rarely satisfied by the collections whereas only 4% from the Group II institutions expressed dissatisfaction.

The questionnaire also asked each respondent to evaluate whether library resources and services in his subject areas were adequate to support his teaching needs. The responses from the Group I and Group II institutions paralleled each other. Fifty-five percent from the Group II institutions reported that acquisitions were adequate and seven percent that they were excellent, whereas 48% from the Group I institutions stated that the acquisitions were adequate and 12% felt the situation was excellent. However, over one-third from both groups indicated that acquisitions were adequate.

The responses to question 1 concerning the adequacy of bibliographic and reference sources needed to pursue research activities was also analyzed by institution. The overall average of those answering never or rarely was 9. 7% and those responding usually or always was 58. 2%. (See Figure 8. 5.)

At two institutions, one out of five users feel that the collection is inadequate. The greatest dissatisfaction was evidenced at a new institution where the collection is acknowledged to be weak. But paradoxically the highest positive response was received from an institution where practically no research is being conducted. Of those who stated that bibliographic and reference sources were either never or rarely adequate to meet their needs, as might be expected, users from the newest institution expressed greatest dissatisfaction, and users of the largest research collection voiced the greatest satisfaction.

Respondent attitudes toward the rate of acquisitions at their institution produced generally a more negative response. One-half of the respondents believe that growth is adequate, see Figure 8. 6; only ten percent of the respondents believe the acquisition rate is excellent. And at one institution almost 55% expressed dissatisfaction with growth of the collections.

In order to study attitudes toward collection growth in greater depth, the responses to question 4 were compared with those to question 7.[11] This was done to determine whether there was any relation ship between those who expressed the greatest need for bibliographic and reference sources and respondents who expressed greatest dissatisfaction with the growth rate of acquisitions. Did those who expressed the least need for bibliographic resources express as great a dissatisfaction with collection growth or were they more inclined to regard growth as adequate?

Figure 8. 5
Response to Questions 1 and 7 (in Percentage)

Question	Response	Average	High%	Low%
1. The bibliographic and reference sources I need for my research activities are available to me at the library(s) on campus:	never - rarely	9. 7	19. 3	3. 0
	usually - always	58. 2	81. 8	38. 7
7. The acquisition by the library of books and periodicals in my subject area is:	insufficient	37. 0	54. 8	21. 2
	adequate	49. 9	57. 1	38. 7
	excellent	9. 9	30. 3	0
	don't know	. 7	2. 4	0

Figure 8. 6
Response to Questions 4 and 7 (in Percentage)

Question	Response	Question	Response	% Response Pattern
4. I am engaged in research activities which require bibliographic and reference sources	never or rarely	7. The acquisition by the library of books and periodicals in my subject area is:	insufficient	21%
			adequate	70%
			excellent	6%
			don't know	2%
			other	1%
4. I am engaged in research activities which require bibliographic and reference sources	usually or always	7. The acquisition by the library of books and periodicals in my subject area is:	insufficient	41%
			adequate	44%
			excellent	11%
			don't know	1%
			other	3%

The analysis clearly indicated that those who expressed the greatest need were the same as those who were most dissatisfied with the growth rate of the collections. Twenty-one percent of those who said that they rarely or never required bibliographic sources expressed dissatisfaction with the rate of acquisition; whereas, forty-one percent of those who answered usually or always to question 4, are unhappy with collection growth.

The preliminary analysis, while by no means conclusive, suggests that as a group the faculty are neither extremely satisfied or dissatisfied with library collections; those who use the collections most frequently are more likely to be dissatisfied than individuals who are not so dependent on them.

The project team, while interviewing faculty respondents occasionally gained the impression that a faculty member was apathetic to the state of the overall collections but was more inclined to react to an issue of the moment; that is, he was satisfied if the library owned or could borrow the titles he needed to write a specific article or prepare a paper, but unhappy if the material he needed was unavailable.

Several respondents did, however, append statements to their questionnaires requesting that if additional funds could be secured, they should not be used to initiate new services but should be spent on improving the library's collections. One respondent wrote, "I much prefer adding to the book and periodical collections before adding various kinds of services.... I'd rather have another nineteenth century periodical than a list of books already in the library." Another observed that "...we need money for books and periodicals more than we need most of the services suggested." One respondent, commenting on the quality of the library collections at the participating institutions, remarked that a statewide network would prove to be a futile gesture in his area of interest because "none of the (services) applies to classics since there is nothing scholarly anywhere in Colorado except Boulder." This individual was more interested in putting extra funds into strengthening existing collections than in providing library network services.

The responses regarding collections were also tabulated according to academic areas of interest. This analysis revealed that those researchers working in the humanities are less satisfied with the quality of library resources than those working within the applied and natural sciences. In question 1, 16% from the humanities reported that resources were either never or rarely available whereas only 3.5% and 7% from the sciences and applied sciences responded in this manner. A similar relationship was noted in question 7 regarding the rate of growth. Fifty-three percent of the humanists felt that growth was insufficient for their needs whereas only 22% from the applied sciences and 34% from the sciences expressed dissatisfaction. Moreover, only 31% from the humanities believe that resources in their subject areas are sufficient whereas 58% from applied sciences and 53% from the sciences are satisfied with the collections available to them.

The analysis by discipline did provide one surprise. Those from the humanities expressed the greatest dissatisfaction with the speed in which materials are processed into the library's collection. Only 10% noted that materials were already in the library at the time they were needed whereas 32% from the applied sciences and 22% from the sciences checked this response. This contradicted somewhat the generally held view that scientists are more concerned than humanists with the speed in which materials are acquired. However, in part, the greater satisfaction of those associated with scientific disciplines might be explained by the fact that scientists are more dependent on periodicals and reports for current developments than are the humanists.

Evaluation of present services: The Card Catalog--The study attempted to gain insights regarding overall faculty reaction to the card catalog. Do they find materials sufficiently indexed to permit retrieval? Do the catalog cards contain sufficient bibliographic information to allow them to locate the books they need?

The general attitude of those responding seemed to be one of tentative acceptance of the catalog. When asked whether or not the catalog was sufficiently subject indexed to meet their needs, 78.4% responded that the catalog was either usually or always sufficiently indexed, whereas only 6.9% checked a never or rarely response. Regarding the adequacy of the descriptive information, 78% indicated that the cards either usually or always supplied them with sufficient information, as compared to only 5% who responded with a "rarely" or "never" answer.

These responses can be interpreted in several ways. One seemingly obvious conclusion is that in spite of the shortcomings of the catalog, the study did not uncover a great deal of dissatisfaction. The follow-up interviews, likewise, did not bring to light latent negative reactions.

Analysis of individual responses revealed a relationship between the responses of those who stated that bibliographic reference resources were important to their research and user satisfaction with the card catalog. The respondent who says he does not need bibliographic resources is more likely to express satisfaction with the adequacy of the card catalog, whereas heavier users of bibliographical resources tend to be more critical. (See Figure 8. 7.)

Another factor that may have biased the attitude of respondents is their ability to use a card catalog. A person who is continually frustrated in his attempts to locate material through the catalog is more likely to attribute his failures on the structure and the weakness of the card catalog rather than on his own ineptitude. This behavioral pattern is familiar to many reference librarians.

Rush Requests--The speed with which books are made available for use is a basic concern of most librarians. The desire to reduce the acquisition/processing time lag is one motivation for establishing a statewide processing center. As reported in Section II, the average acquisition/processing lag for the nine institutions was 186 days. This time is considered unacceptable by the librarians of the participating institutions. All believe that the time lag can and should be significantly reduced.

One might have expected that the long delay would have prompted a significant number of rush requests, but the samples drawn from outstanding order files did not support this view. The rush acquisition rate for the institutions ranged between 2% and 4%. When asked about rush requests, two-thirds of the respondents reported that they had not requested a rush book in the last 12 months. Of those who had submitted a request, two-thirds had submitted requests for less than three books. In general, this finding agrees with the order file sample in that only a minority of the faculty can be expected to submit rush requests.

Figure 8. 7
Response to Questions 4 and 9 (in Percentage)

Question 4	Response	Question 9	Response	% Response Pattern
I am engaged in research activities which require bibliographic and reference resources	never rarely (negative)	The cards in the card catalog contain sufficient information with which I can select the books I need.	never	1
			rarely	1
			sometimes	11
			usually	69
			always	17
			don't use	1
I am engaged in research activities which require bibliographic and reference resources.	usually always (positive)	The cards in the card catalog contain sufficient information with which I can select the books I need.	never	1
			rarely	5
			sometimes	19
			usually	60
			always	11
			don't use	4

When asked whether new books required in their work were available in the library's collection at the time they were needed, thirty percent of the respondents noted that this was never or rarely the case while 45% noted that books were only sometimes available when requested. Based on these responses, it can be concluded that a significant number of library users do not find library materials at the time they need the information. On the other hand, the inconvenience and frustration which this causes is not sufficient to stimulate most faculty users into initiating rush requests. One explanation offered is that the user will "make do" with what is readily accessible to him, if that is at all possible. This conclusion is born out by previously reported studies.

If library users place great stress on speed of acquisitions and processing, a positive correlation should exist between the attitudes of respondents to question 11 and the duration of the acquisition/processing cycle found at each of the institutions. A ranked correlation of . 214 (Figure 8. 8) indicates that a relationship does exist, but the correlation is weak. The institution with the highest favorable response ranks number 7 in processing lag performance, and the library with by far the shortest acquisition/processing time cycle ranks only as number 5 on the attitude response scale.

Figure 8. 8

Ranked Correlation of the Speed Materials are Made Available for Use and the Attitudes of Library Users

Availability of Materials Ranking of the Most Favorable by Institution		Acquisition/Processing Cycle, Institution Ranked According to the Speed in Which Books are Made Available	
Rank	% Favorable Responses	Rank	No. of Days
1	30. 0	7	280
2	26. 4	2	123
3	24. 5	3	126
4	22. 6	6	227
5	19. 0	1	65
6	17. 0	5	205
7	15. 2	4	148
8	3. 1	8	374

$$p = 1 - \frac{6\Sigma d^2}{N(N^2-1)}$$

$$p = 1 - \frac{6.66}{8(8^2-1)}$$

$$p = 1 - \frac{396}{8(63)}$$

$$p = 1 - \frac{396}{504}$$

$$p = 1 - .786$$

$$p = .214$$

x	y	d	d^2
1	7	-6	36
2	2	0	
3	3	0	
4	6	-2	4
5	1	4	16
6	5	1	1
7	4	3	9
8	8	0	
		0	66

The factors which account for these variations are not completely clear. However, the libraries which received the highest favorable responses are both heavily committed to domestic approval plans which provide each library with English language imprints automatically. Although these materials account for only 20 to 30% of the total acquisitions of these institutions, the latest scholarly monographs written in the English language are more likely to be available when requested than would be true if they had been ordered on a title-by-title basis. The weak rank correlation might also be accounted for by differences in services provided at the various libraries, i.e., the willingness to process and expedite special requests.

Although there was very little vocal dissatisfaction with the libraries' performance in acquiring and processing materials, the responses of many users participating in the survey would indicate that materials are not available when they are needed. Several respondents appended comments to their questionnaire suggesting that efforts be made to decrease the time cycle between the ordering of a book and the time the book is available for circulation. One comment summarized this attitude: "Why does it take so long to catalog books that have been received?"

Interlibrary Loan--The performance of interlibrary loan services is of particular importance when collections cannot support ongoing research projects. The responses revealed that for both large and small institutions approximately 60% of the respondents have used interlibrary loan services. Of this number, 5% to 7% believe that the services are excellent whereas 40% of the Group II respondents and 31% of the Group I respondents reported that the services are too slow. This latter attitude is not surprising since the average loan period time cycle averages from three to five weeks. One respondent commented that "Anything done to speed the movement of data from the library to me is appreciated; often the library does not have what I need and by the time it gets here on interlibrary loan (weeks later) it is too late."

Inter-institutional Courier--Three of the participants are cosponsors of a courier service which has drastically reduced the time required to transmit materials between libraries. Much to the amazement of the project team, the responses to question 33 if taken at face value imply that users do not place a high priority on the movement of materials. This attitude could be explained partly by the fact that for those institutions where the service is available, the user may be unaware of the impact the courier service has made. Since they are accustomed to rapid delivery service, they now place a lower priority on it. Further, if the majority of interlibrary loan users stress speed, then these same individuals should place a high priority on a courier service.

The comments of two respondents reveal a general attitude of some faculty. "Personally, I am most interested in those services which make it possible to determine fairly quickly what has been written on relatively narrow subjects... and in determining the availability and location of desired materials, not so much in their rapid delivery to me." Another respondent observed that "availability of my library resource materials is of major importance to me; speed of delivery is of secondary importance."

Bindery Service--The investigation did not probe users to determine their attitude regarding the time required to bind materials, but it became obvious from the telephone interviews and from some of the remarks appended to the questionnaire that the delays incurred when materials are bound are considered unacceptable by the user community. A typical comment included in the questionnaires was:

> I consider it inexcusable for recent journals to be unavailable for one to three months at a time when they are just beginning to be indexed by the various abstracting and bibliographical services and therefore frequently needed. Binding should be organized in small lots so the journals are out of the library only for the actual time needed to do the job. They should never be unavailable for more than one week.

It is safe to say that none of the librarians at the participating institutions is satisfied with the present situation. Unfortunately, even if pre-binding and post-binding processing are reduced to a minimum, it is likely that the average volume will be off the shelf from five to seven weeks, unless the binder is able to process the most frequently requested volumes on a rush basis.

One procedure to make periodicals available at the time of greatest need is to hold them until use diminishes and then prepare them for shipment to the bindery. But if this policy is adopted, a library will have to cope with a higher incidence of multilation and lost issues, which consequently increases the number of incomplete volumes that are bound.

Some commercial binders will accept a certain percentage of Rush binding to be processed and returned within one or two weeks.

The survey suggests that rush binding would be well received by library users.

User Awareness--The study also attempted to gauge faculty awareness of services presently offered. Respondents were asked to indicate how frequently they used services such as photocopying and translation, whether or not they received lists of new acquisitions or were furnished with listings of the table of contents of selected periodicals, and whether their library offered specialized research and reference services such as demand bibliographies. In addition, respondents were asked to comment on the effect reclassification has had on the ease of retrieving library materials from the shelves. The most striking aspect of this part of the survey was that many of faculty either do not need or are not utilizing available services, particularly the specialized reference services that are offered in some of the libraries.

With regard to demand bibliographies, ten percent checked that this service was not provided in their library, but seven percent noted that the service was not only available but promptly provided. These contradictory responses came from individuals at the same institutions. The fact that ten percent of the faculty stated that the service was not provided, when in all cases such service is available upon request, indicated a lack of awareness among some users. That 80% of the users checked that they had not used the service implies either that they were unaware of its availability or had no need for such service, or they are reluctant to use it. The findings of Feinler et al. suggest that some of the faculty may be reluctant to use specialized reference services because they are unwilling to delegate this responsibility to others.[12]

A general lack of awareness was also evident from the responses regarding the provision of a current contents listing of periodicals, and the responses regarding the effect of reclassification. Thirty-two percent indicated they did not know if the library provided a current contents listing service, 26% noted they had never received such a list, and 31% reported that the service was available to them. As far as can be gathered, most of the libraries do not at the present offer such a service to faculty users. One explanation is that many faculty users do not know what a table of contents service actually is. It is possible that some confused this service with acquisitions lists, which are provided by most of the participating libraries.

In the last few years there has been a great deal of interest among academic librarians concerning the effect of reclassification and divided collections on library use. In order to gain an impression as to the attitudes of faculty concerning this issue, users were asked whether or not reclassification of the book collections from Dewey Decimal to the Library of Congress System has affected their ability to retrieve materials. The answers indicated that many of the respondents do not understand what the term reclassification means. Three libraries in the state have never undertaken reclassification; yet four percent of the respondents from one of the institutions reported that reclassification had improved retrievability and 45% indicated that they didn't know whether or not reclassification had been undertaken. In the third, 25% commented on the impact and 20% stated that they didn't know. Conversely, in those libraries that have undertaken reclassification, a significant percentage of the respondents stated that they didn't know if reclassification had been undertaken.

Only 17% of the respondents reported that the collections were now more difficult to use; and 8% that the collections were easier to use, whereas 40% noted that all in all, reclassification had not affected their ability to locate materials.

The responses regarding reclassification produced one surprise. It had been presumed that humanists would express the greatest dissatisfaction. Of those responding, only 13% from the humanities noted that collections were more difficult to use whereas 27% from applied sciences and 18% from the sciences expressed dissatisfaction. It is difficult to interpret the meaning of these reactions. One possible explanation is that the humanistic researchers have become accustomed to the split collections as they utilize them more intensively. But most importantly, divided collections have not produced vocal opprobrium, and most library users become accustomed to working with divided collections.

Possible library services: The questionnaire asked users to rank the significance to them of twelve library services. These ranged from traditional to innovative services that could be offered only through the introduction of computer technology. The services were grouped into five categories: (1) data or information transfer methods; (2) conventional current awareness services; (3) non-conventional current awareness services; (4) specialized information and demand bibliographies; and (5) bibliographic holding record displays.

The responses were ranked according to the number of users who indicated that a particular service was "very significant" to them. The responses were also tabulated according to the number of individuals who ranked the services as being "very significant." By comparing the number of very significant to very insignificant rankings the reader can determine whether the distribution tended to be skewed to one direction or the other. The findings are summarized in Figure 8.9.

The data were further categorized according to Group I and Group II institutions in order to identify significant differences between attitudes of those faculty employed in small colleges and the universities.

Data Transfer Methods--The respondents seemed less interested in the transfer of information than they were in learning about the availability of materials; in fact there seemed to be almost total apathy toward telefacsimile, inter-campus courier service, and a telephone answering service. (See Figure 8.9.) The lack of enthusiasm for the inter-campus courier service was not expected. As mentioned earlier, three institutions have operated such a service for three years. The courier service is heavily used and has expedited the flow of materials between the institutions. It may be that the libraries have failed to explain the importance of this service to users. Perhaps, many users are not aware of its existence. In the three libraries that operate a courier service an average of only 25% of the respondents believe that an expanded courier service would be significant to them whereas only 21% of those responding from the other institutions ranked the courier service as highly significant or as significant.

Figure 8.9
Suggested Library Services as Ranked in Order of Significance by the Respondents

	I	II	Very Significant			Very Insignificant			Ave.
	Rank	Rank	I %	II %	Ave. %	I %	II %	Ave. %	I & II Rank
A. Information Transfer Services:									
Bibliographic network	4	7	37.0	28.1	32.5	4.0	4.9	4.4	6
Telefacsimile Trans.	11	10	10.3	13.8	12.0	8.2	10.8	9.5	10
Intra-campus Delivery	7	4	27.5	35.7	31.6	11.3	7.2	9.2	7
Courier Service	12	12	10.3	10.6	10.4	8.2	10.9	9.5	12
Telephone Answering Ref.	10	11	11.4	10.8	11.1	20.4	15.5	17.9	11
B. Conventional Current Awareness Services:									
Acquisitions Lists	1	1	54.4	55.4	54.9	1.2	2.2	1.7	1
Union Acquisition Lists	3	5	37.9	33.7	35.8	2.0	4.9	3.4	3
C. Non-conventional Current Awareness Services:									
Periodical Contents Service	6	3	31.3	37.0	34.1	3.6	7.8	5.7	4
D. Demand Bibliographies (Manual or machine compiled):	2	2	38.8	40.5	39.6	2.4	5.2	3.8	2
E. Bibliographic Holdings Records:									
Union Serials Catalog	5	6	35.3	32.6	33.9	2.4	5.2	3.8	5
Book Catalog	9	9	22.7	23.1	22.9	6.5	7.5	7.0	9
Union Book Catalog	8	8	26.4	27.2	26.8	5.2	5.6	5.4	8

Several individuals, however, appended comments to their questionnaires stressing the importance of a courier service. One respondent asked that the courier service be extended to his institution. Another stated that a daily bus service between the libraries of two institutions would be particularly useful to him in his research work. Another indicated that he didn't use the university library greatly, but he was interested in quick access to books located in neighboring libraries, such as the National Bureau of Standards Library and the University of Colorado Libraries in Boulder.

The library staffs throughout the state expressed total unanimity that expansion of the courier service could constitute the single greatest improvement in interlibrary loan activities among academic libraries, and that the service would prove to be the greatest contributor to improved services both to faculty and students.

In addition to the inter-campus courier service, users were asked to rate the importance of an intra-campus delivery service; that is, an arrangement that would permit a faculty member to request library materials and receive delivery and pick-up directly at his office on campus. Most respondents did not attach great significance to this service, but there was a positive relationship between the size of the campus and the organization of the collection, with the degree of importance attached to intra-campus delivery. In the smaller colleges, accessibility is not a problem, consequently the service was ranked relatively low. On the other hand, 41% of the respondents from institution #8 ranked the service as highly significant. The collections at #8 are decentralized and the campus sprawls over many acres. Respondents from institution #9 rated the service even higher. At this institution the library is separated from classrooms and offices by several city blocks. At this institution 48% rated the service highly significant. One respondent wrote "great" on his questionnaire. Others commented that intra-campus delivery would be an extremely useful and appreciated service.

The overall concept of a communications network fared better than did the individual components of such a network. Even so, respondents did not attach as high a priority to communications as they did to such services as current awareness and specialized reference services.

Current Awareness Services--Clearly, the services to which respondents attached greatest significance is an accessions list of new materials. It should be noted, however, that accessions lists in one format or another are already supplied at several of the institutions. It may be that the significantly greater priority can be accounted for by the respondents' familiarity with this service.

Union acquisitions lists did not receive as high a priority as the intra-institutional lists. One might assume that the smaller colleges would be more interested in a union list than users at the universities. This turned out to be the case but the response was not significantly greater.

It would appear from the overwhelming interest in acquisitions lists by faculty in both Group I and Group II institutions, that a processing center or network group should grant high priority to the provision of current awareness services. There are many questions to be answered. For instance, what types of lists would users find most useful: exhaustive, selective, those geared to an individual's needs, a single department's needs, or to the needs of a specific research project? Would users be satisfied with citations only, citations with augmented titles, or would their needs best be served by citations accompanied by abstracts?

The comments of a few respondents support the view that current awareness services will have to be geared to satisfy a variety of needs and interests. For example, one individual recommended a MEDLARS-type service. Another stated that "departmental bibliographies (bibliographies listing all books purchased for and by a specific department) would be extremely useful to faculty and students;" whereas another individual requested specialized services in the form of a "periodical article abstract service in selected subject areas." Another respondent asked for a list of books by subjects chosen by a particular professor, not arranged by any library classification scheme. He then added that the list should also be subdivided by subject.

Specialized Information Services and Demand Bibliographies--The high priority attached to demand bibliographies was unexpected since in response to question 16 almost four out of five users reported that they had never asked for a demand bibliography. The contradiction in these two responses is unmistakable. During the telephone interviews, the project staff learned that many respondents did not know that the service was available. Respondents assumed that such services could not be provided. A number volunteered that they would make use of such a service if they were afforded the opportunity.

When several of the librarians were queried on the question of their library's willingness and ability to perform demand literature searching, the general response was that such requests would be honored, but because of limited staff and inadequate collections, only the two university libraries would be able to conduct searches on a regular basis, at any great degree of depth.

Bibliographic Holding Record--The lack of enthusiasm for book catalogs, both institutional and union book catalogs runs counter to prevailing philosophy within the library profession. Great stress is presently placed nationally on the development of union catalogs either in conventional or in non-conventional formats. It is possible that the users placed a low priority on this service because librarians already provide the service in one form or another. The Rocky Mountain Bibliographical Center in Denver has been in operation for over 30 years, and its catalog lists the holdings of libraries throughout the region. A survey conducted three years ago revealed that Colorado academic libraries are the heaviest users of the Bibliographical Center's services.[13] Like the courier service, users may not be aware of the Center's proximity or its role in relation to their research work.

Attitudes by Academic Discipline--The analysis by discipline did not produce conclusive evidence. All responses are subject to different interpretations. Concerning the concept of the bibliographical network, respondents from the humanistic and social sciences disciplines rated a communications network more significant than those responding from the sciences and the applied sciences. Forty-six percent responding from the humanities rated the network as highly significant, whereas only 17% from the applied sciences assigned a highly significant rating. The same pattern was evinced with regard to the inter-campus delivery service. The humanists and social scientists expressed greater enthusiasm than did their counterparts from the sciences and applied sciences. On the surface at least, it would appear that the humanists responding to this survey are more interested in the transfer of information than are their colleagues from the sciences. This merits further investigation.

Humanists are also more interested in the development of book catalogs, both intra-institutional and union catalogs. But both humanists and scientists attach greater significance to the development of a union serials list than they do to a union catalog listing monographs. The humanists rated a union serials catalog higher than the scientists, 45% as compared to 35%.

All groups attached greater significance to accessions lists than other services as follows: applied sciences, 45%; humanities, 63%; interdisciplinary fields, 46%; sciences, 46%; social sciences, 64%; and vocational and technical fields, 51%. Union acquisitions lists were not rated as important. Fifty-two percent responding from the humanities thought that such tools would be highly significant to them; 42% from the social sciences; but only 23% from thc applied sciences and 31% from the sciences noted that union acquisitions lists would be important.

Finally, with regard to demand bibliographies and literature searches, all fields indicated a strong positive response. Thirty-two percent of those responding from the humanities, 40% from the applied sciences, 44% from social sciences, 29% from the sciences checked that these services would be highly significant to them.

Summary

This attitude survey, like most surveys, raised more questions than it answered. The most immediate concern of the project staff, however, was to gain a better understanding of the types of activities that would produce the greatest impact on users if a bibliographic network were put into operation.

The survey revealed that if a processing center were implemented, various types of lists could be usefully produced as by-products of the Center's operations. The heterogeneity of the user groups suggests, however, that lists will have to be tailored to meet many different and sometimes contradictory needs, which implies that the intellectual input and the development of such lists must far exceed the intellectual effort of the customary accessions lists of new books.

In spite of the high priority attached by respondents to demand bibliographies, the investigators remain skeptical that such a service will be utilized by the majority of faculty users. Nevertheless, if bibliographic services are to be extended, every effort should be made to publicize such services, to attempt to learn precisely what researchers from various disciplines are interested in, and what they will accept.

There can be no doubt that a sizeable number of faculty users are not aware of services that libraries now offer. This condition is apparent not only from the answers to the questionnaire but it was brought forth time and time again during telephone interviews. Many of those interviewed said that they would greatly appreciate knowing exactly what services are available to them and under what conditions the services can be provided. Paradoxically most of the libraries have already produced library handbooks in which the services now offered are enumerated. The problem may be that libraries have shied away from tested techniques for advertising.

The faculties' misconceptions and misinformation about the library must be overcome. The lack of familiarity with such concepts as a union card catalog, reclassification, translation service, etc., have already been noted. One respondent wrote "I would like to see a phone service for recommending new books for library acquisitions and ordering. The card system in my case is not very satisfactory and usually time consuming." Later it was learned that the library in question does accept telephone requests for ordering. Another respondent suggested "Instead of a union book catalog why not a union card catalog similar to the one maintained at the University of Pennsylvania? Such a service saves a great deal of time and headaches for the requester; therefore I would place this item at the head of the list of the possible serivces." This respondent has apparently never heard of the Rocky Mountain Bibliographical Center. Still another respondent inquired "Is there any orientation for new faculty to the library and its facilities?" He also wondered whether a handbook of library services and general information were available. The library in question offers both an orientation tour and a handbook for new faculty.

The general lack of awareness among users did not come as a surprise. It does indicate, however, that if the libraries in the state are to band together to pool their resources in an effort to improve and extend bibliographic services, a major effort must be made to publicize programs. In some cases it would be desirable to establish programs to educate interested faculty researchers, even at the risk of offending some users.

The complexity and the magnitude of the problems to be overcome before a bibliographic network can successfully be implemented were pointedly summarized by one respondent when he commented "This all reminds me of Parkinson's Law about work expanding to fill a capacity. The library should do what people ask in sufficient number and without being prompted." The paradox is unmistakable.

Notes

1. Columbia University, Bureau of Applied Social Science, Research (Project Leader: Herbert Menzell) _Review of studies in the flow of information among scientists._ New York, The Bureau, 1960.

2. _Ibid._

3. Dougherty, Richard and Lawrence Leonard _Colorado bibliographic exchange and communications network; Project BEACON, an overview._ Boulder, University of Colorado Libraries, 1967, 13p.

4. Herner, Saul and M. Herner "Information needs and uses in science and technology." _In_ Cuadra, Carlos A., ed. _Annual Review of Information Science and Technology._ New York, 1967, p.1-34.

5. Barber, A. Stephanie "A critical review of the surveys of scientists' use of libraries." _In_ Saunders, W. L., ed. _The Provision and Use of Library and Documentation Services._ Oxford, 1966, p. 145-79.

6. Line, Maurice B. and Mavis Tidmarsh "Student attitudes to the university library: a second survey at Southampton University." _Journal of Documentation_ 22:123-135 (June 1966).

7. _Ibid._

8. *A guide to graduate study; programs leading to the Ph. D. degree.* Washington, D. C., American Council on Education, 1967.

9. *The College Blue Book*, 12th ed. Los Angeles, College Planning Programs, Ltd., 1968.

10. U. S. Office of Education *Earned degrees conferred, 1964-65.* Washington, D. C., U. S. Government Printing Office, 1967, p. 256-265.

11. The Chi Square Test and Kolmogorov-Smirnov Test for differences in distributions will be used to determine significance of difference in response to this attitude survey, and to one to be conducted after a bibliographic network is instituted.

12. Feinler, E. J., C. J. Cook, O. Heinz and C. P. Bourne "Attitudes of scientists toward a specialized information center." *American Documentation* 16:329-333 (October, 1965).

13. Swank, R. C. "The Bibliographical Center for Research, Rocky Mountain Region, Inc., report of a survey." Denver, Colo., 1966.

IX. Conclusions and Recommendations

The specific conclusions may be found at the end of each of the sections. By way of a final review, the most important conclusions are summarized briefly in this section, followed by the recommendations.

Conclusions

A centralized book processing center to serve the needs of the academic libraries in Colorado is a viable approach to book processing. The establishment of a central operation will produce multiple advantages to the participating academic institutions. The most important benefits are:

1. Cost Savings: The unit cost of acquiring and processing volumes will be reduced significantly. The average cost for the nine libraries to acquire and process a volume is $4. 50, or $4. 09 discounting institutional overhead. The comparable CALBPC cost will be $3. 10 as calculated in Section III or $2. 96 as calculated by the mathematical model. If institutional overhead is excluded, the charge is reduced further to processing, and it is known that a certain amount of batch processing can be expected. If an average of twc copies of a title are ordered and processed together, the cost will be reduced to $2. 58 per volume, or $2. 27 excluding institutional overhead.

Overall, the centralized processing center will produce dollar savings of $117, 000. This is a conservative estimate because it assumes single copy processing only, thus a per volume charge of $3. 10. As book budgets and labor costs continue to spiral upwards, the savings will increase. It should be emphasized that this level of savings cannot be realized until the center has completed an operational shake-down of approximately one year. A shake-down period will be needed to perfect procedures and policies, to purchase equipment, and to establish close working liaison arrangements with all of the participating libraries. For example, in order to realize the maximum advantage of centralization, the participating libraries must establish a deposit account with the center so that orders can be placed directly and paid by the center.

Another point that must be understood is that the full benefits of the central operation cannot be realized until a gradual transfer of resources has been effected, and personnel now assigned to technical services are assigned new duties in public service areas of the library. Another benefit that will be realized are cost avoidance savings. As the combined book budgets of the institutions increase, the cost of cataloging can be shared by all of the institutions, thereby obviating the need for individual institutions to increase their own processing staffs.

2. Acquisition/Cataloging Time Lag Reduction: The study showed that a processing center should be able to reduce significantly the time a user must wait before new books are available for use. The greatest savings in time will accrue when the Center is able to purchase materials from a vendor who has built his book stock to reflect the needs of academic institutions. Up to now, vendors have been unwilling to do this because there is insufficient profit motive. Instead of waiting an average of 58 days for domestic materials to arrive from a vendor for processing, these materials should be available in a matter of 2 to 5 days.

Batch processing of multiple copies will also speed the flow of books. Further, the acquistions/cataloging time cycle will be reduced if orders are no longer funneled through institutional business offices. This is an anachronistic practice that many progressive institutions have already abandoned.

3. Personnel Specialization: A processing center will enable the libraries to improve utilization of professional librarians. First, the processing center can employ catalogers with special foreign language capabilities to process materials for all of the institutions. At present, some of the institutions have not been able to employ catalogers with the requisite language qualifications. As a result, some foreign language materials are stored in an unorganized state. As the colleges and universities expand their foreign language teach-

ing programs, the need for specially qualified catalogers will become even more acute.

Second, as the technical processing work load is reduced, the participating libraries will be able to concentrate on eliminating cataloging arrearages, selecting books, and/or developing specialized reference services to faculty and students. The need to employ additional technical service personnel should all but disappear unless book budgets at local institutions are greatly increased in the near future. Even more important, the pressures to expand physical facilities should be reduced as work loads are shifted to the central facility.

4. Library Automation: The volume of work processed by the center may make it economical for the libraries to use data processing equipment that no one of the institutions could afford. From the data collected we can conclude that use of the computer will prove beneficial in certain phases of the center's work. In the short-run, automated procedures operating in a batch-processing-mode will satisfy the system's requirements. This is based on the fact that requests for rush orders were found to be extremely low at all of the institutions (2% to 4%), and on the observation that few inquiries are received from library users. This behavioral pattern was empirically observed at several libraries.

The bibliographic data which will be accumulated at the center will soon become a valuable data resource. It can serve as the nucleus for a union catalog that can be queried on demand when online systems become economically feasible. The development of online capabilities should be the long-range objective of the center's research and developmental program.

5. Transition Problems: On the basis of the study of existing order patterns and cataloging policies, Colorado academic libraries will be able to participate in central processing without seriously disrupting their present procedures and policies. Minor adjustments will have to be made, but the vast majority of books can be processed centrally and added to collections without creating substantial conflicts. Thus, there will be no need for libraries to cross-check and revise books as they are received from the center--at least, no

after the libraries have gained confidence in the center's products. Those few titles that create conflicts, such as differences in classification numbers, can be handled by exception procedures as they are discovered.

6. Approval Plans: The analysis of the approval plan in operation at the two university libraries shows that the plan has proven to be reasonably successful, but that steps should be taken to improve the precision of the selection criteria. However, it was found that the plan as presently constructed is not suitable for the college libraries because only 45% of the approval receipts were found to be listed in Choice, which is a major selection tool at all of the college libraries.

This phase of the investigation did bring to light one major area of conflict. Libraries often process monographic serials differently. One might process the series as classed together with or without analytics, whereas the second might class each title as a separate. Monographic series received on subscriptions comprise a small part of the total acquisitions. While this will not jeopardize the processing center concept, the investigators concluded that only titles which are processed identically by libraries should be acquired and processed centrally.

7. Markov Chain Model: The generalized mathematical model of the book processing center can be used successfully to describe the operations of a processing center on the basis of probability distributions. In this study, the model was used to predict the unit cost of processing materials and manpower requirements under different situations. Among the variable data inputted were the number of copies ordered, the number of books processed, and delays caused by batching work.

The standardized technical services activities used as the basis for the mathematical model simulations provide data that can be used as the basis for management decisions. The generalized model as developed can be used by other libraries to analyze their technical processing activities. If a library's activities differ from those provided for in the model, the model's structure can be modified easily.

8. User Attitudes: The faculty attitude survey showed that users place a much higher priority on learning what is being acquired by the respective libraries than they do in techniques for transferring data within or among institutions. Based on the results of the attitude survey, it was concluded that the processing center should strive to develop capability for providing specialized bibliographies tailored to meet the needs of individuals, academic departments, or research projects. This type of activity should take precedence over the introduction of methods for transmitting data, i. e., teletype, telefacsimile, etc.

Recommendations

1. It is recommended that a book processing center be established. The processing center should acquire and process both English language and foreign language imprints. During the initial operations, processing should be limited to in-print materials. As experience is gained, processing can be extended to include gift materials and out-of-print titles.

2. It is recommended that a processing charge of $2.65 per volume be established. This charge can be reduced once the effect of multiple copy ordering and processing has been documented.

3. It is recommended that separate fee schedules be developed for English language and foreign materials. This can be accomplished during the trial period of operation.

4. It is recommended that the inter-institutional courier service be expanded once processing operations begin. The circuit should include Colorado State University, Colorado State College, the University of Colorado at Boulder and the Denver Center, Metropolitan State College, and the Colorado School of Mines.

Transportation of materials to and from Adams State College can be accomplished more economically by using available commercial transportation.

5. It is recommended that the two university libraries continue the operation of their approval plans. The approval plans should be investigated further to develop more effective methods for the handling and processing of approval materials received by the

institutions which maintain such plans.

6. It is recommended that the college libraries continue ordering materials on a title-by-title basis until the selection criteria for approval plans are sharpened to insure that only needed titles will be acquired.

7. It is recommended that the processing center begin immediately to develop an automated bookkeeping system that will provide the participating libraries with regular financial statements which show outstanding encumbrances, expenditures, outstanding balances, and the state of internal departmental library allocations. The bookkeeping system must also meet all fiscal regulations as established by the State Office of Accounts and Controls.

8. It is recommended that automated procedures be developed that will produce spine labels, book card labels, and book pocket labels and shipping lists. Further, the automated procedures developed as part of the processing center should be compatible with national programs such as the Library of Congress' MARC II Program.

9. It is recommended that procedures be developed to permit the processing center to produce current awareness bibliographies utilizing the data in machine readable form supplied by the Library of Congress. Such a program can be developed without requiring a large expenditure for hardware or software. Procedures should be developed to utilize the data only for those materials acquired by the center. Other data should not be stored in anticipation of acquiring materials unless or until this method is deemed economically feasible.

10. It is recommended that the Resources and Technical Services Division of the American Library Association create a central depository of standard times for performing technical services activities. Only by accumulating standard times like those developed as part of the current investigation will the library profession develop a basis for comparison of time and cost data. Standard times developed as part of the current study are reasonably precise and appear satisfactory for the purposes intended. However, it is recognized that in some instances, where times represent entire sub-procedures such as claiming or handling cancellations, more precise

times can be developed by sub-dividing these procedures further. A dictionary of standard times must include precise definitions of what each task includes so that resulting times can be compared realistically, and only those times which are comparable should be used in a given situtation.

Bibliography

Published

American Library Association. Resources and Technical Services Division, Regional Processing Committee "Guidelines for centralized technical services." Library Resources and Technical Services 10(2):233-240, Spring 1966.

Barber, A. Stephanie "A critical review of the surveys of scientists' use of libraries." In Saunders, W. L., ed. The Provision and Use of Library and Documentation Services. Oxford, 1966, p. 145-79.

Barnes, Ralph M. Motion and time study: design and measurement of work. ed. 5. New York, J. Wiley, 1963.

Bowker annual of library and book trade information, 1967. New York, R. R. Bowker, 1967.

Branscomb, Lewis C. "The Ohio College Library Center." The Rub-Off 18(2):6, March-April 1967.

Bundy, Mary Lee "Behind central processing." Library Journal 88:3539-3543, October 1, 1963.

Catalogers (LC) "Eleven college libraries in beautiful Finger Lakes area beginning cooperative processing center" (classified advertisement). Library Journal 93(2):214, January 15, 1968.

Choice: Books for college libraries, March 1966 - February 1968.

Cochran, W. G. Sampling techniques. New York, Wiley, 1963.

The College blue book, ed. 12. Los Angeles, College Planning Programs, Ltd., 1968.

"Colorado academic librarians to get central processing." Library Journal 92:956, 964-965, March 1, 1967.

Columbia University, Bureau of Applied Social Science, Research (Project Leader: Herbert Menzell). Review of studies in the flow of information among scientists. New York, The Bureau, 1960.

Council on Library Resources "Grant to New England Board of Higher Education to help six-state, inter-university library cataloging project." Recent developments, no. 216, February 1, 1967.

Dewey, Melvil "Co-operative cataloging." Library Journal 1(4-5): 170-175, January 1877.

Dewey, Melvil "Printed catalog cards from a central bureau." Library, 2nd Series 2(5):130-134, January 1901.

Dewey, Melvil Statement made at the Converence of Librarians, Philadelphia, 1876, reported in Library Journal 1:118, November 1876.

Dougherty, Richard M. "A central processing center for Colorado Academic Libraries." The Colorado Academic Library 3(3, 4): 4-6, Summer and Fall 1966.

Dougherty, Richard M. and Fred J. Heinritz Scientific management of library operations. New York, Scarecrow, 1966, p. 113.

Feinler, E. J., C. J. Cook, O. Heinz and C. P. Bourne "Attitudes of scientists toward a specialized information center." American Documentation 16:329-333, October, 1965.

Freund, John E. Modern elementary statistics, ed. 2. Prentice-Hall, 1960, p. 220.

Fristoe, Ashby "Bitter end; the searching process." Library Resources and Technical Services 10:91-95, Winter 1966.

Gardner, Richard K. "Choice: Books for College Libraries, its origin, development, and future plans." Southeastern Librarian 15(1):69-75, Spring 1965.

A guide to graduate study; programs leading to the Ph. D. degree. Washington, D. C., American Council on Education, 1967.

Hendricks, Donald D. Comparative costs of book processing in a processing center and in five individual libraries. Springfield, Ill., Illinois State Library, May 1966, 89 p.

Herner, Saul and M. Herner "Information needs and uses in science and technology." In Cuadra, Carlos A., ed. Annual Review of Information Science and Technology. New York, 1967, p. 1-34.

Hunt, James R. "The historical development of processing centers in the United States." Library Resources and Technical Services 8(1):54-62, Winter 1964.

Jewett, Charles C. "A plan for stereotyping catalogs by separate titles; and for forming a general stereotyped catalog of public libraries in the United States." In: Proceedings of the American Association for the Advancement of Science, 1850 4:165-176, S. F. Baird, 1851.

Jewett, Charles C. Smithsonian Report on the Construction of Catalogues of Libraries ... Washington, Smithsonian Institution, 1852, 78 p.

Kemeny, John George and James Laurie Snell Finite Markov chains. Princeton, N. J., Van Nostrand, 1960.

Kish, L. Survey sampling. New York, Wiley, 1965.

Leonard, Lawrence E. "Cooperative and centralized cataloging and processing: a bibliography, 1850-1967." University of Illinois Graduate School of Library Science, Occasional Papers, No. 93. Urbana, July 1968, 89 p.

Line, Maurice B. and Mavis Tidmarsh "Student attitudes to the university library: a second survey at Southampton University." Journal of Documentation 22:123-135, June 1966.

Arthur D. Little, Inc. "A plan for a library processing center for the State University of New York." Report to the Office of Educational Communications, State University of New York. (Rept. C-69541), November 1967, 127 p.

Merritt, LeRoy Charles "Are we selecting or collecting?" Library Resources and Technical Services 12:140-142, Spring 1968.

Miller, Robert A. "Cost accounting for libraries: acquisition and cataloging." Library Quarterly 7:511-536, October 1937.

Moore, Everett L. "Processing center for California junior college libraries--a preliminary study." Library Resources and Technical Services 9(3):303-317, Summer 1965.

Morrison, Perry D. "A symposium on approval order plans and the book selection responsibilities of librarians." Library Resources and Technical Services 12:133-139, Spring 1968.

Mullen, Evelyn Day "Guidelines for establishing a centralized library processing center." Library Resources and Technical Services 2(3):171-175, Summer 1968.

Mundel, Marvin E. Motion and time study: principles and practice. ed. 3. Englewood Cliffs, N. J., Prentice-Hall, 1960.

Nelson Associates, Inc. Feasibility of school and college library processing through public library systems in New York State. New York, Nelson Associates, 1966.

Oehlerts, Donald E. A study to determine the feasibility of establishing a cooperative technical processing program and direct transmission of Interlibrary loans. Denver, Colo., Association of State Institutions of Higher Education in Colorado, 1962.

Oller, Kathryn "A time study of the Urbana (Illinois) Free Library." University of Illinois Library School, Occasional Papers, no. 16., November 1950, 11 p.

Pearson, E. S. "Random sampling numbers." Tracts for Computors, no. XXIV. Department of Statistics, University College, University of London.

Reichmann, Felix "Costs of cataloging." Library Trends 2:290-317, October 1953.

Rider, Fremont "Library cost accounting." Library Quarterly 6: 331-381, October 1936.

Schultheiss, Louis A., Don S. Culbertson and Edward M. Heiliger Advanced data processing in the university library. New York, Scarecrow, 1962.

Shepard, Stanley A. "Approval books on a small budget." Library Resources and Technical Services 12:144-145, Spring 1968.

"Study on centralization." Library Resources and Technical Services 10(1):50, Winter 1966.

The Suffolk Cooperative Library System. Descriptive brochure, 1967, 8 p.

Swank, R. C. "The Bibliographical Center for Research, Rocky Mountain Region, Inc., report of a survey." Denver, Colo., 1966.

Tauber, Maurice F. and associates Technical services in libraries. New York, Columbia University Press, 1953.

U. S. Office of Education Earned degrees conferred, 1964-65. Washington, D. C., U. S. Government Printing Office, 1967, p. 256-265.

Wilson, Louis Round "The next fifty years." Library Journal 61: 255-260, 1936.

Wright, W. E. "Review (of Colorado College and Head Librarians Conference. Special Committee on Centralized Technical Processes and Book Buying)." Library Journal 68:244, March 15, 1943.

Wulfekoetter, Gertrude Acquisitions work: processes involved in building library collections. Seattle, Wash., University of Washington Press, 1961.

Wynar, Bohdan S. and Harold R. Malinowsky, eds. Cost analysis study, Technical Services Division, University of Denver Library. University of Denver Graduate School of Librarianship,

Studies in Librarianship, no. 4, 1965.

Unpublished

American Library Association. Resources and Technical Services Division, Regional Processing Committee. "Regional processing centers; a preliminary list." July 1, 1966; revised to Spring 1967, 8 p.

California. State Library. Memorandum from Mrs. Carma Leigh, dated June 27, 1967; subject: Automated center for cooperative cataloging and serials control to be established at California State Library. 2 p.

California State Colleges. Committee of Library Development. Second report to the Chancellor. "Recommendations for the support of California state college libraries." December 1965.

Colorado College and Head Librarians Conference. Special Committee on Centralized Technical Processes and Book Buying. _First Report,_ August 1942. _Second Report,_ February 1943.

Dougherty, Richard M. and Lawrence Leonard _Colorado Bibliographic Exchange and Communications Network; Project BEACON, an Overview._ Boulder, University of Colorado Libraries, 1967. 13 p.

Ellsworth, Ralph E. and Richard M. Dougherty _A proposal to National Science Foundation for support of development of an Academic Libraries Cooperative Processing Center for all Colorado colleges and universities._ Stage I: Design of the system. Proposal 65. 5. 242 as revised March, July 1966.

Gregory, L. H. "Xerox card production, cost breakdown per card." Typewritten manuscript, 1967. 5 p.

Hewitt, Joe, Head, Catalog Maintenance Unit, University of Colorado. Typewritten manuscript of results of time in process study completed November 28, 1966. 2 p.

Renfro, Kay "Analysis of Approval Plans at the University of Nebraska Libraries, 1966-1967." Lincoln, University of Nebraska Libraries, July 13, 1967. Typewritten manuscript. 17 p.

Voos, Henry "Standard times for certain clerical activities in technical processing." Ph. D. Thesis, Rutgers, The State University, New Brunswick, N. J., 1964. p. 94.

Appendix 3. 1
Colorado Academic Libraries Book Processing Center
Second Period of Diary Study

Note: All individuals who previously filled out a Daily Time-Function Record are asked to keep this record for a second (and final) five-day period (five completed forms from each participant). If the above named individual has left the library or should he be on an extended leave, assign the forms to an individual performing comparable duties.

Function numbers have been slightly revised for the second study period to be conducted 17-21 July 1967 or as soon afterward as possible, should participant be on vacation during this period. The first study's function numbers have been retained as originally listed. However, some decimal-like numbers have been added to include functions omitted from the first list. These additional numbers should cover many of the items which were handled as "other functions" during the first study.

Please discard all explanatory material from the first study and examine the key functions in the attached list before beginning the second study. When you have completed five forms, return the forms to your Library Administrative Office for forwarding to the project.

Thank you for your excellent cooperation.

Daily Time - Function Record

Each library is asked to keep a record of the amount of time spent in performing regularly assigned functions in technical services during a second five-day period. Through use of this daily record, and through timed observations taken by a member of the study team, an average (mean) performance time will be determined, and the unit cost of acquiring, cataloging and processing a title will be calculated for each member library.

Procedure to follow in completing daily record:

1. Print or type information requested at the top of the form (date, library, department, name and position).
2. Write the number of the function performed in the appropriate hour space under column headed "Function Key." Select the number from the Revised Key to Functions Performed, and write this number as each different function is begun. If several functions are normally combined in the library, indicate the number of each in the combined process under the "function" column.
3. Separate one distinct function from another by drawing a horizontal line through both the "function key" and "number items handled" columns (under the appropriate hour), indicating to the nearest minute the end of one function and the beginning of another (see attached sample).
4. Write in the "number items handled" column the number of items processed or handled during the time indicated for that particular function (i. e., number of multiple order forms typed, books cataloged, cards typed, slips or cards filed, cards revised, etc.).

The lunch hour is not included in the Daily Record; only hours 8:00 a. m. to 12 noon, and 1:00 to 5:00 p. m. If work schedule is other than 8:00 - 5:00, consider the columns as 1st through 8th hour of work.

An estimate of time spent in keeping the Daily Record should be indicated on each daily form (Function 48). Excluding the involvement in recording activity time and number of items processed in this time, the time study periods should reflect normal daily work activity, working at a normal pace.

One number is provided in the Revised Key to Functions Performed in each of the three areas outlined to specify activities not listed (Acquisitions: Number 16; Cataloging: Number 39; General Activities: Number 47). Should a function be performed which is not in the list, record the "other" number for the appropriate area in the "function'' column on the Daily Record and write a brief description of the activity performed on the back of the form.

Please send all completed daily sheets at the end of the time study to:

Lawrence E. Leonard, Project Director
Colorado Academic Libraries Book Processing Center
University of Colorado
Norlin Library, Room 9
Boulder, Colorado 80302

Thank you for your cooperation.

Appendix 3. 1
Colorado Academic Libraries Book Processing Center
Daily Time - Function Record

Library ______________________________

Department ___________________________

Minutes	Function Key	Number Items Handled	Function Key	Number Items Handled	Function Key	Number Items Handled	Function Key
Hour	8:00		9:00		10:00		11:00
05							
10							
15							
20							
25							
30							
35							
40							
45							
50							
55							
60							

Record in the appropriate time space the number of items handled or processed while performing one function. If work schedule is other than 8:00 a. m. - 5:00 p. m., consider the columns as 1st through 8th hour of work.

Date ________________

Name ______________________________

Position ____________________________

Number Items Handled	Func-tion Key	Number Items Handled	Func-tion Key	Number Items Handled	Func-tion Key	Number Items Handled	Func-tion Key	Number Items Handled
	1:00		2:00		3:00		4:00	

Appendix 3. 2
Standardized Technical Processing Activities
Scope of Functions Performed

I. Acquisitions

A. Preliminary Activities

1. Open, sort and distribute incoming mail:
Mail is opened and sorted into like items (publishers advertisements, catalogs, book requests, invoices, incoming books, serials, etc.), and distributed to appropriate processing point.

2a. Review book order requests:
Book order requests are examined to determine their bibliographic completeness, their suitability to the scope of the collection, and the status of the funds against which they will be charged. Book order requests satisfy specific information needs and build the collection in departmental areas.

2b. Review selection media:
Selection media are periodically reviewed to identify new titles which should be added to the collection. Placement of orders by review of selection media satisfies the general subject scope of the collection.

3. Select titles to be ordered:
Titles which satisfy departmental or general interests are selected for order placement, within budgetary limitations.

4. Type library order request card:
Typist prepares library order request card from bibliographic information supplied by the requester. Information may be sent in the form of publishers flyers, brochures, handwritten request lists, catalogs, bibliographies, etc. A single order request card is typed or handwritten for each title selected. Libraries frequently supply order request cards to each academic department, with instructions for orders placement. They can then use the request card completed by the department rather than duplicate work with a separate typing.

B. Bibliographic Searching - Checking

5. Search and verify bibliographic information:
Requests are searched: (1) To establish entry, complete missing bibliographic information, and determine availability of title and LC copy through _Cumulative Book Index_, _National Union Catalog_, _Books in Print_, _Book Publishing Record_,

card catalog, etc.; (2) to determine possible duplication of title, through card catalog and outstanding order file.

Different libraries perform differing levels of searching/verification. Some are primarily interested in verifying form of entry, some want to establish price and others will not place the order until the complete citation has been verified.

C. Orders Placement

6. Assign vendor and fund:
Librarian designates dealer or publisher with whom an order will be placed, and indicates the fund to be encumbered.

7. Prepare multiple order record:
Typist completes multiple-order form for each title ordered, following oral or written instructions for each group of orders. Multiple order form may also be xeroxed or otherwise reproduced.

8. Type purchase requisition, etc.:
Typist prepares requisition or order, either in ordering a group of titles (initial order), or as a confirming request for payment for materials already received.

9a. Revise typing:
Librarian examines typed orders, noting that information is accurately typed and is complete.

9b. Sign and mail requests:
Requests are signed, appropriate vendor copies are placed in addressed envelopes and orders are mailed to assigned vendor or publisher.

10. Burst forms:
All forms are separated and sorted for distribution. Order forms prepared by xerox or other reproduction are cut apart and sorted for distribution.

11. File forms in appropriate files:
Sorted forms are filed in designated files; i.e., outstanding orders file, purchase requisition or order file, fund file, etc.

12. Encumbrance or prepayment routine:
Encumbrance entry is made in ledger under appropriate fund for each title ordered. If library budgetary records are calculated on unit record equipment, an encumbrance card(s) is keypunched from order record information.

Appendix 3. 2 (continued)

D. Receiving, Billing

13a. Unpack books; check against packing list or invoice: Packages containing books are opened, books are arranged for checking, and checked against packing slip and/or invoice. Incoming books are screened to determine which need special handling.

13b. Check outstanding order file: Outstanding order file slips are pulled, or date of receipt of book is noted on the slip which remains in order file until processing is completed.

14. Check in serials on Kardex: Serials are separated from the other titles and are entered in the Kardex records before further processing.

15. Collate books: Book is examined page by page to determine whether signatures have been properly bound and print is clear.

16. Book return procedure (incorrect shipment, defective copy, approval books): Books which have been incorrectly supplied, approval books not selected, and defective copies are prepared for return shipment to the supplying source.

17. Book accessioning routine: Accession number is stamped on book for positive identification of individual title. Number may be stamped or otherwise recorded on one or more records as aid in identification, and in slipping charge cards. Formal accessions record (ledger) may be maintained in which accessions number, author, title, publisher, date, order source, price, etc., are recorded for each item accessioned. Informal accessions record may be in form of notebook of invoices or order slips stamped with accessions number.

18. Write sourcing information: Information on source of order is written in each book, usually on the page following the verso of the title page: (1) Copy number of book; (2) date of receipt of book in library; (3) source of order (vendor or publisher); (4) list price of book.

19. Prepare gift record form: A gift record is prepared for each book given the library which is added to the collection. (Note: A library order request card, or multiple order record may be typed, depending upon how many copies of the record the library

requires in processing gift materials.)

20. Book distribution routine:
A process form may be prepared to be routed with each title. Books are forwarded to the Cataloging Department, or placed in a holding area, depending upon available copy and processing treatment.

21. Prepare receiving report:
A report is prepared certifying receipt of materials for which payment is requested.

22. Prepare invoices for payment:
Invoices are checked to insure that all titles listed on the invoice have been received. Any discrepancies (incorrect shipment, defective copy, etc.) are noted, necessary changes are made, and the invoice is certified for payment, either through preparation of a receiving report or by signature of the librarian on the invoice itself. Forms are sent to the Business Office for payment.

23. Expenditure routine:
Expenditure amounts are posted under appropriate titles and funds in the ledger (or an expenditure card is keypunched for each title paid). Fund encumbrance and expenditure data are maintained on current basis on a ledger or on punched cards. Periodic reports are distributed to academic departments for which library maintains records, and to Purchasing or Fiscal Office. Credit memos are accounted for.

E. Post-Cataloging

24. Clear in-process file:
Order slips are pulled from outstanding orders file when Acquisitions receives notification from Cataloging that title is completely processed, and is ready for circulation.

25. File forms, etc., in completed records or discard:
Prepare forms used in the order process are filed in required completed orders files, or are discarded when removed from the in-process files.

26. Requester notification routine:
Requester is notified that title is processed and is ready for circulation.

27. Periodic accessions list routine:
A list of selected or total recent acquisitions is prepared on a periodic basis, and sent to faculty members.

F. Miscellaneous Activities

28. Vendor status routine:

Write dealers reply on order form in outstanding order file; pull order form if dealer has cancelled order, or if library wants to cancel.

29. Claims routine:
Order files are periodically searched to locate orders which have been outstanding beyond the established period for claims. Form letters are prepared (or multiform slips are reproduced) and mailed to the ordering source, requesting explanation of delay in receiving requested material.

30. Cancellations routine:
Orders which the source can not supply are cancelled, with possible placement to another source (dealer, publisher, out-of-print dealer). Appropriate forms are pulled from all in-process files at time of cancellation, reason noted, and determination made of desirability of a re-order.

31. Out-of-print order routine:
Desired out-of-print materials may be ordered through an out-of-print dealer or advertised in a publication such as the *Antiquarian Bookman* or the *Library Bookseller* (*TAAB*). A letter is prepared for either purpose and mailed to the source. A request form is typed for each title ordered and filed in the in-process file.

32. Process inquiries:
Answer specific inquiries from requester regarding status of an order in process; general inquiries concerning status of in-process order noted in public catalog by patron; general inquiries regarding bibliographic information, i. e., author, title, date of publication, publisher, price, etc.

33. General typing - correspondence, etc. (specify):
Acquisitions typing not noted above is included here: e. g., general correspondence to publishers, dealers or colleagues; request for price quotations; exchange or gift lists; etc.

34. General revision (specify):
Acquisitions revision not noted above is included here: e. g., revision of letters typed in corresponding with dealers, publishers, colleagues, etc.; revision of prepared lists; revision of other tasks performed by Acquisitions personnel.

35. General filing (specify):
Acquistions filing not noted above is included here.

G. Other Acquisitions Activities

36. Other acquisitions activities not listed above (specify): Use this number for processes in the Acquisitions Department which are not included in activities 1-35.

II. Cataloging

A. Pre-Cataloging

37. Sort books, assign and distribute: Books delivered from the Acquisitions Department are sorted into categories for processing: i. e., added volumes, added copies, books with LC copy, books for which LC cards/copy must be searched, original cataloging, etc. Books are placed on book trucks and distributed to the appropriate processing area.

38. Search for LC copy; verify bibliographic information: Additional searching is done to verify bibliographic data and to locate LC copy or copy closely approximating titles to be cataloged.

39. Order LC cards or other unit cards: Cards to be ordered are determined, order is prepared (multiple-form LC slip, or preprinted, typed LC order), LC or other unit card order (Wilson cards, etc.) is sent, and interim (outstanding) order slip is filed. Unit cards are frequently ordered at the time orders for new titles are placed.

40. Receive and arrange LC cards: Upon receipt of cards, LC interim order slip is pulled, LC cards are sorted, and matched, or held for filing (and later matching with incoming books).

41. Receive and arrange LC proof slips or proof sheets: Upon receipt of proof slips, slips are examined, sorted and matched with books or held for filing. Proof sheets are examined, cut apart, sorted, and matched with books or held for filing.

42. File LC copy (cards or proof): LC copy is sorted (unless received pre-sorted) and filed as it is received.

43. Match LC cards or proof copy and books: Upon receipt of both book and LC card set, a match is accomplished through systematic, periodic check of both book holding shelves and LC card holdings drawers, or a proof copy is pulled.

44. Added copies/added volumes routine:

The main entry and shelf list cards are pulled, added copies or volumes are entered on these records (also the kardex record in some cases), and the books are then ready for physical processing.

B. LC Cataloging

45. Catalog and classify with LC cards/copy:
LC cards or copy are compared with book to insure that cards match the book in question. Titles are classified (LC or Dewey Decimal), entries may be checked in the public catalog, subjects established, and modifications made, if necessary. Call number is written inside the book.

C. Original Cataloging

46. Original cataloging and classifying:
Cataloger performs descriptive cataloging, subject analysis, classification, and authority work (i. e. , name subject, etc.) for titles for which no LC copy is available. Cataloger prepares a work slip or work sheet to be used in typing copy for catalog card reproduction.

47. Shelf listing (for 44, 45 and 46):
The shelf list is examined to prevent duplicate assignment of a call number. A temporary shelf list slip/card is prepared and filed to reserve the call number while the book is being processed, and before a permanent shelf list card is prepared and filed.

D. Card Reproduction and Processing

48. Type complete card sets:
Complete card sets are typed; or additional cards are typed as required to complete card sets.

49. Type master card:
A master card is typed, to be used in reproducing sets of unit cards by electrostatic or photoreproductive processes. A complete set of catalog cards may be typed in lieu of reproducing the set.

50. Revise master card:
Master card is proofread to correct any typing errors. If a complete set of catalog cards is typed, each card must be examined for errors.

51. Type modification on a card or proof slip:
Close copy is modified, if little moddification is required. Modified copy then serves as master card for reproduction

of card sets.

52a. Reproduce card sets (other than typing):
Some method of card reproduction is used to duplicate a set of catalog cards from each master card typed.

52b. Sort cards into sets:
Reproduced cards are sorted into sets after reproduction (and cutting, if necessary).

53. Type call number, added entries:
Call number is typed on cards in the set; established added entries are typed at top of cards in the set; shelf list card is typed.

54. Revise typing on card sets:
Cards are revised to verify accuracy of typing, both of call number and added entries.

55. Prepare authority cards:
Authority cards are typed or otherwise prepared as necessary for authority files mentioned.

56. Prepare cross-reference cards:
Cross-reference cards are typed or otherwise prepared as new subject (and corporate) entries are established, and emphasis on established subjects changes.

E. Mechanical Book Processing

57. Prepare circulation card:
A circulation charge card(s) is typed or prepared for all books processed into the library's circulating collection.

58. Prepare book pocket:
Identifying bibliographic elements may be typed on the book pocket; or adhesive label containing elements may be attached to the pocket.

59. Mark call number or place label on spine of volume:
Call number is hand lettered or otherwise placed on the spine of a book (through use of self-adhesive labels, commerical labeling machines, etc.). Special location designation strips and symbols are affixed to spine.

60. Affix pocket and date due slip. Affix gift plate:
Book card pocket is glued into book in a predetermined position. Date due slip is tipped in. Gift plate is pasted in book in a fixed position.

61. Affix biographical and review material in book:
Biographical material about the book's author, and significant reviews found on dust jacket are clipped and pasted in book.

62. Stamp property marks:
The library's identifying stamp is placed on the book at several fixed locations (i. e. , edge stamp, title page, secret page, etc.).

63. Affix plastic jacket to book:
Plastic jacket is placed over dust cover and affixed to the book.

64. Paperback books--library binding routine:
Libraries equipped for "home binding" may bind paper-back books or place plastic covers or jackets on them.

65. Revise completed books before forwarding to circulation:
Completely processed books are checked to insure accuracy of typing and processing.

F. Card Filing

66. Sort and alphabetize shelf list and all catalog cards:
Cards (shelf list, main catalog, authority, cross-reference, etc.) are arranged in order in which they will be filed.

67. File shelf list and all catalog cards:
Cards are filed in the shelf list, public catalog and other files following library's rules for systematic arrangement of card files.

68. Revise filing of shelf list and all catalog cards:
Filing is checked to insure its accuracy; corrections are made where necessary.

G. Miscellaneous Activities

69. Route card sets to departmental libraries:
Card sets for departmental libraries are identified in the sorting process after card reproduction. Card sets are placed in containers and routed through campus mail (or U. S. mail for off-campus departments or library branches).

70. Paperback books--bindery routine (preparation):
Paperback books and other paperbound materials are prepared for shipment to the bindery. Lists of titles may be typed, or order cards filed in bindery control records. Classification and Cutter number may be assigned and shelf listing performed if call number is to be imprinted at bindery.

71. Paperback books--bindery routine (receiving):

Shipment of books from bindery is checked, records are changed to reflect those titles which have been returned, and books readied for processing.

72. Catalog maintenance (other than filing):
Replacement of worn or multilated cards, correction of changed or incorrect entries, etc., is entailed in maintenance of the card catalog.

73. General typing (specify):
Cataloging typing not noted above is included here; e.g., general correspondence, listings, etc.

74. General revision (specify):
Cataloging revision not noted above is included here; e.g., revision of general typing, filing, etc.

75. General filing (specify):
Cataloging filing not noted above is included here.

H. Other Cataloging Activities

76. Other cataloging activities not listed above (specify):
Use this number for processes in the Cataloging Department which are not included in activities 37-75.

Appendix 3. 3
Frequency Computation
Acquisitions

* The use of these functions varied widely.
** Proportions were estimated when no statistics were available

Assumption: Volumes processed entered the system during a given fiscal year.

	Activity Description	Frequency Percentage Formula
1.	Open, sort and distribute incoming mail	1
2.	Review book order requests; review selection media.	titles purchased / volumes processed
3.	Select titles to be ordered.	Same as #2
*4.	Type library order request card.	Same as #2
5.	Search and verify bibliographic information	Same as #2
6.	Assign vendor and fund	Same as #2
7.	Prepare multiple order record.	Same as #2
*8.	Type purchase requisition, etc.	purchase requisitions prepared / volumes processed
9.	Revise typing. Sign and mail requests	Same as #8
10.	Burst forms.	Same as #2
11.	File forms in appropriate files.	Same as #2
12.	Encumbrance or prepayment routine	Same as #2
13.	Unapck books; check against packing list or invoice. Check outstanding order file.	Same as #2 ⟶ 1 (if gifts are handled this way)
14.	Check in serials on Kardex.	added volumes / volumes processed
*15.	Collate books.	0 ⟶ 1
16.	Book return procedure (incorrect shipment, defective copy, approval books).	volumes returned / volumes processed
17.	Book accessioning routine.	0 or 1
*18.	Write sourcing information.	0 or 1
19.	Prepare gift record form.	gift volumes received / volumes processed
20.	Book distribution routine.	1

Activity Description	Frequency Percentage Formula
*21. Prepare receiving report.	Same as #2
22. Prepare invoices for payment.	$\frac{\text{invoices processed}}{\text{volumes processed}}$
23. Expenditure routine.	Same as #22
24. Clear in-process file.	Same as #2 $\longrightarrow$ 1 (if gifts and serials are entered also)
25. File forms, etc., in completed records or discard.	Same as #24
26. Requestor notification routine.	$\frac{\text{titles requested}}{\text{volumes processed}}$
27. Periodic accessions list routine.	0 or 1
28. Vendor status routine.	$\frac{\text{reports processed}}{\text{volumes processed}}$
29. Claims routine.	$\frac{\text{claims sent}}{\text{volumes processed}}$
30. Cancellations routine.	$\frac{\text{orders cancelled}}{\text{volumes processed}}$
31. Out-of-print order routine.	$\frac{\text{out-of-print titles purchased}}{\text{volumes processed}}$
32. Process inquiries.	$\frac{\text{requests handled}}{\text{volumes processed}}$
**33. General typing - correspondence, etc. (specify).	0 $\longrightarrow$ 1
**34. General revision (specify).	0 $\longrightarrow$ 1
**35. General filing (specify).	0 $\longrightarrow$ 1
**36. Other acquisitions activities not listed above (specify).	0 $\longrightarrow$ 1

Appendix 3. 3
Frequency Computation
Cataloging

Activity Description	Frequency Percentage Formula
37. Sort books, assign and distribute.	1
38. Search for LC copy; verify bibliographic information.	$\frac{\text{new titles added}}{\text{volumes processed}}$
*39. Order LC cards or other unit cards.	Same as #38
*40. Receive and arrange LC cards.	Same as #38
*41. Receive and arrange LC proof slips or proof sheets.	0 or 1 (the handling of proof is accomplished independent of the volumes actually processed)
42. File LC copy. (cards or proof)	Same as #2 (for cards) Same as #41 (for proof)

Appendix 3. 3
Frequency Computation
Cataloging (continued)

Activity Description	Frequency Percentage Formula
43. Match LC cards or proof copy and books.	Same as #38
44. Added copies/added volumes routine.	$\frac{\text{added copies} + \text{added volumes}}{\text{volumes processed}}$
45. Catalog and classify with LC cards/copy.	$\frac{\text{titles mass cataloged (or number of LC card sets ordered)}}{\text{volumes processed}}$
46. Original cataloging and classifying.	$\frac{\text{titles originally cataloged}}{\text{volumes processed}}$
47. Shelf listing (for 44, 45 and 46).	1
*48. Type complete card sets.	$\frac{\text{titles originally cataloged}}{\text{volumes processed}}$ ⟶ same as #38
49. Type master card.	Same as #48
*50. Revise master card.	Same as #49
**51. Type modification on a card or proof slip.	$\frac{\text{modifications tallied}}{\text{volumes processed}}$ or 1 (this assumes the modification is on a proof slip of LC card used as a master card)
*52. Reproduce card sets (other than typing). Sort cards into sets.	Same as #38 (assuming typing is never used for reproduction)
53. Type call number, added entries.	Same as #38
54. Revise typing on card sets.	Same as #38
**55. Prepare authority cards.	$\frac{\text{authority cards typed}}{\text{volumes processed}}$
**56. Prepare cross-reference cards.	$\frac{\text{cross-reference cards typed}}{\text{volumes processed}}$
*57. Prepare circulation card.	0 or 1 (if used)
*58. Prepare book pocket.	0 or 1 (if used)
59. Mark call number or place label on spine of volume.	1
60. Affix pocket and date due slip. Affix gift plate.	1
61. Affix biographical and review material in book.	0 or same as #38
62. Stamp property marks.	1 ⟶ number of times per book by local practice
*63. Affix plastic jacket to book.	0 ⟶ 1 depending on local practice

Activity Description	Frequency Percentage Formula
*64. Paperback books--library binding routine.	0 or $\frac{\text{paperbacks homebound}}{\text{volumes processed}}$
65. Revise completed books before forwarding to circulation.	1
66. Sort and alphabetize shelf list and all catalog cards.	$\frac{\text{total cards added}}{\text{volumes processed}}$ = average number of cards per book
67. File shelf list and all catalog cards.	Same as #66
68. Revise filing of shelf list and all catalog cards.	Same as #66
*69. Route card sets to departmental libraries.	$\frac{\text{added copies of volumes sent to departmental libraries}}{\text{volumes processed}}$
*70. Paperback books--bindery routine (preparation).	$\frac{\text{paperbacks commercially bound}}{\text{volumes processed}}$
71. Paperback books--bindery routine (receiving).	Same as #70
72. Catalog maintenance (other than filing).	1
**73. General typing (specify).	$0 \longrightarrow 1$
**74. General revision (specify).	$0 \longrightarrow 1$
**75. General filing (specify).	$0 \longrightarrow 1$
**76. Other cataloging activities not listed above (specify).	$0 \longrightarrow 1$

Appendix 3. 4
Generalized Standard Times Summary
Acquisitions

Activity Description	Normalized			Standardized		
	Low	High	Mean	Low	High	Mean
1. Open, sort and distribute incoming mail.	. 321	1. 348	. 646	. 474	1. 990	. 954
2. Review book order requests; review selection media.	. 472	. 942	. 823	. 697	1. 391	1. 215
3. Select titles to be ordered.	---	---	---			---
4. Type library order request card.	. 675	2. 563	1. 470	. 997	3. 786	2. 171
5. Search and verify bibliographic information.	1. 599	13. 624	4. 274	2. 362	20. 123	6. 313
6. Assign vendor and fund.	. 069	1. 732	. 481	. 102	2. 559	. 711
7. Prepare multiple order record.	. 613	15. 293	2. 800	. 906	22. 590	4. 136
8. Type purchase requisition, etc.	. 352	14. 176	6. 213	. 519	20. 939	9. 177
9. Revise typing. Sign and mail requests.	. 118	1. 679	. 757	. 174	2. 480	1. 118
10. Burst forms.	. 148	3. 746	. 861	. 218	5. 533	1. 272
11. File forms in appropriate files.	. 373	2. 521	1. 523	. 550	3. 724	2. 250
12. Encumbrance or prepayment routine.	. 485	1. 090	. 740	. 716	1. 610	1. 094
13. Unpack books; check against packing list or invoice. Check outstanding order file.	. 654	6. 064	2. 878	. 966	8. 957	4. 252
14. Check in serials on Kardex	. 531	11. 101	4. 398	. 785	16. 398	6. 497
15. Collate books.	. 373	. 884	. 651	. 551	1. 306	. 962
16. Book return procedure (incorrect shipment, defective copy, approval books).	3. 778	6. 032	5. 013	5. 580	8. 910	8. 734

17. Book accessioning routine.	.345	3.403	1.201	.510	5.027	1.774
18. Write sourcing information.	.331	1.005	.678	.489	1.484	1.002
19. Prepare gift record form.	.058	4.662	2.224	.086	6.886	3.286
20. Book distribution routine.	.204	1.165	.616	.302	1.721	.909
21. Prepare receiving report.	1.619	4.021	2.663	2.392	5.940	3.933
22. Prepare invoices for payment.	.361	2.291	.910	.533	3.384	1.344
23. Expenditure routine.	.117	2.866	1.035	.172	4.233	1.529
24. Clear in-process file.	.317	.818	.617	.468	1.208	.912
25. File forms, etc., in completed records or discard.	.406	2.210	1.264	.600	3.265	1.866
26. Requester notification routine.	.028	1.128	.423	.041	1.666	.624
27. Periodic accessions list routine.	.586	10.421	5.964	.866	15.393	8.809
28. Vendor status routine.	1.133	8.076	4.092	1.673	11.929	6.044
29. Claims routine.	3.590	3.590	3.590	5.303	5.303	5.303
30. Cancellations routine.	2.144	6.266	4.473	3.166	9.256	6.608
31. Out-of-print order routine.	2.669	2.808	2.762	3.943	4.148	4.080
32. Process inquiries.	1.529	32.266	10.754	2.258	47.661	15.885
33. General typing - correspondence, etc. (specify).	2.061	16.817	8.213	3.045	24.840	12.132
34. General revision (specify).	.365	4.134	1.818	.540	6.106	2.685
35. General filing (specify).	.226	7.412	2.015	.333	10.948	2.976
36. Other acquisitions activities not listed above (specify).	.241	10.186	6.255	.356	15.046	9.239

Appendix 3.4
Generalized Standard Times Summary
Cataloging

Activity Description	Normalized			Standardized		
	Low	High	Mean	Low	High	Mean
37. Sort books, assign and distribute.	.363	5.139	1.672	.537	7.590	2.470
38. Search for LC copy; verify bibliographic information.	.984	9.318	3.797	1.454	13.764	5.609
39. Order LC cards or other unit cards.	.604	2.805	1.518	.892	4.144	2.243
40. Receive and arrange LC cards.	.450	1.543	1.010	.665	2.279	1.492
41. Receive and arrange LC proof slips or proof sheets.	.188	.617	.392	.278	.912	.579
42. File LC copy. (cards or proof)	.238	.507	.359	.351	.749	.530
43. Match LC cards or proof copy and books.	.167	7.579	1.845	.246	11.195	2.725
44. Added copies/added volumes routine.	2.933	7.489	6.425	4.332	11.063	9.490
45. Catalog and classify with LC cards/copy.	1.586	9.245	6.577	2.342	13.656	9.715
46. Original cataloging and classifying.	12.627	31.669	19.927	18.652	46.778	29.135
47. Shelf listing (for 44, 45 and 46).	1.082	5.181	2.428	1.599	7.653	3.587
48. Type complete card sets.	2.852	5.736	9.294	4.213	8.473	13.728
49. Type master card.	1.539	9.833	3.889	2.273	14.524	5.744
50. Revise master card.	.297	1.140	.694	.439	1.683	1.026
51. Type modification on a card or proof slip.	.170	3.238	1.704	.252	4.783	2.518
52. Reproduce card sets (other than typing). Sort cards into sets.	.495	4.658	2.141	.731	6.880	3.162
53. Type call number, added entries.	.429	5.271	2.802	.634	7.786	4.138
54. Revise typing on card sets.	.109	1.503	.903	.161	2.220	1.334
55. Prepare authority cards.	.584	2.070	1.370	.863	3.058	2.023

56. Prepare cross-reference cards.	.028	3.865	1.812	.041	5.710	2.677
57. Prepare circulation card.	.411	.825	.633	.606	1.219	.934
58. Prepare book pocket.	.477	.851	.640	.705	1.257	.946
59. Mark call number or place label on spine of volume.	.806	2.223	1.438	1.190	3.284	2.124
60. Affix pocket and date due slip. Affix gift plate.	.240	1.111	.506	.354	1.641	.747
61. Affix biographical and review material in book.	.890	1.129	1.009	1.314	1.667	1.491
62. Property stamp.	.162	1.310	.466	.239	1.936	.689
63. Affix plastic jacket to book.	2.595	6.592	4.747	3.833	9.738	7.012
64. Paperback books--library binding routine.	1.529	12.510	4.668	2.258	18.479	6.896
65. Revise completed books before forwarding to circulation.	.122	1.985	.653	.180	2.932	.964
66. Sort and alphabetize shelf list and all catalog cards.	.125	.637	.269	.185	.941	.397
67. File shelf list and all catalog cards.	.470	1.241	.775	.694	1.834	1.145
68. Revise filing of shelf list and all catalog cards.	.145	.865	.379	.214	1.277	.559
69. Route card sets to departmental libraries.	.704	.704	.704	1.040	1.040	1.040
70. Paperback books--bindery routine (preparation).	.848	3.395	2.105	1.253	5.014	3.109
71. Paperback books--bindery routine (receiving).	.754	.829	.799	1.113	1.225	1.180
72. Catalog maintenance (other than filing).	.015	.183	.036	.023	.270	.054
73. General typing (specify).	.350	.350	.350	.517	.517	.517
74. General revision (specify).	.458	1.066	.762	.676	1.574	1.125
75. General filing (specify).	.520	.520	.520	.768	.768	.768
76. Other cataloging activities not listed above (specify).	.900	.900	.900	1.329	1.329	1.329

Appendix 3. 5. 1
Labor (L)
Unit Cost Calculation for Technical Processing Activities

Acquisitions

Library #1

Key:

AF = Another function incorporated this activity at this library.
NA = Not applicable (not performed at this library).
( ) = Simulated data
+ = Standardizing factor (1. 4771)
g_1 = Student Assistant
g_2 = Clerk (full-time)
g_3 = Professional
d = Data taken from the diary.

Activity Description	a	b	c	d	f [+]	g	h	i
	Observed Mean Time	Fre-quency	Adjusted Time	Personal Rating Factor	Standard Time	Cate-gory of Worker	Wage/ Minute	Cost of Activity
1. Open, sort and distribute incoming mail	. 9215 d	1. 0	. 922	1. 10	1. 4981	2	. 0268	. 040
2. Review book order requests; review selection media.	AF	---	---	---	----	-	---	---
3. Select titles to be ordered.	AF	---	---	---	----	-	---	---
4. Type Library order request card.	1. 509	1. 333	2. 011	1. 15	3. 4159	2	. 0268	. 092
5. Search and verify bibliographic information.	3. 077	1. 0	3. 077	1. 15	5. 2269	2	. 0268	. 140
6. Assign vendor and fund.	. 074	1. 0	. 074	1. 20	. 1317	3	. 0815	. 011
7. Prepare multiple order record.	. 998	1. 0	. 998	1. 15	1. 6953	2	. 0268	. 045
8. Type purchase requisition, etc.	. 850	1. 0	. 850	1. 15	1. 4439	2	. 0268	. 039

9. Revise typing. Sign and mail requests.	AF	---	---	---	----	-	---	---
10. Burst forms.	. 241	1. 0	. 241	1. 15	. 4095	2	. 0268	. 011
11. File forms in appropriate files.	1. 172	1. 0	1. 172	1. 13	1. 9563	2	. 0268	. 052
12. Encumbrance or prepayment routine.	. 572	1. 0	. 572	1. 15	. 9716	2	. 0268	. 026
13. Unpack books; check against packing list or invoice. Check outstanding order file.	. 618	1. 0	. 618	1. 15	1. 0498	2	. 0268	. 028
14. Check in serials on Kardex.	NA	---	---	---	----	-	---	---
15. Collate Books	. 605	1. 0	. 605	1. 15	1. 0276	2	. 0268	. 028
16. Book return procedure (incorrect shipment, defective copy, approval books).	(5. 484)	. 013	. 071	1. 10	. 1154	2	. 0268	. 003
17. Book accessioning routine.	. 587	1. 0	. 587	1. 05	. 9105	1	. 0140	. 013
18. Write sourcing information.	. 288	1. 0	. 288	1. 15	. 4892	2	. 0268	. 013
19. Prepare gift record form.	(2. 090)	. 087	. 182	1. 10	. 2957	2	. 0268	. 008
20. Book distribution routine.	AF	---	---	---	----	-	---	---
21. Prepare receiving report.	1. 408	1. 0	1. 408	1. 15	2. 3917	2	. 0268	. 064
22. Prepare invoices for payment.	(. 869)	. 199	. 173	1. 10	. 2811	2	. 0268	. 008
23. Expenditure routine.	. 204	1. 0	. 204	1. 15	. 3465	2	. 0268	. 009
24. Clear in-process file.	. 711	1. 0	. 711	1. 15	1. 2078	2	. 0268	. 032

Appendix 3. 5. 1 (continued)
Acquisitions

Activity Description	a Observed Mean Time	b Fre- quency	c Adjusted Time	d Personal Rating Factor	+ f Standard Time	g Cate- gory of Worker	h Wage/ Minute	i Cost of Activity
25. File forms, etc., in completed records or discard.	. 369 d	1. 0	. 369	1. 10	. 5996	2	. 0268	. 016
26. Requester notification routine.	. 418	1. 0	. 418	1. 17	. 7224	2	. 0268	. 019
27. Periodic accessions list routine.	. 510	1. 0	. 510	1. 15	. 8663	2	. 0268	. 023
28. Vendor status routine.	(3. 871)	. 027	. 105	1. 10	. 1706	2	. 0268	. 005
29. Claims routine.	(3. 264)	. 027	. 088	1. 10	. 1430	2	. 0268	. 004
30. Cancellations routine.	1. 864	. 027	. 050	1. 15	. 0849	2	. 0268	. 002
31. Out-of-print order routine.	(2. 553)	. 010	. 026	1. 10	. 0422	2	. 0268	. 001
32. Process inquiries.	AF	---	---	---	----	-	---	---
33. General typing - correspondence, etc. (specify).	AF	---	---	---	----	-	---	---
34. General revision (specify).	AF	---	---	---	----	-	---	---
35. General filing (specify).	AF	---	---	---	----	-	---	---
36. Other acquisitions activities not [illegible]	AF	---	---	---	----	-	---	---
						Sub-total		. 732

Cataloging

37. Sort books, assign and distribute.	1. 607	1. 0	1. 607	1. 15	2. 7298	3	. 0815	. 222
38. Search for LC copy; verify bibliographic information.	3. 156	1. 0	3. 156	1. 10	5. 1279	2	. 0268	. 137
39. Order LC cards or other unit cards.	NA	---	---	---	----	-	---	---
40. Receive and arrange LC cards.	NA	---	---	---	----	-	---	---
41. Receive and arrange LC proof slips or proof sheets.	. 214	. 1	. 0214	1. 12	. 0355	3	. 0815	. 003
42. File LC copy. (cards or proof)	. 264	. 1	. 0264	. 90	. 0352	1	. 0140	. 001
43. Match LC cards or proof copy and books.	AF	---	---	---	----	-	---	---
44. Added copies/added volumes routine.	6. 580	. 214	1. 408	1. 10	2. 2877	3	. 0815	. 186
45. Catalog and classify with LC cards/copy.	5. 235	. 915	4. 790	1. 10	7. 7828	3	. 0815	. 634
46. Original cataloging and classifying.	15. 781 d	. 085	1. 341	1. 10	2. 1789	3	. 0815	. 178
47. Shelf listing (for 44, 45, and 46).	4. 710	1. 0	4. 710	1. 10	7. 6529	2	. 0268	. 205
48. Type complete card sets.	NA	---	---	---	----	-	---	---
49. Type master card.	2. 033	. 085	. 173	1. 10	. 2811	2	. 0268	. 008
50. Revise master card.	1. 036	. 085	. 088	1. 10	. 1430	2	. 0268	. 004
51. Type modification on a card or proof slip.	AF	---	---	---	----	-	---	---

Appendix 3. 5. 1 (continued)

Cataloging

Activity Description	a Observed Mean Time	b Fre- quency	c Adjusted Time	d Personal Rating Factor	f Standard Time	g Cate- gory of Worker	h Wage/ Minute	i Cost of Activity
52. Reproduce card sets (other than typing). Sort cards into sets.	. 450	1. 0	. 450	1. 10	. 7312	2	. 0268	. 020
53. Type call number, added entries.	1. 644	1. 0	1. 644	1. 10	2. 6712	2	. 0268	. 072
54. Revise typing on card sets.	1. 330	1. 0	1. 330	1. 10	2. 1610	3	. 0815	. 176
55. Prepare authority cards.	NA	---	---	---	----	-	---	---
56. Prepare cross-reference cards.	. 025	. 035	. 001	1. 10	. 0016	2	. 0268	---
57. Prepare circulation card.	. 515	1. 0	. 515	1. 10	. 8368	2	. 0268	. 022
58. Prepare book pocket.	. 678	1. 0	. 678	1. 10	1. 1016	2	. 0268	. 030
59. Mark call number or place label on spine of volume.	2. 021	1. 0	2. 021	1. 10	3. 2837	2	. 0268	. 088
60. Affix pocket and date due slip. Affix gift plate.	. 319	1. 0	. 319	1. 10	5. 1831	2	. 0268	. 139
61. Affix biographical and review material in book.	. 809	. 732	. 592	1. 10	. 9619	3	. 0815	. 078
62. Stamp property marks.	1. 248	1. 0	1. 835	1. 05	1. 9356	1	. 0140	. 027
63. Affix plastic jacket to book.	NA	---	---	---	----	-	---	---

64. Paperback books--library binding routine.	2. 866	. 025	. 072	1. 10	. 1170	1	. 0140	. 002
65. Revise completed books before forwarding to circulation.	1. 002	1. 0	1. 002	1. 15	1. 7021	3	. 0815	. 139
66. Sort and alphabetize shelf list and all catalog cards.	. 579	8. 0	4. 632	1. 10	7. 5261	1	. 0140	. 105
67. File shelf list and all catalog cards.	. 596	8. 0	4. 768	1. 10	7. 7471	1	. 0140	. 109
68. Revise filing of shelf list and all catalog cards.	. 404	8. 0	3. 232	1. 10	5. 2514	1	. 0140	. 074
69. Route card sets to departmental libraries.	NA	---	---	---	----	-	---	---
70. Paperback books--bindery routine (preparation).	1. 255	. 091	. 114	1. 12	. 1886	2	. 0268	. 005
71. Paperback books--bindery routine (receiving).	(. 754)	. 091	. 069	1. 10	. 1121	2	. 0268	. 003
72. Catalog maintenance (other than filing).	. 016	. 732	. 012	1. 10	. 0195	1	. 0140	---
73. General typing (specify).	AF	---	---	---	----	-	---	---
74. General revision (specify).	. 416	. 732	. 305	1. 10	. 4956	2	. 0268	. 013
75. General filing (specify).	AF	---	---	---	----	-	---	---
76. Other cataloging activities not listed above (specify).	AF	---	---	---	----	-	---	---
						Sub-total		2. 680
					Acquisitions			. 732
					Cataloging			2. 680
					Σ L			$ 3. 412

Appendix 3. 5. 2
Labor (L)
Unit Cost Calculation for Technical Processing Activities
Acquisitions

Library #2

Key:
AF = Another function incorporated this activity at this library.
NA = Not applicable (not performed at this library).
( ) = Simulated data.

+ = Standardizing factor (1. 4771)
g_1 = Student Assistant
g_2 = Clerk (full-time)
g_3 = Professional
d = Data taken from the diary.

Activity Description	a Observed Mean Time	b Fre-quency	c Adjusted Time	d Personal Rating Factor	f + Standard Time	g Cate-gory of Worker	h Wage/ Minute	i Cost of Activity
1. Open, sort and distribute incoming mail.	. 279	1. 000	. 279	1. 15	. 4739	2	. 0272	. 129
2. Review book order requests; review selection media.	(. 856)	1. 000	. 856	1. 10	1. 3908	3	. 0874	. 122
3. Select titles to be ordered.	AF	----	---	---	---	-	---	---
4. Type library order request card.	. 641	1. 038	. 665	1. 10	1. 0805	1	. 0233	. 025
5. Search and verify bibliographic information.	2. 359	1. 000	2. 359	1. 10	3. 8329	1	. 0233	. 089
6. Assign vendor and fund.	(. 475)	1. 000	. 475	1. 10	. 7718	3	. 0874	. 068
7. Prepare multiple order record.	. 687	1. 000	. 687	1. 10	1. 1162	2	. 0272	. 030
8. Type purchase requisition, etc.	3. 676	. 013	. 048	1. 10	. 0780	2	. 0272	. 002

9.	Revise typing. Sign and mail requests.	.828	.013	.011	1.10	.0179	2	.0272	.001
10.	Burst forms.	.193	1.000	.193	1.10	.3136	2	.0272	.008
11.	File forms in appropriate files.	1.456	1.000	1.456	1.10	2.3657	2	.0272	.064
12.	Encumbrance or prepayment routine.	NA	---	---	---	---	-	---	---
13.	Unpack books; check against packing list or invoice. Check outstanding order file.	1.776	1.000	1.776	1.10	2.8857	1	.0233	.067
14.	Check in serials on Kardex.	NA	---	---	---	---	-	---	---
15.	Collate books.	NA	---	---	---	---	-	---	---
16.	Book return procedure (incorrect shipment, defective copy, approval books).	(5.484)	.002	.011	1.10	.0179	2	.0272	.001
17.	Book accessioning routine.	.314	1.000	.314	1.10	.5102	1	.0233	.012
18.	Write sourcing information.	NA	---	---	---	---	-	---	---
19.	Prepare gift record form.	(2.090)	.003	.006	1.10	.0097	2	.0272	---
20.	Book distribution routine.	.270	1.000	.270	1.10	.4387	1	.0233	.010
21.	Prepare receiving report.	1.765	1.000	1.765	1.10	2.8678	2	.0272	.078
22.	Prepare invoices for payment.	.658	.013	.009	1.10	.0146	2	.0272	---
23.	Expenditure routine.	AF	---	---	---	---	-	---	---
24.	Clear in-process file.	AF	---	---	---	---	-	---	---

Appendix 3. 5. 2 (continued)

Acquisitions

	a	b	c	d	f	g	h	i
Activity Description	Observed Mean Time	Fre-quency	Adjusted Time	Personal Rating Factor	Standard Time	Cate-gory of Worker	Wage/ Minute	Cost of Activity
25. File forms, etc., in completed records or discard.	NA	---	---	---	---	-	---	---
26. Requester notification routine.	.139	1.000	.139	1.10	.2258	2	.0272	.006
27. Periodic accessions list routine.	(5.715)	1.000	5.715	1.10	9.2858	2	.0272	.253
28. Vendor status routine.	4.166 d	.065	.271	1.10	.4403	1	.0233	.010
29. Claims routine.	AF	---	---	---	---	-	---	---
30. Cancellations routine.	AF	---	---	---	---	-	---	---
31. Out-of-print order routine.	NA	---	---	---	---	-	---	---
32. Process inquiries.	6.875 d	.027	.186	1.10	.3022	3	.0874	.026
33. General typing - correspondence, etc. (specify).	AF	---	---	---	---	-	---	---
34. General revision (specify).	NA	---	---	---	---	-	---	---
35. General filing (specify).	.855	.021	.018	1.10	.0292	2	.0272	.001
36. Other acquistions activities not listed above (specify).	NA	---	---	---	---	-	---	---
						Sub-total		1.002

	Cataloging							
37. Sort books, assign and distribute.	(1. 738)	1. 000	1. 738	1. 10	2. 8239	1	. 0233	. 066
38. Search for LC copy; verify bibliographic information.	1. 400	1. 000	1. 400	1. 10	2. 2747	1	. 0233	. 053
39. Order LC cards or other unit cards.	NA	---	---	---	---	-	---	---
40. Receive and arrange LC cards.	NA	---	---	---	---	-	---	---
41. Receive and arrange LC proof slips or proof sheets.	NA	---	---	---	---	-	---	---
42. File LC copy. (cards or proof)	NA	---	---	---	---	-	---	---
43. Match LC cards or proof copy and books.	AF	---	---	---	---	-	---	---
44. Added copies/added volumes routine.	(6. 736)	. 036	. 242	1. 10	. 3932	2	. 0272	. 011
45. Catalog and classify with LC cards/copy.	6. 065	. 815	4. 943	1. 15	8. 2266	3	. 0874	. 719
46. Original cataloging and classifying.	17. 454 d	. 148	2. 583	1. 10	4. 1969	3	. 0874	. 367
47. Shelf listing (for 44, 45, and 46).	AF	---	---	---	---	-	---	---
48. Type complete card sets.	NA	---	---	---	---	-	---	---
49. Type master card.	1. 306	. 963	1. 258	1. 25	2. 3227	2	. 0272	. 063
50. Revise master card.	AF	---	---	---	---	-	---	---
51. Type modification on a card or proof slip.	AF	---	---	---	---	-	---	---

Appendix 3. 5. 2 (continued)

Cataloging

Activity Description	a Observed Mean Time	b Fre- quency	c Adjusted Time	d Personal Rating Factor	+ f Standard Time	g Cate- gory of Worker	h Wage/ Minute	i Cost of Activity
52. Reproduce card sets (other than typing). Sort cards into sets.	1. 529	. 963	1. 472	1. 22	2. 6526	1	. 0233	. 062
53. Type call number, added entries.	. 980	. 815	---	1. 25	1. 4753	2	. 0272	. 040
54. Revise typing on card sets.	(. 904)	. 963	. 871	1. 10	1. 4152	3	. 0874	. 124
55. Prepare authority cards.	NA	---	---	---	---	-	---	---
56. Prepare cross-reference cards.	(1. 946)	. 002	. 004	1. 10	. 0065	2	. 0272	---
57. Prepare circulation card.	. 370	1. 000	. 370	1. 25	. 6832	2	. 0272	. 019
58. Prepare book pocket.	. 557	1. 000	. 557	1. 25	1. 0284	2	. 0272	. 028
59. Mark call number or place label on spine of volume.	. 655	1. 000	. 655	1. 23	1. 1900	2	. 0272	. 032
60. Affix pocket and date due slip. Affix gift plate.	. 367	1. 000	. 367	1. 23	. 6668	2	. 0272	. 018
61. Affix biographical and review material in book.	AF	---	---	---	---	-	---	---
62. Stamp property marks.	. 207	1. 000	. 207	1. 10	. 3363	1	. 0233	. 008
63. Affix plastic jacket to book.	NA	---	---	---	---	-	---	---
64. Paperback books--library binding routine.	NA	---	---	---	---	-	---	---

65. Revise completed books before forwarding to circulation.	.327	1.000	.327	1.15	.5555	3	.0874	.049
66. Sort and alphabetize shelf list and all catalog cards.	.197	6.000	1.182	1.20	2.0951	1	.0233	.049
67. File shelf list and all catalog cards.	.933	6.000	5.598	1.17	9.6746	2	.0272	.263
68. Revise filing of shelf list and all catalog cards.	.126	6.000	.756	1.15	1.2842	2	.0272	.035
69. Route card sets to departmental libraries.	NA	---	---	---	---	-	---	---
70. Paperback books--bindery routine (preparation).	NA	---	---	---	---	-	---	---
71. Paperback books--bindery routine (receiving).	NA	---	---	---	---	-	---	---
72. Catalog maintenance (other than filing).	.017	.964	.016	1.10	.0260	3	.0874	.002
73. General typing (specify).	NA	---	---	---	---	-	---	---
74. General revision (specify).	NA	---	---	---	---	-	---	---
75. General filing (specify).	NA	---	---	---	---	-	---	---
76. Other cataloging activities not listed above (specify).	NA	---	---	---	---	-	---	---
							Sub-total	2.008
					Acquisitions			1.002
					Cataloging			2.008
					ΣL			$ 3.010

Appendix 3. 5. 3
Labor (L)
Unit Cost Calculation for Technical Processing Activities
Acquisitions

Library #3

Key:
AF = Another function incorporated this activity at this library.
NA = Not applicable (not performed at this library).
( ) = Simulated data.
+ = Standardizing factor (1. 4771)
g_1 = Student Assistant
g_2 = Clerk (full-time)
g_3 = Professional
d = Data taken from the diary.

Activity Description	a Observed Mean Time	b Fre-quency	c Adjusted Time	d Personal Rating Factor	f [+] Standard Time	g Cate-gory of Worker	h Wage/ Minute	i Cost of Activity
1. Open, sort and distribute incoming mail.	(. 410)	1. 000	. 410	1. 10	. 6662	2	. 0362	. 024
2. Review book order requests; review selection media.	. 429 d	1. 000	. 429	1. 10	. 6970	3	. 0813	. 057
3. Select titles to be ordered.	AF	---	---	---	---	-	---	---
4. Type library order request card.	NA	---	---	---	---	-	---	---
5. Search and verify bibliographic information.	2. 990	1. 000	2. 990	1. 20	5. 2998	2	. 0362	. 192
6. Assign vendor and fund.	. 395	1. 000	. 395	1. 15	. 6709	3	. 0813	. 054
7. Prepare multiple order record.	3. 735	1. 000	3. 735	1. 17	6. 4549	2	. 0362	. 234
8. Type purchase requisition, etc.	2. 268	. 054	. 122	1. 10	. 1982	2	. 0362	. 007

9. Revise typing. Sign and mail requests.	.390	1.000	.390	1.15	.6625	2	.0362	.024
10. Burst forms.	1.224	1.000	1.224	1.15	2.0792	2	.0362	.075
11. File forms in appropriate files.	1.001	1.000	1.001	1.18	1.7448	2	.0362	.063
12. Encumbrance or prepayment routine.	NA	---	---	---	---	-	---	---
13. Unpack books; check against packing list or invoice. Check outstanding order file.	2.146	1.000	2.146	1.20	3.8038	2	.0362	.138
14. Check in serials on Kardex.	2.723	.112	.305	1.15	.4517	2	.0362	.016
15. Collate books.	NA	---	---	---	---	-	---	---
16. Book return procedure (incorrect shipment, defective copy, approval books).	3.285 d	.020	.066	1.15	.1121	2	.0362	.004
17. Book accessioning routine.	NA	---	---	---	---	-	---	---
18. Write sourcing information.	NA	---	---	---	---	-	---	---
19. Prepare gift record form.	(2.090)	.039	.082	1.15	.1393	2	.0362	.005
20. Book distribution routine.	1.022	1.000	1.022	1.14	1.7210	3	.0813	.140
21. Prepare receiving report.	2.790	.310	.865	1.10	1.4055	2	.0362	.051
22. Prepare invoices for payment.	.401	.022	.009	1.25	.0165	2	.0362	.001
23. Expenditure routine.	2.260	.126	.285	1.15	.4842	2	.0362	.018
24. Clear in-process file.	.616	1.000	.616	1.10	1.0009	2	.0362	.036

Appendix 3. 5. 3 (continued)

Acquisitions

Activity Description	a Observed Mean Time	b Fre- quency	c Adjusted Time	d Personal Rating Factor	f Standard Time	g Cate- gory of Worker	h Wage/ Minute	i Cost of Activity
25. File forms, etc., in completed records or discard.	AF	---	---	---	---	-	---	---
26. Requester notification routine.	.024	1.000	.024	1.15	.0408	2	.0362	.002
27. Periodic accessions list routine.	NA	---	---	---	---	-	---	---
28. Vendor status routine.	1.585 d	.020	.032	1.10	.0520	2	.0362	.002
29. Claims routine.	(3.264	.010	.033	1.10	.0536	2	.0362	.002
30. Cancellations routine	(4.102)	.010	.041	1.10	.0666	2	.0362	.002
31. Out-of-print order routine.	AF	---	---	---	---	-	---	---
32. Process inquiries.	3.092 d	.091	.282	1.10	.4582	3	.0813	.037
33. General typing - correspondence, etc. (specify).	1.874	.010	.019	1.10	.0309	2	.0362	.001
34. General revision (specify).	AF	---	---	---	---	-	---	---
35. General filing (specify).	AF	---	---	---	---	-	---	---
36. Other acquistions activities not listed above (specify).	9.260	.010	.093	1.10	.1511	2	.0362	.006
						Sub-total		1.191

		Cataloging						
37. Sort books, assign and distribute.	. 316	1. 000	. 316	1. 15	. 5368	2	. 0362	. 019
38. Search for LC copy; verify bibliographic information	8. 246	. 435	3. 587	1. 13	5. 9871	2	. 0362	. 217
39. Order LC cards or other unit cards.	NA	---	---	---	---	-	---	---
40. Receive and arrange LC cards.	NA	---	---	---	---	-	---	---
41. Receive and arrange LC proof slips or proof sheets.	. 456	. 435	. 198	1. 10	. 3217	2	. 0362	. 012
42. File LC copy. (cards or proof)	. 249	. 435	. 108	1. 10	. 1755	2	. 0362	. 006
43. Match LC cards or proof copy and books.	. 775	. 358	. 277	1. 15	. 4706	2	. 0362	. 017
44. Added copies/added volumes routine.	5. 728	. 114	. 653	1. 10	1. 0610	2	. 0362	. 038
45. Catalog and classify with LC cards/ copy.	1. 510	. 358	. 541	1. 05	. 8391	2	. 0362	. 030
46. Original cataloging and classifying.	14. 081 d	. 077	1. 084	1. 10	1. 7613	3	. 0813	. 143
47. Shelf listing (for 44, 45, and 46).	AF	---	---	---	---	-	---	---
48. Type complete card sets.	NA	---	---	---	---	-	---	---
49. Type master card.	2. 288	. 077	. 176	1. 10	. 2860	2	. 0362	. 010
50. Revise master card.	. 635	. 077	. 049	1. 10	. 0796	2	. 0362	. 029
51. Type modification on a card or proof slip	AF	---	---	---	---	-	---	---

Appendix 3. 5. 3 (continued)
Cataloging

Activity Description	a Observed Mean Time	b Fre-quency	c Adjusted Time	d Personal Rating Factor	f Standard Time	g Cate-gory of Worker	h Wage/ Minute	i Cost of Activity
52. Reproduce card sets (other than typing). Sort cards into sets.	. 748	1. 000	. 748	1. 12	1. 2375	2	. 0362	. 045
53. Type call number, added entries.	1. 777	1. 000	1. 777	1. 13	2. 9660	2	. 0362	. 011
54. Revise typing on card sets.	. 960	1. 000	. 960	1. 12	1. 5882	3	. 0813	. 129
55. Prepare authority cards.	(1. 197)	. 036	. 043	1. 10	. 0699	2	. 0362	. 002
56. Prepare cross-reference cards.	(1. 946)	. 026	. 051	1. 10	. 0829	2	. 0362	. 003
57. Prepare circulation card.	NA	---	---	---	---	-	---	---
58. Prepare book pocket.	NA	---	---	---	---	-	---	---
59. Mark call number or place label on spine of volume.	1. 369	1. 000	1. 369	1. 10	2. 2244	1	. 0238	. 053
60. Affix pocket and date due slip. Affix gift plate.	. 218	1. 000	. 218	1. 10	. 3542	1	. 0238	. 008
61. Affix biographical and review material in book.	NA	---	---	---	---	-	---	---
62. Stamp property marks.	. 241	1. 000	. 241	1. 10	. 3916	1	. 0238	. 009
63. Affix plastic jacket to book.	NA	---	---	---	---	-	---	---
64. Paperback books--library binding routine.	3. 075	. 052	. 160	1. 15	. 2718	2	. 0362	. 010

65. Revise completed books before forwarding to circulation.	. 173	1. 000	. 173	1. 15	. 2939	2	. 0362	. 011
66. Sort and alphabetize shelf list and all catalog cards.	. 226	6. 000	1. 356	1. 10	2. 2032	2	. 0362	. 080
67. File shelf list and all catalog cards.	. 458	6. 000	2. 748	1. 10	4. 4650	1	. 0238	. 106
68. Revise filing of shelf list and all catalog cards.	. 786 d	6. 000	4. 716	1. 10	7. 6626	3	. 0813	. 623
69. Route card sets to departmental libraries.	AF	---	---	---	---	-	---	---
70. Paperback books--bindery routine (preparation).	. 771	. 040	. 031	1. 10	. 0537	2	. 0362	. 002
71. Paperback books--bindery routine (receiving).	(. 754)	. 040	3. 016	1. 10	. 0487	2	. 0362	. 002
72. Catalog maintenance (other than filing).	. 017	. 435	. 007	1. 10	. 0114	3	. 0813	. 001
73. General typing (specify).	AF	---	---	---	---	-	---	---
74. General revision (specify).	AF	---	---	---	---	-	---	---
75. General filing (specify).	AF	---	---	---	---	-	---	---
76. Other cataloging activities not listed above (specify).	AF	---	---	---	---	-	---	---
						Sub-total		1. 616
					Acquisitions			1. 191
					Cataloging			1. 616
					ΣL			2. 807

Appendix 3. 5. 4
Labor (L)
Unit Cost Calculation for Technical Processing Activities
Acquisitions

Library #4

Key:
AF = Another function incorporated this activity at this library.
NA = Not applicable (not performed at this library).
( ) = Simulated data.

+ = Standardizing factor (1. 4771)
g_1 = Student Assistant
g_2 = Clerk (full-time)
g_3 = Professional
d = Data taken from the diary.

Activity Description	a	b	c	d	f +	g	h	i
	Observed Mean Time	Fre-quency	Adjusted Time	Personal Rating Factor	Standard Time	Cate-gory of Worker	Wage/ Minute	Cost of Activity
1. Open, sort and distribute incoming mail.	. 249	1.0	. 249	1. 07	. 3935	2	. 0425	. 017
2. Review book order requests; review selection media.	(. 856)	1. 0	. 856	1. 10	1. 3908	3	. 0716	. 100
3. Select titles to be ordered.	AF	---	---	---	---	-	---	---
4. Type library order request card.	1. 734	. 079	. 137	1. 03	. 2084	2	. 0425	. 009
5. Search and verify bibliographic information.	3. 101	1. 0	3. 101	1. 10	5. 0385	1	. 0172	. 087
6. Assign vendor and fund.	. 473	1. 0	. 473	1. 05	. 7335	3	. 0716	. 052
7. Prepare multiple order record.	1. 007	1. 0	1. 007	1. 12	1. 6659	2	. 0425	. 071
8. Type purchase requisition, etc.	12. 657	. 257	3. 253	1. 12	5. 3817	2	. 0425	. 229

9. Revise typing. Sign and mail requests.	1. 569	. 257	. 403	1. 07	. 6369	3	. 0716	. 046
10. Burst forms.	. 132	1. 000	. 132	1. 12	. 2183	2	. 0425	. 009
11. File forms in appropriate files.	1. 683	1. 000	1. 683	1. 09	2. 7097	2	. 0425	. 115
12. Encumbrance or prepayment routine.	AF	---	---	---	---	-	---	---
13. Unpack books; check against packing list or invoice. Check outstanding order file.	4. 245	1. 000	4. 245	1. 05	6. 5837	1	. 0172	. 113
14. Check in serials on Kardex.	. 483	. 187	. 090	1. 10	. 1462	1	. 0172	. 002
15. Collate books.	NA	---	---	---	---	-	---	---
16. Book return procedure (incorrect shipment, defective copy, approval books).	(5. 484)	. 004	. 022	1. 10	. 0357	2	. 0425	. 002
17. Book accessioning routine.	NA	---	---	---	---	-	---	---
18. Write sourcing information.	. 939	1. 000	. 939	1. 07	1. 4840	2	. 0425	. 063
19. Prepare gift record form.	1. 410	. 079	. 111	1. 10	. 1804	2	. 0425	. 008
20. Book distribution routine.	. 191	1. 000	. 191	1. 07	. 3019	1	. 0172	. 005
21. Prepare receiving report.	NA	---	---	---	---	-	---	---
22. Prepare invoices for payment.	. 567	. 257	. 146	1. 10	. 2372	2	. 0425	. 010
23. Expenditure routine.	2. 629	1. 000	2. 629	1. 09	4. 2328	2	. 0425	. 180
24. Clear in-process file.	AF	---	---	---	---	-	---	---

Appendix 3. 5. 4 (continued)

Acquisitions

Activity Description	a Observed Mean Time	b Fre- quency	c Adjusted Time	d Personal Rating Factor	f Standard Time	g Cate- gory of Worker	h Wage/ Minute	i Cost of Activity
25. File forms, etc., in completed records or discard.	1. 199	1. 000	1. 199	1. 07	1. 8950	2	. 0425	. 080
26. Requester notification routine.	. 928	1. 000	. 928	1. 00	1. 3707	2	. 0425	. 058
27. Periodic accessions list routine.	(5. 715)	. 350	2. 000	1. 10	3. 2496	2	. 0425	. 138
28. Vendor status routine.	7. 342 d	. 004	. 029	1. 10	. 0471	2	. 0425	. 020
29. Claims routine.	(3. 264)	. 004	. 013	1. 10	. 0211	2	. 0425	. 001
30. Cancellations routine.	(4. 102)	. 004	. 016	1. 10	. 0260	2	. 0425	. 001
31. Out-of-print order routine.	2. 321	1. 000	2. 321	1. 15	3. 9427	2	. 0425	. 168
32. Process inquiries.	6. 326 d	. 394	2. 492	1. 10	4. 0490	3	. 0716	. 290
33. General typing - correspondence, etc. (specify).	6. 880	. 004	. 028	1. 07	. 0443	2	. 0425	. 002
34. General revision (specify).	. 348	. 004	. 001	1. 05	. 0016	2	. 0425	---
35. General filing (specify).	6. 738	. 004	. 270	1. 10	. 0439	2	. 0425	. 002
36. Other acquisitions activities not listed above (specify).	5. 772	. 004	. 023	1. 10	. 0374	2	. 0425	. 002
						Sub-total		1. 880

		Cataloging						
37. Sort books, assign and distribute.	.724	1.000	.724	1.05	1.1229	1	.0172	.019
38. Search for LC copy; verify bibliographic information.	4.329	.681	2.948	1.10	4.7899	3	.0716	.343
39. Order LC cards or other unit cards.	1.579	.551	.870	1.10	1.4136	2	.0425	.060
40. Receive and arrange LC cards.	.565	.551	.311	1.10	.5053	1	.0172	.009
41. Receive and arrange LC proof slips or proof sheets.	.523	.039	.020	1.18	.0349	2	.0425	.002
42. File LC copy. (cards or proof)	.461	.039	.018	1.10	.0292	2	.0425	.001
43. Match LC cards or proof copy and books.	.524	.138	.072	1.13	.1202	1	.0172	.002
44. Added copies/added volumes routine.	(6.736)	.319	2.149	1.10	3.4917	2	.0425	.148
45. Catalog and classify with LC cards/copy.	11.969	.750	8.977	1.10	14.5859	3	.0716	1.044
46. Original cataloging and classifying.	16.762 d	.099	1.659	1.10	2.6956	3	.0716	.193
47. Shelf listing (for 44, 45, and 46).	1.463	1.000	1.463	1.07	2.3123	3	.0716	.166
48. Type complete card sets.	NA	---	---	---	---	-	---	---
49. Type master card.	1.828	.099	.181	1.10	.2941	2	.0425	.011
50. Revise master card.	AF	---	---	---	---	-	---	---
51. Type modification on a card or proof slip.	2.944 d	.039	.115	1.10	.1869	2	.0425	.008
52. Reproduce card sets (other than typing). Sort cards into sets.	.897	.138	.124	1.15	.2106	2	.0425	.009

Appendix 3. 5. 4 (continued)

Cataloging

Activity Description	a	b	c	d	f	g	h	i
	Observed Mean Time	Fre-quency	Adjusted Time	Personal Rating Factor	Standard Time	Cate-gory of Worker	Wage/ Minute	Cost of Activity
53. Type call number, added entries.	4. 792	1. 000	4. 792	1. 10	7. 7861	2	. 0425	. 331
54. Revise typing on card sets.	. 586	1. 000	. 586	1. 05	. 9089	1	. 0172	. 016
55. Prepare authority cards.	1. 815 d	. 033	. 060	1. 10	. 0975	2	. 0425	. 004
56. Prepare cross-reference cards.	(1. 946)	. 014	. 027	1. 10	. 0439	2	. 0425	. 002
57. Prepare circulation card.	. 785	1. 000	. 785	1. 00	. 1159	2	. 0425	. 005
58. Prepare book pocket.	. 851	1. 000	. 851	1. 00	1. 2570	2	. 0425	. 053
59. Mark call number or place label on spine of volume.	1. 217	1. 000	1. 217	1. 15	2. 0673	2	. 0425	. 088
60. Affix pocket and date due slip. Affix gift plate.	. 546	1. 000	. 546	1. 05	. 8468	1	. 0172	. 015
61. Affix biographical and review material in book.	NA	---	---	---	---	-	---	---
62. Stamp property marks.	. 377	1. 000	. 377	1. 07	. 5959	2	. 0425	. 025
63. Affix plastic jacket to book.	NA	---	---	---	---	-	---	---
64. Paperback books--library binding routine.	(3. 347)	. 049	. 164	1. 10	. 2665	1	. 0172	. 005

65. Revise completed books before forwarding to circulation.	1. 007	1. 000	1. 007	1. 05	1. 5619	2	. 0425	. 066
66. Sort and alphabetize shelf list and all catalog cards.	. 140	5. 000	. 700	1. 10	1. 1374	1	. 0172	. 020
67. File shelf list and all catalog cards.	. 753	5. 000	3. 765	1. 05	5. 8393	2	. 0425	. 248
68. Revise filing of shelf list and all catalog cards.	. 320	5. 000	1. 600	1. 10	2. 5997	3	. 0716	. 186
69. Route card sets to departmental libraries.	NA	---	---	---	---	-	---	---
70. Paperback books--bindery routine (preparation).	2. 295 d	. 054	. 124	1. 10	. 2015	1	. 0172	. 004
71. Paperback books--bindery routine (receiving).	(. 685)	. 054	. 037	1. 10	. 0601	1	. 0172	. 001
72. Catalog maintenance (other than filing).	. 017 d	. 681	. 012	1. 10	. 0195	3	. 0716	. 001
73. General typing (specify).	NA	---	---	---	---	-	---	---
74. General revision (specify).	NA	---	---	---	---	-	---	---
75. General filing (specify).	NA	---	---	---	---	-	---	---
76. Other cataloging activities not listed above (specify).	NA	---	---	---	---	-	---	---

Sub-total	3. 085
Acquisitions	1. 880
Cataloging	3. 085
ΣL	4. 965

Appendix 3. 5. 5
Labor (L)
Unit Cost Calculation for Technical Processing Activities
Acquisitions

Library #5

Key:
AF = Another function incorporated this activity at this library.
NA = Not applicable (not performed at this library).
( ) = Simulated data.

+ = Standardizing factor (1. 4771)
g_1 = Student Assistant
g_2 = Clerk (full-time)
g_3 = Professional
d = Data taken from the diary.

Activity Description	a	b	c	d	f +	g	h	i
	Observed Mean Time	Fre- quency	Adjusted Time	Personal Rating Factor	Standard Time	Cate- gory of Worker	Wage/ Minute	Cost of Activity
1. Open, sort and distribute incoming mail.	1. 225 d	1. 000	1. 225	1. 10	1. 9904	3	. 0643	. 128
2. Review book order requests; review selection media.	AF	---	---	---	---	-	---	---
3. Select titles to be ordered.	AF	---	---	---	---	-	---	---
4. Type library order request card.	2. 373	. 393	. 933	1. 08	1. 4883	2	. 0395	. 059
5. Search and verify bibliographic information.	12. 385	1. 000	12. 385	1. 10	14. 1261	3	. 0643	. 908
6. Assign vendor fund.	. 063	1. 000	. 063	1. 10	. 1024	3	. 0643	. 007
7. Prepare multiple order record.	13. 903	1. 000	13. 903	1. 10	22. 5897	2	. 0395	. 892
8. Type purchase requisition, etc.	7. 755	. 145	1. 124	1. 02	1. 6935	2	. 0395	. 067

9. Revise typing. Sign and mail requests.	.952	1.000	.952	1.00	1.4062	2	.0395	.056
10. Burst forms.	3.637	1.000	3.637	1.03	5.5334	2	.0395	.219
11. File forms in appropriate files.	2.448	1.000	2.448	1.03	3.7244	2	.0395	.147
12. Encumbrance or prepayment routine.	.970	.227	.220	1.00	.3250	2	.0395	.013
13. Unpack books; check against packing list or invoice. Check outstanding order file.	5.765	1.000	5.765	1.15	9.7929	3	.0643	.630
14. Check in serials on Kardex.	1.638	.294	.482	1.10	.7832	2	.0395	.031
15. Collate books.	.804	1.000	.804	1.10	1.3063	3	.0643	.084
16. Book return procedure (incorrect shipment, defective copy, approval books).	(5.484)	.004	.022	1.10	.0357	3	.0643	.002
17. Book accessioning routine.	NA	---	---	---	---	-	---	---
18. Write sourcing information.	NA	---	---	---	---	-	---	---
19. Prepare gift record form.	AF	---	---	---	---	-	---	---
20. Book distribution routine.	AF	---	---	---	---	-	---	---
21. Prepare receiving report.	NA	---	---	---	---	-	---	---
22. Prepare invoices for payment.	1.992	1.000	1.992	1.15	3.3837	2	.0395	.134
23. Expenditure routine.	.676	.227	.153	1.15	.2600	2	.0395	.010
24. Clear in-process file.	NA	---	---	---	---	-	---	---

Appendix 3. 5. 5 (continued)

Acquisitions

Activity Description	a Observed Mean Time	b Fre- quency	c Adjusted Time	d Personal Rating Factor	f Standard Time	g Cate- gory of Worker	h Wage/ Minute	i Cost of Activity
25. File forms, etc., in completed records or discard.	AF	---	---	---	---	-	---	---
26. Requester notification routine.	. 348	1. 000	. 348	1. 00	. 5140	2	. 0395	. 020
27. Periodic accessions list routine.	8. 617	1. 000	8. 617	1. 10	14. 0010	2	. 0395	. 553
28. Vendor status routine.	(3. 871)	. 005	. 019	1. 10	. 0309	2	. 0395	. 001
29. Claims routine.	(3. 264)	. 005	. 016	1. 10	. 0260	2	. 0395	. 001
30. Cancellations routine.	(4. 102)	. 005	. 021	1. 10	. 0341	2	. 0395	. 001
31. Out-of-print order routine.	AF	---	---	---	---	-	---	---
32. Process inquiries.	29. 333 d	. 104	3. 051	1. 10	4. 9573	3	. 0643	. 319
33. General typing - correspondence, etc. (specify).	15. 288 d	. 145	2. 217	1. 10	3. 6022	2	. 0395	. 142
34. General revision (specify).	. 909	1. 000	. 909	1. 05	1. 4097	2	. 0395	. 056
35. General filing (specify).	. 554	1. 000	. 554	1. 10	. 9001	3	. 0643	. 058
36. Other acquistions activities not listed above (specify).	AF	---	---	---	---	-	---	---
						Sub-total		4. 538

	Cataloging							
37. Sort books, assign and distribute.	1.125 d	1.000	1.125	1.10	1.8279	3	.0643	.118
38. Search for LC copy; verify bibliographic information.	.895	.702	.628	1.10	1.0203	3	.0643	.066
39. Order LC cards or other unit cards.	.928	.600	.557	1.00	.8227	2	.0395	.032
40. Receive and arrange LC cards.	1.543	.600	.926	1.00	1.3678	2	.0395	.054
41. Receive and arrange LC proof slips or proof sheets.	(.375)	.036	.014	1.10	.0227	1	.0209	.001
42. File LC copy. (cards or proof)	.451	.036	.016	1.10	.0260	3	.0643	.002
43. Match LC cards or proof copy and books.	.621	.702	.436	1.00	.6440	2	.0395	.025
44. Added copies/added volumes routine.	5.314	.295	1.568	.98	2.2697	2	.0395	.090
45. Catalog and classify with LC cards/copy.	8.560	.636	5.444	1.08	8.6846	3	.0643	.558
46. Original cataloging and classifying.	28.790 d	.066	1.900	1.10	3.0871	3	.0643	.198
47. Shelf listing (for 44, 45, and 46).	AF	---	---	---	---	-	---	---
48. Type complete card sets.	NA	---	---	---	---	-	---	---
49. Type master card.	8.939	.066	.590	1.10	.9586	2	.0395	.038
50. Revise master card.	.584	.066	.039	1.10	.0634	3	.0643	.004
51. Type modification on a card or proof slip.	AF	---	---	---	---	-	---	---

Appendix 3. 5. 5 (continued)

Cataloging

Activity Description	a Observed Mean Time	b Fre-quency	c Adjusted Time	d Personal Rating Factor	f Standard Time	g Cate-gory of Worker	h Wage/ Minute	i Cost of Activity
52. Reproduce card sets (other than typing). Sort cards into sets.	3. 698	. 066	. 244	1. 07	. 3857	2	. 0395	. 015
53. Type call number, added entries.	5. 097	1. 000	5. 097	1. 03	7. 7546	2	. 0395	. 306
54. Revise typing on card sets.	. 305	1. 000	. 305	1. 10	. 4956	3	. 0643	. 032
55. Prepare authority cards.	. 584	. 064	. 037	1. 00	. 0547	2	. 0395	. 002
56. Prepare cross-reference cards.	(1. 946)	. 022	. 043	1. 10	. 0699	2	. 0395	. 003
57. Prepare circulation card.	. 842	1. 000	. 842	. 98	1. 2189	2	. 0395	. 048
58. Prepare book pocket.	. 539	1. 000	. 539	. 98	. 7802	2	. 0395	. 031
59. Mark call number or place label on spine of volume.	1. 020	1. 000	1. 020	1. 10	1. 6573	1	. 0209	. 035
60. Affix pocket and date due slip. Affix gift plate.	1. 010	1. 000	1. 010	1. 10	1. 6411	1	. 0209	. 034
61. Affix biographical and review material in book.	NA	---	---	---	---	-	---	---
62. Stamp property marks.	. 419	1. 000	. 419	1. 10	. 6808	1	. 0209	. 014
63. Affix plastic jacket to book.	5. 993	. 100	. 599	1. 10	. 9733	1	. 0209	. 020
64. Paperback books--library binding routine.	5. 017	. 060	. 301	1. 10	. 4891	1	. 0209	. 010

65. Revise completed books before forwarding to circulation.	.166	1.000	.166	1.10	.2697	3	.0643	.017
66. Sort and alphabetize shelf list and all catalog cards.	.178	6.000	1.068	1.15	1.8142	1	.0209	.038
67. File shelf list and all catalog cards.	1.171	6.000	7.026	1.06	11.0008	1	.0209	.230
68. Revise filing of shelf list and all catalog cards.	.614	6.000	3.684	1.15	6.2579	1	.0209	.131
69. Route card sets to departmental libraries.	NA	---	---	---	---	-	---	---
70. Paperback books--bindery routine (preparation).	NA	---	---	---	---	-	---	---
71. Paperback books--bindery routine (receiving).	NA	---	---	---	---	-	---	---
72. Catalog maintenance (other than filing).	.014	.702	.010	1.10	.0162	3	.0643	.001
73. General typing (specify).	AF	---	---	---	---	-	---	---
74. General revision (specify).	AF	---	---	---	---	-	---	---
75. General filing (specify).	AF	---	---	---	---	-	---	---
76. Other cataloging activities not listed above (specify).	AF	---	---	---	---	-	---	---
					Sub-total			2.153
					Acquisitions			4.538
					Cataloging			2.153
					ΣL			6.691

Appendix 3. 5. 6
Labor (L)
Unit Cost Calculation for Technical Processing Activities
Acquisitions

Library #6

Key:
AF = Another function incorporated this activity at this library.
NA = Not applicable (not performed at this library).
( ) = Simulated data.

+ = Standardizing factor (1. 4771)
g_1 = Student Assistant
g_2 = Clerk (full-time)
g_3 = Professional
d = Data taken from the diary.

Activity Description	a	b	c	d	f +	g	h	i
	Observed Mean Time	Fre-quency	Adjusted Time	Personal Rating Factor	Standard Time	Cate-gory of Worker	Wage/ Minute	Cost of Activity
1. Open, sort and distribute incoming mail.	(. 410)	1. 000	. 410	1. 10	. 6662	2	. 0262	. 018
2. Review book order requests; review selection media.	(. 856)	1. 000	. 856	1. 10	1. 3908	3	. 0759	. 106
3. Select titles to be ordered.	AF	---	---	---	---	-	---	---
4. Type library order request card.	. 540	1. 000	. 540	1. 25	. 9970	2	. 0262	. 026
5. Search and verify bibliographic information.	AF	---	---	---	---	-	---	---
6. Assign vendor and fund.	. 308	1. 000	. 308	1. 15	. 5232	3	. 0759	. 040
7. Prepare multiple order record.	. 707	1. 000	. 707	1. 23	1. 2845	2	. 0262	. 034
8. Type purchase requisition, etc.	. 293	1. 000	. 293	1. 20	. 5193	2	. 0262	. 014

9. Revise typing. Sign and mail requests.	NA	---	---	---	---	-	---	---
10. Burst forms.	.202	1.000	.202	1.25	.3730	2	.0262	.010
11. File forms in appropriate files.	.464	1.000	.464	1.20	.8224	2	.0262	.022
12. Encumbrance or prepayment routine.	.991 d	.055	.054	1.10	.0877	2	.0262	.002
13. Unpack books; check against packing list or invoice. Check outstanding order file.	.545	1.000	.545	1.20	.9660	2	.0262	.025
14. Check in serials on Kardex.	NA	---	---	---	---	-	---	---
15. Collate books.	NA	---	---	---	---	-	---	---
16. Book return procedure (incorrect shipment, defective copy, approval books).	(5.484)	.006	.033	1.10	.0536	2	.0262	.001
17. Book accessioning routine.	.406	1.000	.406	1.20	.7196	2	.0262	.019
18. Write sourcing information.	NA	---	---	---	---	-	---	---
19. Prepare gift record form.	.053	1.000	.053	1.10	.0861	2	.0262	.002
20. Book distribution routine.	AF	---	---	---	---	-	---	---
21. Prepare receiving report.	AF	---	---	---	---	-	---	---
22. Prepare invoices for payment.	AF	---	---	---	---	-	---	---
23. Expenditure routine.	.169	1.000	.169	1.20	.2996	2	.0262	.008
24. Clear in-process file.	(.597)	1.000	.597	1.10	.9700	2	.0262	.025

Appendix 3. 5. 6 (continued)

Acquisitions

Activity Description	a Observed Mean Time	b Fre-quency	c Adjusted Time	d Personal Rating Factor	f Standard Time	g Cate-gory of Worker	h Wage/ Minute	i Cost of Activity
25. File forms, etc., in completed records or discard.	(1. 379)	1. 000	1. 379	1. 10	2. 2406	2	. 0262	. 059
26. Requester notification routine.	(. 417)	1. 000	. 417	1. 10	. 6775	2	. 0262	. 018
27. Periodic accessions list routine.	(5. 715)	. 100	. 572	1. 10	. 9294	2	. 0262	. 024
28. Vendor status routine.	(3. 871)	. 246	. 952	1. 10	1. 5468	1	. 0127	. 020
29. Claims routine.	(3. 264)	. 246	. 803	1. 10	1. 3047	2	. 0262	. 034
30. Cancellations routine.	(4. 102)	. 246	1. 009	1. 10	1. 6394	1	. 0127	. 021
31. Out-of-print order routine.	NA	---	---	---	---	-	---	---
32. Process inquiries.	(10. 492)	. 010	. 105	1. 10	. 1706	3	. 0759	. 013
33. General typing - correspondence, etc. (specify).	4. 916 d	. 010	. 049	1. 10	. 0796	2	. 0262	. 002
34. General revision (specify).	NA	---	---	---	---	-	---	---
35. General filing (specify).	. 205	. 164	. 034	1. 10	. 0552	1	. 0127	. 001
36. Other acquisitions activities not listed above (specify).	NA	---	---	---	---	-	---	---
						Sub-total		. 544

	Cataloging							
37. Sort books, assign and distribute.	AF	---	---	---	---	-	---	---
38. Search for LC copy; verify bibliographic information.	2. 419	. 965	2. 334	1. 10	3. 7923	2	. 0262	. 099
39. Order LC cards or other unit cards.	AF	---	---	---	---	-	---	---
40. Receive and arrange LC cards.	. 4095 d	. 717	. 294	1. 10	. 4777	2	. 0262	. 012
41. Receive and arrange LC proof slips or proof sheets.	NA	---	---	---	---	-	---	---
42. File LC copy. (cards or proof)	NA	---	---	---	---	-	---	---
43. Match LC cards or proof copy and books.	1. 137	. 717	. 815	1. 05	1. 2641	2	. 0262	. 033
44. Added copies/added volumes routine.	AF	---	---	---	---	-	---	---
45. Catalog and classify with LC cards/copy.	4. 080	. 717	2. 925	1. 05	4. 5365	3	. 0759	. 344
46. Original cataloging and classifying.	12. 026	. 248	2. 982	1. 05	4. 6249	2	. 0262	. 122
47. Shelf listing (for 44, 45, and 46).	AF	---	---	---	---	-	---	---
48. Type complete card sets.	12. 240	. 248	3. 036	1. 05	4. 7087	2	. 0262	. 123
49. Type master card.	NA	---	---	---	---	-	---	---
50. Revise master card.	AF	---	---	---	---	-	---	---

Appendix 3. 5. 6 (continued)
Cataloging

Activity Description	a Observed Mean Time	b Fre-quency	c Adjusted Time	d Personal Rating Factor	f Standard Time	g Cate-gory of Worker	h Wage/ Minute	i Cost of Activity
51. Type modification on a card or proof slip.	AF	---	---	---	---	-	---	---
52. Reproduce card sets (other than typing). Sort cards into sets.	NA	---	---	---	---	-	---	---
53. Type call number, added entries.	2. 100	. 965	2. 026	1. 15	3. 4415	2	. 0262	. 090
54. Revise typing on card sets.	1. 431	. 965	1. 381	1. 05	2. 1419	2	. 0262	. 056
55. Prepare authority cards.	. 800	. 005	---	---	---	-	---	---
56. Prepare cross-reference cards.	(1. 946)	. 033	. 064	1. 05	. 0993	2	. 0262	. 003
57. Prepare circulation card.	. 542	1. 000	. 542	1. 10	. 8806	2	. 0262	. 023
58. Prepare book pocket.	. 450	1. 000	. 450	1. 10	. 7312	2	. 0262	. 019
59. Mark call number or place label on spine of volume.	1. 262	1. 000	1. 262	1. 10	2. 0505	1	. 0127	. 026
60. Affix pocket and date due slip. Affix gift plate.	. 473	1. 000	. 473	1. 10	. 7685	1	. 0127	. 010
61. Affix biographical and review material in book.	NA	---	---	---	---	-	---	---
62. Stamp property marks.	. 204	1. 000	. 204	1. 25	. 3767	2	. 0262	. 010
63. Affix plastic jacket to book.	2. 359	1. 000	2. 359	1. 10	3. 8323	1	. 0127	. 049

64. Paperback books--library binding routine.	2. 864	. 100	. 286	1. 10	. 4647	1	. 0127	. 006
65. Revise completed books before forwarding to circulation.	AF	---	---	---	---	-	---	---
66. Sort and alphabetize shelf list and all catalog cards.	. 129	5. 000	. 645	1. 10	1. 0480	1	. 0127	. 013
67. File shelf list and all catalog cards.	. 439	5. 000	2. 195	1. 13	3. 6638	1	. 0127	. 047
68. Revise filing of shelf list and all catalog cards.	. 288	5. 000	1. 440	1. 10	2. 3397	3	. 0759	. 178
69. Route card sets to departmental libraries.	NA	---	---	---	---	-	---	---
70. Paperback books--bindery routine (preparation).	NA	---	---	---	---	-	---	---
71. Paperback books--bindery routine (receiving).	NA	---	---	---	---	-	---	---
72. Catalog maintenance (other than filing).	. 017	. 681	. 012	1. 10	. 0195	3	. 0759	. 002
73. General typing (specify).	. 280	. 079	. 002	1. 25	. 0036	2	. 0262	---
74. General revision (specify).	AF	---	---	---	---	-	---	---
75. General filing (specify).	AF	---	---	---	---	-	---	---
76. Other cataloging activities not listed above (specify).	AF	---	---	---	---	-	---	---
						Sub-total		1. 265
					Acquistions			. 544
					Cataloging			1. 265
					ΣL			1. 809

Appendix 3. 5. 7
Labor (L)
Unit Cost Calculation for Technical Processing Activities
Acquisitions

Library # 7

Key:
AF = Another function incorporated this activity at this library.
NA = Not applicable (not performed at this library).
( ) = Simulated data.

+ = Standardizing factor (1. 4771)
g_1 = Student Assistant
g_2 = Clerk (full-time)
g_3 = Professional
d = Data taken from the diary.

Activity Description	a Observed Mean Time	b Fre- quency	c Adjusted Time	d Personal Rating Factor	f + Standard Time	g Cate- gory of Worker	h Wage/ Minute	i Cost of Activity
1. Open, sort and distribute incoming mail.	. 727 d	1. 000	. 727	1. 25	1. 3424	1	. 0175	. 024
2. Review book order requests; review selection media.	AF	---	---	---	---	-	---	---
3. Select titles to be ordered.	AF	---	---	---	---	-	---	---
4. Type library order request card.	1. 120	1. 000	1. 120	1. 10	1. 8197	1	. 0175	. 032
5. Search and verify bibliographic information.	1. 454	1. 000	1. 454	1. 10	2. 3625	1	. 0175	. 041
6. Assign vendor and fund.	. 106	1. 000	. 106	1. 25	. 1957	3	. 0792	. 016
7. Prepare multiple order record.	. 511	1. 000	. 511	1. 20	. 9058	1	. 0175	. 016
8. Type purchase requisition, etc.	NA	---	---	---	---	-	---	---

9. Revise typing. Sign and mail requests.	NA	---	---	---	---	-	---	---
10. Burst forms.	.455	1.000	.455	1.20	.8065	1	.0175	.014
11. File forms in appropriate files.	2.186	1.000	2.186	1.14	3.6809	1	.0175	.064
12. Encumbrance or prepayment routine.	.438	1.000	.438	1.15	.7440	1	.0175	.013
13. Unpack books; check against packing list or invoice. Check outstanding order file.	1.753	1.000	1.753	1.17	3.0295	2	.0287	.087
14. Check in serials on Kardex.	4.341	.077	.334	1.25	.6167	1	.0175	.011
15. Collate books.	.311	1.000	.311	1.20	.5513	2	.0287	.016
16. Book return procedure (incorrect shipment, defective copy, approval books).	(5.484)	.002	.011	1.10	.0179	2	.0287	.001
17. Book accessioning routine.	2.836	1.000	2.836	1.20	5.0269	1	.0175	.088
18. Write sourcing information.	.597	1.000	.597	1.17	1.0318	2	.0287	.026
19. Prepare gift record form.	(2.090)	.088	.018	1.10	.0292	1	.0175	.001
20. Book distribution routine.	AF	---	---	---	---	-	---	---
21. Prepare receiving report.	3.437	.105	.361	1.17	.6239	2	.0287	.018
22. Prepare invoices for payment.	AF	---	---	---	---	-	---	---
23. Expenditure routine.	.360	1.000	.360	1.25	.6647	2	.0287	.019
24. Clear in-process file.	AF	---	---	---	---	-	---	---

Appendix 3. 5. 7 (continued)

Acquisitions

Activity Description	a Observed Mean Time	b Fre- quency	c Adjusted Time	d Personal Rating Factor	+ f Standard Time	g Cate- gory of Worker	h Wage/ Minute	i Cost of Activity
25. File forms, etc., in completed records or discard.	1. 922	1. 000	1. 922	1. 15	3. 2648	1	. 0175	. 057
26. Requester notification routine.	. 115	1. 000	. 115	1. 15	. 1953	3	. 0792	. 016
27. Periodic accessions list routine.	2. 182	1. 000	2. 182	1. 10	3. 5453	2	. 0287	. 102
28. Vendor status routine.	(3. 871)	. 004	. 015	1. 10	. 0244	1	. 0175	---
29. Claims routine.	(3. 264)	. 004	. 013	1. 10	. 0211	1	. 0175	---
30. Cancellations routine.	4. 414 d	. 004	. 018	1. 10	. 0292	1	. 0175	. 001
31. Out-of-print order routine.	AF	---	---	---	---	-	---	---
32. Process inquiries.	1. 390 d	. 025	. 035	1. 10	. 0569	3	. 0792	. 004
33. General typing - correspondence, etc. (specify).	AF	---	---	---	---	-	---	---
34. General revision (specify).	AF	---	---	---	---	-	---	---
35. General filing (specify).	AF	---	---	---	---	-	---	---
36. Other acquisitions activities not listed above (specify).	. 193	. 210	. 041	1. 25	. 0756	2	. 0287	. 002
						Sub-total		. 669

	Cataloging							
37. Sort books, assign and distribute.	. 357	1. 000	. 357	1. 25	. 6591	3	. 0792	. 052
38. Search for LC copy; verify bibliographic information.	2. 800	. 907	2. 540	1. 25	4. 6898	3	. 0792	. 371
39. Order LC cards or other unit cards.	. 525	. 803	. 422	1. 15	. 7168	1	. 0175	. 012
40. Receive and arrange LC cards.	(1. 159)	. 803	. 931	1. 10	1. 5127	1	. 0175	. 026
41. Receive and arrange LC proof slips or proof sheets.	NA	---	---	---	---	-	---	---
42. File LC copy. (cards or proof)	NA	---	---	---	---	-	---	---
43. Match LC cards or proof copy and books.	1. 700 d	. 803	1. 365	1. 10	2. 2179	1	. 0175	. 039
44. Added copies/added volumes routine.	2. 666 d	. 093	. 248	1. 10	. 4030	1	. 0175	. 007
45. Catalog and classify with LC cards/copy.	6. 701	1. 000	6. 701	1. 25	9. 9353	3	. 0792	. 787
46. Original cataloging and classifying.	(17. 980)	. 024	. 432	1. 20	. 7657	3	. 0792	. 061
47. Shelf listing (for 44, 45, and 46).	. 902	1. 000	. 902	1. 20	1. 5988	3	. 0792	. 127
48. Type complete card sets.	4. 780	. 024	. 115	1. 20	. 0204	1	. 0175	---
49. Type master card.	1. 304	. 024	. 031	1. 18	. 0541	1	. 0175	. 001
50. Revise master card.	AF	---	---	---	---	-	---	---
51. Type modification on a card or proof slip.	AF	---	---	---	---	-	---	---

Appendix 3. 5. 7 (continued)

Cataloging

Activity Description	a Observed Mean Time	b Fre- quency	c Adjusted Time	d Personal Rating Factor	f Standard Time	g Cate- gory of Worker	h Wage/ Minute	i Cost of Activity
52. Reproduce card sets (other than typ- ing). Sort cards into sets.	NA	---	---	---	---	-	---	---
53. Type call number, added entries.	3. 340	. 803	2. 682	1. 20	4. 7539	1	. 0175	. 083
54. Revise typing on card sets.	. 095	1. 000	. 095	1. 15	. 1613	3	. 0792	. 013
55. Prepare authority cards.	NA	---	---	---	---	-	---	---
56. Prepare cross-reference cards.	AF	---	---	---	---	-	---	---
57. Prepare circulation card.	. 680	1. 000	. 680	1. 15	1. 1551	1	. 0175	. 020
58. Prepare book pocket.	. 598	1. 000	. 598	1. 15	1. 0158	1	. 0175	. 018
59. Mark call number or place label on spine of volume.	. 774	1. 000	. 774	1. 25	1. 4291	1	. 0175	. 025
60. Affix pocket and date due slip. Affix gift plate.	. 215	1. 000	. 215	1. 25	. 3970	1	. 0175	. 007
61. Affix biographical and review material in book.	. 903	1. 000	. 903	1. 25	1. 6674	1	. 0175	. 029
62. Stamp property marks.	. 461	1. 000	. 461	1. 24	. 8443	1	. 0175	. 015
63. Affix plastic jacket to book.	NA	---	---	---	---	-	---	---

64. Paperback books--library binding routine.	NA	---	---	---	---	-	---	---
65. Revise completed books before forwarding to circulation.	1. 614	1. 000	1. 614	1. 23	2. 9323	3	. 0792	. 232
66. Sort and alphabetize shelf list and all catalog cards.	. 125	2. 000	. 250	1. 00	. 7386	1	. 0175	. 013
67. File shelf list and all catalog cards.	. 603	2. 000	1. 206	1. 17	4. 1684	1	. 0175	. 073
68. Revise filing of shelf list and all catalog cards.	. 157	2. 000	. 314	1. 20	1. 1131	3	. 0792	. 088
69. Route card sets to departmental libraries.	NA	---	---	---	---	-	---	---
70. Paperback books--bindery routine (preparation).	2. 952	. 049	. 145	1. 15	. 2464	1	. 0175	. 004
71. Paperback books--bindery routine (receiving).	(. 754)	. 049	. 037	1. 10	. 0601	1	. 0175	. 001
72. Catalog maintenance (other than filing).	. 017	. 907	. 015	1. 10	. 0244	3	. 0792	. 002
73. General typing (specify).	NA	---	---	---	---	-	---	---
74. General revision (specify).	NA	---	---	---	---	-	---	---
75. General filing (specify).	NA	---	---	---	---	-	---	---
76. Other cataloging activities not listed above (specify).	NA	---	---	---	---	-	---	---
					Sub-total			2. 106
					Acquisitions			. 669
					Cataloging			2. 106
					ΣL			2. 775

Appendix 3. 5. 8
Labor (L)
Unit Cost Calculation for Technical Processing Activities
Acquisitions

Library # 8

Key:
AF = Another function incorporated this activity at this library.
NA = Not applicable (not performed at this library).
( ) = Simulated data.

+ = Standardizing factor (1. 4771)
g_1 = Student Assistant
g_2 = Clerk (full-time)
g_3 = Professional
d = Data taken from the diary.

Activity Description	a	b	c	d	f +	g	h	i
	Observed Mean Time	Fre-quency	Adjusted Time	Personal Rating Factor	Standard Time	Cate-gory of Worker	Wage/ Minute	Cost of Activity
1. Open, sort and distribute incoming mail.	. 471	1. 000	. 471	1. 15	. 8001	1	. 0222	. 018
2. Review book order requests; review selection media.	NA	---	---	---	---	-	---	---
3. Select titles to be ordered.	NA	---	---	---	---	-	---	---
4. Type library order request card.	AF	---	---	---	---	-	---	---
5. Search and verify bibliographic information.	3. 366	1. 000	3. 366	1. 09	5. 4193	2	. 0360	. 195
6. Assign vendor and fund.	1. 604	1. 000	1. 604	1. 08	2. 5588	1	. 0222	. 057
7. Prepare multiple order record.	. 580	1. 000	. 580	1. 06	. 9081	2	. 0360	. 033
8. Type purchase requisition, etc.	8. 256	. 003	. 025	1. 06	. 0391	2	. 0360	. 001

9. Revise typing. Sign and mail requests.	.112	.003	.0003	1.05	.0005	2	.0360	---
10. Burst forms.	NA	---	---	---	---	-	---	---
11. File forms in appropriate files.	1.691	1.000	1.691	1.08	2.6976	1	.0222	.060
12. Encumbrance or prepayment routine.	.453	1.000	.453	1.07	.7160	2	.0360	.026
13. Unpack books; check against packing list or invoice. Check outstanding order file.	5.615	1.000	5.615	1.08	8.9574	1	.0222	.199
14. Check in serials on Kardex.	10.092	.038	.383	1.10	.6223	2	.0360	.022
15. Collate books.	NA	---	---	---	---	-	---	---
16. Book return procedure (incorrect shipment, defective copy, approval books).	6.676	.003	.020	1.08	.0319	2	.0360	.001
17. Book accessioning routine.	NA	---	---	---	---	-	---	---
18. Write sourcing information.	NA	---	---	---	---	-	---	---
19. Prepare gift record form.	4.238	.041	.174	1.10	.2827	2	.0360	.010
20. Book distribution routine.	.724	1.000	.724	1.10	1.1764	2	.0360	.042
21. Prepare receiving report.	NA	---	---	---	---	-	---	---
22. Prepare invoices for payment.	.334	.810	.271	1.08	.4323	2	.0360	.016
23. Expenditure routine	.108	.810	.087	1.08	.1388	2	.0360	.005
24. Clear in-process file.	.302	1.000	.302	1.05	.4684	2	.0360	.017

Appendix 3. 5. 8 (continued)

Acquisitions

	a	b	c	d	f	g	h	i
Activity Description	Observed Mean Time	Fre- quency	Adjusted Time	Personal Rating Factor	± Standard Time	Cate- gory of Worker	Wage/ Minute	Cost of Activity
25. File forms, etc., in completed records or discard.	. 641	1. 000	. 641	1. 12	1. 0604	2	. 0360	. 038
26. Requester notification routine.	. 122	1. 000	. 122	1. 14	. 2055	1	. 0222	. 005
27. Periodic accessions list routine.	NA	---	---	---	---	-	---	---
28. Vendor status routine.	. 985	. 107	. 105	1. 15	. 1784	2	. 0360	. 006
29. Claims routine.	3. 264	. 016	. 052	1. 10	. 0845	2	. 0360	. 003
30. Cancellations routine.	5. 595	. 036	. 201	1. 12	. 3325	2	. 0360	. 012
31. Out-of-print order routine.	(2. 553)	. 004	. 010	1. 10	. 0162	1	. 0222	---
32. Process inquiries.	10. 208 d	. 015	. 153	1. 10	. 2486	2	. 0360	. 009
33. General typing - correspondence, etc. (specify).	8. 802	. 053	. 467	1. 07	. 7381	2	. 0360	. 027
34. General revision (specify).	3. 533	1. 000	3. 533	1. 17	4. 0267	3	. 0759	. 306
35. General filing (specify).	. 806	1. 000	. 806	1. 10	1. 3096	2	. 0360	. 047
36. Other acquisitions activities not listed above (specify).	7. 850	. 001	. 008	1. 05	. 0124	2	. 0360	---
						Sub-total		1. 155

	Cataloging							
37. Sort books, assign and distribute.	4. 894	1. 000	4. 894	1. 05	7. 5904	2	. 0360	. 273
38. Search for LC copy; verify bibliographic information.	3. 766	. 468	1. 762	1. 10	2. 8629	2	. 0360	. 103
39. Order LC cards or other unit cards.	NA	---	---	---	---	-	---	---
40. Receive and arrange LC cards.	NA	---	---	---	---	-	---	---
41. Receive and arrange LC proof slips or proof sheets.	. 171 d	. 468	. 080	1. 10	. 1300	1	. 0222	. 003
42. File LC copy. (cards or proof)	. 244	. 468	. 114	1. 15	. 1936	1	. 0222	. 004
43. Match LC cards or proof copy and books.	6. 890	. 229	1. 578	1. 10	2. 5640	2	. 0360	. 092
44. Added copies/added volumes routine.	6. 871	. 532	3. 655	1. 09	5. 8848	2	. 0360	. 212
45. Catalog and classify with LC cards/ copy.	2. 935	. 292	. 857	1. 10	1. 3925	3	. 0759	. 106
46. Original cataloging and classifying.	20. 964 d	. 176	3. 690	1. 10	5. 9955	3	. 0759	. 455
47. Shelf listing (for 44, 45, and 46).	2. 619	1. 000	2. 619	1. 09	4. 2167	2	. 0360	. 152
48. Type complete card sets.	NA	---	---	---	---	-	---	---
49. Type master card.	6. 777	. 176	1. 193	1. 10	1. 9384	2	. 0360	. 070
50. Revise master card.	. 270	. 176	. 048	1. 10	. 0780	2	. 0360	. 003
51. Type modification on a card or proof slip.	. 155	1. 000	. 155	1. 10	. 2518	2	. 0360	. 009

Appendix 3. 5. 8 (continued)

Cataloging

Activity Description	a Observed Mean Time	b Fre-quency	c Adjusted Time	d Personal Rating Factor	f Standard Time	g Cate-gory of Worker	h Wage/ Minute	i Cost of Activity
52. Reproduce card sets (other than typing). Sort cards into sets.	average 4. 273	1. 000	4. 273	1. 09	6. 8797	2	. 0360	. 248
53. Type call number, added entries.	. 401	1. 000	. 401	1. 07	. 6338	2	. 0360	. 023
54. Revise typing on card sets.	1. 048	1. 000	1. 048	1. 08	1. 6718	2	. 0360	. 060
55. Prepare authority cards.	1. 882	. 010	. 019	1. 10	. 0309	2	. 0360	. 001
56. Prepare cross-reference cards.	3. 514	. 031	. 109	1. 10	. 1771	2	. 0360	. 006
57. Prepare circulation card.	NA	---	---	---	---	-	---	---
58. Prepare book pocket.	NA	---	---	---	---	-	---	---
59. Mark call number or place label on spine of volume.	1. 703	1. 000	1. 703	1. 10	2. 7671	2	. 0360	. 100
60. Affix pocket and date due slip. Affix gift plate.	. 434	. 041	. 018	1. 10	. 0292	2	. 0360	. 001
61. Affix biographical and review material in book.	NA	---	---	---	---	-	---	---
62. Stamp property marks.	. 147	1. 000	. 147	1. 10	. 2388	2	. 0360	. 009
63. Affix plastic jacket to book.	NA	---	---	---	---	-	---	---

64. Paperback books--library binding routine.	1. 390	. 044	. 061	1. 10	. 0991	1	. 0222	. 002
65. Revise completed books before forwarding to circulation.	. 111	1. 000	. 111	1. 10	. 1804	2	. 0360	. 006
66. Sort and alphabetize shelf list and all catalog cards.	. 449	9. 500	. 427	1. 10	6. 9314	2	. 0360	. 250
67. File shelf list and all catalog cards.	. 9463	9. 500	8. 990	1. 08	1. 4341	1	. 0222	. 032
68. Revise filing of shelf list and all catalog cards.	. 208	9. 500	1. 976	1. 08	3. 1523	2	. 0360	. 114
69. Route card sets to departmental libraries.	. 640	. 381	. 244	1. 10	. 3965	2	. 0360	. 014
70. Paperback books--bindery routine (preparation).	2. 138	. 094	. 201	1. 10	. 3266	2	. 0360	. 012
71. Paperback books--bindery routine (receiving).	. 685	. 094	. 064	1. 10	. 1040	2	. 0360	. 004
72. Catalog maintenance (other than filing).	. 017	. 468	. 008	1. 10	. 0130	2	. 0360	. 001
73. General typing (specify).	AF	---	---	---	---	-	---	---
74. General revision (specify).	1. 015	. 020	. 020	1. 05	. 0310	3	. 0759	. 002
75. General filing (specify).	. 473 d	. 020	. 009	1. 10	. 0146	1	. 0222	---
76. Other cataloging activities not listed above (specify).	. 818	1. 000	. 818	1. 10	1. 3291	1	. 0222	. 029
						Sub-total		2. 413
					Acquisitions			1. 155
					Cataloging			2. 413
					ΣL			3. 568

Appendix 3. 5. 9
Labor (L)
Unit Cost Calculation for Technical Processing Activities
Acquisitions

Library # 9

Key:
AF = Another function incorporated this activity at this library.
NA = Not applicable (not performed at this library).
( ) = Simulated data.

\+ = Standardizing factor (1. 4771)
g_1 = Student Assistant
g_2 = Clerk (full-time)
g_3 = Professional
d = Data taken from the diary.

Activity Description	a Observed Mean Time	b Fre- quency	c Adjusted Time	d Personal Rating Factor	f + Standard Time	g Cate- gory of Worker	h Wage/ Minute	i Cost of Activity
1. Open, sort and distribute incoming mail.	. 491	1. 000	. 491	1. 05	. 7616	3	. 0751	. 057
2. Review book order requests; review selection media.	. 778	1. 000	. 778	1. 05	1. 2066	3	. 0751	. 091
3. Select titles to be ordered.	AF	---	---	---	---	-	---	---
4. Type library order request card.	(1. 448)	2. 000	2. 896	1. 10	4. 7054	1	. 0166	. 078
5. Search and verify bibliographic information.	1. 667	1. 000	1. 667	1. 30	3. 2010	1	. 0166	. 053
6. Assign vendor and fund.	see U							
7. Prepare multiple order record.	1. 038	1. 000	1. 038	1. 00	1. 5332	1	. 0166	. 026
8. Type purchase requisition, etc.	10. 000	. 027	. 270	1. 10	. 4387	2	. 0632	. 028

9. Revise typing. Sign and mail requests.	. 362	1. 000	. 362	1. 20	. 6417	3	. 0751	. 048
10. Burst forms.	. 258	1. 000	. 258	1. 15	. 4383	1	. 0166	. 007
11. File forms in appropriate files.	. 324	1. 000	. 324	1. 15	. 5504	1	. 0166	. 009
12. Encumbrance or prepayment routine.	(. 669)	. 027	. 018	1. 10	. 0292	2	. 0632	. 002
13. Unpack books; check against packing list or invoice. Check outstanding order file.	. 693	1. 000	. 693	1. 17	1. 1976	1	. 0166	. 020
14. Check in serials on Kardex.	NA	---	---	---	---	-	---	---
15. Collate books.	NA	---	---	---	---	-	---	---
16. Book return procedure (incorrect shipment, defective copy, approval books).	(5. 484)	. 001	. 005	1. 10	. 0081	2	. 0632	. 001
17. Book accessioning routine.	. 986	1. 000	. 986	1. 17	1. 7040	1	. 0166	. 028
18. Write sourcing information.	NA	---	---	---	---	-	---	---
19. Prepare gift record form.	AF	---	---	---	---	-	---	---
20. Book distribution routine.	NA	---	---	---	---	-	---	---
21. Prepare receiving report.	NA	---	---	---	---	-	---	---
22. Prepare invoices for payment.	(. 869)	. 027	. 023	1. 05	. 0357	2	. 0632	. 002
23. Expenditure routine.	AF	---	---	---	---	-	---	---
24. Clear in-process file.	NA	---	---	---	---	-	---	---

Appendix 3. 5. 9 (continued)

Acquisitions

Activity Description	a Observed Mean Time	b Fre- quency	c Adjusted Time	d Personal Rating Factor	f Standard Time	g Cate- gory of Worker	h Wage/ Minute	i Cost of Activity
25. File forms, etc., in completed records or discard.	(1. 379)	1. 000	1. 379	1. 05	2. 1388	3	. 0751	. 161
26. Requester notification routine.	. 940	1. 000	. 940	1. 20	1. 6662	3	. 0751	. 125
27. Periodic accessions list routine.	9. 474	1. 000	9. 474	1. 10	1. 5393	2	. 0632	. 097
28. Vendor status routine.	(3. 871)	. 940	3. 639	1. 10	5. 9127	1	. 0166	. 098
29. Claims routine.	AF	---	---	---	---	-	---	---
30. Cancellations routine.	AF	---	---	---	---	-	---	---
31. Out-of-print order routine.	NA	---	---	---	---	-	---	---
32. Process inquiries.	(10. 492)	. 057	. 598	1. 10	. 9716	3	. 0751	. 073
33. General typing - correspondence, etc. (specify).	AF	---	---	---	---	-	---	---
34. General revision (specify).	NA	---	---	---	---	-	---	---
35. General filing (specify).	NA	---	---	---	---	-	---	---
36. Other acquisitions activities not listed above (specify).	NA	---	---	---	---	-	---	---
						Sub-total		1. 004

	Cataloging							
37. Sort books, assign and distribute.	see U							
38. Search for LC copy; verify bibliographic information.	see U							
39. Order LC cards or other unit cards.	2. 158	. 106	. 229	1. 30	. 4397	1	. 0166	. 007
40. Receive and arrange LC cards.	(1. 159)	. 106	. 129	1. 10	. 2096	1	. 0166	. 004
41. Receive and arrange LC proof slips or proof sheets.	NA	---	---	---	---	-	---	---
42. File LC copy. (cards or proof)	NA	---	---	---	---	-	---	---
43. Match LC cards or proof copy and books.	. 145	. 106	. 015	1. 15	. 0254	1	. 0166	---
44. Added copies/added volumes routine.	(6. 736)	. 172	1. 159	1. 10	1. 8832	3	. 0751	. 141
45. Catalog and classify with LC cards/copy.	see U							
46. Original cataloging and classifying.	see U							
47. Shelf listing (for 44, 45, and 46).	1. 389	1. 000	1. 389	1. 05	2. 1542	1	. 0166	. 036
48. Type complete card sets.	see U							
49. Type master card.	see U							
50. Revise master card.	see U							
51. Type modification on a card or proof slip.	see U							

Appendix 3. 5. 9 (continued)

Cataloging

Activity Description	a Observed Mean Time	b Fre-quency	c Adjusted Time	d Personal Rating Factor	+ f Standard Time	g Cate-gory of Worker	h Wage/ Minute	i Cost of Activity
52. Reproduce card sets (other than typing). Sort cards into sets.	see U							
53. Type call number, added entries.	see U							
54. Revise typing on card sets.	see U							
55. Prepare authority cards.	NA	---	---	---	---	-	---	---
56. Prepare cross-reference cards.	(1. 946)	. 001	. 002	1. 10	. 0032	3	. 0751	---
57. Prepare circulation card.	. 357	. 106	. 038	1. 15	. 0645	3	. 0651	. 005
58. Prepare book pocket.	. 415	. 106	. 044	1. 15	. 0747	3	. 0751	. 006
59. Mark call number or place label on spine of volume.	1. 442	. 106	. 153	1. 15	. 2600	3	. 0751	. 020
60. Affix pocket and date due slip. Affix gift plate.	. 487	. 106	. 052	1. 15	. 0883	3	. 0751	. 007
61. Affix biographical and review material in book.	NA	---	---	---	---	-	---	---
62. Stamp property marks.	. 515	. 106	. 055	1. 05	. 0854	1	. 0166	. 001
63. Affix plastic jacket to book.	(4. 594)	. 106	. 487	1. 10	. 7913	1	. 0166	. 013

64. Paperback books--library binding routine.	11. 373 d	. 024	. 273	1. 10	. 4436	1	. 0166	. 007
65. Revise completed books before forwarding to circulation.	. 127	1. 000	. 127	1. 15	. 2158	3	. 0751	. 016
66. Sort and alphabetize shelf list and all catalog cards.	. 141	6. 000	. 846	1. 25	1. 5620	1	. 0166	. 026
67. File shelf list and all catalog cards.	. 376	6. 000	2. 256	1. 25	4. 1654	1	. 0166	. 069
68. Revise filing of shelf list and all catalog cards.	. 145	6. 000	. 870	1. 15	1. 4778	3	. 0751	. 111
69. Route card sets to departmental libraries.	NA	---	---	---	---	-	---	---
70. Paperback books--bindery routine (preparation).	NA	---	---	---	---	-	---	---
71. Paperback books--bindery routine (receiving).	NA	---	---	---	---	-	---	---
72. Catalog maintenance (other than filing).	. 166	. 828	. 137	1. 10	. 2226	3	. 0751	. 017
73. General typing (specify).	NA	---	---	---	---	-	---	---
74. General revision (specify).	NA	---	---	---	---	-	---	---
75. General filing (specify).	NA	---	---	---	---	-	---	---
76. Other cataloging activities not listed above (specify).								

Sub-total	. 486
Acquisitions	1. 004
Cataloging	. 486
ΣL	1. 490

Appendix 5. 1
Overall Standard Times
Acquisitions

Key:

AF = Another function incorporated this activity at this library.
NA = Not applicable (not performed at this library).

Activity Description	#1	#2	#3
1. Open, sort and distribute incoming mail.	1. 4971	. 4739	. 6662
2. Review book order requests; review . . .	AF	1. 3908	. 6970
3. Select titles to be ordered.	AF	AF	AF
4. Type library request card.	2. 5633	1. 0415	NA
5. Search and verify bibliographic . . .	5. 2269	3. 8329	5. 2998
6. Assign vendor and fund.	. 1312	. 7718	. 6709
7. Prepare multiple order record.	1. 6953	1. 1162	6. 4549
8. Type purchase requisition, etc.	1. 4439	5. 9728	3. 6851
9. Revise typing. Sign and mail requests.	AF	1. 3453	. 6625
10. Burst forms.	. 4095	. 3136	2. 0792
11. File forms in appropriate files.	1. 9563	2. 3657	1. 7448
12. Encumbrance or prepayment routine.	. 9716	NA	NA
13. Unpack books; check against packing . . .	1. 0498	2. 8857	3. 8038
14. Check in serials on Kardex.	NA	NA	4. 6254
15. Collate books.	1. 0278	NA	NA
16. Book return procedure (incorrect shipment . . .)	8. 9104	8. 9104	5. 5802
17. Book accessioning routine.	. 9105	. 5102	NA
18. Write sourcing information.	. 4892	NA	NA
19. Prepare gift record form.	3. 3959	3. 3959	3. 5502
20. Book distribution routine.	AF	. 4387	1. 7210

Note: These times are the product of observed mean time, the personal rating factor and the standardizing factor (1. 4771).

Library #4	#5	#6	#7	#8	#9	Mean
. 3935	1. 9904	. 6662	1. 3424	. 8000	. 7616	. 9546
1. 3908	AF	1. 3908	AF	NA	1. 2066	1. 2152
AF	AF	AF	AF	NA	AF	AF
2. 6381	3. 7855	. 9970	1. 8198	AF	2. 3527	2. 1711
5. 0385	20. 1232	AF	2. 3625	5. 4193	3. 2010	6. 3130
. 7335	. 1024	. 5232	. 1957	2. 5588	see U	. 7109
1. 6659	22. 5897	1. 2845	. 9058	. 9081	1. 5332	4. 2393
20. 9391	11. 6840	. 5193	NA	12. 9267	16. 2481	9. 1774
2. 4798	1. 4062	NA	NA	. 1737	. 6417	1. 1182
. 2183	5. 5334	. 3730	. 8065	NA	. 4383	1. 2715
2. 7097	3. 7244	. 8224	3. 6809	2. 6976	. 5504	2. 2502
AF	1. 4328	1. 6102	. 7440	. 7160	1. 0870	1. 0936
6. 5837	9. 7929	. 9660	3. 0295	8. 9574	1. 1976	4. 2518
. 7848	2. 6614	NA	8. 0150	16. 3976	NA	6. 4968
NA	1. 3063	NA	. 5513	NA	NA	. 9618
8. 9104	8. 9104	8. 9104	8. 9104	10. 6500	8. 9104	8. 7337
NA	NA	. 7196	5. 0269	NA	1. 7040	1. 7742
1. 4840	NA	NA	1. 0318	NA	NA	1. 0017
2. 2910	AF	. 0816	3. 3959	6. 8859	AF	3. 2858
. 3019	AF	AF	AF	1. 1764	NA	. 9095

Appendix 5. 1 (continued)

Acquisitions

Activity Description	#1	#2	#3
21. Prepare receiving report.	2. 3917	2. 8678	4. 5332
22. Prepare invoices for payment.	1. 4120	1. 0691	. 7403
23. Expenditure routine.	. 3465	AF	3. 8390
24. Clear in-process file.	1. 2077	AF	1. 0009
25. File forms, etc., in completed records ...	. 5996	NA	AF
26. Requester notification routine.	. 7224	. 2258	. 0408
27. Periodic accessions list routine.	. 8663	9. 2858	NA
28. Vendor status routine.	6. 2896	6. 7690	2. 5753
29. Claims routine.	5. 3034	AF	5. 3034
30. Cancellations routine.	3. 1663	AF	6. 6650
31. Out-of-print order routine.	4. 1481	NA	AF
32. Process inquiries.	AF	11. 1706	5. 0304
33. General typing - correspondence ...	AF	AF	3. 0449
34. General revision (specify).	AF	NA	AF
35. General filing (specify).	AF	1. 3892	AF
36. Other acquisitions activities ...	AF	NA	15. 0457
Acquisitions sub-total	58. 1323	66. 5427	89. 0599

Cataloging

Activity Description	#1	#2	#3
37. Sort books, assign and distribute.	2. 7297	2. 8239	. 5368
38. Search for LC copy; verify bibliographic ...	5. 1279	2. 2747	13. 7636
39. Order LC cards or other unit cards.	NA	NA	NA
40. Receive and arrange LC cards.	NA	NA	NA

#4	Library #5	#6	#7	#8	#9	Mean
NA	NA	AF	5. 9399	NA	NA	3. 9332
. 9213	3. 3837	AF	AF	. 5328	1. 3477	1. 3438
4. 2328	1. 1483	. 2996	. 6647	. 1722	AF	1. 5290
AF	NA	. 9700	AF	. 4684	NA	. 9118
1. 8950	AF	2. 2406	3. 2648	1. 0604	2. 1388	1. 8665
1. 3707	. 5140	. 6775	. 1953	. 2055	1. 6662	. 6242
9. 2858	14. 0010	9. 2858	3. 5454	NA	15. 3934	8. 8091
11. 9294	6. 2896	6. 2896	6. 2896	1. 6733	6. 2896	6. 0439
5. 3034	5. 3034	5. 3034	5. 3034	5. 3034	AF	5. 3034
6. 6650	6. 6650	6. 6650	7. 1719	9. 2561	AF	6. 6078
3. 9427	AF	NA	AF	4. 1481	NA	4. 0796
10. 2785	47. 6606	17. 0475	2. 2585	16. 5861	17. 0475	15. 8850
10. 8738	24. 8401	7. 9876	AF	13. 9115	AF	12. 1316
. 5397	1. 4097	NA	AF	6. 1057	NA	2. 6850
10. 9480	. 9001	. 3331	AF	1. 3096	NA	2. 9760
9. 3784	AF	NA	. 3563	12. 1750	NA	9. 2388
146. 1275	217. 4932	75. 9684	76. 8082	143. 1756	83. 7158	141. 8990
1. 1229	1. 8279	AF	. 6591	7. 5904	see U	2. 4701
7. 0338	1. 4542	3. 9304	5. 1699	6. 1190	see U	5. 6091
2. 5656	1. 3707	AF	. 8919	NA	4. 1438	2. 2430
. 9180	2. 2792	. 6653	1. 8832	NA	1. 7120	1. 4915

Appendix 5. 1 (continued)
Cataloging

Activity Description	#1	#2	#3
41. Receive and arrange LC proof slips ...	.3541	NA	.7409
42. File LC copy. (cards or proof)	.3510	NA	.4046
43. Match LC cards or proof copy and books.	AF	AF	1.3164
44. Added copies/added volumes routine.	10.6912	10.9447	9.3069
45. Catalog and classify with LC cards/ copy.	8.5059	10.3025	2.3419
46. Original cataloging and classifying.	25.6411	28.3594	22.8789
47. Shelf listing (for 44, 45, and 46).	7.6529	AF	AF
48. Type complete card sets.	NA	NA	NA
49. Type master card.	3.3032	2.4114	3.7176
50. Revise master card.	1.6833	AF	1.0318
51. Type modification on a card or proof slip.	AF	AF	AF
52. Reproduce card sets (other than typing) ...	.7312	2.7554	1.2375
53. Type call number, added entries.	2.6712	1.8094	2.9660
54. Revise typing on card sets.	2.1610	1.4688	1.5882
55. Prepare authority cards.	NA	NA	1.9449
56. Prepare cross-reference cards.	.0406	3.1619	3.1619
57. Prepare circulation card.	.8368	.6832	NA
58. Prepare book pocket.	1.1016	1.0284	NA
59. Mark call number or place label on ...	3.2837	1.1900	2.2244
60. Affix pocket and date due slip ...	.5183	.6668	.3542
61. Affix biographical and review material ...	1.3145	AF	NA
62. Stamp property marks.	1.9356	.3363	.3916
63. Affix plastic jacket to book.	NA	NA	NA

Library #4	#5	#6	#7	#8	#9	Mean
. 9115	. 6093	NA	NA	. 2778	NA	. 5785
. 7490	. 7328	NA	NA	. 4145	NA	. 5304
. 8746	. 9173	1. 7634	2. 7622	11. 1949	. 2464	2. 7250
10. 9447	7. 6923	AF	4. 3317	11. 0626	10. 9447	9. 4898
19. 4474	13. 6555	6. 3279	12. 3725	4. 7688	see U	9. 7153
27. 2351	46. 7783	18. 6518	31. 8699	34. 0625		29. 4346
2. 3122	AF	AF	1. 5988	4. 2167	2. 1542	3. 5870
NA	NA	18. 9837	8. 4726	NA	see U	13. 7282
2. 9702	14. 5242	NA	2. 2728	11. 0113	see U	5. 7444
AF	. 9489	AF	AF	. 4387	see U	1. 0257
4. 7834	AF	AF	AF	. 2518	see U	2. 5176
1. 5238	5. 8447	NA	NA	6. 8797	see U	3. 1620
7. 7861	7. 7546	3. 5672	5. 9202	. 6338	see U	4. 1386
. 9088	. 4956	2. 2195	. 1613	1. 6718	see U	1. 3344
2. 9490	. 8626	1. 2998	NA	3. 0579	NA	2. 0228
3. 1619	3. 1619	3. 0182	AF	5. 7096	3. 1619	3. 0722
1. 1595	1. 2189	. 8806	1. 1551	NA	. 6065	. 9344
1. 2570	. 7802	. 7312	1. 0158	NA	. 7049	. 9456
2. 0673	1. 6573	2. 0505	1. 4291	2. 7671	2. 4495	2. 1243
. 8468	1. 6411	. 7685	. 3970	. 7052	. 8273	. 7472
NA	NA	NA	1. 6674	NA	NA	1. 4910
. 5959	. 6808	. 3767	. 8443	. 2388	. 7988	. 6888
NA	9. 7375	3. 8329	NA	NA	7. 4644	7. 0116

Appendix 5. 1 (continued)
Cataloging

Activity Description	#1	#2	#3
64. Paperback books--library binding . . .	4. 6567	NA	5. 2233
65. Revise completed books before . . .	1. 7021	. 5554	. 2939
66. Sort and alphabetize shelf list . . .	. 9408	. 3492	. 3672
67. File shelf list and all catalog cards.	. 9684	1. 6124	. 7442
68. Revise filing of shelf list and all . . .	. 6564	. 2140	1. 2771
69. Route card sets to departmental libraries.	NA	NA	AF
70. Paperback books--bindery routine . . .	2. 0762	NA	1. 2527
71. Paperback books--bindery routine. . .	1. 2251	NA	1. 2251
72. Catalog maintenace (other than filing).	. 0260	. 0276	. 0276
73. General typing (specify).	AF	NA	AF
74. General revision (specify).	. 6759	NA	AF
75. General filing (specify).	AF	NA	AF
76. Other cataloging activities not listed . . .	AF	NA	AF
Cataloging sub-total	93. 5624	72. 9754	80. 3192
Acquisitions sub-total	58. 1323	66. 5427	89. 0599
Cataloging sub-total	93. 5624	72. 9754	80. 3192
Grand total	151. 6947	139. 5181	169. 3791

Library #4	#5	#6	#7	#8	#9	Mean
5. 4382	8. 1517	4. 6534	NA	2. 2585	18. 4790	6. 9801
1. 5619	. 2697	AF	2. 9323	. 1804	. 2156	. 9639
. 2275	. 3024	. 2096	. 1846	. 7295	. 2603	. 3968
1. 1678	1. 8335	. 7328	1. 0421	1. 5096	. 6942	1. 1450
. 5199	1. 0430	. 4679	. 2783	. 3318	. 2464	. 5594
NA	NA	NA	NA	1. 0399	NA	1. 0399
3. 7289	NA	NA	5. 0144	3. 4738	NA	3. 1092
1. 1130	NA	NA	1. 2251	1. 1130	NA	1. 1803
. 0276	. 0227	. 0276	. 0276	. 0276	. 2697	. 0538
NA	AF	. 5170	NA	AF	NA	. 5170
NA	AF	AF	NA	1. 5743	NA	1. 1251
NA	AF	AF	NA	. 7685	NA	. 7685
NA	AF	AF	NA	1. 3291	NA	1. 3291
117. 9093	138. 2488	75. 6759	95. 5792	127. 4089	55. 3796	137. 7312
146. 1275	217. 4932	75. 9684	76. 8082	143. 1756	83. 7158	141. 8990
117. 9093	138. 2488	75. 6759	95. 5792	127. 4089	55. 3796	137. 7312
264. 0368	355. 7420	151. 6443	172. 3874	270. 5845	139. 0954	279. 6302

Appendix 5. 2
Operational Comparison and Standardization
Section I: Acquisitions

Li-brary	Order Request Card	Multiple-Order Record
#1	Demco 18-263.	Demco, 5-part, with carbon.
#2	Demco 257-B1.	Bro-Dart #24286 6-part form with carbon. Library imprinted.
#3	Job printed. White stock. One side only.	Two procedures: 1) Photocopies (SCM) purchase request card (5 at a time) on sheets pre-stacked in five colors, cuts to 3 x 5 size. 2) Types speed-kraft 6-part form, with carbon. Library imprinted.
#4	Job printed. White stock. Retyped if necessary. Heavy paper stock. Both sides.	Job printed with consecutive numbering. Seven-part with carbon. Library imprinted.
#5	Job printed. Yellow stock. Retyped if necessary. Library imprint and directions for requesting library books on verso.	Time-saver 10-part with self-carboning paper. Tenth copy is buff card stock. Library imprinted.
#6	Gaylord Form 101-L.	Gaylord #555, 5-part with carbon.
#7	Gaylord Form 101-L, received typed from faculty. One side only.	Gaylord 5-part with carbon #55 Library imprinted.
#8	Job printed. White stock. Library imprint. Both sides used for search information.	Assigns number and photocopies purchase request card (6 at a time) on Xerox on sheets pre-stacked in 5 colors. Cuts to 3 x 5 size with electric cutter. Staples into packs for encumbering
#9	Uses the sixth part of the multiple-order form provided by Professional Library Service. This is on buff card stock.	Uses other 5 parts of the PLS form. Form is with carbon.

CALBPC Proposed	Two-part order request, similar to # 8's to facilitate searching. Second copy remains at requesting library.	Participating libraries will be notified whenever a basic title is ordered centrally.
Decision of Council of Librarians 11/8/67	As proposed.	As proposed.

Section II: Bookkeeping

Library	Orders Placement Procedure	Library Accounting Procedure
# 1	Types purchase requisition on which the author, title, number of copies wanted, and price for each book is given. Forwards purchase request to business office which types a purchase order and sends the library an information copy.	Enters each book in ledger according to fund. Files white 3 x 5 slip on department outstanding order file.
# 2	Sends white 3 x 5 slip with letter to vendor	(None. Treats all orders as confirming.)
# 3	Sends white copy of multiple-order form to vendor.	Same as Library # 2.
# 4	Sends white multiple-order slips to vendor and pink slip to business office to prepare a purchase order.	Ledgers under "Outstanding Orders" and by fund. Files multiple-order slips by vendor pack.
# 5	Types buff card, remainder of multiform, and purchase requisition. Sends white copy and five white carbon copies attached to requisition to business office. Types vendor card and bands other slips with it.	Ledgers only expenditures on gift funds.
# 6	Types a purchase order for each vendor listing author, title, number of copies, and list price of each book. Files order pack except for pink slips by main entry.	Files pink 3 x 5 slips in departmental encumbrance file. Ledgers purchase order by date, order number, dealer, and amount and sends to business office. Retains carbon of purchase order.

Appendix 5.2 (continued)
Section II: Bookkeeping

Library	Orders Placement Procedure	Library Accounting Procedure
#7	Types purchase requisitions; submits to business office.	Ledgers by fund. Files green slip by requester as encumbrance.
#8	Punches encumbrance card for each title according to fund. Sends white 3 x 5 slip to vendor.	Every two weeks submits all punched cards to University Data Processing and obtains run off ledger from same.
#9	Sends white, blue, and yellow 3 x 5 slips to PLS. PLS prepares machine run off of the titles they can provide and sends this list back in 5 copies. Library types purchase requisition, attaches lists, and sends to business office.	Ledgers each purchase requisition in by date. Logs in purchase order number when purchase order is received from business office indicating placement.
CALBPC Proposed	One copy of multiform will be sent to vendor. Encumbrance card punched for each title.	Each participating library will receive a monthly statement of its account. The statement will include: 1) encumbrances, 2) expenditures, and 3) free balance.
Decision	As proposed.	As proposed.

Section III: Cataloging, Classification, Card Reproduction, and Related Operations

Library	Receiving-Payment Procedure	Classification
#1	Pulls purchase request card & green & white slips from outstanding order file. Also pulls requisition & purchase order. Records actual cost on these. Ledgers in receipts under book fund. Prepares budget report & departmental book funds reports each month. Types receiving report listing author, title, number of copies & actual cost, attaches 3 copies of invoice & sends to business office for payment.	Dewey, 17th edition.

# 2	When book arrives, types requisition, writes out receiving report, attaches invoice and green 3 x 5 slip and purchase request and receiving report. Sends all to business office for payment.	L. C.
# 3	Bookkeeper types purchase order and receiving report. Enters expenditure in ledger fund. Sends receiving report, purchase order and invoice to business office for payment.	L. C.
# 4	Sends purchase order, invoice, and pink slips to business office. Enters expenditure in ledger. Updates vendor slip and refiles it.	Dewey, 13th edition.
# 5	Pulls vendor pack, house card, and purchase request. Stamps date inside top left corner of front board and ownership on top edge. Sends invoice to secretary. Secretary routes invoice to business office for payment.	LC.
# 6	Checks books received against multiple order file, purchase order and invoice. Ledgers and forwards completed invoices to business office for payment. Pulls pink slips from encumbrance file and discards. Files green slips in fund expenditure file.	L.C., modified if deemed necessary.
# 7	Types receiving report for each title. Sends receiving report and invoices to business office for payment. Enters expenditure in ledger. Staples order request card to green slip.	Dewey number suggested by L. C.
# 8	Uses pink slip to pull encumbrance cards, punches actual price plus postage on it. Submits all punched cards to Data Processing every two weeks. Sends invoices and pink expenditure slips to business office for payment.	L. C.
# 9	Upon receipt of invoice, checks it against packing slip. Sends completed invoice to business office to initiate payment. If invoice is received by business office first, business office checks status of order by telephone.	L. C.
ALBPC roposed	Checks from member libraries will be recorded on punched cards and forwarded to the business office for payment. Expenditure data will be punched; and collated	L. C.

Appendix 5. 2 (continued)
Section III: Cataloging, Classification, Card Reproduction, and Related Operations

Library	Receiving-Payment Procedure	Classification
	against encumbrance cards. Invoices and accounting slip will be forwarded for payment.	
Decision	As proposed.	As proposed.

Library	Cuttering	Author and Subject Heading Authority
# 1	Cutter-Sanborn	L. C. for both author and subject.
# 2	L. C.	L. C. for both author and subject.
# 3	L. C.	L. C. for both author and subject.
# 4	Cutter-Sanborn	L. C. for both author and subject.
# 5	L. C.	L. C. for both author and subject.
# 6	Cutter-Sanborn with modifications.	L. C. for both author and subject.
# 7	Cutter-Sanborn	L. C. for author. L. C. and/or Sears for subject.
# 8	L. C.	L. C. for both author and subject.
# 9	L. C.	L. C. for both author and subject.
CALBPC Proposed	L. C.	L. C. for both author and subject.
Decision	As proposed.	As proposed.

Library	Authority and Cross-Reference Cards	Catalog Card Reproduction and Processing
#1	Maintains series authority file. Types cross references.	Types master card from National Union Catalog. Reproduces on Ektafax. *
#2	No authority files. Types cross reference cards.	Two procedures: 1) Orders card sets from L. C. when available. 2) Types master card and runs it on Ektafax. *
#3	Maintains name, series, and subject authority files. Types cross reference cards.	Xeroxes proof slip when available. If no proof slip, photocopies page in National Union Catalog of useable entry. Types master card. Xeroxes master card.
#4	No author or subject authority files. Has series authority file. Types cross reference cards.	Orders sets of cards from L. C. or xeroxes set if proof sheet available (education only). Types and xeroxes master cards. Uses perforated stock.
#5	Maintains official series and subject authority files. Types cross reference cards.	Same as #4 except maintains proof sheet file given to them by another library.
#6	Maintains series authority file. Types cross references.	Orders L. C. card sets. If not available, types complete sets using lined catalog cards (Gaylord #306).
#7	No authority files. Types cross reference cards.	Monographs: Types card sets; types added entries in black, subject headings in red; childrens' literature: reproduces card sets on xerox.
#8	Same as #3	Three procedures: 1) Obtains L. C. copy in form of either proof copy or enlargement from National Union Catalog. Xeroxes either. 2) If entry is to be several cards long & there is no L. C. copy available, cuts tape & runs cards on Flexowriter. 3) Types master card & xeroxes.
#9	No authority files. Types cross reference cards.	Two procedures: 1) Cards arrive with books already processed from PLS. 2) For books locally cataloged, orders sets of L. C. cards.

*Carbon paper no longer manufactured.

Appendix 5. 2 (continued)

Section III: Cataloging, Classification, Card Reproduction, and Related Operations

Library	Authority and Cross-Reference Cards	Catalog Card Reproduction and Processing
CALBPC Proposed	Believe this can better be accomplished at the local library.	Xerox reproduction using die cut stock; cards photo reproduces six-up; power cut to size. May use perforated stock four-up.
Decision	As proposed.	Subject headings will be in red. Pattern of capitalization will follow tracings on L. C. card. Call number will be formated as per example: DS 35 W4 1966

Library	Sourcing Information	Accessioning Procedure
#1	Writes date received, initials of vendor, & actual cost along inside edge of page following verso of title page.	Stamps accession number on right front flyleaf verso of title page and left back flyleaf. Ledgers only the inclusive numbers for the number of books accessioned at any one time.
#2	Not applicable.	Stamps accession number on verso of title page. Later types accession number on upper right corner of circulation card and pocket.
#3	Not applicable.	Not applicable.
#4	Writes date received, vendor, & price on inside edge of page following verso of title page.	Not applicable.
#5	Not applicable.	Not applicable.
#6	Not applicable.	Stamps accession number on verso of title page, page 99 of book, L. C. order slip (yellow multiple order form), buff card of multiple order form, blank white circulation card, blank card pocket. Shelves books in holding area by accession number. Writes number on purchase request

		card and files in in-process file.
#7	Writes date received, vendor, price, fund, & requester along inside edge of title page.	Formal accessions record; in four sections: 1) Monographs, 2) Periodicals, 3) Childrens' Literature, 4) Government Documents. Accessions number in book: 1) Top of fly leaf, right corner, 2) Top of contents page, 3) Bottom of page 50.
#8	Not applicable.	Not applicable.
#9	Not applicable.	Stamps accession numbers 6 times for each book on 1) Blue slip, 2) shelf list, 3) pocket, 4) circulation card, 5) packing slip, 6) verso of title page. Keeps packing slip in a notebook.
CALBPC Proposed	Local operation.	No accessioning. (Copy numbers will be used to distinguish multiple copies ordered by one library.)
Decision	As proposed.	As proposed.

Section IV: Mechanical Preparation

Library	Book Pocket	Spine Label
#1	Demco 25-310 with library imprint and circulation policy. Types call number, author, title and accession number. Pastes on inside back board.	Types label using Se-Lin label strip. Trims corners of label. Seals to spine with teflon iron.
#2	Gaylord style F plain. Types like circulation card. Pastes on inside back board of book.	Same as #8 except trims off all excess white.
#3	Not applicable.	Types label using Se-Lin label strip. Trims excess white off. Applies on several spines at once with teflon iron.
#4	Pastes pocket on front inside board, centered at bottom.	Types label using Se-Lin label strip. Trims corners. Applies with teflon iron individually.

Appendix 5. 2 (continued)
Section IV: Mechanical Preparation

Library	Book Pocket	Spine Label
#5	Gaylord style F. Types call number only. Pastes it on inside front board.	Hand letters with stylus and transfer tape, white or black. Applies drop of paint under call number if for reading rooms.
#6	Gaylord style F. Types call number. Pocket has library imprint. Pastes pocket on inside front board.	Hand letters spine with electric stylus. Applies mystic tape beforehand if texture of binding is rough. Sprays spine.
#7	Gaylord style F; printed with library name and circulation policy. Types call number, author, title, and accessions number. Pastes pocket on inside back cover.	Hand letters spine in white or black ink. Sprays spine with lacquer.
#8	Not applicable.	Types label using Se-Lin labeler. Cuts but does not trim label. Applies to each spine individually.
#9	Bro-Dart #25-310, with library imprint. Types call number, author, title and accession number. Pastes on right front flyleaf.	Types pressure sensitive "Avery" label. Applied to spine, coats label and immediate border with plastic glue. Same method as used by PLS.
CALBPC Proposed	Pocket with machine printed label (call number, title) pasted inside front board. Hinged if flyleaf contains a map.	A machine printed label applied with plastic glue: coating.
Decision	As proposed.	As proposed.

Library	Date Due Slip	Circulation Card
# 1	Gaylord # 3533, gummed. Places on verso back flyleaf opposite pocket.	Bro-Dart # 23102, notched, blank white. Types call number, author, title, and accession number.
# 2	Gaylord # 3533, gummed. Places on inside back flyleaf opposite book pocket.	Gaylord # 45, white. One card system. White only. Types call number, complete author, title and accession number.
# 3	Gaylord # 3533 gummed. Moistens several at one time with brush. Applies to inside front board.	One - Two card (McBee).
# 4	Demco # 38-297.	One card system. White only. Types call number, author, title and copy number.
# 5	Demco # 38-297. Pastes slip on front flyleaf.	Gaylord # 40. Two-card system. White - circulation; Blue - closed reserve. 10-1/8". Types call number, author, and title.
# 6	Gaylord # 3533, gummed. Applies to pocket.	Gaylord # 40, white. One card system.
# 7	Demco # 38-297, gummed. Pastes slip on verso of back flyleaf opposite pocket.	Gaylord # 45 One-card system white - circulation; blue - reference. Types call number, author and title. Accessions number typed on upper right corner.
# 8	Gaylord # 3533, gummed. Moistens and applies individually to lower part of front flyleaf.	One - Two card (McBee).
# 9	Bro-Dart, gummed. Moistens and applies to inside front board opposite pocket.	Bro-Dart # 23250, White, one-card system. Types call number, author, title, and accession number.
CALBPC Proposed	Slip located inside front flyleaf opposite pocket.	One circulation card. Call number and title.
Decision	As proposed.	As proposed.

Appendix 5. 2 (continued)
Section IV: Mechanical Preparation

Library	Property Stamp	Plastic Jacketing
# 1	Stamps 3 edges, inside front board, verso of title page, page 25, bottom of last page of text, bottom of verso of back flyleaf, top of inside board.	Not applicable.
# 2	Stamps at time of receipt in 3 places; verso of title page, lower right corner of inside back board, and bottom page.	Not applicable.
# 3	Stamps top edge of book and bottom edge of page after title page.	Not applicable.
# 4	Stamps 3 edges, inside front board at upper left corner, front flyleaf at bottom right corner, page after title page, middle back flyleaf, several times within body on right.	Not applicable.
# 5	Stamps 3 edges, title page, lower right corner inside back board.	Only books for reading lounge. Uses jackets of exact sizes.
# 6	Stamps 3 edges, top of title page, bottom of verso of title page, page 99, top of back flyleaf.	Applies duplex jackets to all books with dust covers. Cuts hole in backing paper so that call number can be seen.
# 7	Stamps 3 edges, embosses library seal on title page.	Only of children's collection. Books come with plastic jacket.
# 8	Stamps middle edge only.	Not applicable.
# 9	PLS stamps books on 3 edges only.	PLS jackets all books with dust covers. Books locally processed get the Bro-Dart duplex jacket.

CALBPC Proposed	Stamp middle edge.	May furnish at an extra charge.
Decision	CALBPC will not do any property stamping.	CALBPC will not do any plastic jacketing.

Section V: Miscellaneous

Library	Biographical - Review Information	Paperback Books
# 1	Trims blurb and any author information from dust jacket and pastes it on verso of front flyleaf with extra clippings on right hand page following it.	Sends quality paperbounds to commercial bindery after receipt. Puts other paperbounds in pamphlet casings. Pastes label to front cover.
# 2	Clips significant biographical material from dust jacket. Pastes on verso of front flyleaf.	Orders paperbacks prebound when known to be paperbound. Others homebinds or treats like hardbounds.
# 3	Not applicable.	Same as # 1.
# 4	Not applicable.	Catalogs and sends to bindery.
# 5	Not applicable.	Home binds books in pamphlet casings. Applies pressure-sensitive labels to front covers.
# 6	Not applicable.	Applies plastic jacket.
# 7	Pastes pertinent biographical and review information on front inside cover and flyleaf of book.	Librarian sorts books of lasting value, catalogs and sends to bindery. Other paperbacks: accessions, assigns "PB" number, places in "BP" collection.
# 8	Not applicable	Four procedures: 1) Sends order to paperback jobber, 2) sends to university bindery after cataloging, 3) homebinds, 4) labels and shelves as is.
# 9	Not applicable.	Orders all books known to be paperback through PLS

Appendix 5. 2 (continued)
Section V: Miscellaneous

Library	Biographical - Review Information	Paperback Books
		where the standing instruction is to bind before processing. Homebinds other paperbacks.
CALBPC Proposed	None. Book jackets will be forwarded with book.	Cataloged and forwarded to University or a commercial bindery when a paperback is received instead of hardback, or when requested by a library. Pre-bounds will be ordered from a dealer when so requested.
Decision	As proposed.	As proposed.

Library	Periodic Accessions List
# 1	Quarterly list arranged by broad subject discipline. Each book cited by call number, author, title and date of publication. Mimeographed for general distribution.
# 2	Monthly list arranged by broad L. C. class, and within that by main entry. Typed from shelf list cards on mimeograph mats. Sent to all faculty members.
# 3	Not applicable.
# 4	Semi-annual list arranged by broad L. C. classification. Typed from process slips onto a mimeograph master. Duplicated and distributed to Division Heads.
# 5	Monthly list arranged within broad subject categories by call number. Types rough draft from shelf list cards. Stencils draft. Printing office duplicates. Clerk routes copy to each faculty member.
# 6	Reference Librarian selects and annotates

about a dozen new books each week. This information is mimeographed for general distribution.

#7	Monthly list arranged by broad Dewey classification prepared using entries in accessions record. Dittoed and distributed generally.
#8	Several departmental libraries prepare and distribute selected accessions lists on a periodic basis.
#9	Quarterly when staff time permits. By broad L. C. classification. Prepared from process slips.
CALBPC Proposed	Special lists produced by computer as by-products will be one goal, but development of such a system will take some time.
Decision	As proposed.

Appendix 8. 1
Library Services Questionnaire

Please return questionnaire to the library no later than ____________

Department ____________ College Teaching Experience: ______ Years

Degrees ____________ Subject Fields ____________

Institution ____________ ____________

Please answer the following questions on the rating scale provided to the right of the column. Place an x on the appropriate line.

1. The bibliographic and reference sources I need for my research activities are available to me at the library(s) on campus:
   - never a. ____
   - rarely b. ____
   - sometimes c. ____
   - usually d. ____
   - always e. ____
   - don't know f. ____

2. Resources in my subject field are available to me in sufficient quantity to support the courses offered at the institution:
   - yes a. ____
   - no b. ____
   - in part c. ____
   - not used in course work d. ____
   - don't know e. ____

3. Resources in my subject field are available to me in sufficient quality to support the courses offered at the institution:
   - yes a. ____
   - no b. ____
   - in part c. ____
   - not used in course work d. ____
   - don't know e. ____

4. I am engaged in research activities which require bibliographic and reference sources:
   - never a. ____
   - rarely b. ____
   - sometimes c. ____
   - usually d. ____
   - always e. ____

5. The services of the reference librarian are:
   - never helpful a. ____
   - rarely helpful b. ____
   - sometimes helpful c. ____
   - usually helpful d. ____
   - always helpful e. ____
   - I've never sought help f. ____

6. In my usual research activities the immediate availability of reference materials is:
   - never important a. ____
   - rarely important b. ____
   - sometimes important c. ____
   - usually important d. ____
   - always important e. ____

7. The acquisition by the library of books and periodicals in my subject area is:
   - insufficient a. ____
   - adequate b. ____
   - excellent c. ____
   - don't know d. ____

8. The card catalog is sufficiently subject indexed for my needs:
   - never a. ____
   - rarely b. ____
   - sometimes c. ____
   - usually d. ____
   - always e. ____
   - do not use f. ____

Note: Responses 1f, 2e, 3e, 7d, 9f, 10d, 11f, and 14e were added after the general mailing. See pag 220 for explanation.

9. The cards in the card catalog contain sufficient information with which I can select the books I need:
   - never a. ____
   - rarely b. ____
   - sometimes c. ____
   - usually d. ____
   - always e. ____
   - do not use f. ____

10. Library resources and services in my subject area are adequate to the support of my teaching needs:
    - yes a. ____
    - no b. ____
    - in part c. ____
    - don't teach d. ____

11. New books pertinent to my work are already in the library's collection at the time I request them:
    - never a. ____
    - rarely b. ____
    - sometimes c. ____
    - usually d. ____
    - always e. ____
    - don't know f. ____

12. Interlibrary loan service is (for my needs):
    - too slow a. ____
    - adequate b. ____
    - excellent c. ____
    - do not use d. ____

13. Photocopying service (i. e., xeroxing, thermofax, SCM, etc.) for library materials is:
    - difficult to obtain a. ____
    - available but slow b. ____
    - adequate c. ____
    - usually satisfactory d. ____
    - always satisfactory e. ____
    - do not use f. ____

14. Organized translation service is:
    - not available a. ____
    - available but slow b. ____
    - adequate c. ____
    - not needed d. ____
    - don't know if there is one e. ____

15. I have need for a translation of an article or a portion of a book:
    - never a. ____
    - one to three times a year b. ____
    - four to six times a year c. ____
    - seven to ten times a year d. ____
    - more than ten times a year e. ____

16. Demand bibliographies (literature searches) on special subjects are:
    - not provided by the library a. ____
    - provided, but slowly b. ____
    - promptly provided c. ____
    - never asked for one d. ____

17. The library informs me of current books acquired in my areas of interest:
    - never a. ____
    - rarely b. ____
    - sometimes c. ____
    - usually d. ____
    - always e. ____

18. The library provides a current contents listing of periodicals in my areas of interest received by the library:
    - never a. ____
    - rarely b. ____
    - sometimes c. ____
    - usually d. ____
    - always e. ____

19. The library provides specialized reference and research services in my subject area:
    - yes a. ____
    - no b. ____
    - don't know c. ____

Appendix 8. 1 (continued)
Library Services Questionnaire

20. I have requested:
    one to three a. ____
    four to six b. ____
    seven to ten c. ____
    more than ten d. ____
    not any e. ____
    rush books within the past year.

21. The library provides rush book requests to me within:
    one week a. ____
    two weeks b. ____
    three weeks c. ____
    four weeks d. ____
    five or more weeks e. ____
    never requested one f. ____

22. Reclassification of the book collection from Dewey to the Library of Congress classification in our library:
    has made locating books difficult a. ____
    has not affected my ability to locate books b. ____
    has made locating books easier c. ____
    is not being done at our library d. ____
    do not know if it is being done e. ____

May a member of the research project's staff discuss your questionnaire reply with you during the month of December or January?

yes a. ____
no b. ____

Possible Services

Note: Funds are not now available for initiation of any of the following suggested services. However, your reaction is sought to those services which you would most like to have, should funding be provided to begin one or more services on a test basis.

Instruction for Completing Possible Services Section

Here are 12 items describing services which may, or may not be of significance to you. If you feel that the item is very significant to your research-study needs, circle #1. If you believe the item is somewhat significant, circle #2. If you feel that the item is very insignificant to your needs, circle #5. If you believe it to be somewhat insignificant, circle #4.

If you cannot make up your mind whether an item is significant, circle #3.

Very Significant	Somewhat Significant	Neutral	Somewhat Insignificant	Very Insignificant
1	2	3	4	5

A. Bibliographic Network 1 2 3 4 5
A rapid communication system (teletype, dataphone, etc.) linking the state's libraries, to speed book requests and interlibrary loans.

B. Library Acquisitions List 1 2 3 4 5
A complete, or selected list of books and other materials recently acquired by your library, subject arranged.

C. Union Library Acquisitions List 1 2 3 4 5
A complete, composite list of books and other materials recently acquired by all participating libraries. (Would include B, Individual Library Acquisitions List.)

D. Book Catalog 1 2 3 4 5
A catalog of library holdings in book form, which can be located at as many designated areas on campus as the institution is prepared to finance. This would not be a retrospective catalog, but a holdings catalog as of a specified beginning date.

E. Union Book Catalog 1 2 3 4 5
A composite catalog in book form of all participating libraries holdings; catalog would be located at each library and at as many designated areas on campus as each institution is prepared to finance. (Would include D, Individual Book Catalogs.)

F. Bibliographies 1 2 3 4 5
Specific subject bibliographies/literature searches compiled by the library for requesters on a demand basis. Should the Center obtain the equipment to search magnetic tape files, use could be made of the machine readable output of the Library of Congress, Atomic Energy Commission, Department of Defense, National Aeronautics and Space Agency, etc., in producing subject bibliographies.

G. Periodical Contents Service 1 2 3 4 5
Reproduced contents pages of selected periodicals routed to academic departments on a routine basis.

H. Union List of Serial Holdings 1 2 3 4 5
A composite listing of the serial/periodical holdings of all participating libraries. Such a list would be available at each library and at designated locations on each campus.

I. Telefacsimile Transmission 1 2 3 4 5
Telefacsimile transmission equipment would be located in those libraries for which there was sufficient demand for rush of materials, and where normal interlibrary loan procedures would not suffice. Economics of telefacsimile transmission would have to be examined in each case.

J. Delivery Service for Specific Requests 1 2 3 4 5
Demand delivery and pickup of library materials to any office on

Very Significant 1	Somewhat Significant 2	Neutral 3	Somewhat Insignificant 4	Very Insignificant 5

campus. Researcher would phone request to library, attendant would locate materials in library, and deliver to researcher. Attendant would call researcher if materials were not in collection and arrange for an interlibrary loan or purchase if researcher so desired.

K. Expanded Courier Service 1 2 3 4 5
Extend the twice-weekly book request and delivery service now operating between Fort Collins and Denver, to a daily service between Fort Collins and Pueblo.

L. Telephone Answering Service 1 2 3 4 5
An answering service to receive requests for library materials during hours when library is closed. Messages would be placed with the tape recording answering service, and requests would be filled the next morning.

Perhaps none of the above services would aid you in research/study; or you may favor another service not listed above which the Center and your library could provide.

Please list any such service(s) and include in the rating scale:

_______________________________ 1 2 3 4 5

_______________________________ 1 2 3 4 5

Please list any additional comments:

Thanks again for your coopeation.

Appendix 8. 2
Attitude Survey Interview Check List

Institution__________________ Date__________________

Subject__________________ Phone # __________________

Interviewer__________________ Preparation__________________

	Comments	Validated Question	Yes	No	Alt. Answer
General Use					
1. When you are compiling a bibliography, writing a paper or doing other research, do you use the library collection?		4			
2. Do you usually phone for specific requests, or do you go to the library?		1			
3. Are you generally interested in finding a specific, referenced title, or do you browse in the stacks in your general area of interest?		8, 9, 19			
4. How do you use the card catalog? (author__; title__; subject__)		8, 9			
5. From examination of a card in the catalog, can you determine if you need to examine the book?		9			
6. Do you feel that the information given on the card is adequate for your needs? (too much__; too little__)		8, 9			
7. Can you obtain assistance in locating materials or finding answers to specific questions while at the library?		5, 19			
8. What kind of information needs do you have?		1, 4, 6-11, 14-19			
9. Do you ask for help?		5, 19			
10. Who do you ask?					
Collection					
11. Are the standard works in your field represented in the book collection?		3, 7			

Appendix 8. 2 (continued)
Attitude Survey Interview Check List

	Comments	Validated Question	Yes	No	Alt. Answer
12. Do you find that there are enough indexes, bibliographies, encyclopedias, and other source materials in your field?		1			
13. What do you find lacking most often?		2, 3, 7, 10			
14. Are new books in your field in the library when you need them?		11			
15. Is it important that new books be immediately available?		6, 11			
16. Would knowledge of and availability to new books affect your teaching or reading habits?		6, 11			
17. Do you feel confident when assigning term paper topics that your students will have enough in-depth source material with which to work?		7, 10			
18. Are there enough books in your subject field in the library to go around at term paper time?		2			
19. Do you have a hard time in determining what subjects are really represented in the library's book collection?		8			
20. What are the weakest areas of coverage in the fields of interest to you?		1, 2, 3, 7, 10			
Services					
21. Have you ever had need for a copy of a book on a "rush" basis?		20			
22. Did you order the book(s) through the library ?		20			
23. Was the "rush" service satisfactory?		21			
24. Have you ever requested a book on inter-library loan through		12			

	Comments	Question	Validated Yes	Validated No	Alt. Answer
your library?					
25. Did you get the book?		12			
26. Did it arrive in time to meet your needs?		12			
27. Can you obtain copies of material from books and periodicals quickly and easily?		13			
28. Do you use this service often?		13			
29. How long does the photocopying take?		13			
30. What would be a satisfactory delay time?		13			
31. Do you ever have need for a translation of an article or book?		14, 15			
32. How do you determine if a translation already exists?		14, 15			
33. Is there a translation service available in the library or on campus?		14, 15			
34. If so, who provides it?		14, 15			
35. Can you get useful reading lists from the library to use in conjunction with course assignments?		10, 16			
36. Do you need demand bibliographies; What kind; What subjects; In what format?		16			
37. How often do you receive from the library a list of current books in your field?		17			
38. What kind of a list is it? How is it organized?		17			
39. Are you interested in a current contents service for periodicals?		18			

Possible Services

Cross-check ratings on pages 3 and 4 for possible conflict with responses on pages 1 and 2; if such a conflict exists, ask individual about rating on specific services. Otherwise verify that services are clear to respondent, and accept ratings.

40. Interviewer's Observations ______________________

____

Appendix 8. 3
Response Percent by Library for Each Question

Question 1

Lib.	a	b	c	d	e	f	Unusable Data
1	3. 13	9. 38	46. 87	37. 50	3. 13	0.	0.
2	4. 76	9. 52	42. 86	33. 33	9. 52	0.	0.
3	0.	7. 14	28. 57	59. 29	4. 29	0.	. 71
4	1. 22	6. 10	32. 93	53. 66	4. 88	0.	1. 22
5	0.	8. 16	22. 45	57. 14	10. 20	0.	2. 04
6	0.	0.	0.	0.	0.	0.	0.
7	0.	6. 06	1. 12	66. 67	15. 15	0.	0.
8	. 60	2. 40	22. 75	67. 07	4. 79	1. 80	. 60
9	6. 45	12. 90	41. 94	25. 81	12. 90	0.	0.

Question 2

Lib.	a	b	c	d	e	f	Unusable Data
1	43. 75	18. 75	37. 50	0.	0.	0.	0.
2	42. 86	19. 05	33. 33	4. 76	0.	0.	0.
3	27. 86	10. 00	56. 43	5. 00	0.	0.	. 71
4	30. 49	18. 29	47. 56	3. 66	0.	0.	0.
5	51. 02	6. 12	26. 53	8. 16	4. 08	0.	4. 08
6	0.	0.	0.	0.	0.	0.	0.
7	54. 55	12. 12	27. 27	6. 06	0.	0.	0.
8	38. 92	10. 78	40. 72	6. 59	1. 20	0.	1. 80
9	19. 35	19. 35	61. 29	0.	0.	0.	0.

Question 3

Lib.	a	b	c	d	e	f	Unusable Data
1	37. 50	12. 50	50. 00	0.	0.	0.	0.
2	33. 33	14. 29	47. 62	4. 76	0.	0.	0.
3	37. 14	8. 57	50. 00	4. 29	0.	0.	0.
4	29. 27	9. 76	54. 88	3. 66	1. 22	0.	1. 22
5	53. 06	8. 16	22. 45	8. 16	4. 08	0.	4. 08
6	0.	0.	0.	0.	0.	0.	0.
7	51. 52	6. 06	36. 36	6. 06	0.	0.	0.
8	46. 11	3. 59	38. 92	7. 19	. 60	0.	3. 59
9	38. 71	12. 90	45. 16	3. 23	0.	0.	0.

Question 4

Lib.	a	b	c	d	e	f	Unusable Data
1	3. 13	12. 50	53. 12	25. 00	6. 25	0.	0.
2	14. 29	28. 57	42. 86	9. 52	0.	0.	4. 76
3	4. 29	10. 00	26. 43	29. 29	30. 00	0.	0.
4	2. 44	15. 85	46. 34	18. 29	14. 63	0.	2. 44
5	6. 12	10. 20	34. 69	24. 49	22. 45	0.	2. 04
6	0.	0.	0.	0.	0.	0.	0.
7	6. 06	27. 27	42. 42	21. 21	3. 03	0.	0.
8	. 60	7. 19	31. 14	36. 53	22. 75	0.	1. 80
9	9. 68	22. 58	48. 39	12. 90	6. 45	0.	0.

Question 5

Lib.	a	b	c	d	e	f	Unusable Data
1	0.	0.	6. 25	43. 75	43. 75	6. 25	0.
2	0.	0.	4. 76	28. 57	66. 67	0.	0.
3	0.	5. 71	15. 00	32. 86	32. 14	12. 86	1. 43
4	0.	1. 22	8. 54	30. 49	51. 22	8. 54	0.
5	2. 04	2. 04	8. 16	30. 61	40. 82	16. 33	0.
6	0.	0.	0.	0.	0.	0.	0.
7	0.	0.	3. 03	21. 21	63. 64	9. 09	3. 03
8	0.	2. 99	20. 36	37. 72	24. 55	13. 77	. 60
9	0.	0.	9. 68	41. 94	29. 03	19. 35	0.

Question 6

Lib.	a	b	c	d	e	f	Unusable Data
1	3. 13	6. 25	31. 25	40. 62	18. 75	0.	0.
2	4. 76	9. 52	28. 57	28. 57	28. 57	0.	0.
3	0.	2. 14	31. 43	43. 57	22. 14	. 71	0.
4	0.	8. 54	24. 39	36. 59	30. 49	0.	0.
5	4. 08	10. 20	28. 57	44. 90	12. 24	0.	0.
6	0.	0.	0.	0.	0.	0.	0.
7	3. 03	12. 12	27. 27	39. 39	18. 18	0.	0.
8	0.	2. 99	22. 75	51. 50	22. 16	0.	. 60
9	3. 23	12. 90	25. 81	41. 94	16. 13	0.	0.

Question 7

Lib.	a	b	c	d	e	f	Unusable Data
1	37. 50	53. 12	9. 38	0.	0.	0.	0.
2	38. 10	57. 14	0.	0.	0.	0.	4. 76
3	39. 29	55. 71	2. 86	0.	0.	0.	2. 14
4	42. 68	42. 68	10. 98	1. 22	10. 98	0.	2. 44
5	30. 61	51. 02	12. 24	2. 04	0.	0.	4. 08
6	0.	0.	0.	0.	0.	0.	0.
7	21. 21	48. 48	30. 30	0.	0.	0.	0.
8	32. 34	52. 69	10. 18	2. 40	0.	0.	2. 40
9	54. 84	38. 71	3. 23	0.	0.	0.	3. 23

Question 8

Lib.	a	b	c	d	e	f	Unusable Data
1	0.	6. 25	9. 38	75. 00	9. 38	0.	0.
2	0.	4. 76	14. 29	42. 86	33. 33	4. 76	0.
3	. 71	7. 86	21. 43	60. 00	7. 14	2. 86	0.
4	0.	7. 32	3. 66	60. 98	24. 39	3. 66	0.
5	4. 08	6. 12	6. 12	55. 10	14. 29	14. 29	0.
6	0.	0.	0.	0.	0.	0.	0.
7	0.	6. 06	9. 09	63. 64	18. 18	0.	3. 03
8	0.	5. 39	16. 17	60. 48	11. 38	4. 19	2. 40
9	0.	0.	12. 90	58. 06	19. 35	9. 68	0.

Question 9

Lib.	a	b	c	d	e	f	Unusable Data
1	0.	0.	15. 62	78. 12	6. 25	0.	0.
2	0.	4. 76	4. 76	76. 19	9. 52	0.	4. 76
3	2. 14	4. 29	22. 86	62. 86	6. 43	. 71	. 71
4	0.	3. 66	6. 10	69. 51	19. 51	0.	1. 22

Appendix 8.3 (continued)
Response Percent by Library for Each Question

Lib.	a	b	c	d	e	f	Unusable Data
5	0.	6.12	12.24	55.10	20.41	4.08	2.04
6	0.	0.	0.	0.	0.	0.	0.
7	0.	6.06	0.	63.64	30.30	0.	0.
8	0.	5.99	20.96	57.49	9.58	2.99	3.00
9	3.23	0.	22.58	51.61	19.35	3.23	0.
Question 10							
1	40.62	9.38	50.00	0.	0.	0.	0.
2	52.38	9.52	33.33	4.76	0.	0.	0.
3	40.71	14.29	44.29	0.	0.	0.	.71
4	40.24	13.41	42.68	2.44	0.	0.	1.22
5	59.18	12.24	20.41	4.08	0.	0.	4.08
6	0.	0.	0.	0.	0.	0.	0.
7	57.58	3.03	39.39	0.	0.	0.	0.
8	46.11	5.99	40.72	2.99	0.	0.	0.
9	29.03	16.13	51.61	0.	0.	0.	3.23
Question 11							
1	3.13	31.25	59.37	3.13	0.	0.	3.13
2	9.52	23.81	42.86	19.05	0.	0.	4.76
3	3.57	20.00	43.57	30.00	0.	.71	2.14
4	4.88	32.93	40.24	17.07	0.	0.	4.88
5	6.12	18.37	42.86	20.41	4.08	4.08	4.08
6	0.	0.	0.	0.	0.	0.	0.
7	9.09	30.30	42.42	15.15	0.	3.03	0.
8	1.20	19.76	47.90	25.75	.60	3.59	1.20
9	6.45	51.61	16.13	22.58	0.	0.	3.23
Question 12							
1	15.62	43.75	9.38	31.25	0.	0.	0.
2	9.52	14.29	4.76	66.67	0.	0.	4.76
3	27.14	33.57	5.71	30.71	0.	0.	2.85
4	23.17	32.93	3.66	35.37	0.	0.	4.88
5	16.33	44.90	8.16	30.61	0.	0.	0.
6	0.	0.	0.	0.	0.	0.	0.
7	12.12	30.30	18.18	36.36	0.	0.	3.03
8	22.16	29.34	3.59	38.32	0.	0.	6.58
9	22.58	19.35	3.23	54.84	0.	0.	0.
Question 13							
1	0.	3.13	31.25	28.12	9.38	28.12	0.
2	4.76	0.	9.52	19.05	4.76	61.90	0.
3	2.86	9.29	22.86	25.00	15.00	25.00	0.
4	3.66	8.54	19.51	20.73	24.39	23.17	0.
5	2.04	8.16	18.37	18.37	30.61	22.45	0.
6	0.	0.	0.	0.	0.	0.	0.
7	0.	0.	6.06	24.24	51.52	18.18	0.

Lib.	a	b	c	d	e	f	Unusable Data
8	4. 19	8. 98	16. 77	25. 15	13. 77	28. 74	2. 40
9	9. 68	3. 23	25. 81	6. 45	25. 81	29. 03	0.

Question 14

Lib.	a	b	c	d	e	f	Unusable Data
1	37. 50	0.	0.	62. 50	0.	0.	0.
2	28. 57	0.	0.	71. 43	0.	0.	0.
3	30. 00	2. 86	5. 00	57. 14	2. 86	0.	2. 14
4	12. 20	2. 44	0.	74. 39	2. 44	0.	8. 54
5	24. 49	4. 08	6. 12	55. 10	0.	0.	10. 20
6	0.	0.	0.	0.	0.	0.	0.
7	15. 15	3. 03	6. 06	69. 70	6. 06	0.	0.
8	12. 57	4. 79	2. 99	68. 86	4. 19	0.	6. 59
9	12. 90	0.	0.	74. 19	9. 68	0.	3. 23

Question 15

Lib.	a	b	c	d	e	f	Unusable Data
1	65. 62	28. 12	0.	3. 13	3. 13	0.	0.
2	76. 19	23. 81	0.	0.	0.	0.	0.
3	48. 57	40. 00	6. 43	3. 57	1. 43	0.	0.
4	80. 49	13. 41	3. 66	0.	0.	0.	2. 44
5	46. 94	40. 82	8. 16	0.	2. 04	0.	2. 04
6	0.	0.	0.	0.	0.	0.	0.
7	72. 73	21. 21	0.	0.	3. 03	0.	3. 03
8	50. 30	35. 93	4. 79	1. 80	5. 39	0.	1. 80
9	58. 06	32. 26	0.	3. 23	6. 45	0.	0.

Question 16

Lib.	a	b	c	d	e	f	Unusable Data
1	12. 50	6. 25	0.	78. 12	0.	0.	3. 13
2	0.	0.	9. 52	90. 48	0.	0.	0.
3	15. 00	4. 29	4. 29	75. 00	0.	0.	1. 42
4	4. 88	6. 10	17. 07	67. 07	0.	0.	4. 88
5	16. 33	0.	6. 12	75. 51	0.	0.	2. 04
6	0.	0.	0.	0.	0.	0.	0.
7	0.	6. 06	12. 12	81. 82	0.	0.	0.
8	6. 59	2. 99	4. 19	82. 04	0.	0.	4. 19
9	6. 45	3. 23	12. 90	74. 19	0.	0.	3. 23

Question 17

Lib.	a	b	c	d	e	f	Unusable Data
1	6. 25	3. 13	12. 50	34. 37	43. 75	0.	0.
2	4. 76	0.	0.	42. 86	47. 62	0.	4. 76
3	56. 43	12. 14	15. 00	11. 43	3. 57	0.	1. 42
4	35. 37	10. 98	9. 76	28. 05	12. 20	1. 22	2. 44
5	2. 04	2. 04	8. 16	34. 69	48. 98	0.	4. 08
6	0.	0.	0.	0.	0.	0.	0.
7	0.	0.	3. 03	18. 18	78. 79	0.	0.
8	30. 54	12. 57	12. 57	18. 56	20. 36	0.	5. 39
9	16. 13	6. 45	9. 68	38. 71	29. 03	0.	0.

Appendix 8. 3 (continued)
Response Percent by Library for Each Question

Question 18

Lib.	a	b	c	d	e	f	Unusable Data
1	18. 75	9. 38	15. 62	18. 75	12. 50	25. 00	0.
2	19. 05	0.	4. 76	9. 52	9. 52	47. 62	9. 52
3	40. 00	6. 43	4. 29	6. 43	2. 86	37. 86	2. 14
4	20. 73	3. 66	10. 98	13. 41	9. 76	40. 24	1. 22
5	20. 41	4. 08	0.	12. 24	10. 20	51. 02	2. 04
6	0.	0.	0.	0.	0.	0.	0.
7	12. 12	3. 03	9. 09	3. 03	42. 42	30. 30	0.
8	24. 55	5. 39	4. 79	5. 99	10. 18	44. 91	4. 20
9	12. 90	9. 68	9. 68	6. 45	12. 90	48. 39	0.

Question 19

Lib.	a	b	c	d	e	f	Unusable Data
1	12. 50	34. 37	43. 75	0.	0.	0.	9. 38
2	9. 52	28. 57	61. 90	0.	0.	0.	0.
3	17. 14	31. 43	50. 00	0.	0.	0.	1. 41
4	26. 83	19. 51	52. 44	0.	0.	0.	0.
5	10. 20	28. 57	59. 18	0.	0.	2. 04	0.
6	0.	0.	0.	0.	0.	0.	0.
7	30. 30	18. 18	51. 52	0.	0.	0.	0.
8	16. 17	18. 56	62. 28	0.	0.	0.	3. 00
9	16. 13	32. 26	51. 61	0.	0.	0.	0.

Question 20

Lib.	a	b	c	d	e	f	Unusable Data
1	28. 12	15. 62	6. 25	9. 38	40. 62	0.	0.
2	4. 76	9. 52	4. 76	4. 76	66. 67	0.	9. 52
3	20. 00	. 71	. 71	2. 86	75. 00	0.	. 71
4	19. 51	10. 98	6. 10	8. 54	52. 44	0.	2. 44
5	30. 61	4. 08	2. 04	2. 04	61. 22	0.	0.
6	0.	0.	0.	0.	0.	0.	0.
7	15. 15	6. 06	0.	3. 03	75. 76	0.	0.
8	25. 15	5. 99	2. 40	2. 99	61. 08	0.	2. 40
9	9. 68	9. 68	6. 45	6. 45	64. 52	0.	3. 23

Question 21

Lib.	a	b	c	d	e	f	Unusable Data
1	3. 13	15. 62	18. 75	9. 38	12. 50	40. 62	0.
2	4. 76	4. 76	0.	4. 76	0.	71. 43	14. 29
3	3. 57	7. 14	3. 57	2. 14	6. 43	75. 00	2. 14
4	4. 88	4. 88	8. 54	10. 98	18. 29	47. 56	4. 88
5	10. 20	10. 20	2. 04	2. 04	10. 20	59. 18	6. 12
6	0.	0.	0.	0.	0.	0.	0.
7	6. 06	6. 06	9. 09	0.	3. 03	72. 73	3. 03
8	8. 38	7. 19	4. 79	5. 99	10. 18	57. 49	6. 00
9	6. 45	6. 45	0.	9. 68	3. 23	67. 74	6. 45

Question 22

Lib.	a	b	c	d	e	f	Unusable Data
1	0.	25. 00	0.	40. 62	28. 12	0.	6. 25
2	14. 29	47. 62	23. 81	0.	14. 29	0.	0.
3	32. 86	35. 71	10. 71	0.	15. 71	0.	4. 99
4	1. 22	19. 51	3. 66	25. 61	45. 12	0.	4. 88
5	10. 20	61. 22	10. 20	0.	18. 37	0.	0.
6	0.	0.	0.	0.	0.	0.	0.
7	3. 03	33. 33	9. 09	15. 15	39. 39	0.	0.
8	20. 96	50. 90	7. 19	1. 80	16. 17	0.	3. 00
9	3. 23	48. 39	6. 45	6. 45	35. 48	0.	0.

Question 23

Lib.	a	b	c	d	e	f	Unusable Data
1	43. 75	28. 12	18. 75	6. 25	3. 13	0.	0.
2	47. 62	28. 57	23. 81	0.	0.	0.	0.
3	34. 29	31. 43	24. 29	6. 43	3. 57	0.	0.
4	44. 44	30. 86	18. 52	3. 70	2. 47	0.	0.
5	22. 45	30. 61	36. 73	4. 08	6. 12	0.	0.
6	0.	0.	0.	0.	0.	0.	0.
7	39. 39	36. 36	12. 12	6. 06	6. 06	0.	0.
8	22. 89	33. 73	22. 29	14. 46	6. 02	0.	. 60
9	25. 81	35. 48	19. 35	12. 90	6. 45	0.	0.

Question 24

Lib.	a	b	c	d	e	f	Unusable Data
1	46. 87	40. 62	9. 38	0.	0.	0.	3. 13
2	66. 67	23. 81	4. 76	0.	0.	0.	4. 76
3	61. 43	31. 43	5. 00	0.	2. 14	0.	0.
4	64. 20	29. 63	6. 17	0.	0.	0.	0.
5	34. 69	34. 69	24. 49	2. 04	2. 04	0.	2. 04
6	0.	0.	0.	0.	0.	0.	0.
7	51. 52	27. 27	12. 12	3. 03	6. 06	0.	0.
8	50. 00	32. 53	7. 83	6. 63	2. 41	0.	. 60
9	58. 06	25. 81	12. 90	3. 23	0.	0.	0.

Question 25

Lib.	a	b	c	d	e	f	Unusable Data
1	37. 50	46. 87	15. 62	0.	0.	0.	0.
2	28. 57	33. 33	28. 57	9. 52	0.	0.	0.
3	37. 86	36. 43	19. 29	2. 86	2. 86	0.	. 71
4	45. 68	30. 86	18. 52	3. 70	0.	0.	1. 23
5	28. 57	28. 57	34. 69	4. 08	4. 08	0.	0.
6	0.	0.	0.	0.	0.	0.	0.
7	42. 42	33. 33	15. 15	6. 06	3. 03	0.	0.
8	29. 52	30. 72	24. 10	7. 23	6. 63	0.	1. 81
9	32. 26	35. 48	19. 35	3. 23	6. 45	0.	3. 23

Question 26

Lib.	a	b	c	d	e	f	Unusable Data
1	31. 25	28. 12	31. 25	9. 38	0.	0.	0.
2	14. 29	52. 38	23. 81	4. 76	4. 76	0.	0.
3	18. 57	29. 29	30. 71	11. 43	8. 57	0.	1. 42
4	27. 16	24. 69	35. 80	7. 41	4. 94	0.	0.

Appendix 8. 3 (continued)
Response Percent by Library for Each Question

Lib.	a	b	c	d	e	f	Unusable Data
5	6. 12	30. 61	40. 82	14. 29	8. 16	0.	0.
6	0.	0.	0.	0.	0.	0.	0.
7	21. 21	27. 27	18. 18	18. 18	12. 12	0.	3. 03
8	26. 51	34. 34	25. 90	6. 02	6. 63	0.	. 60
9	35. 48	29. 03	19. 35	6. 45	9. 68	0.	0.
Question 27							
1	34. 37	43. 75	18. 75	3. 13	0.	0.	0.
2	19. 05	42. 86	23. 81	9. 52	4. 76	0.	0.
3	25. 00	24. 29	32. 86	10. 00	6. 43	0.	1. 43
4	29. 63	33. 33	25. 93	6. 17	4. 94	0.	0.
5	14. 29	32. 65	38. 78	8. 16	6. 12	0.	0.
6	0.	0.	0.	0.	0.	0.	0.
7	30. 30	30. 30	21. 21	6. 06	9. 09	0.	3. 03
8	28. 31	30. 12	24. 10	10. 84	4. 82	0.	1. 80
9	29. 03	29. 03	19. 35	12. 90	6. 45	0.	3. 23
Question 28							
1	56. 25	28. 12	12. 50	3. 13	0.	0.	0.
2	33. 33	38. 10	28. 57	0.	0.	0.	0.
3	42. 14	35. 00	15. 00	2. 86	4. 29	0.	. 71
4	44. 44	40. 74	9. 88	3. 70	1. 23	0.	0.
5	30. 61	34. 69	28. 57	4. 08	2. 04	0.	0.
6	0.	0.	0.	0.	0.	0.	0.
7	21. 21	45. 45	21. 21	6. 06	6. 06	0.	0.
8	38. 55	30. 72	18. 07	5. 42	6. 02	0.	1. 20
9	41. 94	25. 81	16. 13	9. 68	6. 45	0.	0.
Question 29							
1	28. 12	43. 75	12. 50	12. 50	0.	0.	3. 13
2	42. 86	33. 33	19. 05	4. 76	0.	0.	0.
3	38. 57	30. 71	20. 00	4. 29	5. 71	0.	. 71
4	27. 16	44. 44	17. 28	7. 41	3. 70	0.	0.
5	32. 65	18. 37	38. 78	4. 08	6. 12	0.	0.
6	0.	0.	0.	0.	0.	0.	0.
7	24. 24	39. 39	24. 24	6. 06	6. 06	0.	0.
8	35. 54	30. 72	18. 07	6. 02	9. 64	0.	0.
9	41. 94	38. 71	6. 45	9. 68	3. 23	0.	0.
Question 30							
1	50. 00	18. 75	28. 12	0.	3. 13	0.	0.
2	42. 86	33. 33	19. 05	4. 76	0.	0.	0.
3	35. 71	30. 71	24. 29	4. 29	5. 00	0.	0.
4	35. 80	34. 57	20. 99	6. 17	2. 47	0.	0.
5	26. 53	30. 61	36. 73	4. 08	2. 04	0.	0.
6	0.	0.	0.	0.	0.	0.	0.

Lib.	a	b	c	d	e	f	Unusable Data
7	33. 33	36. 36	15. 15	9. 09	3. 03	0.	3. 03
8	30. 12	38. 55	24. 10	1. 81	5. 42	0.	0.
9	29. 03	25. 81	19. 35	22. 58	3. 23	0.	0.

Question 31

1	18. 75	31. 25	43. 75	3. 13	3. 13	0.	0.
2	19. 05	33. 33	28. 57	19. 05	0.	0.	0.
3	14. 29	20. 71	42. 14	13. 57	9. 29	0.	0.
4	13. 58	38. 27	39. 51	3. 70	4. 94	0.	0.
5	2. 04	34. 69	46. 94	8. 16	8. 16	0.	0.
6	0.	0.	0.	0.	0.	0.	0.
7	27. 27	15. 15	45. 45	3. 03	9. 09	0.	0.
8	13. 25	21. 69	42. 17	9. 64	12. 05	0.	1. 20
9	6. 45	29. 03	35. 48	12. 90	9. 68	0.	6. 45

Question 32

1	18. 75	21. 87	40. 62	9. 38	9. 38	0.	0.
2	23. 81	42. 86	14. 29	9. 52	9. 52	0.	0.
3	27. 86	26. 43	22. 14	10. 71	11. 43	0.	1. 43
4	35. 80	30. 86	20. 99	7. 41	4. 94	0.	0.
5	12. 24	20. 41	32. 65	10. 20	24. 49	0.	0.
6	0.	0.	0.	0.	0.	0.	0.
7	21. 21	33. 33	12. 12	18. 18	15. 15	0.	0.
8	41. 57	30. 12	15. 66	7. 83	3. 61	0.	1. 20
9	48. 39	19. 35	12. 90	12. 90	6. 45	0.	0.

Question 33

1	6. 25	0.	84. 37	6. 25	3. 13	0.	0.
2	9. 52	9. 52	52. 38	0.	23. 81	0.	4. 76
3	12. 14	24. 29	43. 57	12. 14	6. 43	0.	1. 43
4	19. 75	16. 05	54. 32	4. 94	2. 47	0.	2. 47
5	2. 04	12. 24	44. 90	30. 61	8. 16	0.	2. 04
6	0.	0.	0.	0.	0.	0.	0.
7	3. 03	12. 12	60. 61	3. 03	15. 15	0.	6. 06
8	9. 04	15. 66	50. 60	8. 43	14. 46	0.	1. 81
9	9. 68	22. 58	48. 39	9. 68	9. 68	0.	0.

Question 34

1	12. 50	12. 50	46. 87	18. 75	9. 38	0.	0.
2	19. 05	4. 76	42. 86	14. 29	19. 05	0.	0.
3	8. 57	19. 29	34. 29	16. 43	20. 00	0.	1. 43
4	18. 52	18. 52	40. 74	8. 64	9. 88	0.	3. 70
5	0.	28. 57	30. 61	10. 20	30. 61	0.	0.
6	0.	0.	0.	0.	0.	0.	0.
7	3. 03	42. 42	18. 18	21. 21	15. 15	0.	0.
8	12. 65	23. 49	30. 72	12. 05	20. 48	0.	. 60
9	12. 90	29. 03	32. 26	16. 13	9. 68	0.	0.

Appendix 8.4
Response by Major Academic Areas*

Question 1

Academic Area	a	b	c	d	e	f	Unusable Data
Administrative	1	1	9	28	3	0	0
Applied Sciences	0	3	18	55	7	0	1
Humanities	3	16	37	49	9	0	2
Interdisciplinary	0	3	13	43	2	2	0
Sciences	2	6	35	59	4	0	1
Social Sciences	0	4	36	59	6	1	0
Vocational-Technical	0	1	9	23	4	0	0

Question 2

Academic Area	a	b	c	d	e	f	Unusable Data
Administrative	17	6	12	4	2	0	1
Applied Sciences	40	4	34	6	0	0	0
Humanities	26	24	64	2	0	0	0
Interdisciplinary	21	7	24	7	2	0	2
Sciences	51	10	41	4	0	0	1
Social Sciences	31	17	52	4	0	0	2
Vocational-Technical	15	2	19	1	0	0	0

Question 3

Academic Area	a	b	c	d	e	f	Unusable Data
Administrative	14	2	17	5	3	0	1
Applied Sciences	45	5	29	5	0	0	0
Humanities	31	18	63	2	0	0	2
Interdisciplinary	29	3	20	8	1	0	2
Sciences	55	3	43	4	0	0	2
Social Sciences	38	11	51	4	0	0	2
Vocational-Technical	15	1	20	1	0	0	0

Question 4							
Administrative	1	6	21	8	5	0	1
Applied Sciences	2	6	28	20	27	0	1
Humanities	2	17	52	33	11	0	1
Interdisciplinary	3	5	16	21	16	0	2
Sciences	8	12	25	32	30	0	0
Social Sciences	4	16	40	28	16	0	2
Vocational-Technical	1	8	17	8	3	0	0
Question 5							
Administrative	0	0	8	10	22	2	0
Applied Sciences	0	3	10	30	30	10	1
Humanities	0	4	9	45	46	12	0
Interdisciplinary	0	2	7	24	23	7	0
Sciences	1	4	20	36	25	20	1
Social Sciences	0	1	16	35	42	11	1
Vocational-Technical	0	1	3	9	18	5	1
Question 6							
Administrative	1	2	12	19	8	0	0
Applied Sciences	0	5	18	42	19	0	0
Humanities	0	10	33	44	28	0	1
Interdisciplinary	1	4	14	28	15	1	0
Sciences	2	7	28	48	22	0	0
Social Sciences	1	4	31	45	25	0	0
Vocational-Technical	1	0	13	18	5	0	0

* The difference between the total number who responded to the questionnaire and the number of respondents who are categorized by academic discipline is due to the fact that some respondents did not supply enough information to permit categorization by discipline.

Appendix 8.4 (continued)
Response by Major Academic Areas

Question 7

Academic Area	a	b	c	d	e	f	Unusable Data
Administrative	12	22	5	2	0	0	1
Applied Sciences	19	59	5	0	0	0	1
Humanities	62	39	10	0	0	0	5
Interdisciplinary	20	32	7	2	0	0	2
Sciences	37	55	12	1	0	0	2
Social Sciences	42	54	8	1	0	0	1
Vocational-Technical	11	22	3	0	0	0	1
Question 8							
Administrative	0	4	2	23	11	2	0
Applied Sciences	0	9	12	55	5	2	1
Humanities	1	7	18	73	15	2	0
Interdisciplinary	1	4	7	39	7	5	0
Sciences	1	6	17	56	16	11	0
Social Sciences	0	3	14	67	18	2	2
Vocational-Technical	0	1	6	21	6	1	2
Question 9							
Administrative	0	1	8	24	9	0	0
Applied Sciences	2	4	10	57	7	1	3
Humanities	1	4	21	79	9	0	2
Interdisciplinary	0	3	11	37	7	5	0
Sciences	1	8	18	61	14	3	2
Social Sciences	0	3	15	68	20	0	0
Vocational-Technical	0	2	8	20	5	0	2

Question 10							
Administrative	21	3	11	3	0	0	4
Applied Sciences	49	7	27	1	0	0	0
Humanities	37	20	58	0	0	0	1
Interdisciplinary	33	5	18	2	0	0	5
Sciences	57	6	42	2	0	0	0
Social Sciences	35	14	54	2	0	0	1
Vocational-Technical	16	3	17	0	0	0	1
Question 11							
Administrative	2	12	16	10	0	1	1
Applied Sciences	3	16	35	27	1	1	1
Humanities	5	43	51	12	0	0	5
Interdisciplinary	1	8	28	23	0	3	0
Sciences	7	25	41	24	1	4	5
Social Sciences	3	22	55	23	1	1	1
Vocational-Technical	1	12	16	7	0	0	1
Question 12							
Administrative	5	16	3	18	0	0	0
Applied Sciences	21	26	3	31	0	0	3
Humanities	20	32	11	48	0	0	5
Interdisciplinary	15	21	1	20	0	0	6
Sciences	32	36	5	32	0	0	2
Social Sciences	25	40	3	36	0	0	2
Vocational-Technical	2	7	6	19	0	0	3

Appendix 8. 4 (continued
Response by Major Academic Areas

Question 13

Academic Area	a	b	c	d	e	f	Unusable Data
Administrative	0	3	10	10	9	10	0
Applied Sciences	1	8	18	16	17	24	0
Humanities	4	11	22	28	22	29	0
Interdisciplinary	3	3	14	9	12	20	2
Sciences	8	8	13	30	16	31	1
Social Sciences	3	5	22	30	21	24	1
Vocational-Technical	0	3	8	3	11	12	0
Question 14							
Administrative	7	0	4	27	1	0	3
Applied Sciences	22	2	4	52	2	0	2
Humanities	26	4	0	76	4	0	6
Interdisciplinary	9	4	3	37	4	0	6
Sciences	34	2	1	59	5	0	6
Social Sciences	10	5	4	81	2	0	4
Vocational-Technical	4	0	1	32	0	0	0
Question 15							
Administrative	27	9	2	1	2	0	1
Applied Sciences	41	33	7	1	2	0	0
Humanities	72	30	4	3	4	0	3
Interdisciplinary	31	24	3	2	2	0	1
Sciences	40	54	6	2	5	0	0
Social Sciences	79	23	2	0	0	0	2
Vocational-Technical	30	5	0	1	1	0	0

Question 16							
Administrative	6	3	4	27	0	0	2
Applied Sciences	13	4	7	59	0	0	1
Humanities	7	3	10	90	0	0	6
Interdisciplinary	6	3	3	50	0	0	1
Sciences	15	1	1	87	0	0	3
Social Sciences	3	6	11	83	0	0	3
Vocational-Technical	0	1	4	32	0	0	0
Question 17							
Administrative	15	5	5	12	3	0	2
Applied Sciences	35	7	16	11	13	0	2
Humanities	39	12	8	26	27	0	4
Interdisciplinary	21	4	6	11	18	0	3
Sciences	22	9	8	31	34	0	3
Social Sciences	27	9	16	23	29	1	1
Vocational-Technical	9	5	3	11	8	0	1
Question 18							
Administrative	6	6	7	5	2	15	1
Applied Sciences	20	5	4	9	4	42	0
Humanities	44	4	6	9	8	41	4
Interdisciplinary	18	2	1	5	8	26	3
Sciences	29	5	5	4	12	48	4
Social Sciences	18	5	8	9	21	44	1
Vocational-Technical	7	3	4	6	3	13	1

Appendix 8.4 (continued)
Response by Major Academic Areas

Question 19

Academic Area	a	b	c	d	e	f	Unusable Data
Administrative	8	8	26	0	0	0	0
Applied Sciences	19	17	48	0	0	0	0
Humanities	17	42	51	0	0	0	6
Interdisciplinary	11	16	36	0	0	0	0
Sciences	10	35	60	0	0	1	1
Social Sciences	29	17	57	0	0	0	3
Vocational-Technical	5	3	28	0	0	0	1

Question 20

Academic Area	a	b	c	d	e	f	Unusable Data
Administrative	9	2	1	1	28	0	1
Applied Sciences	16	3	2	2	61	0	0
Humanities	20	11	6	9	66	0	4
Interdisciplinary	17	2	1	4	37	0	2
Sciences	27	8	2	1	68	0	1
Social Sciences	24	7	3	7	63	0	2
Vocational-Technical	6	1	1	0	29	0	0

Question 21

Academic Area	a	b	c	d	e	f	Unusable Data
Administrative	3	3	3	1	3	27	2
Applied Sciences	6	5	2	3	7	60	1
Humanities	3	10	7	9	16	62	9
Interdisciplinary	8	3	6	3	3	36	4
Sciences	4	13	4	5	8	67	6
Social Sciences	9	7	6	9	11	62	2
Vocational-Technical	1	0	2	0	4	28	2

Question 22							
Administrative	3	22	1	1	14	0	1
Applied Sciences	23	31	4	2	21	0	3
Humanities	15	51	10	16	19	0	5
Interdisciplinary	13	30	5	1	12	0	2
Sciences	19	46	10	7	23	0	2
Social Sciences	13	34	12	13	29	0	5
Vocational-Technical	6	11	3	4	13	0	0
Question 23							
Administrative	13	15	9	2	2	0	0
Applied Sciences	14	29	28	10	3	0	0
Humanities	53	27	17	13	5	0	0
Interdisciplinary	20	23	10	7	3	0	0
Sciences	34	42	17	9	5	0	0
Social Sciences	39	30	28	3	5	0	1
Vocational-Technical	5	12	16	2	2	0	0
Question 24							
Administrative	22	15	3	1	0	0	0
Applied Sciences	38	32	10	2	2	0	0
Humanities	77	22	8	4	3	0	1
Interdisciplinary	29	24	5	3	2	0	0
Sciences	49	40	13	2	1	0	2
Social Sciences	68	26	7	2	2	0	1
Vocational-Technical	19	15	3	0	0	0	0

Appendix 8. 4 (continued)
Response by Major Academic Areas

Academic Area	a	b	c	d	e	f	Unusable Data
Question 25							
Administrative	14	12	13	0	2	0	0
Applied Sciences	19	31	24	4	4	0	2
Humanities	60	32	15	4	4	0	0
Interdisciplinary	18	23	15	2	5	0	0
Sciences	33	36	25	8	3	0	2
Social Sciences	44	34	18	6	2	0	2
Vocational-Technical	7	17	11	2	0	0	0
Question 26							
Administrative	16	11	11	0	2	0	1
Applied Sciences	11	22	32	6	11	0	2
Humanities	36	30	28	13	8	0	0
Interdisciplinary	14	24	16	6	3	0	0
Sciences	21	36	31	11	7	0	1
Social Sciences	20	35	36	11	4	0	0
Vocational-Technical	8	13	8	4	4	0	0
Question 27							
Administrative	16	9	14	1	1	0	0
Applied Sciences	14	25	31	7	5	0	2
Humanities	44	30	24	9	7	0	1
Interdisciplinary	14	18	17	11	3	0	0
Sciences	21	38	30	9	7	0	2
Social Sciences	28	39	24	8	5	0	2
Vocational-Technical	10	10	10	5	2	0	0

Question 28							
Administrative	17	10	13	0	0	0	1
Applied Sciences	34	33	12	1	3	0	1
Humanities	49	38	18	3	7	0	0
Interdisciplinary	27	16	13	4	2	0	1
Sciences	31	39	21	8	8	0	0
Social Sciences	47	38	15	5	1	0	0
Vocational-Technical	14	16	3	3	1	0	0
Question 29							
Administrative	14	17	5	4	1	0	0
Applied Sciences	27	30	17	5	5	0	0
Humanities	41	38	23	6	6	0	1
Interdisciplinary	19	21	11	6	6	0	0
Sciences	43	28	22	4	9	0	1
Social Sciences	37	37	20	6	6	0	0
Vocational-Technical	9	14	11	3	0	0	0
Question 30							
Administrative	9	14	15	3	0	0	0
Applied Sciences	26	28	23	3	4	0	0
Humanities	52	29	25	2	7	0	0
Interdisplinary	20	18	17	4	4	0	0
Sciences	38	43	18	5	3	0	0
Social Sciences	35	36	23	8	3	0	1
Vocational-Technical	7	15	12	2	1	0	0

Appendix 8. 4 (continued)
Response by Major Academic Areas

Question 31

Academic Area	a	b	c	d	e	f	Unusable Data
Administrative	3	12	21	3	2	0	0
Applied Sciences	5	16	34	13	15	0	1
Humanities	26	33	37	11	8	0	0
Interdisciplinary	9	12	28	6	7	0	1
Sciences	8	33	48	10	7	0	1
Social Sciences	20	29	45	5	7	0	0
Vocational-Technical	4	9	17	4	2	0	1

Question 32

Academic Area	a	b	c	d	e	f	Unusable Data
Administrative	12	11	12	4	2	0	0
Applied Sciences	22	20	21	9	11	0	1
Humanities	35	32	28	8	11	0	1
Interdisciplinary	27	19	9	6	2	0	0
Sciences	25	27	23	19	12	0	1
Social Sciences	41	35	16	6	8	0	0
Vocational-Technical	14	11	5	2	4	0	1

Question 33

Academic Area	a	b	c	d	e	f	Unusable Data
Administrative	5	4	30	1	1	0	0
Applied Sciences	7	15	38	16	6	0	2
Humanities	14	19	58	10	13	0	1
Interdisciplinary	4	11	31	5	12	0	0
Sciences	12	16	52	14	9	0	4
Social Sciences	13	22	55	6	6	0	4
Vocational-Technical	2	5	20	4	6	0	0

Question 34

Administrative	6	9	17	1	6	0	2
Applied Sciences	4	16	31	14	17	0	2
Humanities	16	30	32	22	14	0	1
Interdisciplinary	6	19	17	4	17	0	0
Sciences	7	13	36	21	30	0	0
Social Sciences	19	27	37	10	12	0	1
Vocational-Technical	3	9	17	4	4	0	0

Appendix 8. 5
Tabulation for Group I Institutions

Question	a	b	c	d	e	f	Unusable Data
1	5	20	79	121	21	0	2
2	97	38	99	10	2	0	2
3	98	25	108	11	3	0	3
4	14	44	110	48	28	0	4
5	1	2	18	80	120	26	1
6	6	24	67	97	54	0	0
7	94	117	29	2	0	0	6
8	2	14	19	149	49	14	1
9	1	9	24	162	46	3	3
10	114	28	97	5	0	0	4
11	15	77	101	41	2	3	9
12	45	82	18	97	0	0	6
13	8	13	47	49	64	67	0
14	49	5	5	169	7	0	13
15	168	62	7	2	5	0	4
16	18	10	27	186	0	0	7
17	38	13	20	78	93	1	5
18	45	12	21	28	37	101	4
19	48	63	132	0	0	1	4
20	49	23	11	15	145	0	5
21	15	19	17	17	26	141	13
22	11	90	18	41	82	0	6
23	92	78	54	13	10	0	0
24	133	76	29	3	3	0	3
25	93	83	54	10	5	0	2
26	56	73	76	25	16	0	1
27	65	85	64	18	13	0	2
28	96	90	44	11	6	0	0
29	77	91	51	18	9	0	1
30	87	76	59	18	6	0	1
31	33	79	101	17	15	0	2
32	68	68	57	26	28	0	0
33	25	32	139	25	20	0	6
34	28	57	88	33	38	0	3

Appendix 8. 6
Tabulation for Group II Institutions

Question	a	b	c	d	e	f	Unusable Data
1	1	14	78	195	14	3	2
2	104	32	147	18	2	0	4
3	129	18	135	18	1	0	6
4	7	26	89	102	80	0	3
5	0	13	55	109	86	41	3
6	0	8	82	147	68	1	1
7	109	166	21	4	0	0	7
8	1	20	57	185	29	11	4
9	3	16	67	184	25	6	6
10	134	30	130	5	0	0	8
11	7	61	141	85	1	7	5
12	75	96	14	107	0	0	15
13	11	28	60	77	44	83	4
14	63	12	12	195	11	0	14
15	152	116	17	8	11	0	3
16	32	11	13	242	0	0	9
17	130	38	42	47	39	0	11
18	97	18	14	19	21	128	10
19	51	75	174	0	0	0	7
20	70	11	5	9	207	0	5
21	19	22	13	13	26	201	13
22	81	135	27	3	49	0	12
23	86	100	71	33	15	0	1
24	169	98	20	11	7	0	1
25	102	102	67	16	15	0	4
26	70	98	86	26	23	0	3
27	82	84	86	32	17	0	5
28	123	100	51	13	16	0	3
29	113	94	58	16	24	0	1
30	100	107	74	9	16	0	0
31	42	65	129	35	33	0	2
32	108	87	57	28	22	0	4
33	32	60	145	31	33	0	5
34	33	66	99	43	62	0	3

Appendix 8. 7
Attitude Survey --- Academic Coding

Academic Departments	Administrative	Applied Sciences	Humanities	Interdisciplinary	Sciences	Social Sciences	Vocational-Technical
1. Accounting							x
2. Aerospace Engineering Sciences		x					
3. Agricultural Engineering		x					
4. Agriculture		x					
5. Agronomy		x					
6. Anatomy		x					
7. Animal Science		x					
8. Anthropology						x	
9. Architecture			x				
10. Art			x				
11. Astro-Geophysics				x			
12. Astronomy					x		
13. Atmospheric Science		x					
14. Biochemistry				x			
15. Biology					x		
16. Botany & Plant Pathology					x		
17. Business (General)							x
18. Business Education							x
19. Chemical Engineering				x			
20. Chemistry					x		
21. Child Development						x	
22. Civil Engineering		x					
23. Classics			x				
24. Consumer Sciences & Housing						x	
25. Culinary Arts							x
26. Data Processing							x
27. Drafting Engineering							x
28. Economics						x	
29. Education						x	
30. Electrical Engineering		x					
31. Engineering, Basic		x					
32. Engineering Design & Economic Evaluation				x			
33. Engineering English (Technical Journalism)				x			
34. English			x				
35. Entomology					x		
36. Finance						x	

Academic Departments	Study Category						
	Administrative	Applied Sciences	Humanities	Interdisiplinary	Sciences	Social Sciences	Vocational-Technical
37. Fine Arts			x				
38. Fishery & Wildlife Biology		x					
39. Food Science & Nutrition		x					
40. Foreign Languages			x				
41. Forest & Wood Sciences		x					
42. French			x				
43. Geography						x	
44. Geophysics				x			
45. Geological Sciences					x		
46. Germanic Languages & Literature			x				
47. Hearing & Speech Science		x					
48. History			x				
49. Home Economics							x
50. Horticulture		x					
51. Industrial Arts							x
52. Italian			x				
53. Journalism							x
54. Language & Literature			x				
55. Law						x	
56. Library Science			x				
57. Literature			x				
58. Marketing							x
59. Mathematics & Statistics					x		
60. Mechanical Engineering		x					
61. Medicine		x					
62. Metallurgical Engineering		x					
63. Microbiology		x					
64. Military Science						x	
65. Mining Engineering		x					
66. Musicology			x				
67. Music			x				
68. Music, Instrumental			x				
69. Nursing		x					
70. Occupational Therapy							x
71. Office Administration							x
72. Pathology		x					
73. Petroleum Engineering		x					
74. Pharmacy		x					
75. Philosophy			x				
76. Physical Education						x	
77. Physics & Astrophysics					x		
78. Physiology & Biophysics		x					
79. Police Science							x

Appendix 8. 7 (continued)
Attitude Survey --- Academic Coding

Academic Departments	Administrative	Applied Sciences	Humanities	Interdisciplinary	Sciences	Social Sciences	Vocational-Technical
80. Political Science						x	
81. Poultry Science		x					
82. Production & Manpower							x
83. Psychology, Counseling & Guidance						x	
84. Quality Assurance Engineering		x					
85. Radiation & Radiation Biology		x					
86. Range Science		x					
87. Recreation & Watershed Resources		x					
88. Science					x		
89. Science Education				x			
90. Slavic & Eastern Languages			x				
91. Social Studies Education						x	
92. Sociology						x	
93. Spanish & Portuguese			x				
94. Special Education						x	
95. Speech Arts (includes Drama)			x				
96. Speech Therapy							x
97. Textiles & Clothing							x
98. Veterinary Clinics & Surgery		x					
99. Veterinary Medicine		x					
100. Vocational Education							x
101. Zoology					x		
200. Research Organizations				x			
JILA							
LASP							
Inst. Arctic & Alpine Research							
Inst. Developmental Biology							
Bureau of Research							
300. Interdisciplinary				x			
400. Administrative	x						

Appendix 8.8
Response by Time Returned

Question 1 Follow-up	a	b	c	d	e	f	Unusable Data
0	6	29	126	256	25	3	4
1	0	4	23	48	6	0	0
2	0	1	5	9	4	0	0
3	0	0	3	3	0	0	0
Question 2							
0	163	57	197	22	4	0	6
1	29	10	38	4	0	0	0
2	6	2	9	2	0	0	0
3	3	1	2	0	0	0	0
Question 3							
0	183	35	196	22	4	0	9
1	36	8	32	5	0	0	0
2	7	0	10	2	0	0	0
3	1	0	5	0	0	0	0
Question 4							
0	17	59	157	119	90	0	7
1	2	8	32	23	16	0	0
2	2	2	9	5	1	0	0
3	0	1	1	3	1	0	0
Question 5							
0	1	10	51	150	179	54	4
1	0	5	18	28	21	9	0
2	0	0	4	7	6	2	0
3	0	0	0	4	0	2	0
Question 6							
0	5	28	120	194	100	1	1
1	1	1	22	38	19	0	0
2	0	3	5	9	2	0	0
3	0	0	2	3	1	0	0
Question 7							
0	168	221	43	5	0	0	12
1	27	46	7	0	0	0	1
2	6	12	0	1	0	0	0
3	2	4	0	0	0	0	0

Question 8 Follow-up	a	b	c	d	e	f	Unusable Data
0	3	30	48	276	63	24	5
1	0	4	17	48	11	1	0
2	0	0	8	8	3	0	0
3	0	0	3	2	1	0	0
Question 9							
0	4	22	63	286	59	7	8
1	0	2	22	47	8	2	0
2	0	1	5	9	3	0	1
3	0	0	1	4	1	0	0
Question 10							
0	198	46	188	8	0	0	9
1	39	10	28	1	0	0	3
2	8	1	10	0	0	0	0
3	3	1	1	1	0	0	0
Question 11							
0	20	114	193	95	3	10	14
1	2	18	39	22	0	0	0
2	0	5	8	6	0	0	0
3	0	1	2	3	0	0	0
Question 12							
0	87	150	24	169	0	0	19
1	27	19	7	26	0	0	2
2	5	9	1	4	0	0	0
3	1	0	0	5	0	0	0
Question 13							
0	14	33	84	96	93	126	3
1	3	6	17	25	12	17	1
2	1	1	6	3	2	6	0
3	1	1	0	2	1	1	0
Question 14							
0	92	11	14	296	13	0	23
1	16	6	3	49	3	0	4
2	3	0	0	14	2	0	0
3	1	0	0	5	0	0	0
Question 15							
0	266	136	23	6	14	0	4
1	37	36	1	2	2	0	3
2	13	5	0	1	0	0	0
3	4	1	0	1	0	0	0

Appendix 8. 8 (continued)
Response by Time Returned

Question 16 Follow-up	a	b	c	d	e	f	Unusable Data
0	38	17	32	350	0	0	12
1	10	3	6	58	0	0	4
2	2	1	2	14	0	0	0
3	0	0	0	6	0	0	0
Question 17							
0	135	39	51	106	105	1	12
1	23	9	9	13	23	0	4
2	7	2	1	6	3	0	0
3	3	1	1	0	1	0	0
Question 18							
0	112	22	31	38	45	189	12
1	24	5	2	6	11	31	2
2	5	2	2	3	2	5	0
3	1	1	0	0	0	4	0
Question 19							
0	77	104	257	0	0	1	10
1	18	25	37	0	0	0	1
2	3	6	10	0	0	0	0
3	1	3	2	0	0	0	0
Question 20							
0	95	28	13	20	284	0	9
1	20	4	0	4	52	0	1
2	3	2	2	0	12	0	0
3	1	0	1	0	4	0	0
Question 21							
0	23	33	26	29	39	277	22
1	9	4	3	1	11	49	4
2	2	3	0	0	2	12	0
3	0	1	1	0	0	4	0
Question 22							
0	62	183	38	39	112	0	15
1	24	32	6	4	12	0	3
2	4	9	0	1	5	0	0
3	2	1	1	0	2	0	0

Question 23

Follow-up	a	b	c	d	e	f	Unusable Data
0	143	143	108	32	20	0	3
1	27	27	13	12	2	0	0
2	7	6	4	0	2	0	0
3	1	2	0	2	1	0	0

Question 24

Follow-up	a	b	c	d	e	f	Unusable Data
0	244	141	39	11	8	0	6
1	44	25	8	3	1	0	0
2	11	6	1	0	1	0	0
3	3	2	1	0	0	0	0

Question 25

Follow-up	a	b	c	d	e	f	Unusable Data
0	153	158	95	23	14	0	6
1	32	22	18	3	4	0	2
2	8	3	6	0	2	0	0
3	2	2	2	0	0	0	0

Question 26

Follow-up	a	b	c	d	e	f	Unusable Data
0	91	134	138	47	34	0	5
1	27	27	19	4	3	0	1
2	8	6	3	0	2	0	0
3	0	4	2	0	0	0	0

Question 27

Follow-up	a	b	c	d	e	f	Unusable Data
0	110	136	125	44	28	0	6
1	29	22	20	6	1	0	3
2	8	6	4	0	1	0	0
3	0	5	1	0	0	0	0

Question 28

Follow-up	a	b	c	d	e	f	Unusable Data
0	175	156	77	21	15	0	5
1	36	22	15	2	6	0	0
2	6	10	1	1	1	0	0
3	2	2	2	0	0	0	0

Question 29

Follow-up	a	b	c	d	e	f	Unusable Data
0	142	152	93	31	27	0	4
1	34	26	13	3	5	0	0
2	12	4	3	0	0	0	0
3	2	3	0	0	1	0	0

Question 30

Follow-up	a	b	c	d	e	f	Unusable Data
0	149	151	106	21	19	0	3
1	28	22	23	5	3	0	0
2	9	8	2	0	0	0	0
3	1	2	2	1	0	0	0

Appendix 8.8 (continued)
Response by Time Returned

Follow-up	a	b	c	d	e	f	Unusable Data
Question 31							
0	53	114	197	43	38	0	4
1	19	21	25	7	8	0	1
2	2	8	5	1	2	0	1
3	1	1	3	1	0	0	0
Question 32							
0	129	128	93	46	48	0	5
1	36	23	15	6	1	0	0
2	8	4	4	2	0	0	1
3	3	0	2	0	1	0	0
Question 33							
0	46	68	236	47	42	0	10
1	8	16	39	8	8	0	2
2	2	8	6	1	2	0	0
3	1	0	3	0	1	0	1
Question 34							
0	40	99	156	64	84	0	6
1	14	21	22	12	10	0	2
2	5	3	7	0	4	0	0
3	2	0	2	0	2	0	0

Index